ÆSTHETIC

EDUCATION

University of Illinois Press

CONCEPTS and

edited by Ralph A. Smith

Urbana Chicago London

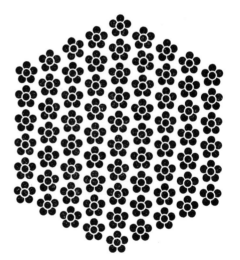

*At a time when institutions
of higher education are much
abused I am happy to dedicate
this volume to the University of
Illinois, for creating the
conditions to advance studies
in aesthetic education.*

CONTENTS

INTRODUCTION

Aesthetics and Education

The essays in this volume are intended to indicate the relevance of certain key concepts in the discipline of aesthetics to both the philosophy of aesthetic education proper, i.e., the philosophy of education in the arts, and general educational theory. An effort of this kind constitutes a relatively new type of venture. Although it is sometimes lamented that short shrift is given to the aesthetic aspects of education, little has been done to fill this lacuna in educational theory. The situation is improving, however, and in recent years a small but substantial foundational literature has appeared. To reflect this trend, writers who have thought seriously about the role of the aesthetic in education were invited to contribute to this collection. A reading of the essays, including footnote references, may thus serve as something of an introduction to contemporary philosophical thinking about aesthetic education.

Types of Aesthetics

The mere mention of "aesthetics," however, is not sufficient to suggest the character of the writings contained herein, especially since the term does not enjoy popular currency in educational parlance. The need for a brief account of the various meanings the term has acquired is evidenced not only by the uncomprehending reactions of many persons upon first hearing the word, but also by the common mistake of confusing "aesthetics," the name for an area of scholarly study and inquiry, with "aesthetic experience," an expression referring to the perceptual focus or structural cast of experience under certain conditions. In brief, aesthetics as a field of study is one thing and aesthetic experience something else.

Understanding is further complicated by the belief that aesthetics is best construed as the psychology of art, or as psychological aesthetics. Thus conceived, aesthetics is a branch of empirical science. Yet during the modern era aesthetics has also come to be viewed as a branch of philosophical inquiry. In brief, the question "What is aesthetics?" does not admit of a simple answer. Fortunately, however, recent scholarship has greatly facilitated the task of gaining orientation in this somewhat unwieldy subject. For the purposes of this volume it will be sufficient to accept a classification of aesthetics into roughly three types: *scientific, analytic,* and *synoptic* or programmatic.

In *Aesthetics from Classical Greece to the Present*[1] Monroe C. Beardsley points out that one of the important achievements of twentieth-century thinking about the arts has been to clarify a distinction between two kinds of aesthetic inquiry. The first type is *scientific aesthetics.* As interpreted by its leading advocate in this country, Thomas Munro,[2] this approach to aesthetics is broadly experimental and empirical, even if not exclusively devoted to the quantification of research data. Ideally, scientific aesthetics is said to exploit the insights of art criticism and philosophy of art in framing hypotheses but it tends to derive its principal ideas from the history and analysis of form and from psychological studies of the production, appreciation, and teaching of the arts. Scientific aesthetics thus encompasses a rather large cluster of empirical studies. I don't

1 (New York: Macmillan, 1966), pp. 376–88.
2 *Toward Science in Aesthetics* (New York: Liberal Arts Press, 1956).

think much harm is done, however, if scientific aesthetics is assimilated to psychological aesthetics, which typically inquires into what happens when persons experience art or aesthetic objects in a variety of experimentally controlled situations. The research studies discussed in C. W. Valentine's *The Experimental Psychology of Beauty*[3] are instances of this type of aesthetics. Psychological aesthetics, however, is not exclusively concerned with investigations of aesthetic preference and judgment. There is another important type that inquires into the nature of perception in art and artistic creation. The studies of Rudolf Arnheim, for example, are good instances of this type of psychological aesthetics.[4]

Then there is *analytical aesthetics*, which, according to Beardsley, takes as its central task "the critical examination of basic concepts and basic assumptions involved in all our [aesthetic] beliefs. The aim is to increase the rationality of those beliefs by clarifying the concepts and testing the reasoning." Beardsley's own work, e.g., *Aesthetics: Problems in the Philosophy of Criticism*,[5] is a good specimen of this type. Analytical aesthetics may take various forms. It may rest content simply to analyze the ways in which a term is used in ordinary language in an attempt to discover the term's meaning. Or it may try to reconstruct the meaning of a term so as to make it a more useful tool in theory and practice. Beardsley conceives of his own brand of aesthetics as essentially metacriticism—the philosophical study of the problems which arise when critical statements are made about works of art. Insofar as analytical aesthetics of this sort results in aesthetic theory, it consists of general principles that provide a foundation for art criticism. Such unity as analytical aesthetics has derives from a concern with a family of concepts typical of which are the ones surveyed in this collection, e.g., the concepts of aesthetic experience, metaphor, style, intention, aesthetic argument, and so

[3] (London: Methuen, 1962).
[4] E.g., *Art and Visual Perception* (Berkeley: University of California Press, 1954), and *Picasso's Guernica* (Berkeley: University of California Press, 1962).
[5] (New York: Harcourt, Brace, 1958).

on. Hence if a scientific aesthetician typically asks what happens when a person asserts an aesthetic preference or has an aesthetic experience of a work of art or other object, an analytical aesthetician typically analyzes the logical structure of the basic concepts of art. Accordingly, in an oft-anthologized essay, "The Role of Theory in Aesthetics," Morris Weitz asks not "What is art?" but rather "What is the logic of the concept of art?"[6] Now just as scientific aesthetics may be roughly assimilated to psychological aesthetics, so analytical aesthetics may be equated with philosophical aesthetics, albeit of a certain kind; for the third kind of aesthetics, *synoptic aesthetics*, is also philosophical in character.

Synoptic or programmatic aesthetics is best illustrated by specimens, and John Dewey's *Art as Experience*,[7] D. W. Gotshalk's *Art and the Social Order*,[8] and Susanne Langer's *Feeling and Form*[9] may be singled out. Such works are typically referred to as systematic "philosophies of art," and they are synoptic in the sense that they comprise a synthesis of several topics, ideas, and concepts which have to do not only with the nature of artistic creation, appreciation, and criticism, but also with the role of art and aesthetic experience in the good life. It is in this latter respect that such works are programmatic. Different types of aesthetics may, of course, overlap. Indeed, while it is easy enough to observe divisions of labor and to assign labels, the analytical or scientific aesthetician may have his synoptic moments just as the synoptic aesthetician may also do some analytical or scientific aesthetics from time to time. Still, the foregoing classification is helpful, especially if the reader is only recently come to an interest in aesthetics and aesthetic education.

This volume, then, may be described as an effort in the application of the methods and techniques of philosophical

6 *Journal of Aesthetics and Art Criticism* XV (1956), 27–35.

7 (New York: Minton, Balch, 1934. Reprinted as a Capricorn paperback).

8 2nd ed. (New York: Dover, 1962).

9 (New York: Charles Scribner's Sons, 1953. Reprinted as a Scribner Library Edition paperback).

aesthetics to the problems of aesthetic education, broadly conceived. It is designed to shorten the distance between work being done in the disciplines and the practical problems and tasks of teachers and learners. It takes cognizance of the observation that the application of the major disciplines to education has not been carried nearly far enough and that much work remains to be done.

Aesthetic Concepts

As Beardsley points out in his opening essay, "Aesthetic Theory and Educational Theory," the expression "aesthetic concepts" has been preempted in the literature of philosophical aesthetics to refer to certain interesting or admirable qualities of things, e.g., such qualities as "elegance," "vitality," "gracefulness," or what Beardsley in his own writings calls "human regional qualities." Thus Beardsley chooses to call the kinds of concepts discussed in this volume "critical concepts." I take it, however, that it will be no source of great confusion if in this collection such concepts are also referred to as "aesthetic concepts." An aesthetic concept, then, is simply one that gets discussed and analyzed by aestheticians in their articles and books. Anthologies in particular are often organized around such concepts. The recent collection of articles from the *Journal of Aesthetics and Art Criticism*,[10] for example, lists the following topical headings: art and aesthetics, form and style, meaning and truth, aesthetic experience, and critical judgment. Or perhaps it should be said that these are words which philosophers study in aesthetic contexts, for when is a concept an aesthetic concept? I think it is clear that the domain membership of a word is often indeterminate, and several universes of discourse may lay claim to the same term. Thus F. E. Sparshott opens his essay by saying that he is not certain at all whether the concept of play belongs to this collection, the reason being that the term "play" figures in several contexts where aesthetic considerations are not emphasized. For others, however, "play" obviously is an aesthetic category. Similar contextual implica-

[10] Monroe C. Beardsley and Herbert M. Schueller, eds., *Aesthetic Inquiry* (Belmont, Calif.: Dickenson Publishing Co., 1967).

tions attach to "intention," "metaphor," "style," and other concepts analyzed in this volume. This acknowledges a commonplace, but it is one of those commonplaces that causes confusion when overlooked; that is, just because a term has a certain meaning in one context, it doesn't follow that it necessarily means the same thing in other contexts. "Growth," for example, has different meanings in biology, economics, and agriculture, none of which can be assimilated to the meaning of "aesthetic growth."

Aesthetic Concepts and Education

Invitations to contribute to this volume suggested that in addition to indicating the pertinence of key aesthetic concepts to aesthetic education proper, a further application might be made to the problems of general educational theory. In several instances this was done while in others the application is restricted to considerations of arts instruction, leaving the reader to ponder further ramifications.

A word about the methods used by contributors: they exhibit a variety of philosophical techniques ranging from what may be called the methods of traditional philosophical criticism to styles characteristic of recent modes of linguistic analysis. But the volume's lack of stylistic unity is hopefully offset by its variety and vitality. Further, in contrast to my earlier anthology, *Aesthetics and Criticism in Art Education*,[11] the essays in this collection (with one exception) were especially invited for this volume. The exception, Joseph Margolis's "Aesthetic and Moral Judgments: Against Compartmentalization," is an expanded version of an article that first appeared in *The Journal of Aesthetic Education*.[12]

That the authors are professional aestheticians or professional educators also deserves to be mentioned. It is becoming clear

11 (Chicago: Rand McNally, 1966).

12 A new journal devoted to understanding the problems of aesthetic education, broadly conceived. The *Journal* prints articles on the problems of formal instructions in the arts and humanities at all levels of schooling and also on the aesthetic problems of the larger society created by modern life. Published by the University of Illinois Press at Urbana.

that the formation of policy for aesthetic education, which is part of the larger problem of formulating educational policy, must involve both subject-matter specialists in the disciplines and professional educators whose special mission is the bridging of the distance between frontier scholarship and the classroom. This volume, to which both types of professional scholars have volunteered their competence and concern, is hopefully a sign that bridges can be built between professional domains. It is further hoped that readers will be persuaded that aesthetics is relevant to understanding the problems of education, perhaps in ways they will find surprising and uncommonly illuminating. Should this be the case, then perhaps this collection will have performed that persuasive function of criticism which Brian Crittenden in his essay says characterizes good teaching.

Finally, the volume does not pretend to present the complete range of aesthetic concepts relevant to an understanding of the problems of aesthetic education: "form" and "expression," for instance, are conspicuously absent. Yet I think that the essays constitute more than a casual start in a philosophical enterprise that is certain to become more important in the years ahead. As aesthetic problems loom larger in a modern mass society, and as conditions are created which will make aesthetic studies an important element in a person's educational development, the need for more philosophical analysis will be felt. It is clear that we have not thought nearly enough, for example, about the contributions of aesthetics to re-definitions of work, recreation, and leisure, or about how aesthetic studies might be shown to contribute not only to intrinsic satisfaction but also to have inherent value, i.e., long-range beneficial effects in the life of individuals and society directly attributable to aesthetic education. It seems that ours will be the first civilization able to give significant time and attention to the cultivation of a first-rate existence for a large proportion of people. Once this obligation is accepted it does not seem that educators can long afford to neglect the role of the aesthetic foundations of education.

ACKNOWLEDGMENTS

Foremost among the many people responsible for this volume are of course the contributors, and my gratitude is first of all expressed to them. I am also indebted to Harry S. Broudy, William P. McLure, Miodrag Muntyan, Rupert N. Evans, and J. Myron Atkin of the University of Illinois who in various ways have lent support and encouragement to my efforts to advance work in aesthetic education. I also wish to extend my thanks to the several people at the University of Illinois Press who helped see the volume through publication, especially Mrs. Gay E. Menges, Mrs. Elizabeth G. Dulany, Mrs. Bonnie J. Depp, and Miss Martha S. Bergland.

Ralph A. Smith
University of Illinois, 1970

ÆSTHETIC
CONCEPTS
and
EDUCATION

ÆSTHETIC THEORY AND

EDUCATIONAL THEORY / 1

Monroe C. Beardsley

Considering the exploratory nature of any attempt to discover what light aesthetics is able to throw on problems in the theory of education, I hope I am permitted to begin with some general remarks, by way of getting my bearings. Despite all that has been written about each of these subjects, their central concepts remain too problematic to be taken for granted. So it will not be out of order, I think, to explain at least my own assumptions—without claiming that they are shared by all.

As far as aesthetics is concerned, I can be fairly succinct. In my view, aesthetics, as a branch of philosophy, is essentially metacriticism. It deals with philosophical problems that arise when we make statements about works of art and other aesthetic objects. And aesthetic theory, as a body of knowledge (or at least reasoned belief), consists of general principles that provide solutions to those problems and thus serve as theoretical underpinnings for art criticism.[1] The unity of aesthetic

[1] For a fuller account, see my *Aesthetics: Problems in the Philosophy of Criticism* (New York: Harcourt, Brace, 1958), Introduction.

theory is derived partly from its preoccupation with a set of concepts that play an important role in reasonable discussion of works of art. Since the handiest term for these concepts of aesthetic concern, "aesthetic concepts," has already been pre-empted for a quite different class of concepts (namely, aesthetically interesting qualities of objects), I suggest that we use the term "critical concepts" for them (e.g., *form, expression, beauty*).

Turning to the theory of education, I find myself on much less familiar ground. I am in need, for one thing, of a concept of education such as might be at least roughly marked out by a definition. But I have the impression that there is a prevailing uneasiness about all such definitions, and as much skepticism about their possibility as about their utility. I shall offer a quasi-definitional description of what I take education to be and work from that. To the extent to which my concept of education deviates from the reader's, to that extent aesthetics may be less relevant to educational theory in your sense of "education" than it is (if I am right) to educational theory in my sense.

A *developmental experience*, in my sense, is an experience that contributes materially to the formation or strengthening of a person's powers—that is, his capacities or dispositions to act in ways that are valuable to him (including mental acts). When these capacities are chiefly physical or when they are fairly isolated and independent skills, we are likely to speak of developmental experiences as "training." But when a developmental experience contains a cognitive component— when the person acquires not only a particular power, but an awareness of having that power and some understanding of its worth and of its relationship to other powers—then his experience is an *educational experience.*[2]

[2] In framing this concept, I have profited from the arguments of R. S. Peters, "Education as Initiation," in Reginald D. Archambault, ed., *Philosophical Analysis and Education* (London: Routledge, 1965), and *Ethics and Education* (Glenview, Ill.: Scott, Foresman, 1967), chap. 1. Cf. John Dewey, *Experience and Education* (New York: Macmillan, 1938).

4 /

If education consists of educational experiences, then, as has often been remarked, it can occur outside of any institutional setting such as the classroom; and it can even occur unsought. But there is also such a thing as the deliberate creation and control of situations in order to provide educational experiences, and this I shall refer to, broadly, as *instruction*. In my sense, then, an instructor is one who arranges educational experiences (either for himself or for others).

Instruction may be improvised or it may be thought out (at least in main strategic outlines) in advance. Such an advance plan or design for an educational experience or a sequence of educational experiences is (if I may be permitted a somewhat tainted contemporary term) an *educational scenario*, which might be drawn up as a textbook or a syllabus or a "unit-plan."[3] Finally, the *theory of instruction* (which I take to be at least a substantial part of what is often called "educational theory") consists of general principles—both normative and nonnormative—for constructing educational scenarios of various sorts for various kinds of persons.[4] Since its nonnormative principles are general facts about human beings, the theory of instruction is, as Michael Scriven has clearly shown,[5] an applied social science (where social science includes psychology).

[3] Under this heading we might even include such broad systems of curricular proposals as those of Hampshire College (Franklin Patterson and Charles Longsworth, *The Making of a College*, Cambridge: M.I.T. Press, 1966) and Swarthmore College (*Critique of a College*, Swarthmore, Pa., 1967).

[4] Cf. Jerome S. Bruner, *Toward a Theory of Instruction* (Cambridge: Harvard University, Belknap Press, 1966), chap. 3.

[5] See Michael Scriven, "The Contribution of Philosophy of the Social Sciences to Educational Development," in George Barnett, ed., *Philosophy and Educational Development* (Boston: Houghton Mifflin, 1966). Scriven uses the term "education" rather than "instruction," but the context indicates, I believe, that he has in mind what I am calling "instruction." The view of instructional theory as applied social science is objected to by Marc Belth, *Education as a Discipline* (Boston: Allyn and Bacon, 1965), pp. 2–4, but his objections are misplaced. It does not follow from regarding the theory of instruction as applied social science that "there is no such subject as education" (p. 2) or that "almost everything now being offered in education programs could be eliminated except practice teaching" (p. 3).

I

When we ask how, if at all, one field of study or inquiry can illuminate another, we cannot expect an answer until we are clear about their logical relationship. But when we are assured of logical relationship, the answer may be comparatively easy. For example, if we agree with Scriven that the theory of instruction is an applied social science, then we may expect a study of social science to have a bearing upon the theory of instruction—indeed, to form an essential basis of it; and we may expect, less confidently perhaps, that a knowledge of the theory of instruction will suggest ideas that are usable in other applied social sciences (such as welfare economics or clinical psychology). The first connection is in part deductive, of course, and therefore intimate; the second is only inductive, and tenuously inductive at that—any suggestions carried over from one applied social science to another have to be regarded as hypotheses until subjected to independent test in the new field. Or, to take one more example, if aesthetics deals with problems that arise in discussing aesthetic objects, and if part of the theory of instruction concerns aesthetic instruction (instruction in the creation or understanding of aesthetic objects), then evidently some of the discoveries that aestheticians make —assuming that they make discoveries—may be expected to be of interest to the theorist of instruction, insofar as he is concerned with aesthetic instruction.

But the question here being posed has to do with a different sort of field-to-field cognitive illumination. For there is no logical connection between aesthetic theory, taken generally, and instructional theory, taken generally. If we ask how elements of the former help us to understand elements of the latter, we cannot answer by showing how one is subsumed under the other, or how both are coordinate species of a significantly proximate genus (they are, of course, both species of the genus "subjects" or "fields of inquiry"). So we must look for a different sort of linkage.

Given two logically separate fields of inquiry between which we seek illuminating connections, there seem to be two kinds of connection that might be found. They differ in candlepower (if my figure of speech may be momentarily sustained), and the second connection might be regarded as a bundle of connections of the first kind.

The first, and weaker, kind of interfield illumination can come about in the following way. As I have said, aesthetics is directly concerned with criticism, and criticism with aesthetic objects, primarily works of art. Now works of art have their own noteworthy properties—if not indispensable and exclusive properties (which some would deny to them) then at least properties which they may be said to *feature,* in that these properties are highly prevalent, or often present to a high degree, or connected with their peculiar values, or in some other way especially notable. The terms designating these featured properties will naturally play a central role in critical talk about these objects, and so they will be brought to the attention of aestheticians and carefully examined by them. In this way, we would expect that aestheticians, if they put their minds to their job and are reasonably successful, will have something helpful to say about these critical concepts: about precisely what is and what is not involved in them, about the analytical connections among them, and so forth. But though these critical concepts have an important role—perhaps their most important role—to play in criticism, they may well have roles in other fields of study, as, for example, the theory of instruction. And so it may turn out that the aesthetician's work can be put to the uses of the instructionist, in that the latter's inquiries can benefit from the work of the former.

A number of these critical concepts that seem eligible for conceptual crossover are discussed in other essays in this book. So I turn to the second sort of interfield illumination. In this case, the critical concept is not taken over directly into instructional theory, after having been clarified in aesthetics, but the object or process that it stands for is used as a *model.*

There has been much talk about models of educational situations or processes.[6] It is now pretty well recognized, I think, that they can be useful in calling our attention to significant features of instruction that we might without them fail to perceive so clearly; but also that they have their limitations and can easily be overextended. The term "model" may itself be misleading in this context, where it cannot be supposed to have as much content as it does in the philosophy of natural or social science. What I have in mind, at any rate, is something rather modest: that if we understand an important aspect of our relationship to works of art, and try looking at instruction with its help, we may find that certain features of instruction become plainer or sharper from this point of view. Moreover, we may derive some useful suggestions about what *good* instruction is.

I propose to discuss one rather fundamental notion in aesthetics and consider its possible application in instructional theory. My question is: to what extent, and in what respects, can the aesthetic experience serve as a useful model of the educational experience? Or, in somewhat plainer terms: to what extent, and in what ways, should an educational experience *be* an aesthetic experience?

II

Two preliminary points should be noted at once. In the first place, when one speaks of "the aesthetic experience" and "the educational experience," there need be no implication that either of these is all of a piece. There are, indeed, many varieties of aesthetic experiences and of educational experiences; but I suppose that each of these terms marks out a reasonably though somewhat vaguely defined class of experiences. In the second place, the concepts of the two kinds of experience appear to be logically independent, in that a particular experience might be one but not the other, or might be both or neither.

[6] See, for example, Israel Scheffler, "Philosophical Models of Teaching," *Harvard Educational Review* XXXV (1965): 131–43. Earlier Scheffler had discussed similar concepts as metaphors in *The Language of Education* (Springfield, Ill.: Charles Thomas, 1960), chap. 3. See also Belth, *Education as a Discipline*, esp. chap. 6.

In some aesthetic and educational theories, this second proposition would be disputed. Some hold, for example, that all educational experiences are problem-solving experiences and thus are necessarily patterned according to certain stages of the problem-solving process.[7] Some hold that aesthetic experiences can only occur in the absence of any intellectual activity, such as is involved in framing hypotheses, inferring consequences, and testing them. If both of these views were correct, it would follow that no experience could be both an educational experience and an aesthetic experience. But I do not accept either of these views.

In order to see what use there may be in a model, the first step, of course, is to examine the model itself. What is aesthetic experience? I say that it is an experience having the following five characteristics:

1. It involves attention to a portion of a phenomenally objective field, either sensuous (such as the colors in a painting) or intentional (such as the events in a novel), and to its elements and internal relationships. Whether or not we should call an experience "aesthetic" when its phenomenal object consists entirely of abstract entities (such as numbers or positions on a chess board) and their relationships is a question I cannot decide how to answer, and so must leave open here.

2. It involves an awareness of form, i.e., relationships among the elements of the phenomenal field, especially (but not exclusively) relationships of similarity/contrast and serial order. More specifically, it involves perceiving the phenomenal field as a stratified design, in which a complex appears to possess a certain unity just because of the relationships among the parts of which it is (or appears to have been) composed.

3. It involves an awareness of regional quality—by which I mean simple qualities of complexes, and especially (but not exclusively) those qualities that are described by words taken over metaphorically from human contexts. (The class of re-

[7] This view is interestingly and acutely presented by Donald Arnstine, *Philosophy of Education: Learning and Schooling* (New York: Harper and Row, 1967).

gional qualities corresponds roughly to the class of aesthetic concepts alluded to above: beauty, elegance, grace, dignity, frivolity, irony, wit.)

4. It is characterized by a fairly high degree of unity, in comparison with ordinary everyday experiences. Unity has two distinguishable parts: coherence and completeness. An aesthetic experience is unusually coherent, in that the various perceptions, feelings, inferences, recognitions, memories, desires, etc., that occur in the course of its development (and not all of these kinds of mental state need occur) have a character of belonging or fitting together or succeeding one another with continuity. An aesthetic experience is unusually complete, in that the experience marks itself off fairly definitely from other experiences—both from contemporaneous items of awareness that do not belong to it and from experiences that precede and follow it.

5. It is intrinsically gratifying, or, in other words, brings with it both a continuing enjoyment that is felt as part of the development of the experience, and a final satisfaction or fulfillment that may linger after the experience has ended. I am not certain that this gratifying character should be included in the definition of "aesthetic experience," as I am proposing here; however, for my present purposes I do not think it matters very much if one decides that the connection between aesthetic experience and aesthetic gratification is a synthetic, contingent one.

As one would expect, many of our experiences have some of these five characteristics without having them all, and we are often inclined, I think, to assimilate some of them to aesthetic experiences, or perhaps to say that they have "aesthetic quality" or a "quasi-aesthetic character." Some such terminology might well be useful—for example, in talking about the experience of smelling a rose, which clearly satisfies conditions 1 and 5, but not the others. (In a limiting sense, it could be said to satisfy condition 4, but it is not a unity of diverse elements.)

Except for the disputed points that I have mentioned, my characterization of an aesthetic experience would generally be regarded as quite conventional, and even boringly so. John Dewey did more than anyone else, I think, to make it vivid and convincing, but in the past thirty years it has been repeated over and over with little variation and very little critical examination—until recently. Now George Dickie has called into serious question condition 4, which to followers of Dewey is perhaps the most crucial of all. His significant attack has been made in two stages. First, in a deservedly well-known essay he questioned the usual way of talking about aesthetic experience: "Some philosophers, however, have talked about aesthetic experience as if it were some unique sort of entity which can become the object of experimental inquiry. (Beardsley is not one of these theorists.) There is something odd about any attempt to make experience an object of inquiry, as if experience were of the same type as a piece of copper, a frog, or even an example of behavior."[8] Second, he questioned the applicability of terms like "coherent" and "complete" to experiences as such, and argued that, strictly speaking, there cannot be a "unity of experience," though there can be an "experience of unity," which has been misdescribed as a "unity of experience."[9] Taken together, these two theses are, in my judgment, of considerable significance and demand careful consideration. I have offered a reply to them elsewhere,[10] defending both (1) the legitimacy of inquiring into the traits of experiences as such, including traits that could serve to distinguish one kind of experience from another, and (2) the propriety of speaking of the "unity [including the coherence and completeness] of experience." But I don't wish to imply that the debate is closed, or my argument conclusive, even though on the present occasion I will not repeat my defense of aesthetic experience.

At the very least, Dickie has made an extremely valuable point and forced us to a new level of scrupulousness in our talk

[8] George Dickie, "Is Psychology Relevant to Aesthetics?" *Philosophical Review* LXXI (1962): 297.

[9] George Dickie, "Beardsley's Phantom Aesthetic Experience," *Journal of Philosophy* LXII (1965): 129–36.

[10] Monroe C. Beardsley, "Aesthetic Experience Regained," *Journal of Aesthetics and Art Criticism* XXVIII (Fall, 1969): 3–11.

about experience and experiences—a kind of talk in which it is all too easy to fall into looseness and vagueness. In moments of lyric exaltation, aestheticians—and instructionists as well—sometimes talk about such things as the *quality* of an experience, the *rhythm* of an experience, the *structure* of an experience. In Dewey's *Art as Experience*, experiences are spoken of as "refined and intensified," "crude," having "form," having "unity," "inchoate," having "individualizing quality and self-sufficiency," being such that "every successive part flows freely, without seam and without unfulfilled blanks, into what ensues," having "no holes, mechanical junctions, and dead centers," having "fulfillment reached through ordered and organized movement," "slack and discursive"—this list is far from exhaustive.[11] But which of these descriptions are literally correct, which metaphorically acceptable, which nonsensical? Dickie's argument obliges us to take these questions seriously.

One guide we have in trying to be clear about such terms is the fundamental distinction between the phenomenally objective and the phenomenally subjective in our experience—that is, between those qualities that we perceive as belonging to a world that presents itself as external to, and independent of, our awareness of it, and those qualities that we perceive as qualities of our own egos. The painting is red; I am annoyed. The music is sad; I am delighted. When we speak of the "quality of an experience," then, do we mean (1) a regional quality of the phenomenally objective field, such as the continually unfolding gracefulness of the dancer, or (2) a phenomenally subjective content, a pervasive affect such as joy or sorrow, or (3) something that can be predicated of the whole experience at a given time, including both its phenomenally objective and phenomenally subjective elements? When I speak of the "coherence" or "completeness" of an experience I am speaking in the third way, as I have indicated. But sometimes terms are applied to experiences as such when, in fact, they properly

11 John Dewey, *Art as Experience* (New York: Minton, Balch, 1934), pp. 3, 11, 15, 19, 35, 35, 36, 36, 38, 40.

apply only in the first or second way, and the confusion arises from a failure to keep these distinctions clearly in mind.

III

One of Dewey's most remarkable claims in *Art as Experience* is that aesthetic experience is a model for all experience—even an ideal model, to which other experience should as far as possible be brought to conform. This conclusion derived, first, from his connection of aesthetic experience with what it is to have "*an* experience," and thus with what it is to be fully alive; and, second, from his conviction that when our lives are not as worthwhile as they might be, this is because they are infected by various dualisms, both theoretical and social, which Dewey's whole philosophy was designed to repair and which are so notably and happily absent from aesthetic experience. I don't want to try to defend Dewey's claim in all its generality, but I think the peculiar self-sufficiency and satisfyingness of aesthetic experience, its ability to combine intensity of livingness with harmony of the self, do justify us in using it as the kind of exploratory model I have described above. What makes a good aesthetic experience is not what makes a good religious experience, or a good educational experience, and the same may be said of all the other varieties of experience, such as verifying a scientific theory, making a moral decision, performing a political act, etc. But the traits that distinguish aesthetic experience and determine its peculiar goodness are highly generic and independent of practical contexts and interests. So it is natural to inquire whether this kind of goodness can be, or should be, an ingredient in other kinds of goodness.

There are, moreover, certain affinities between aesthetic experience and educational experience that suggest the possibility of deeper bonds. Both artistic creation and instruction consist in the deliberate setting up of conditions for experiences, which implies a common concern about such matters as medium and form. And the enjoyment of a work of art is a process of discovery: if it does not necessarily issue in heightened personal powers, it has the feel of growing insight and mastery, at least with regard to the object directly confronted.

I know of two attempts that have been made to throw light on educational experience by using aesthetic experience as a model. The first is an article by Villemain and Champlin,[12] which proposes a broadening of Dewey's educational theory by bringing to bear upon it part of his work in aesthetics. Unfortunately (in my view) the authors rely mainly on one of the most puzzling things that Dewey says about aesthetic experience: that "the existence of this unity [i.e., the unity of *an* experience] is constituted by a single *quality* that pervades the entire experience in spite of the variation of its constituent parts."[13] First, there is the oddity—already touched on—of talking about the quality of an *experience*. Second, even if there can be such qualities, I do not think it is correct to say that typical aesthetic experiences owe their unity to a single all-pervasive quality. I find my experience of listening to Haydn's *String Quartet in D Major* (Op. 76, No. 5) highly unified, but I cannot discriminate a single quality that appears throughout. Third, Villemain and Champlin confuse matters somewhat by the identification implicit in their statement that "The qualitative or esthetic is generic to *all* experience."[14] What does it mean to place "qualitative" and "esthetic" in apposition? What these writers seem to be saying (and claiming Dewey's authority for saying) is (1) that an aesthetic experience is one in which there is an all-pervasive quality and (2) that every experience is an aesthetic experience (perhaps they would add, in some *degree*). But (1) and (2) are surely both false, unless they are taken in trivial senses. I think one can grant that art takes a special interest in quality (see my third condition of aesthetic experience, above), and also that there is a kind of "qualitative thinking" involved in art creation, something different from intellectual inquiry or

12 Francis T. Villemain and Nathanial L. Champlin, "Frontiers for an Experimentalist Philosophy of Education," *Antioch Review* XIX (1959): 345–59.

13 Dewey, *Art as Experience*, p. 37, quoted by Villemain and Champlin, "Frontiers," p. 347.

14 Villemain and Champlin, "Frontiers," p. 347.

problem-solving.[15] These are important points, and they have implications for the *content* of general education; but they do not show that, or how, the process of education as such can be an aesthetic experience.

The second and more recent approach to these problems is that made in a carefully argued book by Donald Arnstine.[16] He takes learning to consist in the acquisition of dispositions, and he holds that dispositions can only be acquired in situations that involve emotional response. Thus, in reference to one method of instruction, he says: "Generally speaking, then, if a lecture is to facilitate change in the kinds of dispositions that have an appropriate place in schools, it must not only arouse emotions (which is to say, enlist interest), but it must also focus emotion so that it will be relevant to the topic of the lecture."[17] If I understand Arnstine's view, the phrase "which is to say" is misleading here; the point is not that "to arouse emotion" and "to enlist interest" are synonymous expressions, but that arousing emotion in the relevantly focused way will in fact enlist interest and facilitate learning.

It is this emphasis on emotion in learning that leads Arnstine to connect learning with aesthetic experience. In giving his characterization of aesthetic experience, he, too, talks about "aesthetic quality in experience" and sometimes "aesthetic qualities,"[18] but it turns out that in his rather strange usage aesthetic quality is the "immediately and directly felt perception of form."[19] What he seems to be saying, then, is (1) that aesthetic experience is the experience of perceiving form, (2) that "perception of form is affective in quality—that is, it has a particular feel to it,"[20] and (3) that therefore aesthetic ex-

[15] See my "On the Creation of Art," *Journal of Aesthetics and Art Criticism* XXIII (1965): 291–304. Villemain and Champlin are concerned to emphasize "qualitative thinking" (pp. 347 ff.), but they regard it as a kind of problem-solving; there are "qualitative" and "theoretical" problems, in their view.
[16] Arnstine, *Philosophy of Education.*
[17] *Ibid.*, pp. 169–70.
[18] *Ibid.*, pp. 176–77.
[19] *Ibid.*, p. 186.
[20] *Ibid.*, p. 185.

perience is always, and notably, "emotional." From this he draws the important conclusion that pedagogical techniques and materials must be judged by aesthetic as well as other criteria: their style, their dramatic shape, their inherent expressiveness become subject to criticism, since these properties are essentially connected with the emotional response that learning requires.[21]

I believe there are two confusions in Arnstine's argument; a clarification narrows his conclusion without invalidating it. First, it may be granted that (except perhaps in the simplest cases) the perception of form is affective—we are interested, expectant, pleased, etc.—but it is a mistake to jump from this to talk about "emotions" and to speak of "the vast range of emotions that may become aesthetic in quality."[22] If "emotion" denotes such things as fear, hope, jealousy, sadness, then it is evident that emotion is not at all necessary for aesthetic experience, and in fact it is doubtful that emotions, in a strict sense, even occur in those aesthetic experiences which are obtained from nonverbal works of art. The problem is complex. The matter is obscured in this context by Arnstine's second confusion, as it seems to me—one that emerges in the following passage: "Hence it is the case that the sounds and colors of 'formal' or nonobjective art works are meaningful only insofar as they call forth or are expressive of particular emotions (for emotions *are* recognizable members of the community of human meanings), whether these emotions are clear-cut enough to be nameable. Unless such works have an emotional impact, they are quite literally meaningless, and they have failed artistically."[23] The term "emotional impact" seems to be the equivocal pivot that permits the easy identification of "calling forth" and "being expressive of." Emotions are phenomenally subjective affective states. But the sadness of the music or the joyousness of the abstract expressionist painting are, of course, not emotions at all but perceptual qualities.

21 *Ibid.*, p. 255.
22 *Ibid.*, p. 187.
23 *Ibid.*, p. 211.

16 /

This has been noted by many writers and should not be a source of confusion here. It is one thing to hear sadness and quite another to feel sad, nor need the former involve the latter.

Arnstine's argument can be interpreted to be that learning requires a satisfying arousal of affect; that aesthetic experience consists essentially in the arousal of affect through form, which is thus inherently satisfying; and therefore that for successful instruction, the educational experience should be an aesthetic experience. Apart from questions about its logic, this argument rests on a dubious premise about the nature of aesthetic experience. However, it might be reformulated in the following way: that learning requires a certain intensity of experience; that the peculiar intensity of aesthetic experience derives from an integrative response to form and to aesthetic (regional) qualities; and therefore that the techniques that achieve artistic success (in producing aesthetic experience) are conditions of instructional success as well. If we understand the intensity of an experience to consist in its concentration of attention, its heightened vitality, its engagement of the whole self, then I think we can say that there is important truth in what Arnstine proposes. In this respect it could be said that aesthetic experience does serve as a valid model of educational experience.

But a more significant feature of aesthetic experience, from the educational point of view, is its unusual degree of wholeness, its coherence and completeness. If we want to know what a unified experience can be, aesthetic experiences provide paradigm cases. They sharpen our sensitivity to factors that contribute to the unity of an experience, as well as to those that subtly or grossly interfere with it. They show us how to increase the wholeness of an experience, to make it richer and deeper and at the same time more individual and memorable. And in both of these ways they may guide us in understanding and controlling educational experience to make it effective. I will try to be more specific—though I am afraid not exact or definitive.

First, in aesthetic experience at its best there is unusual interrelatedness. We are in a state in which everything counts, so to speak—whether for or against. Our grasp is inclusive, not abstracting or rejective: every word of the poem, every gesture of the drama, is, ideally, to be registered and connected with the rest. Now it is a commonplace among educators—though it has not yet universally become ingrained as habit—that on the pupil who is aware, everything that goes on in the classroom may have its effect. The teacher of arithmetic, it is said, is never merely a teacher of arithmetic; by her forms of speech, her manners, her movements, her tone of voice, and in numerous other ways, she teaches (inevitably) many things at once: not only, say, that the product of two fractions is equal to the product of their numerators over the product of their denominators, but that arithmetic is pointless, that learning is largely memorization, that it is important to have good handwriting, that children should not question what they are told, that adults are obtuse, etc., etc. It helps us to perceive this fact, and take account of it, when we consider whether an educational experience should be an aesthetic experience.

On the other hand, the factors that make for disruption in what would otherwise be a unified experience can also be pointed up from an aesthetic point of view, which thus helps to make us aware of failure in instruction. One of the verses that Jonathan Kozol found in his "Course of Study" for the fourth-grade black children in his Boston ghetto school went like this:

> There is beauty in the sunshine
> An' clouds that roam the sky;
> There is beauty in the Heavens,
> An' the stars that shine on high.
> There is beauty in the moonbeams
> That shine both pale an' fair—
> An' it matters not where'er we go
> There is beauty everywhere.[24]

24 Jonathan Kozol, *Death at an Early Age* (Boston: Houghton Mifflin, 1967), p. 171; cf. p. 188. Poem by P. F. Freeman.

My present point has nothing to do with the literary ghastliness of this verse or the question of its aesthetic worth to fourth graders. Suppose that it could provide some measure of aesthetic satisfaction to some young readers. But these were children who came to school from broken-down slum apartments, through streets littered with abandoned cars, trash, winos, decaying storefronts, and prospects of the New York, New Haven, and Hartford Railway tracks. It is our recognition of the need for some degree of wholeness in the educational experience that makes us doubt that an educational experience could result from bringing such a verse to children who live with such images.

I believe that this line of inquiry could fruitfully be extended, but my purpose here is primarily to see what kind of question we have on hand, and, indeed, whether we have a significant question at all. It seems to me clear, now, that the question is worth asking; it is important to know how far, and in what ways, educational experiences ought to have the character of aesthetic experiences. The superficial positive answers are not far to seek: it is fairly obvious that lectures can be improved by audio-visual aids of various kinds, that they can benefit from dramatic shaping, that discussions and dialogues are better—educationally speaking—as they have the right change of pace, balance, dynamic contrast, fluidity of movement toward a climax, etc. These points belong to the *decorative* use of artistry in education. The more fundamental positive answers, along the lines suggested above, concern the *structural* use of artistry; they involve the role of coherence and completeness and their derivative and related concepts.

It remains to note, however, that part of the answer is negative; there must be limits to the aestheticizing of instruction. From the aesthetic point of view, an experience ought to be self-sufficient, that is, complete in itself. But there is something inimical to education in such an ideal when it is realized to a high degree. First, the experience of a rounded form, of a completed closure, may be less likely to leave a trace than an experience that is open-ended, unfinished. Second, the more complete an experience is, the less it connects with other experiences, earlier and later; but the development of active powers depends on sequences of related experiences rather than single ones.

Though we have come to understand how important it is to make the experience of learning intrinsically satisfying for purely educational reasons, that is not the same as making it aesthetic. And we must also bear in mind that the continuity and cumulativeness of the educational process require something more than individual experiences that are enjoyed for their own sake. Something unsatisfied, something still in the making, something that leads on to further questions and inquiries, is also necessary. Thus the best educational experiences will seldom, if ever, be the best aesthetic experiences. And, of course, vice versa.

Here is an example of the ineluctable tension between our aesthetic interest and our other interests—however successful we may be in harmonizing them for certain parts of our lives. This tension, we may remind ourselves, is what makes art possible and necessary; were we to realize the Deweyan dream of making all our works and days aesthetically rewarding, we would have no wish or need to design special objects for aesthetic purposes. But the ultimate pluralism of values and of obligations should not surprise us—or discourage us from seeking fruitful combinations of mutually supporting or overlapping interests to give some coherence to our lives. And it is good to find our interests in art and education combinable to a significant extent, even though not without limit.

ÆSTHETIC QUALITIES

IN EXPERIENCE AND LEARNING / 2

Donald Arnstine

In experience that is aesthetic in quality, and in experience from which learning results, there can be found important common elements. These elements have great significance for educators, for they indicate more effective ways in which learning in schools can be promoted. An effort will be made in this essay both to delineate what is common to learning and the aesthetic and to show how events which are aesthetic in character can be made to serve processes that eventuate in learning. Throughout the discussion, the concept of learning will be used with reference to what may happen within any field of study or inquiry; it will not be restricted to the field of the arts.

At first, there seems nothing more in common between learning and the aesthetic than there is between grapefruit and happiness. Indeed, some people are happy when they eat grapefruit, and others maintain that they learned something from Charles Dickens. But after all, so what? Accidents are slim pickings for the development of theoretical generalizations.

It would be rather novel for a theorist to assert that *everyone* who eats grapefruit is *always* made happy. Yet such an assertion, if true, would serve as a sound basis for claiming that if everyone is to be made happy, everyone should be given grapefruit to eat. Aside from the particulars about grapefruit and happiness, this is just the form of argument I shall try to pursue here. I shall propose that learning does in fact result from experiences that can properly be described as aesthetic in character, and that if learning is what teachers are after, the promotion of experiences having aesthetic qualities is an important way (although not the only way) of promoting learning. I shall try to show that these proposals are not such radical ones by subjecting to analysis the concepts of learning and the aesthetic, and by referring to some recent and reasonably well-established empirical research.

The Concept of Learning

For our purposes it is important first to acknowledge a crucial distinction between the use of the term "aesthetic" and the use of the term "learning." The concept of the aesthetic has reference to a quality of experience—to how experience is felt. The concept of learning, on the other hand, refers to an outcome of experience and has no implications for how experience might feel. Thus it would be quite possible, in considering a single experience or set of experiences, to speak both of its aesthetic quality and of its outcome in terms of what was learned. This is the approach that will be followed in the discussion later on.

To what is one committed when he speaks about learning? It has just been said that the term "learning" refers to an outcome of experience and not to its felt quality. Yet the expression "learning experience" is sometimes used to indicate a sort of experience which has a characteristic feel to it. This usage has had very misleading consequences. For example, students are judged with respect to how much and how well they have learned. Sometimes the student is keenly disap-

22 /

pointed because the judgments of others do not accord with his own self-judgment. How did the student come to believe that he learned? He claims that he *felt* he did. But it is observation, inference, and judgment that afford knowledge of whether a person learned or not. The mere having of feelings does not yield such knowledge.

In the course of a semester's time—or of a lifetime—we feel a great many things, but the feelings we have offer no clues about whether anything was learned at the time. We may learn from what was delightful, what was frightening, what was tragic. And then again, we may not have learned. But the way the experience felt offers no reliable guide to what was learned, just as our later realization that something had been learned implies nothing about the felt qualities of the experiences from which the learning resulted.

Just as "learning" refers to nothing directly felt, neither does it refer to anything directly observed or observable. In fact, it refers to no specific event at all, for it functions more like the word "recuperating" than it does like the word "swimming." That is, "learning" is a judgment-making term. Although the judgment "He learned" is about the outcome of past events, its principal *use* is predictive. For it means, at the very least, that with regard to some range of behavior, an individual will not act as he did before.

Minimally, then, "He learned" means "He has changed and, under the appropriate conditions, his future behavior will show it." The future becomes focal, for whenever the statement is made of anyone, at least these two things are meant: (1) he has changed and (2) that change can be expected to persist in some form in the future.

To say that this is minimally meant by the claim "He learned" is not to hide the two glaring ambiguities in the second of the above two meanings. Those two ambiguities lie at the heart of all of the confusion and all of the dispute among learning theories. *In what form* must the change persist? And for *how long* in the future must it persist? Differences in the answers to these questions stake out the boundaries between behaviorists, gestaltists, functionalists, etc. Although these ambiguities can never be eliminated, they can be reduced. Let us first consider the question of how long the change must persist.

It makes sense to say that someone learned something but that he forgot it the next day. To last for a day justifies calling a change a case of learning. But it is surely a trivial case. More important, it is wholly inadequate to any consideration of the learning sought by schools. If those learnings last for only a day, instruction will be judged unsuccessful—even if an exam was passed before it was forgotten.

How long, then, must a change persist in a person before we are willing to regard it as a case of learning in a nontrivial sense? Surely the question cannot be answered simply in terms of calendar time, for it will depend on what was learned and on the purpose for which it was learned. My purpose in learning the phone number of the drugstore was to be able to order a prescription. No further purpose is served by being able to recite the number later on. But when a child learns his name, he doesn't ever forget it, for he often has good reason for responding to it or being able to say it.

The sense of these observations amounts to this: for a change in a person to permit the term "learning," it must persist at least long enough to serve the learner's purpose. If that purpose is a specific and short-range one (ordering a prescription), then the specific content of what is learned (a telephone number) becomes reduced in importance, and it is appropriate to say that *what* was learned was just a way of achieving a certain purpose.

This feature of the persistence implied in the concept of learning helps us to analyze some of the events promoted in school settings. A student who can supply enough correct answers to pass an examination on Friday may be unable to do so the following Monday. To say that he learned would be to use the term "learning" in a peculiar sense. If it was the student's purpose always to have available those particular answers for anyone who asked for them,[1] then he didn't learn except in a very trivial sense. But if his purpose was simply the short-term one of passing the examination, then he did learn. But in this case, the learning that mattered was not the information embodied in the answers but rather how to pass the examination. And indeed, for the successful student, it is this latter learning which will persist long after the information sought by the exam has altogether disappeared.

Persistence or longevity, at least in terms of the learner's purpose, will thus be implied whenever the term "learning" is used in the discussion that follows. Excluded from consideration, then, will be cases of the acquisition of information or of skill which is then lost in a relatively short time. Much of the effort of teachers, of course, is expended in just such activities: asking, cajoling, and demanding that students acquire information and skills which are destined for early extinction. Thus our subsequent discussion of the aesthetic dimensions of learning must exclude much of what is traditionally done in schools. This does not suggest that the discussion is therefore "inapplicable" to school practices. It does suggest that these practices call for change. An idea that did *not* imply changes in current practices would be an idea not worth serious consideration.

Assuming a measure of persistence in any sort of learning which schools are concerned to foster, we are ready to examine the second of the major ambiguities built into the concept of learning: *in what form* must changes persist, in order for us to be able to say "He learned"? Must the change be preserved on future occasions in just the same form in which it originally appeared? Or can a change indicative of learning take a variety of different forms on future occasions?

A strict behaviorist opts for the first alternative; a change in behavior is called learning when it is repeated on the appropri-

[1] This is admittedly an odd sort of purpose, seldom found in students. Even so, school personnel behave as if most students either did or at least should have such a purpose.

ate cue. A series of responses of the same form to repeated occasions of similar stimuli is called a habit. Thus what is called learning in this context would also be called habituation. To say "He learned" would mean "He acquired a habit." Yet this meaning will not be useful for the present discussion, for we are concerned with those deliberate processes of education which are appropriate for schools. The cultivation of habits is only peripheral to these processes. Since this is a point that is crucial to the present discussion and is also subject to some disagreement, it calls for explanation and defense.

It is sometimes claimed that school learning in the various subject areas—English, science, history, etc.—is nothing more than the cultivation of complex verbal habits. This claim is the principal support for the use of programmed instruction techniques which seek to produce certain verbal habits in students by what is thought to be a process of conditioning. To learn chemistry, on this view, would be to acquire the habit of saying "H_2O" when asked, "What is the chemical name for water?" Chemists, of course are people who have learned chemistry, and in the course of learning it they acquired many verbal habits. But they are not called chemists by virtue of those verbal habits. They are chemists because of their attitudes, the skills they can perform, and the dispositions on which they act. They retain jobs in laboratories and in universities because of the characteristic ways in which they treat novelties and problems of certain sorts—the ways they bring information, ideas, and techniques to bear upon procedures of analysis, hypothesis-generation, testing, verification, and generalization. In the course of learning to do this, certain verbal habits are acquired, but the simple acquisition of verbal habits hardly enables one to think and act in these refined and discriminating ways.

It may be objected that to learn chemistry is not to come to act like a chemist, but is just to acquire some knowledge of what generations of chemists have discovered. Since this sort of knowledge is subject to early erosion through forgetting, verbal habits are again called upon to produce "informed" students. Unfortunately, these students do not *act* very "informed" if they are not asked appropriate questions—as, for example, those questions they were habituated to answer.

Cultivating verbal habits can get students past examinations, but it serves little purpose beyond that. If schools are maintained for purposes beyond preparing pupils to pass examinations, then merely to cultivate habits would be to fail to achieve those purposes. This would be true for learnings in all the subjects of the curriculum, and even more true for learnings in the area of personality and character development.

In order to say of a person, "He learned," changes in him must persist, but not merely in the form of habits. In what form, then, shall these changes persist? A change in a person which is not simply a new habit, but which affects his future action, might best be understood as the acquisition of a new disposition—that is, a new way of approaching, of looking at, or of dealing with some range of topics or problems. To have a disposition is to be disposed to act, but it is not simply to be prepared to run off a specific set of responses.

Because dispositions are not just habits, they are not simply automatic. Thus the possessor of a disposition exercises choice in action; his action is discriminating. To this extent, and in contrast to habits, dispositions imply intelligence. Gregariousness and problem-centeredness can be dispositions. People who have such dispositions can be expected to act in certain ways. But while the *habitually* gregarious person seeks the company of others whenever the occasion allows, the person who is *disposed* to be gregarious exercises choice about when to be with other people. Thus a man seeking isolation on a certain occasion may still accurately be called gregarious, and a man who at the moment has become quite self-conscious can still be called a problem-centered person. But a person who is disposed to be problem-centered is one who usually forgets about himself as he deals with situations, who usually is not rendered ineffective in action by his own self-doubts, and who usually is not dominated by a desire to seek the good opinion of others.

When a person has changed in such a way that the change

persists over time and is a change in patterns of action which allows for both variability in specific acts and the possibility of intelligent choice, the change can be described as a change in disposition and not merely the addition of a new habit. Changes in dispositions, with their necessary reference to patterns of action, are an appropriate focus for the efforts of teachers. And it is such changes which will hereafter be indicated by the term "learning." It is the promotion of these kinds of changes, and this kind of learning, which can be helped by a fuller understanding of the aesthetic dimension of experience.

The Conditions of Learning

Before seeking the origin and focus of experience that is aesthetic in quality, it is first necessary to examine the conditions under which dispositions come to be acquired or changed. To acquire a disposition is to acquire a tendency toward patterns of action different from those acted on before. What we seek, then, is an answer to the question, why should one's patterns of action change? It may be worth reemphasizing here that unless patterns of action change, there is not sufficient reason to suppose that learning has taken place. That is, if there is no change in action, whatever has been acquired (e.g., "information") must be accounted trivial; while if there is only a change in a particular action rather than in a continuing pattern of action, there is no reason to describe it as learning, since there is no way of telling whether the learner will act any differently in the future.

Insofar as things run smoothly, there is little impulsion to change. This rule of thumb for political incumbents seeking reelection holds equally for teachers trying to promote learning. For if a person's characteristic patterns of action—if the ways in which he approaches and deals with his world—produce reasonably satisfactory results without undue effort, then his dispositions will not change. It is when his customary approaches fail that he is most likely to try something different. Since patterns of action cannot be acquired without being performed, a situation promoting learning must involve activity on the learner's part. The teacher's task is then the seemingly perverse one of insuring failure on the part of his active student. More specifically, the teacher must so arrange conditions that obstacles appear in the path of his student's activity, such that characteristic modes of action will not overcome the obstacles.

Yet simply to interfere with a course of action is not necessarily to produce learning. The student may simply quit and look for something else to do. He may blindly repeat his unsuccessful action. Or he may get someone else—through force or fraud or supplication—to overcome the obstacle for him. Thus merely to face the student with an obstacle to action is not enough to insure learning. Besides providing encouragement and guidance, the teacher must also insure that the obstacle itself be of a certain sort: it must not discourage the learner from continued action, and it should have an attractiveness that encourages the learner to try new modes of action with regard to it. In other words, a situation appropriate to the promotion of learning is one which, without overwhelming or discouraging a person, yet interferes with the normal expectations which guide his characteristic modes of action.

If such an interference or discrepancy is to produce thoughtful changes in action rather than the relatively thoughtless acts mentioned above, it must have some attraction for the learner —something which holds his attention and commands his effort. Speaking broadly, there are two types of situations which will satisfy this condition. In the first, a situation may be perceived by a learner to be directly relevant to purposes of his own which he wishes to fulfill. In the second, a situation may simply have intrinsic interest for a learner regardless of its possible connections to other things. In either type of situation the appearance of a discrepancy—if it is not too great—is likely to elicit even greater attention and effort from a learner.

The first sort of situation—that which is perceived by the learner to be connected with his own purposes—is one familiar to educators. It has traditionally been called the problematic situation: the sort of situation which introduces problem-solving. The setting is what has been called an ongoing, purposeful activity in which some obstacle or blockage is encountered. To the extent that a learner in such a situation comes increasingly to seek information ("data") relevant to overcoming the obstacle, to generate ideas ("hypotheses") that bridge the gap between an understood present and a desired outcome, to reject inadequate ideas and to try out ("test") those that successfully pass imaginative testing, and to make his own actions more effective by working cooperatively with others—to the extent that these modes of action alter earlier characteristic modes of action, then dispositions are being acquired, at least with respect to certain ranges of problems or topics. Learning is taking place.

That a situation of the sort just described will result in those changes of disposition we call learning has been discussed in detail by John Dewey[2] and needs no further elaboration here. What is of special concern, however, is that this is not the only sort of situation from which learning results, nor is it the only sort of situation which initiates problem-solving.[3]

The Concept of the Aesthetic

It has been observed that with appropriate guidance from a teacher, two broad types of situations may lead to thoughtful problem-solving and result, in the long run, in learning. The first type of situation has already been discussed briefly; it is the problematic one in which the student's purposes are involved. The second type of situation, in which the student finds immediate, intrinsic interest, must now undergo closer examination. For it is in this situation that aesthetic factors are most explicit. This also appears to be the type of situation least

[2] John Dewey, *Democracy and Education* (New York: Macmillan, 1916), chaps. 11 and 13; and *How We Think* (Boston: D. C. Heath, 1933).

[3] Situations in which students are simply authoritatively told what to do (e.g., read an assignment or solve a problem), or are given freedom to do as they wish, are not considered to be learning situations here. The former leads to the cram, exam, and forget-it cycle, mistaking for learning whatever devious devices the student has adopted to satisfy his teacher and pass his course. The latter simply allows students to behave as they are already disposed to, and thus substitutes accident for deliberate education.

understood by educators and therefore least exploited in school settings.

There are times when we are so completely absorbed in something that we lose all awareness of its wider context and its consequences; indeed, we lose awareness even of ourselves. No single, particular emotion attends such absorption. When so occupied, we may feel pleased or irritated, happy or sad, euphoric or despondent. But however we feel, our attention is bounded by the situation itself, and does not focus on its antecedents or its consequences. It is in just such situations of rapt attention to the immediate and here-and-now that experience is said to be aesthetic in quality. Although there are disagreements among aestheticians, there is virtually complete agreement[4] on this issue: if a situation is an aesthetic one, it must have value for the individual independent of any subsequent event, experience, or idea to which it might lead. The experience of beholding any work of art has this feature. Aside from its possible instrumental values, the experience is consummatory; it is enjoyed "for its own sake."

Yet such a characterization of aesthetic quality in experience is obviously incomplete. For it applies equally to eating ice cream cones, taking sunbaths, and burning one's fingers. All these experiences share, with the experience of works of art, an absorption in the value (pleasant or otherwise) of the immediate present, independent of possible consequences. The above characterization of the aesthetic also embraces the experiencing of sunsets, birdcalls, and sporting events. Indeed, if consummatory value were all that distinguished aesthetic from other qualities of experience, the realm of the aesthetic would become unaccountably large and would include types of experience so different from one another as to render practically useless the conceptual category, "aesthetic."

---

[4] In the past some theorists insisted that a work had to possess some positive didactic or moral value in order to qualify as a work of art. See, for example, Leo Tolstoy, *What is Art?* trans. Aylmer Maude (Boston: Small, Maynard and Co., 1924). Views like this one, however, can rarely be found among contemporary English-speaking aestheticians.

There is, to be sure, another set of conditions which any consummatory experience must meet in order to qualify as aesthetic. Such an experience must also involve the perception of form. Everything that is presented to experience—whether it be something seen, something heard, or some combined presentation—can be conceived as being made up of parts or elements. These parts are themselves perceived as being in some relation to one another. This relation of perceptible parts to the whole is referred to as form, or aesthetic form. If the parts of a whole are not so regular and repetitive as to be boring and not so unorganized as to seem virtually formless, they may be perceived as a pattern that is interesting. When such a formal pattern is perceived and attended to for its own sake —that is, for its immediate, consummatory value—then the experience can properly be said to be aesthetic in quality. All things which are traditionally called works of art present at least this much to experience: a patterned arrangement of formal elements which has been found interesting to behold by someone.

To say that experience has aesthetic quality when it is consummatory and when it involves the perception of form is not to say that this is all that can characterize such experience. For the form that is perceived may also be representative; it may contain or embody references to recognizable features of the world. When it does, the quality of the experience is enhanced. The embodiment of ideas, opinions, and beliefs in recognizable symbols creates occasions for people to share values. Although such occasions may appear in any experience which has aesthetic quality, they are often deliberately cultivated by artists.

Yet this characterization of aesthetic quality does not limit it to works of art that are deliberately created by men. The criteria for aesthetic quality mentioned here—being consummatory and involving the perception of form—do exclude the experiences of eating ice cream, taking sunbaths, and burning one's fingers. All may be attended to for their own sakes, but none involves perception of form. But these criteria do not necessarily exclude sunsets, birdcalls, or sporting events, all of which *can* be perceived aesthetically. This is to say that there are no "aesthetic objects"—works of art, or anything else— which, if simply perceived, will afford aesthetic quality to the experience of the beholder. On the contrary, the appearance of aesthetic qualities in experience is the outcome of a transaction between some object or event and a perceiving person who has adopted a particular posture toward it. This essentially Deweyan[5] point of view has recently been summarized thus: "Anything which, when attended to in the proper way, can lead to the satisfaction . . . outlined above, can be an aesthetic object. On the face of it we should say that anything *might*, and that what actually *will* is an empirical question. That entities with certain properties have in the past is a good reason for thinking that they, and other entities with the same or resembling properties, will in the future. But it is not a conclusive reason. . . ."[6]

The Appearance of Aesthetic Qualities in Experience

We have spoken of a particular posture to be adopted toward objects and events, a particular way of attending to things. It is this posture, or mode of attention, which is crucial in determining whether or not experience will have aesthetic quality. To ask what it is that a person does to achieve such quality is to inquire after the conditions under which experience becomes aesthetic. This inquiry will take us an important step closer to an understanding of the relation between aesthetic qualities and the conditions under which people learn.

To an observer, a music listener or a poetry reader may not appear very active; they may be both silent and motionless. Thus they present a sort of puzzle to psychologists whose behavioristic presuppositions have led them to focus their investigations on the active engagements of organisms with their environment. This particular research focus may be in part responsible for the tacit assumption that organisms are simply

[5] See John Dewey, Art as Experience (New York: Minton, Balch, 1934).
[6] Robert L. Zimmerman, "Can Anything Be an Aesthetic Object?" *Journal of Aesthetics and Art Criticism* XXV (1966): 186.

inactive when not engaging in goal-directed, instrumental behavior. Of course this is false, for it contradicts the most ordinary sort of daily observation. When people have not got something that needs doing, a purpose to fulfill, an obstacle to overcome, a problem to solve, then they normally look for something else to do. This is the case whether we are observing animals[7] or men.[8] It is at such times—when the environment makes no strong demands, and instrumental behavior is held in abeyance—that we engage in activities that are intrinsically interesting: in art, in play, and in curiosity that sometimes is developed into science and philosophy. D. E. Berlyne has called all of this "ludic" behavior.[9] It often happens, of course, that for many people what begins as an intrinsically interesting and enjoyable activity later develops into a highly demanding and instrumentally useful career.

When engaging in these ludic activities, men are not confronting or compelled to deal with a demanding, problematical environment. But it is important to note that when freed from demands and problems, men make the situations confronting them into problems—problems that can be played with, contemplated, entered into imaginatively, enjoyed.

The appearance of ludic (or "non-coping"[10]) behavior suggests a connection between the aesthetic and problem-solving that bears a closer examination. That a creative artist is engaged in problem-solving cannot be doubted; the painter Matisse's account of his own work[11] is an exemplar of such

---

[7] See F. A. Beach, "Current Concepts of Play in Animals," *American Naturalist* LXXIX (1945): 523–41; or H. F. Harlow, "Learning and Satiation of Response in Intrinsically Motivated Complex Puzzle Performance by Monkeys," *Journal of Comparative Physiological Psychology* XLIII (1950): 289–94.

[8] See J. McVicker Hunt, "Experience and the Development of Motivation: Some Reinterpretations," *Child Development* XXXI (1960): 489–504; or Robert W. White, "Motivation Reconsidered," *Psychological Review* LXV (1959): 297–333.

[9] D. E. Berlyne, *Conflict, Arousal, and Curiosity* (New York: McGraw-Hill, 1960).

[10] See Abraham Maslow, *Toward a Psychology of Being* (Princeton, N.J.: Van Nostrand, 1962).

[11] Henri Matisse, *Henri-Matisse*, Introduction by Alfred H. Barr, Jr., Notes

activity. What is less obvious, but just as important, is the fact that the beholder, too, is engaged in a form of problem-solving. That is, given a degree of freedom from immediate, practical concerns, and given an alert focusing of attention unencumbered by wool-gathering, this form of problem-solving is the sort of active doing that will be found whenever experience can be said to be aesthetic in quality. What sort of process is this which a percipient undertakes? If it is a form of problem-solving, what is the problem, and how is it solved?

When a situation is seen neither to advance nor to block a person's practical goals, he is not impelled to deal with it actively. Yet such a situation does not suddenly render a person passive and inert. Unlike a camera or a tape recorder, he does not simply register everything in his visual and auditory field without bias or presupposition. Because he is alive, he has a history of dealing with the world; thus he exists as a collection of habits, dispositions, presuppositions. It is because of this that any situation—whether or not it is a practical one—will arouse one's expectations, even if he is not concerned to alter the situation so that his expectations will be met.

When we ask what it is that a person expects when his experience is aesthetic in quality, we must first recall that whatever enters experience comes in the form of sensuously perceptible elements. When these elements are the sounds of music, the shapes and colors of painting, or the meaningful sounds of poetry, patterns are perceived as being organized in certain ways. The pattern can never be perceived in an instant, all at once. This is obvious in music, where the listener must wait for the pattern of sounds to unfold. It is less obvious but just as important in the visual arts, where the viewer must continue to attend to a picture for a period of time if he is fully to understand the nuances of its pattern.

When I hear a piece of music, just as when I come into contact with any other part of the world, I have expectations. But

---

by the Artist, Museum of Modern Art (New York: Norton, 1931); also in Eliseo Vivas and Murray Krieger, eds., *The Problems of Aesthetics* (New York: Rinehart, 1953), pp. 255–61.

when music is being played, the focus of these expectations is on what pattern of sounds will be played next. Even though I have not heard this particular piece before, I have expectations about it because I am familiar with the style of which it is an instance. But I don't know what sounds will come next, so I listen to the music as it continues, expecting it to maintain its characteristic form. My expectation is not so much deliberate and articulated as it is spontaneous and inchoate; it is the way I perceive things.

The reason a person deliberately attends to an expectation of this kind is to see whether, and in what way, his expectation will be fulfilled. This is the problem a percipient sets himself when he confronts art or when he takes an aesthetic posture toward anything in his environment. His orientation is not one of seeking ways of changing a situation but rather is one of seeing how the situation will change over time, either in virtue of its own momentum or of his own continued attention and increase of information. This form of activity, accompanied, at the very least, by feelings of tension and release, will be found in a percipient whenever his experience is aesthetic in quality.

If a perceived pattern develops just as we expected it to, it no longer holds our attention; interest disappears and we turn to other things. Experience is not marked by aesthetic quality. This happens when we hear the ticking of a clock, but it also happens when a familiar piece of music is played repeatedly: after a while, we literally fail to hear it. This also happens to paintings in our homes which, exposed to view every day, are eventually not "seen" at all. Thus in Western culture, reproductions of the finest masterpieces come to function as wallpaper does. Instead of exhibiting the taste and educating the children of middle-class householders, the practice of hanging pictures more probably dulls the taste and innoculates the children against meaningful confrontations with art.[12]

12 See Margaret Mead, "Work, Leisure, and Creativity," *Daedalus* LXXXIX (1960): 13–23.

If on the other hand, we are exposed to a pattern with which we have no familiarity at all, or the development of which eludes our efforts to find any organization in it, then we either ignore it (as in overhearing a conversation held in a foreign language) or become anxious or frustrated about it (if we think the conversation is about us). The beholder who lacks experience with baroque music or with cubism may be unable to find the organizational patterns in Vivaldi or in Braque. Such a beholder will not experience these works aesthetically, whatever the opinions of connoisseurs.

But when experience is attracted by some pattern that begins to develop almost as we expect it to, but varies a little from that expectation, then our attention is held. This discrepancy from what we expected brings us up short, creates some tension, and impels us to attend further to the developing pattern, in quest of a resolution.

The role of discrepancies in emotional life has recently received much attention in empirical psychology. There are some differences in the language used, for example the term "adaption level" may be employed to mean "what the organism is accustomed to," and may correspond to the concept of expectation used in the present context; but generalizations based on empirical studies tend to support what is being claimed here. Thus David McClelland and his associates have concluded that the holding of attention and positive affect (what we might call "satisfaction") result from exposure to discrepancies that are not too slightly or too greatly deviant from one's adaptation level.[13] D. O. Hebb's views about the initiation of satisfying affective arousal are also based on a conception of the role of discrepancies.[14] What has been called "expectation" here is called a "personal construct" by G. A. Kelly, and deviations in events (that is, discrepancies) from this personal construct are

[13] David C. McClelland *et al.*, *The Achievement Motive* (New York: Appleton-Century-Crofts, 1953), pp. 43, 60–62.
[14] D. O. Hebb, "Drives and the C.N.S.," *Psychological Review* LXII (1955); 243–54.

viewed by him as the source of all behavior change.[15] Finally, Leon Festinger has claimed that the actions of people can be understood as efforts to reduce cognitive dissonance, and he has defined dissonance as a discrepancy between one's belief about a situation and one's perception of that situation.[16]

Just as a conception of discrepancy or dissonance figures in a general theory of human experience, it also can be held to account for the appearance of particular qualities within experience. A conception of the aesthetic based upon a discrepancy theory has been carefully worked out with regard to music,[17] and it has elsewhere been more broadly applied to other forms of art.[18] But in the arts, as in any other realm of experience, what is to be called a discrepancy depends as much on the particular percipient and his own background of experience as it does on the nature of the particular cue for experience. To a novice listener of the 1960's, Louis Armstrong's recordings of the 1920's were just examples of good trumpet playing. But to the experienced listener, Armstrong was much more than that. One characteristic that made him exceptional was the way in which he played just behind, or after, the beat. The experienced listener, unlike the novice, expects the pattern of notes to coincide in a particular way with the rhythmic pattern; his expectations are thwarted when it doesn't. By creating a slight delay in what was expected, Armstrong captured the attention of his listeners and distinguished himself from other performers.

Contemporary poetry presents clear examples of the ways in which discrepancies may jolt both our expectations of sound patterns and our expectations of patterns of meaning. In the following poem of Aram Saroyan's, interest is won by the un-

[15] G. A. Kelly, *The Psychology of Personal Constructs* (New York: Norton, 1955).

[16] Leon Festinger, *A Theory of Cognitive Dissonance* (Evanston, Ill.: Row, Peterson, 1957).

[17] Leonard B. Meyer, *Emotion and Meaning in Music* (Chicago: University of Chicago Press, 1956).

[18] Donald Arnstine, *Philosophy of Education: Learning and Schooling* (New York: Harper and Row, 1967), chap. 6.

expectedness of the imagery, as the conclusion of each phrase
is simultaneously the beginning of a new image:

whistling in the street a car turning in the room ticking[19]

In another work by the same poet, discrepancies extend along
even more dimensions:

> my knees are in my knees
> my eyes are in my eyes

In this case, the poem functions much as op art does, for in
reading it we do a double-take; we read, and then we read again,
to make sure we read it correctly the first time. In our everyday reading we have become accustomed to finding in a predicate something different from what was in the subject. This
poem is so discrepant that the words "knees" and "eyes" seem
to jump from line to line. The discrepancy, and our desire to
see it resolved, holds our attention. Not for a very long time,
because it is only a short poem and probably not a very great
poem. But for a far longer time than it would have held us had
all its words been strung out in a single line.

Experience As Aesthetic in Quality and
Instructive in Consequence

We have now examined both the occurrence of learning and
the appearance of aesthetic quality in experience. Learning
has been discussed as a fairly long-lived change in disposition—
that is, as a change in one's patterns of action rather than
simply in one's specific behaviors. It has been claimed that the
conditions under which such changes appear are obstacles or
interferences with one's customarily successful patterns of action and nonhabitual, nonrandom ways of managing those
obstacles. Problem-solving is the term normally assigned to
such behavior. It has also been claimed that experience is aesthetic in quality when it is both consummatory—enjoyed for
its own sake—and attended by the perception of form. The
perception of form is a function of perceived discrepancies
from one's expectations—discrepancies not so great as to be

---

[19] From Aram Saroyan, *Aram Saroyan* (New York: Random House, 1966).

chaotic or confusing, and not so slight as to go unnoticed. It remains now to see how intimately related are both these sets of conditions (resulting in learning on the one hand and in the aesthetic on the other), and to suggest what difference this might make for the organization and conduct of classroom teaching.

There is an important truth and a misleading ambiguity in the cliché that we learn by experience. The ambiguity lies in the fact that every waking moment could be called "experience," and it is just as true that we don't learn by experience (that is, some of it) as it is that we do. But "experience" may be taken to mean active experience—that is, those waking moments during which a person is doing something in a nonroutine, nonrandom way. And it is true that we *do* learn from that sort of experience, just as we don't learn from experience that is thoughtless and routine. Much of schooling, unfortunately, is of this latter sort. Myths die hard, and it is a myth that students will learn if they are simply told to read something or to listen to something that someone else thinks they ought to know.

Once it is seen that learning, or changes in dispositions, results from forms of thoughtful (i.e., nonroutine and nonrandom) activity on the part of the learner, it becomes clear that instruction is a matter of getting something for students to think about. People do not commence thinking just at random. They will not think about what bores them or simply because they have been told to. They do think (or try to) when they have reason or cause to think, and finding and presenting the latter is the principal task for the ingenuity of the teacher. (Helping students to think is a much easier task for the teacher, once the students are already trying.)

We have seen that an obstacle to some purposeful activity is just such an occasion for thinking. This obstacle may be characterized as a discrepancy, although not one of the same sort as we found in experience that was aesthetic in quality. An obstacle to purposeful activity is a discrepancy between the meanings found in what is directly perceived (rather than just in the perceived elements themselves) and the purposes that we entertain.

We have also seen that a discrepancy in a perceived pattern of sensuous elements is the occasion for the sort of thoughtful activity that occurs when experience is aesthetic in quality. Thus the occasion for thinking—and ultimately for learning— is a perceived discrepancy from our expectations, *whether we are actively pursuing some purpose or not.*

Progressive educators were quite right in believing that purposeful problem-solving was the road to learning. But it is not the only road. For it is not the obstacle to a purpose (that is, a problem) that is the key to the initiation of thinking; rather, it is a discrepancy which initiates thought, and the discrepancy may simply be something unexpected in one's environment— something which triggers curiosity[20] or something which leads to the appearance of aesthetic quality in experience. Problem- solving, then, is a species of a broader genus which might be called discrepancy-resolution.

In experience that is aesthetic in quality, the tension of the perceived discrepancy and the release that comes at its reso- lution are felt as satisfying. The same tensions and the same release, however, may also be felt in the activity of purposeful problem-solving. For this reason, solving a problem can have a satisfying felt quality which is properly termed aesthetic. Solving a problem, then, can be looked at in two ways: in its immediate aspect, it may have aesthetic quality; in its long- run, consequential aspect, it may result in learning. Learning and aesthetic quality, then, are not disparate, distinct events; they are but different dimensions, or ways of looking at, the same sort of thing. Thus it can be said that if an experience had aesthetic quality, it resulted in learning (even if the learning was unintended). And if one has learned (i.e., if his dis- position has changed), he has had experiences which were aesthetic in quality.

[20] See Donald Arnstine, "Curiosity," *Teachers College Record* LXVII (1966): 595–602.

It is this last claim which is especially suggestive for a re-examination of school procedures. Purposeful activities and problem-solving cannot always be called upon to initiate learning in the classroom. They need to be supplemented, and they can be, if teachers will attend to other (and often easier) ways of putting students into situations of discrepancy. Confronting students with that which will make them curious is one such sort of situation; it will not be treated here, although there are available several excellent discussions of the arousal and exploitation of curiosity for purposes of learning in varied subject-matter fields.[21] It might be added that teachers might also attend more deliberately to the classroom practices which discourage curiosity and creativity.[22]

Another way of initiating a situation from which learning might result is to make possible for students the kinds of discrepancies which lead to aesthetic qualities in experience. As in cases of the arousal of curiosity, a situation must be created which is intrinsically interesting for the student. At the very least, this means that teachers of any subject must be sensitive to the points at which they are boring their classes; it also means that the humdrum and the erratic must be eliminated from classroom activities.[23] But since these things should *always* be sought in classrooms, the cultivation of the aesthetic must mean more than just this. It means, in the first place, that the teacher's performance should be seen—and analyzed—as a work of art, as either successful or unsuccessful in making an aesthetic impact on learners. In order to perform in this way, teachers must see themselves as both dramatists and dramatic

---

[21] See, for example, Max Beberman, *An Emerging Program of Secondary School Mathematics* (Cambridge: Harvard University Press, 1958); O. K. Moore, "Orthographic Symbols and the Preschool Child," *Proceedings of the Third Minnesota Conference on Gifted Children* (Minneapolis, 1960), pp. 91–101; and Richard J. Suchman, "Inquiry Training: Building Skills for Autonomous Discovery," *Merrill-Palmer Quarterly* VII (1961): 147–69.

[22] See R. E. Myers and E. Paul Torrance, "Can Teachers Encourage Creative Thinking?" *Educational Leadership* XIX (1961): 156–59.

[23] See Clyde E. Curran, "Artistry in Teaching," *Educational Theory* III (1953): 134–39.

actors.[24] And in the second place, works of art should be far more widely used throughout the entire range of school studies than they are at present.

The study of the arts in schools has traditionally been isolated, pursued at a special time and in a special place, segregated from all else that goes on in school. On the basis of such a practice, it is little wonder that students come to think that matters of beauty and taste, creativity and imagination, and above all, affairs of intrinsic interest and enjoyment are different from and unrelated to the study and pursuit of history, mathematics, and science. This is, of course, a tragic misapprehension.[25] It has resulted in art teaching that is effete and decorative in the most trivial of ways, and it has led to teaching in the other school subjects that has deadened the senses, crushed the imagination, and made learning synonymous with drudgery.

Unless the arts and other human enterprises are both understood and studied in schools in relation to one another, they are both bound to become sterile. Without an aesthetic dimension, history and the sciences become just so many facts to be acquired and to be forgotten when examination time is past. And without some vital connection to the real world about which students are concerned, mere exposure to fine art is not likely even to improve standards of artistic taste.[26] This is not to reject the teaching of the arts as separate pursuits. On the contrary, a degree of isolation is necessary for those students who have made a major commitment to the study or

[24] For a further discussion of the training relevant to helping teachers perform as artists, see Arnstine, *Philosophy of Education*, pp. 258–63.

[25] See John Dewey, "The School and Society," in Martin S. Dworkin, ed., *Dewey on Education* (New York: Bureau of Publications, Teachers College, Columbia University, 1959), pp. 69, 70.

[26] See Irvin L. Child and Rosaline S. Schwartz, "Exposure to Better and Poorer Art," *The Journal of Aesthetic Education* II (1968): 111–24. It has been suggested that exposure, combined with careful criticism, will improve standards of taste; see Ralph A. Smith, "Aesthetic Criticism: The Method of Aesthetic Education," *Studies in Art Education*, IX (1968): 13–31. However, no serious criticism of art proceeds far without consideration of its social context.

creation of art. Yet even art taught as a separate study will make a greater impact on a larger number of students if it is united with the concerns those students have for the world in which they live.[27]

But what is being emphasized here is the use of the arts in the course of studying other fields. What makes these fields so difficult to pursue for so many students is the fact that they cannot see why these fields are worth pursuing. An answer to this question is an important contribution of the arts. Art can have an impact on students if it is chosen appropriately— if it is admitted that Bob Dylan and the Beatles, Andy Warhol and Roy Lichtenstein, are more appropriate points from which to begin[28] than the more traditional exemplars that plod through textbooks and curriculum guides. To have an impact is to involve the student emotionally in whatever ideas, values, or beliefs are conveyed by the work of art in question. Without this emotional involvement, and the attitudes and dispositions to which it gives rise, the academic study of these ideas, values, and beliefs may seem to students rather pointless. If, in short, the judicious use of all of the arts can engage the emotions by throwing a highlight on the human dimensions of what often seems to be a very complex, problematical, and impersonal world, then learners may be motivated to examine and even study that world more carefully—in the hope, perhaps, of finding more intelligent ways of dealing with it than their fathers or their teachers found.

27 The implications of this notion for art teaching are elaborated in Donald W. Crawford, "Philosophical Aesthetics and Aesthetic Education," *The Journal of Aesthetic Education* II (1968): 37–49, and in Donald Arnstine, "The Concepts of Art and Teaching Art," *The Journal of Aesthetic Education* I (1966): 95–108.
28 See Crawford, "Philosophical Aesthetics," p. 44.

Louis Arnaud Reid

Introduction

It would be difficult, whatever one's aesthetic theories, to deny altogether that feeling must play some part in the making and appreciation of the arts. Art may or may not express or evoke "emotion"; but without feeling in some sense surely art could hardly exist for us. Feeling seems to be a condition, at one stage or another, of being able to understand art at all. Perhaps feeling is even a component of the understanding of art. But what is "feeling," and what is "understanding"? And can an account of feeling in its relation to understanding of the arts throw light upon the relation of feeling and understanding in other fields?

In this paper I shall put forward a view of feeling which may possibly throw some light not only on aesthetic understanding but upon other forms of understanding too. I shall not, however, attempt to analyze the various forms of understanding. We speak of understanding a word, a concept, a proposition, an argument. We speak of understanding the facts of nature, animate or inanimate. We speak of understanding a person, a moral or historical situation, a work of art. Each use of "understanding" could be analyzed at length. We can, however, do without all that here. Such analysis of "understanding" as there has to be will be purely *ad hoc*, as the need arises.

My first topic, then, is Feeling. Feeling, not Emotion. It is necessary to say this at the outset, because there is a tendency to run feeling and emotion together. Writers on aesthetics, for example, speak of "expression of feeling and emotion" almost as though "feeling" were just another word for "emotion"; writers on education speak as though "education of the emotions" were the same thing as "education of feeling." Connections between the two there certainly must be, but they are not identical. I hold—though I shall not argue it here—that feeling is the basic notion and that the nature of emotion is a further question logically dependent upon a proper account of feeling.

Feeling: Older Views, and a Possible Alternative

The treatment of feeling by psychologists in the earlier part of this century was thin. "Feeling" was conceived by them in a highly abstract way and was identified with *hedonic tone.* Feeling was a subjective state, varying continuously in intensity from pleasure to pain or unpleasure.[1] For Stout, "The affective attitude consists in being pleased or displeased with something, with liking or disliking it."[2] Others say much the same. Hedonic tone, identified with feeling, was supposed to be a positive or negative quality which varied in intensity, sharply distinguished from the character of the concrete mental states of which it was the quality.

Feeling was sometimes used in another, nonhedonistic sense (as when one says "I feel tired, lazy, hungry"). It was in this case denied to be *transitive*. Although one sometimes uses the word "feel" as equivalent to "perceive," one should strictly use it, it was said, only in the intransitive sense. For this reason

[1] James Ward, *Psychological Principles* (Cambridge: Cambridge University Press, 1920), p. 45.

[2] G. F. Stout, *Manual of Psychology*, 3rd ed. (London: University Tutorial Press, 1924), p. 113.

it was argued that feeling is not *cognitive*: ". . . it does not consist of knowing facts of the world outside us nor even in knowing facts regarding ourselves. Feeling is, rather, 'the way you feel.' "[3]

Let me make a preliminary comment on the three points italicized.

1. It is, I think, far too limiting to *identify* feeling with hedonic tone. The subjective state, affect, feeling, may be characterized (not necessarily always) by hedonic tone, may be pleasant or unpleasant. But when we speak of "feeling" we do not, surely, mean simply the abstracted quality, pleasure or unpleasure. It seems nearer the mark to say that feeling states have, or may have, the *characteristic* of being pleasant or unpleasant. It is true that by usage "affect" has come to mean feeling-tone. I shall try to show that a wider use is far more fruitful in trying to understand the life and function of feeling.

2. We must agree that "to feel" is not, grammatically, a transitive verb in the primary sense of "feeling"—e.g., immediate experience of our own states—though "feeling" can have the extended use, as when I say "I feel the shape." But if "feeling" in its primary sense has not, grammatically speaking, an *object*, it does, I shall argue, always (logically) have a *content*, distinguishable though never separate from the feeling of it.

3. Feeling is being affected by something, by whatever it is that affects us. This is the content of feeling, what it is feeling *of*. In this sense, and in this sense only, feeling in its primary sense is *cognitive* of its content, immediately cognitive of a content of which there is awareness, without any intermediary or third term or concept, as there must be in all other cognition. I am not saying that cognitive feeling of content without any third item, the concept, often, or more than rarely, occurs. It may do so in very borderline cases, as when we are halfway between consciousness and unconsciousness, e.g., when waking from deep sleep or from an anaesthetic. Or if I receive a sudden unexpected blow from behind, I may feel something before

[3] Robert S. Woodworth, *Psychology: A Study of Mental Life*, 18th ed. (London: Methuen, 1946), p. 405.

there is time to raise the question "What's that"? Normally, when one feels something, it is interpreted by means of a concept like "toothache," "tiredness," "anxiety," "joy"—and this of course happens when we are not thinking of the words or the concepts as such. Nevertheless, whether immediate feeling of content without any concept actually occurs or not, the very use of a concept which is meaningful and relevant *presupposes* an immediately cognized datum or content of feeling.

Many philosophers thoroughly disapprove of the idea of primary feeling as a unique two-term form of cognition. My defense of it is that we do talk of feeling as immediate awareness of something, and that this is far more illuminating than the older view of feeling as identical with hedonic tone and as being noncognitive.

Feeling as Cognitive

Feeling—according to Susanne Langer, the mark of mentality[4]—emerges at a certain state of evolution. A neurophysiological process can be said to "break through to feeling."[5] The phenomenon usually described as a feeling is really that the organism feels something, i.e., something is felt. Being felt, Mrs. Langer holds, is a phase of the process itself—and a phase is a mode of appearance, not an added factor.[6] There is an analogy, but only an analogy, of feeling with the incandescence of a piece of iron at high temperature. Feeling is living process becoming aware of itself. At the human level feeling is so inseparable from what is felt, that in *experience* itself it is impossible to distinguish between them. In the experience of acute toothache how can we distinguish between feeling and what is felt? The unfelt ache is inconceivable (though, of course, an unfelt state of the disturbed organism which causes it is not). Yet, as so often happens with things existentially inseparable, it is possible and necessary to make a conceptual distinction;

[4] Susanne K. Langer, *Mind: An Essay on Human Feeling* (Baltimore: Johns Hopkins Press, 1967), I, 4.
[5] *Ibid.*, p. 9.
[6] *Ibid.*, p. 21.

and here one may and must distinguish between something which is not so much a mental activity as a mental happening, that of feeling, and the content of this feeling, what is felt. Since the word "feeling" is so highly ambiguous, sliding from one of these meanings into the other, it may be convenient to give each a technical label to avoid confusion. The word "awareness" is useful. When we are aware, it is true that we are always aware of something; but the word "awareness" can be and sometimes is used in a more general, open, less specific way than is usual with "feeling." This use is vague, but it does happen. "To be aware" often has a more open and less specific suggestion than "to feel"; awareness may therefore be borrowed to distinguish technically between the subjective, cognitive aspect of feeling and its content. Feeling is an immediate awareness. I shall therefore, when relevant, distinguish between Feeling (IE) (= immediate awareness) and feeling (C) (= content). (I hasten to add that this is purely a verbal device to point a distinction and implies no special theory of "awareness" or of its relation to feeling.)

Feeling (IE) is primarily of our own processes and states, bodily and mental, psychophysical. It is cognitive in the sense that we immediately and indubitably know the content of feeling—in one sense of the word "know." In that sense, too, feeling (IE) shares the character of all cognition of having content, knowing, feeling, *something.* Indeed this is saying just the same thing in a different way.

But although it is true that the something which we feel is primarily our own psychophysical organic states, it is a truth which would be wholly misleading if we stopped there. For the psychophysical organism of course dwells in a world external to itself, a world in which, as mind, it is interested, a world which it comes to know bit by bit and with some discrimination, to which it responds actively as well as reactively. The life of the psychophysical organism is its life in the world (in the case of human beings, the whole of the humanly known world) and to attend to the inner life of feeling of the organism by itself is to perform an artificial if necessary abstraction. Moreover, if this is true, and if feeling is cognitive and (though purely as feeling not grammatically transitive) shares the transitiveness of all cognition, there must be a sense in which feeling participates in our total psychophysical intercourse with the world we live in. Some forty to forty-five years ago, I suggested some of the implications of this in three published papers.[7] I would not now want to express in the same way everything that was said there; but one main theme I still think true: that feeling does share in the objectively directed character of our cognitive-conative relationships with the world. Cognition and conation are in different ways focusing, grasping, acting, and reacting functions in relation to the world, and feeling includes feeling *of all that*. We feel the whole transitive cognitive-conative process, outwardly directed toward the world. Feeling is the feeling of oneself, dwelling within the psychophysical organism, in total cognitive-conative relation to the world. In this sense, feeling is not only cognitive of immediate content; as sharing in cognition and conation it is also cognitive of *objects* in the world.

The account of what we feel has, so far, stressed two things: (1) the intra-psychophysical content as such (the content of my feeling when I try to attend, with some artificial concentration, on what is going on within my organism); and (2) what I feel, not just as within myself, but as functioning in cognitive-conative relationship with the independent world. I feel myself-living-in-the-world. This is the more normal and less artificial state, though the sense of it fades into the background when I am concentrating hard on what I am doing or thinking.

There is, nevertheless, an important question whether, fading or not, my feeling of participating in my life in the world has

[7] Louis Arnaud Reid, "Instinct, Emotion and the Higher Life," *British Journal of Psychology* XIV (1923), 78–93; "Towards Realistic Psychology," *Journal of Philosophy* XXL (1924), 492–98; "Immediate Experience, Its Nature and Content," *Mind* XXXIX (1931), 154–74.

not a very important part to play in my knowing and acting
and responding, and in its efficiency. If the feeling is there all
the time (and though we may not be thinking of it, there is
always the accompanying feeling of being alive), it would be
surprising if it only remained passively on the sidelines, so to
speak, and had no retroactive effect upon our knowing and
acting. Feeling may be compared to incandescence at its elementary and primitive stages, but it may take on a more positively active function of its own in highly intelligent conscious
and self-conscious life.

There may, in fact, be said to be a sense in which we feel not
simply our own private states, not simply the participation in
our life in the world, but feel, cognitively, something of the
character of the world itself, in which we increase, or illuminate, knowledge through the infiltration of feeling. We "size
up" a situation; we take a decision, moral or otherwise; we
"balance things up." In all this (it may be taken for granted
without argument here), all the mechanisms of perceptual and
conceptual thinking are involved. (Feeling (IE) by itself is a
nonentity). We feel (IE) (or we can feel) ourselves as active
in these ways in our coming to terms with the world. But is not
our feeling more—or may it not be more—than the mental
"incandescence" of all the rest that is happening? If feeling
shares in, is inseparable from, cognition and conation, can it
not intimately affect their active enterprise too? May not sensitive feeling be a positive asset in knowing or otherwise coming to terms with the world? It does certainly seem to be so in
our knowledge of the arts at least—music or painting or poetry
—though it is not confined to them. There does seem to be a
sense in which to "feel" the structures of things and their values is a way in which we positively come to know more of
them.

This may seem strange language to a philosopher, though it
is commonly used in ordinary speech. We speak of "feeling"
the sense of the argument; we say "he has a nose for the
important things." "Being sensitive to the atmosphere, he

showed much more understanding than some of the other, cleverer, people." But is such language strictly justified?

Feeling: The "Proximal" and the "Distal"

It can be clarified, I think, by referring to a distinction frequently used by Professor Polanyi in his discussion of "tacit" knowledge. In a paper entitled "Science and Man's Place in the Universe," for example, he writes as follows: "In his book on freedom of the will, Austin Farrar has spoken of *disattending from* certain things for attending to others. I shall adopt a similar usage by saying that in an act of tacit knowing we *attend from* something for *attending to* something else; namely, *from* the first term *to* the second term of the tacit relation. In many ways the first term of this relation will prove to be nearer to us, the second farther away from us. Using the language of anatomy, I shall call the first term *proximal* and the second term *distal*."[8] A familiar case (mine, not Polanyi's) of the functioning of the proximal and the distal is ordinary perception of things at a distance from the body. The way in which we see an object is determined by our awareness of events inside our bodies; by means of these processes and through them we become aware of position, size, shape, color, etc. We attend from experienced internal qualities to the characters of things outside us, and these characters are what in a sense the internal qualities "mean" to us. We know the world by attending to it from our bodies. The same thing is made very lucid when we consider Polanyi's frequently used illustration of the use of a tool, say a stick, as a probe to explore a cavern. If we use a probe for the first time, we feel impacts of various sorts in our fingers and arms, through kinaesthetic sensations. But as we learn to use the probe, our awareness of its impact on our hand is transformed into a sense of its point touching the hole being explored: "meaningless" feelings become changed into "meaningful" ones. The "meaning" is located at a distance from the body.

---

[8] In Harry Woolf, ed., *Science as a Cultural Force* (Baltimore: Johns Hopkins Press, 1969), pp. 57–58.

Since feeling is the subjective side of all we think and desire and do, the account of meaning as tending to be displaced away from ourselves can be applied to feeling. We may attend at will to various aspects of the total content of feeling—as private, as participating-in-our-life-in-the-world, and as feeling cognitively (as well as, of course, conatively) the very character of the world.

Ordinarily, although the feeling of being alive and involved is never absent, the fact that, in our practical knowledge of the world or in our thinking abstractly, the presence of feeling is not particularly noticeable may mislead us into thinking it absent or superfluous. We are attending to clues for action or to the structure of things or of thought. But feeling is certainly present, and moreover (I believe) often actively auxiliary in what we do and think. We notice clues sufficiently for efficient action, but in acting by means of them we are constantly "feeling" our way. We walk along the street in a directed way, guided partly by feeling. We avoid lampposts and other pedestrians not just by locating them in impersonal cognition as discrete objects but by feeling as well as perceiving the total gestalt, and by feeling our way along. (This becomes very much more obvious when walking along a very dark road, when the awareness of proximal feelings becomes more prominent.) In driving a car through a narrow passage, or in reversing, we know largely what to do by feeling toward the distal from the proximal. The totality and concreteness of massive feeling is indeed an indispensable condition of success. If the particular bits of the situation remain as discrete bits, and the feeling of the whole gestalt is lost, everything goes wrong; either, like the overintellectual centipede, we are paralyzed for action, or we crash into the gatepost! Success is the result of a fine balance between the proximal and the distal, and the balance is known by feeling. The pure "intellectual" without feeling (if such a person could even exist) could never get anywhere because, like one of Achilles's tortoises, before he could reach any point he would have to reach another intermediate point first and another before that, ad infinitum!

Feeling and the Understanding of the Arts

Feeling has an important part to play in the discriminating understanding of the arts. We may assume here, without argument, that sophisticated and mature knowledge of an art-structure presupposes vastly complex processes—perceptual, conceptual, symbolic, and all the rest—involved in the understanding of any structure. Taking all that for granted, what is the function and place of feeling in the understanding and knowledge of a piece of art?

Art, in its aesthetic aspect, I hold, is meaning-embodied. Though art draws meanings from life, it is not just the expression of these meanings other than itself, but new meaning, so embodied that any attempted translation of it into terms other than its own is, strictly, bound to break down. The poem, the painting, the piece of music each embody their own, untranslatable meaning. This meaning, in turn, is apprehended in a *personally* embodied experience of which we are aware in feeling. As a personally embodied experience, it is a felt one, and feeling participates in all three emphases of attention—to the intraorganic, to our participation-in-the-work as objective, and to the feeling (illuminated by the proximal-distal concept) *of* the work itself. Attention to any of the three aspects is legitimate—but on different occasions and with different purposes in mind.

As philosophers experiencing art we are entitled to attend to all three, and to any of them we please, as suits our purpose. We may notice the intraorganic, e.g., the feelings of the psychophysical manifestations of our experience of listening to music, or these *as directed* more focally toward the music; or we may be fully absorbed in cognitively "feeling" the music itself being aware of subjective aspects only by a special effort retrospectively. The artificiality—necessary as it may be for philosophical-analytic purposes—of attention to our own feelings is most clearly seen in this last: we cannot properly attend to the music and to our own feelings strictly at the same moment. Full aesthetic attention must be to the music itself, the distal aspect, the "meaning," and that meaning is not to be identified with our own feelings. On the other hand, the musical meaning is apprehended through and along with our own feelings, and if in a sense they are always tacitly there and function tacitly, there is no reason we should not become aware of them provided they are intrinsic to our attention to the music. And this awareness of our own feelings as we intensely attend to and intensely enjoy the music is certainly a fact of much of our experience. In listening (or playing) we are not only very much alive in our attention to the "life" of the music, but we feel much alive too. Absorption in what we hear is not only not incompatible with acute subconscious awareness of the enjoyment of it; this awareness is a part of it, and as a part of it is even necessary to full discriminating understanding. We can, by sympathy and empathy, see it happening as we watch a master performer at work. If he did not "feel the music," feel his way through it with his whole being—which must include awareness of feeling it with his organism—he could not make it speak. Feeling is here cognitive in an important sense. Likewise we "feel" the forms of space in sculpture, or the weight and rhythm of the meaningful words in poetry.

It is important in all this that aesthetic feeling should be attentively concentrated upon the work of art itself. Sensitive feeling takes place via the organism, and it is feeling for embodiment in the medium—for the right words, right weight, pause, stress, for the proportion of the parts in relation to the whole. Sensitive feeling keeps the proper balance between the proximal and the distal, a proper concern for objective aesthetic meaning, so that the proximal is instrumental to the apprehension of the meaning and does not obtrude itself. If this does not happen, the proximal may get in the way. Feeling, and sometimes emotion, instead of being directed and relevant to artistic meaning, obtrudes irrelevantly its own stirrings-up. Instead of disciplined feeling instrumental to finer aesthetic perception, we may get a self-indulgent wallowing in feeling, a kind of emotionalism.

Feeling, then, seems to be a necessary component in the making and appreciation of art. One seems to see this very clearly

/ 55

in the rendering of music in performance, as I have suggested. In a "Master Class" series on British television, the viewer has the immense advantage of watching professional musicians learning to interpret under a master. The pupils are always, technically and otherwise, highly competent, but a musically experienced viewer can see (or believes that he can see) subtle differences in musical sensitiveness between the pupils. Of two equally competent players, one will get the flow, the balance, the subtle nuances; the other, seeming to perceive intelligently with intellect only, "drier," "harder," does not. (The same sort of thing can, of course, be seen in the performance of other arts —acting, dancing, reading poetry.) The differences, if validly judged, are differences in what is called "musicality." Musicality requires high intelligence—and it seems to be intelligence which cannot fully operate (possibly cannot fully exist?) without the presence and operation of feeling. Feeling seems to be a necessary component of musical understanding: there is a sort of imaginative psychophysical identification in feeling with the musical events as they flow along. It is very hard to understand or express all this clearly. Perhaps because quality in art can never be stated adequately by propositions expressed verbally, it is intrinsically impossible to state it with complete clarity. Anyhow, I hope that in what is only an exploratory essay some vagueness may be excused. The questions involved, if not the answers, may become plainer in what follows—an attempt to puzzle out how feeling may function in fields of understanding other than the arts.

The Positive Functioning of Feeling in Understanding

I shall from now on be thinking of feeling as participating in the total life of the mind, in its cognitive and conative relationships to what is beyond itself rather than (except incidentally) with primary feeling, the feeling of one's own states. One is (as was said at the outset) aware, at least subconsciously, of oneself in feeling all the time one is alive and awake; but attention is normally outwardly directed, and it is feeling as outwardly directed which I shall be discussing, feeling in its distal rather than its proximal aspect. Here questions of truth and falsity arise as they do not in primary feeling of one's own states.

It is important to realize that feeling (and particularly here feeling as entering into outgoing enterprises) *can* be controlled in various ways—inhibited, allowed to have its way, summoned, cultivated, harnessed, directed—in general brought under the control of will, and that this is humanly and educationally important. Feeling may be primarily "incandescence," something which happens to us rather than something which we do. But what we do, and what we choose to do in the ways just mentioned, can affect the happening, the extent, the degree, the quality of feeling and its value for human enterprises. Feeling is a fact, in itself neither moral nor immoral, in itself making neither for truth (except in the very special sense of being veridically aware of its immediate content, as argued above) or falsity. But feeling as part of total conscious human life, life in which character and "will" are operative, can be morally beneficial or destructive, can open up the way to truth and understanding or can obscure or block it. People can be ethically unbalanced in two opposite ways, by being far too inhibited in feeling or by letting feeling rule by running riot. *Zorba the Greek* is a fascinating image of the interplay between Zorba, with his strain of enchanting and lovable "madness," and his intellectual and inhibited young boss—with a refreshing bias towards "madness." The dangers of letting rip are familiar; perhaps the dangers of respectable inhibition are less recognized. (The dance of Zorba is an interesting symbolic release.) Likewise the life of understanding can be obscured by feeling and emotion or made thin and arid by the inhibition, sometimes the fear, of feeling and emotion. What I am arguing for here is (1) the possibility of the control and direction of feeling where "control" is not to be identified with repression, and (2) the desirability of control and direction of feeling in the enterprises of moral, intellectual, and artistic understanding.

Feeling can be marshaled up in identification with situations or with other people; it is an instrument in the use of imagination. Feeling, far from being merely a private subjective event of one's own organism, can be made to function distally—with empathy in relation to things and with sympathy in relation to other living beings, especially persons. Thinking about art, or science, or history, or people, can, we know, be voluntarily directed and controlled. So can feeling be summoned and directed and controlled in acts of relevant attention; and it can condition the success of understanding. Perhaps it may even be said to increase power of understanding. A very obvious example of this is moral education. A parent or teacher may say to a thoughtless child willing to listen: "But can't you put yourself in his position? Can't you *feel* what he must be feeling?" The appeal here is to make the effort to imagine, and to imagine with feeling, the ongoing life (with all *its* feeling) of the other person. Without imaginative feeling, understanding here is incomplete. As a feeling of one's own states is a feeling from inside of one's own life as it flows along, so sympathy —sym-pathy, feeling along with—is imaginative entry into the flow of another person's life. And this is a condition—or a part— of the fuller understanding of that life.

Feeling is inseparably bound up with the whole of mental life. Nevertheless, it has its own distinctive function of reflecting the ongoing flow of life. As in its primary form it reflects the process of one's own internal life, so in its distal functioning it is transferred, or projected, into things and events. We become involved, we have a feeling of the totality and indivisibility, of the flowingness and continuity, of things and events other than our own internal experiences; we become imaginatively identified with their existence, sometimes with their life. In the driving or reversing of the car the feeling of the whole situation is an essential part of the control. Feeling partakes of intuition in the Bergsonian sense. Feeling in its primary functioning gives us immediate knowledge of motion as it occurs in the raising of an arm. Imaginatively projected, it gives knowledge of the movement of the plane overhead. We can come to understand this motion in all kinds of ways, e.g., by mathematical analysis of it. But in the absence, at some stage, of felt experience of motion our analyses could not be of actual motion (which can only be known in intuitive felt experience). It could only be, as Bergson says, a dividing up of static trajectories left by motion. (And from that, all the paradoxes of Zeno arise.) This would be the "understanding" of something, certainly: but could it be said to be (without the presupposition of felt intuition) the understanding of motion? The analyses have to be supplemented by renewed imaginative intuition.

This may be a simple case, but it may not be a bad paradigm for other forms of understanding. Feeling is inside knowledge of a direct kind, of internal relations as events, as they occur. Is this kind of knowledge a general precondition of the significance of other, abstract knowledge? Without it, does abstract knowledge tend to fly into discrete fragments, or to become a substitute for concrete understanding?

Feeling and the Understanding of Values, Chiefly Moral Values

The function of feeling, as an important condition or adjunct of understanding or even as a part of understanding, varies with different subject matters. Without drawing too hard and fast a line, we may distinguish between a relatively value-free understanding, and understanding which is valuation or where valuing is intimately involved. The distinction is probably one mainly of emphasis, and it is dangerous to suggest that there are any situations in which human beings are involved which are entirely and at all points value free.

Moral thinking, judging, deciding—this is valuational thinking in which feeling at some stage is necessarily involved. What does one think about contraception, abortion, the keeping alive of Thalidomide babies, of old people hopelessly and painfully ill? What does one think of the use of force within the state or in international disputes? When should a marriage which has broken down be broken up? What are the rights and wrongs of premarital and extramarital sexual intercourse?

These and countless other similar questions challenge hard thinking, often very subtle and complex thinking. But the thinking presupposes feeling (at some stage) about the issues. It presupposes imaginative feeling about the actual situations, about the value of life in itself, human suffering and human happiness, the importance of respect for persons. It presupposes feeling both for the particular circumstances in which these problems occur, and for broad, general, moral principles —compassion, mercy, justice, freedom, equality. Without feeling there could be no real grasp of the issues, though this certainly does not mean that we are having emotional feelings all the time. Philosophers do not talk much nowadays about their basic feelings of conviction; they used to do so more. The late Olaf Stapledon (better known for his imaginative writings than for his philosophical ones) wrote in a paper to the Aristotelian Society (1943–44): "Briefly, the root of my conviction is the personal experience of practical living, that a certain way of behaving is satisfying in a manner which is more fundamental than the kind of satisfaction afforded by any other way of behaving. This experience is satisfying to something more essentially myself than my ordinary self of current desires and fears, satisfying to me in my most clearly conscious state. In that state, however, I will do it for its own sake, not primarily as a means to satisfaction. . . ."

Moral thinking, then, involves definite feelings at different levels, and, basically, feelings positively toned for what is good and right, negatively toned for what is bad and wrong. One takes "pleasure" in the good and right, finds the bad and wrong "painful"—though "pleasure" and "pain" can be misleading words. And an important part of moral education is to try to get young people to feel about moral matters. Feeling is a condition of moral understanding, though of course it is not a sufficient condition; rational thinking is required.

The same thing, we assumed, is true of the understanding of art, both in making and appreciation. If the master is teaching music, he may have to do a good deal of explaining, of analysis. But he also conveys the musical meaning of a passage by getting his pupil to feel, sometimes by a sort of infection from his (the master's) expressive gestures. Through sympathetic rapport with his pupil, his pupil may also come to feel the musical structure as he does, illuminating the pupil's understanding. Without this, as I have suggested, he may succeed here and there; but the music does not "come together." Exercise of feeling, too, is necessary in the fully personal understanding of another human being. Being in some sense a "psychologist" is not enough without imaginative feeling of the other person's life. Polanyi, as we shall see, says the same thing of certain aspects of biological understanding: one must have imaginative feeling for the life of organisms.

Feeling is an essential aspect of all occurrent values. And if we distinguish between feeling (IE) and its content (C) (or, most often, its object), value may be generically defined as the relation between the two. Value is feeling-for-content (or object); or, content (or object) has value because it is felt. Being cold or hungry, we get warmed by the fire or we eat. Warmth and eating in these instances are positive values; the fire or the food is an object of value. The value really inheres in the whole situation, feeling-for-content or object, but common speech attaches the value to the content or object. Thus being too cold (content of feeling), or a too cold room (object of feeling) is a negative value, as is the state of unsatisfied hunger or the empty cupboard. The warm room, plenty of food, is "good."[9]

Feeling-of-a-content, or feeling-about-an-object, or contents or objects felt, is only value in the most generic and basic sense. It has nothing, or not very much, to do with truth or falsity, with what is "really" good or bad, as distinct from what only appears so. To the unhappy heroin addict, the drug he craves is a positive value which he seeks, a good as it begins to work upon him. In a wider perspective, we all know that this "good" is an appalling evil; and when we think on that level we have

[9] This account, it has been pointed out to me, is exactly parallel to an argument in an excellent early volume of John Dewey. See J. J. Findlay, ed., *Educational Essays* (London: Blackie and Sons, 1906), pp. 90–95. My own view, however, was not derived from Dewey.

moved infinitely beyond immediate feeling to thought and reason of a far-reaching kind. But even there, as we have said, there has to be feeling for human good and evil at a deep level.

Feeling as Integral, and as Auxiliary, to Understanding

Moral and aesthetic thinking, then, are examples of valuational thinking which require feeling at some stage for the fuller and deeper understanding of their problems and situations, understanding which calls for the use of a wide range of mental powers. We must now have a look at the other sorts of understanding—those which are relatively value-free. Accepting the distinction—a very rough one, of emphasis only—I now want to make a general suggestion. It is that whereas feeling is *integral* to, ingredient in, valuational thinking and understanding, to some other sorts of thinking—mathematics and science are examples—feeling is not integral in the same way, but is in some respects a condition of thinking, in others auxiliary to it, a means to its ends.

In art criticism, an example of valuational thinking, feeling for aesthetic value is *integral* to critical thinking. Criticism has many sides, historical, technical, analytic, descriptive, psychological, sociological, philosophical. But unless these bear upon, are relevant to, and are integrated with something quite different, namely an immediate judgment in which feeling of the individual works of art is involved, criticism misses its central mark. The critical verdict may have very complex grounds, but without sensitive feeling they cannot fully contribute to its fulfillment.

On the other hand, in some intellectual thinking—in logic, in mathematics, in scientific understanding of facts in physics, in some parts of philosophical exploration—although feeling has some part to play, it is mainly (1) as a general *condition* of understanding, necessary as a basis for the understanding of anything whatever and not peculiar to any one form. Or (2), feeling is *auxiliary* to something else and a means on the way to something else, namely clear and relatively impersonal thinking issuing in lucid statement in which the subjective factor is minimized. We want to understand logical relations, the mathematical proof, the exact structure of an object in nature, the degree to which an observation supports an hypothesis. The focus, when any of these ends are attained, is a condition of clear understanding of which feeling is at least not a very prominent component. Clear understanding, and understanding which can be expressed in propositional form in symbols of some kind, publicly testable in a straightforward way—this is the aim. All this is in contrast to, say, the clear understanding of a work of art. Such understanding cannot be achieved with the same sort or degree of impersonality, and it can *never* be fully or adequately expressed lucidly and literally in impersonal propositional form. And, although I think that the understanding of art can be tested, and tested in one sense publicly, the testing is by no means a "straightforward" affair as in mathematics or science, and is complex, tenuous, and perhaps never quite final. Although I am sure the understanding of aesthetic meaning is not just a "subjective" affair (it would not be "understanding" if it were), the personal subject is involved, and involved in feeling, as the subject is not involved in mathematical or much of scientific thinking.

In logic, mathematics, and some scientific thinking, feeling in a general sense is presupposed in the thinking, is a necessary *condition*. It is the feeling of the intuition which is a necessary condition of all thinking whatsoever. I referred earlier to the feeling of the intuition of motion as necessary if the analysis of motion is to be truly the analysis of motion and not just the dividing up of a static line, the drawn trajectory of a body in motion. So in all analytic and synthetic thinking there has to be an intuition of wholeness (or of the whole situation, whatever it is) within which the analysis and synthesis take place and, since feeling is the subjective side of the whole of mental life, there is feeling of the intuition of wholeness. We could not understand the relations of terms in a complex were there not an underlying intuitive feeling of the complex, of terms in relation. But, as far as I can see, this very general truth has no special relevance to the kind of thinking we have in mind here at the moment.

Feeling may be *auxiliary* in logical, mathematical, scientific, and indeed in all kinds of thinking. In the processes of working toward intellectual or factual clarity, feeling may be involved, and is familiarly so. We do not understand at once; we grope, we "feel" our way. This direction of thinking feels more hopeful than that; it has a more positive hedonic tone (or less of a negative one), and this reinforces efforts of thinking in one direction rather than another. We feel balance and imbalance almost in our bones before we understand why. These feeling processes are guides on the way to something else, toward the achievement of clarity of understanding, stated in clear propositions. They are the means to its (relatively) feeling-free ends. This is in contrast to art where, as we have seen, feeling has to be incorporated in making judgment. The meaning of a mathematical proposition can be expressed impersonally: the meaning of a work of art (we said) never can be stated in definitive propositional language at all. Propositions of all kinds can help in understanding of art, but in the end the propositions have to become assimilated into a sort of knowledge by acquaintance of which feeling is an intrinsic ingredient. Feeling is incorporated in aesthetic understanding; it is not merely a means on the way to understanding. But in logical and scientific and philosophical thinking, or in other thinking about matters of fact, the function of feeling at the "groping" stage is to eliminate itself; in that sense it is not integral to the judgment as it is in value judgments.

One must not exaggerate this distinction between value judgments and the rest, or suppose that feeling is not at all operative (and in more than the two ways mentioned) in the thinking which has clarity of propositional statement as its supreme aim. It may be true that impersonal clarity is the aim; but we rightly speak of intellectual "passions" without which the search for clarity would never get going, passions which, inspired by their high ends, induce certain qualities of self-sacrifice, even asceticism, in the enterprise of objective truth-seeking. The passion for truth permeates the discipline of the search for it, a moral discipline serving the categorical imperative of truth. Furthermore, both in the groping after truth (in which feeling is involved) and in the enjoyment of its realization when the required clarity is attained, there is feeling which has something of an aesthetic character. This feeling is feeling after a certain beauty of form, feeling away from confusion toward structure. There is some quality of the aesthetic in the finding of the right formulation, in the elegance and beauty of an economical conceptual system. Many thinkers have stressed this aesthetic motive and its aesthetic consummation in the process of scientific discovery.

Feeling and Understanding: Biology and History

In the light of these very general distinctions it may be interesting to take a quick glance at one or two examples of different fields of study, in order to see how the cultivation of sensitive feeling may in various ways enter into understanding; this can have obvious relevance to education.

We often talk about the importance of being on "the inside" of a subject. It is a telling metaphor and brings out the importance of feeling. We are on the "inside" of our own lives; we feel life flowing along. This, we have said, is distinct from and logically prior to any analysis of it. The image can be extended. By imaginative identification with the objects of concern, e.g., the objects of science or art or history, by empathy, sympathy, projection, we can enter, by the distal process, into the inner side of these subjects, into the flow of them, into their unity and continuity, imaginatively living in their structures and processes. This imaginative sympathy and empathy is something which can and ought to be cultivated in education.

This "feeling into" things, into structures and processes, may be less obvious and prominent (as we said) in our concerns with logical structures or with factual understanding of inanimate nature. Logic, pure mathematics, and the mathematics in which physics expresses its most exact concepts are necessarily high abstractions from the unity and continuity of existing things, and they can stand independently on their own as formulated abstractions.

On the other hand, in the sciences of life the part which feeling may play may be much more important. Polanyi points out[10] that although all knowledge involves the person (and therefore, we must add, feeling), the degree of involvement varies with the subject matter. It is least in the exact sciences, greater in degree as we move from inanimate wholes to living wholes, greatest of all in man's knowledge of man. In trying to understand different levels of wholeness, it is extremely important to employ the full personal intuitive powers appropriate to that level in order to understand the ordering principle. Physics and chemistry cannot adequately account for our knowledge of animals. We have to be aware of animals as active, resourceful living beings; we often have to make a conscious effort which involves projections, identifications, sympathetic and empathic feeling. We have to feel something of the queer thing we call "purposiveness," for example in rats, or in the adaptations of insects, spiders, water-beetles, etc., to the amputation of a leg or legs. When we come to man we can only understand him as a man if we accept all of what it is to be a man—conscious, sentient, intelligent, responsible, creative. Any view which regards men as thoughtful automata is logical nonsense. Polanyi observes that as we proceed to survey the ascending stages of life our subject matter will tend to include more and more of the very faculties on which we rely for understanding. "Biology is life reflecting on itself." In particular, without the active exercise of directed, imaginative feeling for the life of others which we first know in the feeling of our own life, the prime condition of understanding life is absent. Once again, feeling is not a substitute for all the other forms of study, but is a condition of their fruitfulness. The opposite of fruitful study is the dry accumulation of abstractions culled from text-

[10] Michael Polanyi, *Personal Knowledge* (London: Routledge, 1958), p. 347.

66 /

books, learned and reproduced without understanding. The difference between study in which the imaginative feeling for life is a basis, and the mechanical ingestion of inert abstractions, is symbolically pictured in the difference between the long strenuous studies of animals in their natural habitat in the open air and the contemplation of the stuffed objects in museums. (In the light of Polanyi's observations, and of our own observations on feeling, we might ask whether there are essential limits, limits in principle, to the expression of biological truths mathematically.)

Imaginative feeling for the interplay between the contingencies of events and human decisions is a condition of *historical* understanding. The historian, surely, has to make history live, in the first instance for himself, then for others. How otherwise can he do it than by the distal process of imaginative feeling? Even more clearly than with science, history cannot be taught or learned as a set of abstractions of which dates and the names of kings and statesmen are the usual paradigms. Professor W. B. Gallie in *Philosophy and the Historical Understanding* puts in the central place of historical understanding the following of a narrative and what is involved in that. We do not, historically, characterize a historical event or sequence of events as instances of a general law or an inevitable causal sequence. One of the interests of history is that there could be a number of alternative outcomes which we do not know in advance. It may be true that the later event is the outcome of the earlier, but to find out the historical outcome we have to go through imaginatively with the events and wait to discover what the outcome is to be: the later event cannot be infallibly predicted from the earlier. For Gallie, study of history is something like following a game or a story. We have to enter and go through it as something acceptable and unpredictable yet not entirely subjective. This involves, of course, intelligent human sympathies and antipathies of all kinds as well as the exercise of the critical intellect, but the basis of it all is the imaginative entry in feeling into the dynamics of the interaction between

/ 67

events and human actions. History is a journey, intelligently followed through a succession of contingencies, into the time of which we have to *live*, in feeling as well as in thought.

Three Levels of the Operation of Feeling

I hope that the emphasis I have been giving in this article to feeling, and the contrast drawn between feeling and abstract thinking, will not be taken to be in any sense anti-intellectual, anti-rational. It seems necessary to repeat, even *ad nauseam*, that feeling cannot be separated from all the rest that is mind, from everything else in human understanding. It functions, as we have seen, in more important ways at some levels and in some situations than in others. And some of the most important ways in which it should be allowed to function are not by any means always recognized in intellectual pursuits. In order to make this clearer, I want to distinguish three different levels at which feeling may operate, three orders of the functioning of feeling.

There is the order of firsthand experience itself. We live within the "flow" of our own lives, immersed in process, psychophysical organisms engaged with the world of nature and persons around us. All this we feel, both as inward private life and, by sympathy, empathy, projection, and other processes, we "feel" the characters of things beyond us. We feel the earthiness of the wet earth, the stoniness of the rocks on the seashore, the motion of the breaking waves, the sensitiveness of the limpet when, stirred, it clings the harder to its rock face. By sympathy, we feel the tensions and problems, the despairs and joys of other people. When we perceive art we feel the dynamics of the sculptured forms, the ebb and flow of the music, the drama on the stage, the significant gestures of the dance. Or we enter into the life of history in imagination. In such experiences we accept in feeling life and things much as they come, as they present themselves. The basic feeling of life is of something which happens to us (including what happens in our participation with other things) and, as far as it can be distinguished from other elements in life, feeling is at

68 /

this level uncomplicated by criticism; it is what it is, and feels as it is. It is good that this should happen and that it should be cultivated and enjoyed.

But of course this *is* only a moment, an aspect of experience which it is important to be aware of; and this feeling is but a distinguishable side of something which is inseparable from all the rest. We may, in relaxation, flow along with life, live within ourselves and other things. But feeling, for human beings, is the feeling of a psychophysical organism whose consciousness and feeling is what it is, has the content which it has, because of its always active powers of discrimination, a conceiving, thinking, interpreting, judging organism. We come to any fresh situation with a vast store of experience and knowledge. Our experiences of nature, people, and art are concept-influenced throughout. The art critic has to feel intuitively the wholeness of the work of art. But the whole is a complex whole of discriminated parts in unique aesthetic relationship; it is something which is shown in complex context—historical, social-contemporary, economic, psychological. It occurs at a particular moment in art history, it has style which is influenced, it employs certain techniques and media, its forms as well as being individual also belong to certain classes. Criticism is of many kinds, according as this or that aspect is emphasized, so that what is being intuited and felt is apprehended, is interpreted *as* this or that. In making the distinction between felt intuition, the relaxed and accepting aspect, and critical activities with all their conceptual and other apparatus, it is important not to forget that qualified appreciation of art can be neither feeling without critical scrutiny nor critical scrutiny without feeling. Mature understanding of art demands both at the same time, sensitiveness to *this* thing with its qualities, as well as long experience, much knowledge of various kinds (including knowledge of one's own limitations and bias) and, underlying all, some very general system of aesthetic concepts within which judgment is made.

The same thing is true, *mutatis mutandis* and with varying emphasis, of understanding at this level in other spheres. Practical moral judgment requires feeling for self and others, sensitiveness, imagination, sympathy, projection: without feeling, as we said, moral thinking may be unperceptive and go awry. But it is all these capacities used in the service of something else, concern for fair and just assessment of situations, just and fair judgment, just and fair action. I am using the terms "just" and "fair" not in a limited sense—for morality is much more than fairness and justice—but in the sense of general concern for principles of moral objectivity and truth. Moral concern is a seeking after what is *truly* good and, in the light of that, seeking for what is right, which is, I believe, definable[11] as the best which it is possible to do within the limitations of any particular situation. It is the feeling of this kind of concern for good and right—morally and intellectually a highly disciplined concern—which is a basic principle in moral life. Not, on the one hand, just an impersonal knowledge that X is good or right and not, on the other hand, just a warm vague feeling, but a highly discriminating feeling of moral concern for the truly good and right. It is a concern for actual moral situations under the domination and control of general feeling for the obligatoriness of good and right.

It is unnecessary in the light of these observations to enlarge upon how the feeling for principles operates in other fields of understanding. Historical understanding requires, we said, a sensitiveness to the flow and tensions of human events of the past. But it is feeling in the service of discriminating analysis and synthesis, and it, too, is under the supreme authority of the feeling of the obligation to objectivity and truth. Like the art critic, the historian has his own private feelings, preferences, biases. He must be aware of these and must in turn submit them to the "authority" acknowledged in his passion for objectivity and truth. In mathematics and the different sciences (e.g., physics and biology) feelings, as we saw, operate in different ways. But sensitiveness to the structures and the facts is united to the conceptual thinking of them, and they

[11] See my *Ways of Knowledge and Experience* (New York: Oxford University Press, 1961), pp. 212ff.

come under the authority of a dominating concern for the imperative of truth, exacting in its demands for precise and definitive testing.

The first and second levels at which feeling contributes to understanding are more like stages on a continuous slope than step-like "levels." Anyhow, whatever the metaphor, they are inseparable. The second state represents thinking at the level of direct confrontation with the "felt" facts of life: artistic, moral, historical, scientific. It is perhaps easier to distinguish, or even to separate, the third level from the other two. It is the level at which understanding is as theoretical as understanding ever can be. I have in mind such fields of study as philosophical aesthetics, ethics, philosophy of history, philosophy of science, and, perhaps, purely theoretical (as distinct from experimental) physics.

These studies (third-order, in my classification) are conceptual studies, of the concepts involved in the second order. Each has its own logical discipline in the very wide, perhaps loose, sense in which one might say that the "logic" of aesthetics is different from the "logic" of ethics because of their different subject matters. Each is autonomous in this same sense. On the other hand, *qua* subject matter, each is in a sense a parasite upon the second and first orders. Aesthetics—or at least the aesthetics of art—considers the conceptual assumptions involved in the direct work of the critic face to face with individual works, who in turn must feel intuitively the differentiated wholeness of the works if he is to do his work properly. This twofold character of third-order studies, autonomy and dependence, sets up a certain tension, demands a certain self-discipline on the part of the student of any of them. If the tension is lost, one or other of two opposite things may happen. If on the one hand, say in aesthetics, the philosopher is too "near" to the critic or too much preoccupied in his mind with particular works of art or with one sort of art (e.g., music or painting), or with schools of art within one type, his theory of general aesthetics will go wrong; his generalizations will be too particularly derived for his general theoretical construction to be fair and all-round. The same could happen in theoretical ethics. Perhaps the rigoristic moral temperament of Kant, or, nearer our own time, of Sir David Ross, may induce a one-sided ethical system. Too easygoing hedonism in real life could induce the opposite mistake, reducing duty to desire or good to satisfaction or pleasure.

A contrasting mistake occurs when theory is too much isolated from practice, experience, and the feelings that go along with them. Thinking certainly in a sense must be detached and has a life of its own. But thinking has an alluring character which can be a temptation to the intellectual. Thinking is fun, if intellectual fun, and every thinker knows that he can get carried along by the sheer exhilaration of the game. Ideas breed ideas, and the interplay between them can be so fascinating that it is possible to forget the concreteness of the original problem which set the thinking going. Of course the profession of thinking for its own sake is an honorable one. (Possibly in mathematics it can be said to be completely self-justifying.) Free thinking, whether speculative or analytic, can, like imagination, lead to new vistas of understanding. But it has, as I am saying, its dangers and temptations. The linguistic or conceptual analyst or the metaphysician can be so busy with his own professional preoccupations that he loses sense of proportion and of what is important. A besetting temptation of intellectualism is a kind of idolatry, constructing intellectual images, then bowing down and worshiping them, setting up the image and mistaking it for the true god. Or, to vary the metaphor, there can be a pygmalionism of thinking; the images walk away in a world of unreal fantasy. This can be harmless, but it can also be destructive when the construction is genuinely but mistakenly thought to be the reality. Scientism is one example of this: when nothing which will not conform to the (legitimate) methods of scientific testing is accounted true. Behavioristic philosophy, which admits as mind only that which is capable of being observed, is a form of it. Logical Positivism, which allowed as meaningful only those statements capable of one very limited kind of testing, was another. In all those cases, limited, isolated patterns of thinking go wrong because they are taken as substitutes or forced in a procrustean way upon the facts of life. Robust life always in the end rejects them and proves them false. But in the meantime they do damage. It is difficult to estimate the damage they may do. How far, for instance, are they responsible for the unspeakable cruelties of ideological wars?

Conceptual thinking must not be too near to the ground of experience and not too far off. Thinking should be in very frequent, if not constant, dialogue with firsthand experience, sustaining its intellectual character, but also submitting to the facts of experience of different kinds. It is the latter which I wish to stress here, and particularly in its aspect of feeling. At this stage it is only necessary to mention or recall, without enlarging on them, a few examples.

I have mentioned aesthetics and how necessary it is for the philosopher of aesthetics to be in touch all the time with the critical experience of art and for himself to possess the capacity for intuitive feeling. Aesthetics is in danger when it is too much dependent upon deduction from some philosophical system. Personally I feel this in the (admittedly very difficult) writings of Maritain upon art. And were not Croce, and even the far more robust Collingwood, misled by their metaphysical idealisms? Collingwood, as I knew from personal contact, was something of an artist himself. Yet how could Croce and he alike be so blind to the importance of artistic discovery through working in *physical* media? The "spiritualization" of art, derived from idealist metaphysics, does not stand up to the facts of *feeling* for the material facts, facts to which Bosanquet, also an idealist, did ample justice.

In general philosophy intellectual isolationism is illustrated in the philosophical system of Hegel, against which the desperate, anguished emphasis of Existentialism upon feeling, the feeling of "existence," was the natural reaction. It can also be illustrated in ethics in some of the writings of Oxford philosophers between the wars. The interesting problems of theoretical ethics, and perhaps the tests of the validity of the treatment of them, must be related to practical moral experience and ought (in a distraught world) to include really significant examples from experience. Some of the Oxford writers did not show much sense of this. No doubt they had their feelings like other people, but their morally important experience did not show in the examples they habitually chose. Their moral feelings seemed too often to be limited to agonies produced in the donnish mind when a book went missing in the post! What on earth could the poor scholar do in this desperate dilemma? Or (to take another actual example) if a lady faints, what should the philosopher do? (The suggested but hesitating answer given was, "Shout!") The feelings, as I say, were evidently there. But a bit more depth of felt moral experience might have lent additional interest to what was, in other respects, superbly acute writing.

One more example of the need to unite thinking with sensitive feeling for firsthand experience is philosophy of education. There was a period after the war, when the low status of what was called—too charitably—"philosophy" of education needed boosting. One method chosen to do this was to invite professional philosophers of standing to "apply" their philosophies to the field of education; one had essays on the bearings of Realism, Idealism, Existentialism, etc. upon education. Such projects tended, I think, to be unsuccessful, not because the writers were not able and distinguished, or that they did not try with great conscientiousness to carry out their prescribed assignments, but because some lacked first hand, mature, reflective experience of the kind of education which goes on in schools and of the problems which practicing teachers have to face daily. The living problems of philosophy of education arise—directly or indirectly—out of actual educational situations, and these have to be known pretty intimately if the philosopher is to talk relevant sense. As the teacher in the classroom, over and above such theoretical equipment as he may have, must, above all things, have a *feeling* for the complex totality of the situations which he has to face in the classroom, so philosophy of education requires feeling for the

74 /

relevant questions. Of course philosophy of education is not only concerned with questions arising directly out of classroom experience; but the philosopher of education, rightly more detached than the classroom teacher, has to be aware "in his bones" of where the tensions are and the problems press. The difficulty in the past was that although the practitioners who tried to write "philosophy" of education had great feeling for education, teaching, and its practical problems, they had, most often, no philosophical training. They did not know how to think or talk with philosophical rigor about education. The professional philosophers, on the other hand, were trained to think and talk philosophically; but they did not really know what they were talking *about*! Hence came a mixture of practical wisdom and waffle on the one hand and competent but sometimes irrelevant writing on the other.

Today it is changing, and my thesis is supported by what is actually happening. Philosophers are no longer deducing thoughts about education from general philosophy. They are, in some places at least, starting to philosophize from within concrete educational experience, and from their *feeling* from within, to select for conceptual examination and systematic exposition those questions which are warmly relevant to education and teaching. It is essential, I think, for the good health of philosophy of education that on the one hand the philosopher of education should be recognized as philosopher in his own right; and this may mean, perhaps, that he is within the department of philosophy as well as in the department of education. On the other hand, it is vital that he should be living within education and its problems so that he is getting the "feel" all the time, from association with his students, his educational colleagues, with practicing teachers, with children, of the dynamics of the educational situation. For this reason it is dangerous—and particularly dangerous if the only motive is to make philosophy of education appear more academically respectable—to consign the teaching of philosophy of education to the "pure" philosopher coming out only at set periods from the isolation of his department of pure philosophy. The phi-

/ 75

losopher of education must, in a sense, think feelingly and feel thinkingly about education.

I hope that this, and all the rest that has been said, will not be misinterpreted as advocating "thinking with the emotions." Thinking with "the emotions" as usually interpreted means thinking distorted by emotional bias, which might be personal or ideological. But the thinking (and understanding) feelingly, and feeling thinkingly (and understandingly) has nothing to do with what is called "emotional thinking"—nothing, that is, if all is done under the dominating imperative of the feeling, the passion, for truth and objectivity. This passion is a condition of understanding, of whatever kind. Or it is something which ought to permeate all thinking, judging, understanding, deciding—whether in criticism or aesthetics, practical living or ethics, science, history, education, or the philosophy of it. Feeling is a datum in all experience, the importance of which ought to be recognized, and it also plays, as passion for truth, a supreme part in the ordering and disciplining of human understanding. To learn when and how to use feeling profitably is a vitally important part of education.

TACIT KNOWING AND

ÆSTHETIC EDUCATION / 4

Harry S. Broudy

Demand for Behavioral Objectives

One of the major obstacles to any proposal regarding aesthetic education in the schools is the demand for behavioral objectives. Implicit in this demand is the assumption that objectives of instruction which are not described behaviorally cannot be evaluated, and that what cannot be evaluated is probably not worth teaching in the first place.

These assumptions require somewhat different modes of support. To contest the first, it would be sufficient to find some way of evaluating an objective that cannot be or has not been translated into observable items of behavior, and whether this can be done, I submit, is still an open question. The second assumption rests on a complicated metaphysics and value system, and I do not know of criteria that would enable us to decide what sort of evidence would count decisively as between incompatible systems of metaphysics.

The demand for behavioral objectives is not very threatening at the level of psychomotor skills, information, solutions of problems, and indeed at any level where the educational outcome can be formulated explicitly or formalized according to some set of statable rules. In this domain—and it is a very extensive and important domain—the demand for behavioral objectives is no more than a call to exercise clarity and precision. The testing people are quite right in insisting on this clarity and, in principle, there is no insuperable difficulty in meeting the demand.

With regard to objectives of instruction in the humanities and the arts, and with respect to all outcomes having to do with the individual's value schema, his attitudes, and his interpretations of experience, the situation is radically different. One can attribute to the demand for behavioral objectives much of the difficulty that besets the humanities in maintaining a position in the curriculum either at the college or the secondary school level. The benefits claimed for instruction in the humanities, e.g., "deepened appreciation," "an understanding of human nature," "a respect of human values," and the like do not lend themselves to unambiguous translation into items of observable behavior. To achieve objectivity in grading, learning in the humanities tends to be measured by the student's responses to informational questions about the work studied, because this kind of learning lends itself to objective testing. Unfortunately, these test results have little demonstrable relationship to the broader outcomes stated above.

On the contrary, these outcomes are concrete individual states of being, necessarily particular and unique. It is not a matter of clearing up the ambiguity and indeterminateness of these outcomes, but rather of preserving them. This is another way of saying that art is not science, that wisdom and folly are not synonymous with accurate and inaccurate information. Accordingly, ambiguity, multilevel meanings, overlapping images, uniqueness, and subjectivity are worth having even though, and perhaps just because, they cannot be stated behaviorally. The blatant insistence on behavioral objectives may, therefore, throw out the baby with the bathwater, and to a considerable extent this has already occurred. The humanities and the arts owe their position in the curriculum more to traditional respect for them than to any strong belief in their usefulness.

"Down with nonbehavioral objectives" is a slogan rather than a claim to empirical truth. As such it has no probative force against the hypothesis that school learnings can function in experience even though neither their objectives nor their outcomes can be made explicit. Are there things that we know but cannot tell? This seems to be an empirical question that is not precluded by any slogan.

Freudian psychology, for example, would be totally senseless unless some *important* items of experience could not be recalled at will. It is by now a commonplace that very early childhood experiences will function in adult life even though they cannot be remembered and in some instances precisely because they have been forgotten. Associationistic psychology is based on the fact that our experience ordinarily is not organized into tightly logical nets. If association of ideas is by contiguity, vividness, frequency, and effect, then the routes of prediction are not so much logical as psychological; which items will be associated and by which principle is a matter of personal history. But man did not have to wait for either associationist psychologists or Freud to observe the tricks of memory. Schooling has always been an attempt to circumvent the capriciousness of memory.

Another branch of psychological theory—Gestalt psychology —also gives evidence in the same direction. This it does in several ways, but especially by its insistence that perception is not an additive process that mechanically, or by the laws of association, summates discrete sensa into objects. Wholeness is taken to be the primary feature of perception and has principles of its own (e.g., closure, inclusiveness, etc.) that operate regardless of the specific content of the perception.

These considerations, it seems to me, are sufficient grounds for challenging the hegemony of behavioral objectives in education. However, they do not by themselves provide the theoretical grounds for justifying instruction (determinate school input) for indeterminate outcomes (pupil outputs). For this purpose it is necessary to show (1) that many and perhaps all forms of knowing necessarily have indeterminate or nonexplicitly formalizable elements, (2) that determinate inputs under certain circumstances contribute to the knowing act in a subsidiary rather than in a direct way, and (3) that the value or the functioning of a school learning (input) is not necessarily or sufficiently tested by its recall or recognition.

I believe this challenge to the behaviorist dogma in educational theory is salutary for schooling as a whole, but it is especially crucial for the humanities, and the arts considered as parts of the humanities, i.e., aesthetic education.[1] A somewhat fuller statement of the reasons for this is in order.

Insofar as aesthetic education aims at skill and knowledge, its objectives are in principle as statable as similar outcomes in other areas of instruction. These outcomes range from technical skill in drawing, painting, and playing a musical instrument through knowledge of styles and biographies of artists to theories of art and theories about such theories.

To a considerable extent such outcomes, like those of chemistry or history, can be correlated with school inputs designed to produce them. Whether a one-to-one correspondence between them can be set up is more debatable. For example, suppose one objective of aesthetic education is an understanding of articles on art written by the critic in the *New York Times*. What school input can correspond one to one with such understanding? Surely "understanding" does not mean repeating a set of statements written by this critic and learned in school. The understanding we have in mind implies a highly flexible interpretation of an interpretation. It brings into play the results of many years of instruction in reading and in many other subjects, not to speak of an indeterminable number of nonschool learnings. The more knowledge is used to interpret experience, the less we replicate our school learnings. We use

[1] For fuller discussion on this concept of aesthetic education see my "The Role of the Humanities in the Curriculum," *The Journal of Aesthetic Education* I (1966): 17–29.

these learnings to think *with*, and in doing so, as will become clear later, we do not necessarily or even usually explicitly think *of* them.

But there is another way of characterizing the outcome of aesthetic education. It is to establish by instruction habits of perception and judgment characteristic of aesthetic experience. This is not the place to elaborate on what is involved here. Roughly, aesthetic education can be directed at heightening the pupil's sensitivity to the sensory, formal, technical, and expressive properties of works of art. It also hopes to equip him with internalized authentic norms for making appropriately reasoned evaluations of works of art. The criterion of good aesthetic experience and, therefore, of the life outcome of aesthetic education is the degree to which it approximates the artist's mode of perception or that of the artist as critic (or, if you like, the critic as artist).

Now it is clear that the possibility of correspondence between school input and life output on this conception of aesthetic education varies over a wide range, depending on how much agreement can be achieved in aesthetic perception and judgment. There can be a good deal of agreement about the sensory components of a work of art and considerably less—but nevertheless an appreciable amount—agreement as to a work's formal structure. But when it comes to the expressive dimension, not only is the task of finding agreement difficult; it is self-defeating, for it is the indeterminacy of the response that makes it an experience of art rather than of history, mathematics, physics, or mechanical drawing. In other words, even if it could be brought off, we would not want all the life outcomes of aesthetic education to correspond unambiguously with the items of instruction. On the contrary, the goal of aesthetic education is to prevent stereotyped perception and judgment.

In aesthetic education the intensification and refinement of the aesthetic response is central. The distinctive feature of this response may be characterized as the interpretation of a metaphor. This metaphor depends for its effectiveness on the fact that there is not a complete literal or logical equivalence between the proffered analogues. The effectiveness of the work of art depends on its expressiveness, but this expressiveness is achieved when feelings are made perceptible by sensory structures that only metaphorically, albeit precisely, resemble them. If a predetermined response to the work of art is insisted upon, there can be no aesthetic education, for there can be no aesthetic experience. Thus, although the behaviorist's demand for the abolition of nonbehavioral objectives is a threat to all education in any save the most rudimentary sense of skill-training and rote memory, it inhibits aesthetic education in a more radical and fundamental sense.

Now if the aesthetic experience itself is unimportant, the behavioristic stricture may be regarded as a salutary sweeping out of mystical nonsense from the curriculum. I do not believe the behaviorists want to say this. They do not reject the enjoyment that aesthetic experience affords, but they prefer to keep that enjoyment and the means for achieving it a personal matter—as a matter of taste and temperament over which no pedagogical control is feasible and perhaps not even desirable. This last reason, of course, gets us back to the starting point, the alleged impossibility of defining explicitly the outcomes and the criteria for such outcomes.[2]

The justification of formal aesthetic education, therefore, calls for an argument that the effects of aesthetic experience go beyond spontaneous enjoyment. The added importance, it seems to me, lies in the effect of art on values, preference, and choice. The connecting factor between action and art is feeling, and in many theories of art the aesthetic experience is characterized by some such phrase as the "understanding of feeling," "cognized feelings," and "felt cognitions." Aesthetic education can justify itself on the grounds that it intensifies, refines, and broadens the capacity of its beneficiaries to perceive and understand feeling in the manner of art. If such an understanding does affect action, then aesthetic experience is

[2] I take it that the relation of this view of the value judgment to a positivistic theory of knowledge needs no elaboration.

even more than its own excuse for being; it has social import and so has aesthetic education.

Yet if art is to be important, it must not only be something; it must in being something reveal something. I shall not rehearse the standard arguments for and against the cognitive status of value judgments in general or of the aesthetic judgment in particular. I find no plausibility in the attempt to regard aesthetic objects as making assertions about matters of fact or value. Indeed, even if conceivably they could, I think it about the most awkward and wasteful way of conveying information. The work of art is cognitive insofar as it presents perceptually in images of one sort or another the feeling import, or the potential for feeling import, of anything whatsoever in nature or dream that interests the artist.

The revelation, therefore, is cognitive in a very special sense, and aesthetic knowing is a unique kind of knowing. Nevertheless, it involves features that it shares with virtually all other forms of knowing. In the remainder of the paper I shall argue that aesthetic "knowing" can be assimilated to what Michael Polanyi calls "tacit knowing." If this can be done successfully, then it would constitute an argument for aesthetic education even though it cannot satisfy the demand for behavioral objectives that correlate point for point with school inputs. For if aesthetic experience is an instance of tacit knowing, then school learnings that constitute aesthetic education can be construed as the subsidiary elements that bear on the focal experience of the work of art. One would have the aesthetic experience with them, but not necessarily of them.

If Polanyi is right, aesthetic education benefits in two ways. First, one can argue for aesthetic education and yet evade the demand for behavioral objectives; second, while doing justice to the distinctive character of aesthetic knowing, it nevertheless brings it into relation with all other forms of knowing.

Tacit Knowing

The most ambitious attempt to substantiate the claim for tacit knowing is that of Michael Polanyi, whose *Personal*

Knowledge has been received with great interest but not without some shrugging of scientific shoulders. In numerous works Polanyi has reiterated the theme of tacit knowing, and in at least one article he attempted to trace the bearings of tacit knowing on some very central problems of philosophy.[3]

I shall explicate briefly some of Polanyi's arguments that all knowing, from perception to the most advanced phases of scientific discovery, have a tacit element and that this tacit element is the most important dynamic of the thought process.

According to Polanyi, there are two kinds of knowing which enter "jointly into any act of knowing a comprehensive entity." There is (1) knowing a thing *by attending to it,* in the way we attend to an entity as a whole, and (2) knowing a thing by *relying on our awareness of it for the purpose of attending to an entity to which it contributes.* It is the latter knowledge which he refers to as tacit. As an example of tacit knowing Polanyi discusses viewing through a stereopticon two pictures of an object taken from slightly different positions. We see one image, however, and this is at the focus of our attention; of the two separate pictures we are aware—if we are aware of them at all—only as "guides to the image on which we focus our attention." The two pictures function as subsidiaries "to our

3 Polanyi's best known work is probably *Personal Knowledge* (Chicago: University of Chicago Press, 1958; London: Routledge, 1958; and New York: Harper Torchbooks, 1964). Among his other books are *Science, Faith and Society* (Chicago: University of Chicago Press, 1946; Oxford: Oxford University Press, 1946; and Phoenix edition, Chicago, 1964), *The Logic of Liberty* (Chicago: University of Chicago Press, 1951; London: Routledge, 1951), *The Study of Man* (Chicago: University of Chicago Press, 1959; London: Routledge, 1959), and the Terry Lectures of 1962, *The Tacit Dimension* (New York: Doubleday, 1966, Anchor Books edition, 1967).

Among the papers bearing on tacit knowing used in the preparation of this chapter are: "Tacit Knowing and Its Bearing on Some Problems of Philosophy," *Review of Modern Physics* XXXIV (1962): 601–16; "The Logic of Tacit Inference," *Philosophy* XL (1966): 369–86; "The Creative Imagination," *Chemical and Engineering News* XLIV (1966): 85–93; "Logic and Psychology," *American Psychologist* XXIII (1968): 27–43. For a thorough discussion of Polanyi's theory of knowledge see Marjorie Grene, *The Knower and the Known* (New York: Basic Books, 1966).

seeing their joint images which is their joint meaning."[4] He holds that these two kinds of knowing are not only distinct but also in an important sense mutually exclusive. In other words, if we try to concentrate our attention on our fingers while we play the piano, then our piano playing is bound to suffer. If we attend carefully to each word as we utter it or if we utter a word repeatedly while concentrating on the word as such, its meaning seems to evaporate.

However, these forms of knowing are disjunctive in a more fundamental sense. According to Polanyi, if subsidiary knowing is a knowing by relying on our awareness of something for the purpose of attending to something else, we cannot at the same time not rely on it for this purpose, as would be the case if we attended to it exclusively in itself and for itself. Tacit knowing, like symbolic knowing, is always relational in that we know the sign for the sake of its referent and not for itself, even though it has a character which could be known for itself and by itself. If this analogy is apt, then subsidiary knowing is a species of symbolic knowing except that it is knowing by means of a cluster of symbols, and the entities serving as signs may not be in full awareness. It is almost as if without clearly perceiving the nature of arrows, pointers, and signs we nevertheless find our way about a city by means of them. The usual language in the literature of signs and symbols tends to make the awareness of that which acts as a sign quite clear and explicit, and in this respect Polanyi's use of clues differs markedly. Polanyi cites a number of experiments on "subception" and what might be called subliminal perception in support of his contention that there are things we know but cannot tell, including M. D. Vernon's conclusion that there is "a type of perception of which we are not directly aware, but which nevertheless affects our actions in some ways."[5]

[4] Polanyi, "Logic and Psychology," p. 29.
[5] Polanyi, "Tacit Knowing," p. 602. Also Polanyi says ". . . accordingly, wherever I shall speak of the unspecifiable particulars that are known to us in terms of a comprehensive entity to which they contribute, I may be taken to speak of a form of subception" (*ibid.*, p. 603).

Polanyi indicates that the whole notion of tacit knowing is based on Gestalt psychology, especially on the whole-part and figure-ground relations. As to the first, Polanyi relies on the principle that the *Gestaltqualität* is not a simple addition of components experienced serially. The "set" or the meaning of the whole, according to this psychology, determines the meaning of the constituent parts. This has been demonstrated by the familiar ambiguous figures which, although made up of the same geometrical constituents, function differently in one whole rather than in another. It is essential for Polanyi to maintain that the meaning of an experience—whether in perception, inference, or in theory-building—is constituted by the *bearing on that experience of its constituents.* Presumably for X to "bear on" Y is more than to be a part of the whole Y.

The figure-ground relationship, which is also characteristic of Gestalt psychology, is used by Polanyi to distinguish between "focal" awareness and "subsidiary" awareness. Just as in any perceptual experience figure is at the forefront of attention and ground on its periphery, so in tacit knowing we perceive, understand, or seek something at the focus by means of clues to which we do not directly attend. Polanyi insists that the items at the periphery or in the background need not be in the unconscious; they can be the contents of various degrees of awareness; the important point is that they are not being attended to directly. Further, as with figure-ground phenomena, the moment one attends directly to items in the background they become focal and something else recedes into the background. The clues of which we are aware subsidiarily are the things we "know but cannot tell," or at least may not be able to tell on demand.

Polanyi holds, as perhaps some Gestalt psychologists who think of the Gestalt as the phenomenological equivalent of the equilibrium of brain states do not, that knowing in any form and at any level consists of a dynamic integrating process whereby items of experience become clues by virtue of having some bearing on a goal.

The subsidiaries, e.g., each of the two pictures in the stereop-

86 /

ticon, cause or contribute to the cause of the single stereoscopic image, but presumably do not constitute the meaning of the final image. Instead, Polanyi says, these subsidiaries have a bearing on the final image and receive their meaning from it, i.e., from the final image. Hence the causes of the final image are not its meanings, but rather the contrary; this reversal of direction is not easy to keep straight.

Polanyi distinguishes three types of relation that he believes are characteristic of tacit knowing. One is the focal-subsidiary one or, as he calls it elsewhere, the from-to relation or a functional relation. Another is the phenomenal transformation of the particulars when combined into a focal target, and the third is the one in which the focal target gives sense or meaning to the particulars, which he calls a semantic relation. Presumably *having a bearing on* is a functional expression, and the focus *giving sense to a particular* is its semantic equivalent.[6]

Of course, the difficulty lies in the relation of "bearing on." The features of a face can be said to be *part* of the facial configuration, but is this the same as saying that these features *bear on* the configuration we recognize as the face of Abraham Lincoln? A good caricaturist proves that not all parts of the face have the same bearing on the physiognomy because he omits most of them from his drawings. The guiding principle for the caricaturist probably is the facial whole.

It seems, therefore, that the whole already has a meaning that determines what shall have a "bearing." Did it derive this meaning from some or all of its constituent parts, or do parts have no meaning until bearing on some whole? This can become a chicken-egg impasse if it is not kept in mind that wholes can be of varying scope, so that wholes can be parts of larger wholes, and that a given item can retain its characteristics and yet have a different bearing on different configurations.

A somewhat different consideration is involved in the question of whether the integration Polanyi refers to in tacit knowing is a temporal process or an intuition that in some sense has

---

[6] Polanyi, "Logic and Psychology," pp. 29ff.

no serial growth. Use of the word "process," of course, answers this question in the affirmative, yet Polanyi uses the language of intuition freely, and he would certainly object to describing the recognition of a face, for example, as a serial process in which clue is added to clue until the process of recognition is completed. However, one can speak without self-contradiction about temporal processes that eventuate in an all-or-none intuition, and in education we would certainly want to keep open the possibility of learning to intuit configurations that at the beginning of instruction were not so intuited.

Tacit knowing is a factor in all knowing but it does not entail the denial of the existence or value of explicit knowing. But Polanyi would hold that explication is always after the fact. After a theory has been envisioned and worked out, it can in retrospect reveal steps and structures that can be made explicit and formalized. However, he would deny that his theory was simply a psychological description of knowing whose logical structure was more truly represented by its explicit formulation. Polanyi asks:

Is an act or perception which sees an object in a way that assimilated it to past instances of the same kind, a psychological process or a logical inference? We have seen that it can be mistaken and its results be false; and it certainly has a considerable likelihood of being true. To me this suggests that it is a logical process of inference even though it is not explicit. In any case, to perceive things rightly is certainly part of the process of scientific inquiry and to hold perceptions to be right, underlies the holding of scientific propositions to be true. And if, in consequence, we must accept the veridical powers of perception as the roots of empirical science, we cannot reasonably refuse to accept other tacit veridical processes having a similar structure. This is what I have been urging all along since I first wrote ". . . that the capacity of scientists to guess the presence of shapes as tokens of reality differs from the capacity of our ordinary perception only by the fact that it can integrate shapes presented to it in terms which the perception of ordinary people cannot readily handle."[7]

Polanyi undertakes to show how the tacit element functions

[7] Polanyi, *Science, Faith and Society*, p. 10.

in many forms of knowing. In addition to the "know-how" involved in motor skills, there is a tacit vector in the identification of a species to which a plant or an animal belongs and in diagnosing a disease. All of these, together with recognizing the identity of a person or the mood in a face, he groups together as the kind of knowing which recognizes a physiognomy, and its structure resembles that of a skill.

It is an intellectual skill in which a complex pattern of delicately graded features takes the place of a dexterously coordinated set of muscular acts. We do not attend to these features and their pattern in themselves but rely on our awareness of them for attending to the physiognomy to which they jointly contribute. Hence, we know a physiognomy but cannot tell, or can only inadequately tell, how we recognize it.[8]

Diagnostic and taxonomic skills are learned by practice under a teacher's guidance, and the *key* learning product is a characteristic Gestalt. Once apprehended, the pupil uses the Gestalt as a criterion for further comparisons and analysis. The essential class characteristics (which themselves are hard to identify until someone points to instances of them) are used to check on doubtful cases, i.e., those with misleading resemblances or differences.

The resemblance of this physiognomic understanding to aesthetic cognition is obvious, for in aesthetic experience one recognizes the physiognomy of a feeling. Yet there is a significant difference because while my friend's identity is recognized tacitly and by means of details that I cannot make fully explicit, the facial pattern is the same to all who know it. My friend John's physiognomy could not be replicated by a wholly different set of subsidiary particulars; indeed even a few small variations might be fatal.

The physiognomy of a feeling, on the contrary, is not a fixed pattern of particulars. Sadness, for example, can be recognized by means of any number of artistic presentations. There may be sad music, sad painting, and sad poetry. And even within these media any number of particulars in any number of pat-

[8] Polanyi, "Tacit Knowing," pp. 603–4.

terns might give rise to the recognition of the face of sadness. The problem of mistaken identity—when two or more individuals have facial features so similar as to permit the mismatching of their names and faces—does not arise when the physiognomy of feeling is aesthetically apprehended. Facial patterns, for example, are made up of shapes into a geometrical whole that remains constant. A picture, a poem, or a musical composition as a perceptual whole may have a geometrical pattern, but it may also be a pattern of motions and tensions.[9] The latter may be embodied in a variety of perceptual images, e.g., the tension created by contrast can be exemplified in many analogues. However, a more important factor is touched when Polanyi notes: "The characteristic physiognomy of a man may be said to be the meaning of the clues which point to it; but a physiognomy in itself is a clue to something else, namely, to the mood that it expresses, or, more generally, to the mind at work in it."[10]

This extension makes it sensible to say that although X and Y do not have the same facial features, they express the same feeling, e.g., the mood of the two characters in Grant Wood's *American Gothic*. But the quotation from Polanyi has even greater significance for aesthetic knowing if we concentrate on the possibility of a work of art by its physiognomy expressing the mind at work in it. For the moment we can evade the question as to which mind's work is expressed in the work of art. Whether it is the artist's mind or a "culture's mind" is less important than that the work betray the presence of some mind, because any object, to be expressive in the manner of art, must be anthropomorphic, i.e., attribute human import to objects or images that are not sentient. To make a tree look lonely or a song sound sad is typical of the work of art. It is in this sense that one would want to insist that all works of art contain

[9] Compare Carroll Pratt's theory which tries to account for the expressive power of music, *The Meaning of Music* (New York: McGraw-Hill, 1931), pp. 187–88. Cf. also Susanne K. Langer, *Feeling and Form* (New York: Charles Scribner's Sons, 1953) and *Mind: An Essay on Human Feeling*, I (Baltimore: Johns Hopkins Press, 1967), chap. 7.

[10] Polanyi, "Tacit Knowing," p. 604.

clues to the mind, or better, the life import at work in it.

The notion of tacit knowing serves to give a similar form to the use of tools, perception, and inference, and Polanyi seems to regard the use of the tool as the basic model of them all, perhaps because it illustrates so well such notions as subsidiary functioning, indwelling, and the displacement of stimuli. A word or two about each of these may not be amiss. We rely on the tool to accomplish something to which we attend, while not focally attending to the tool itself. We are all familiar with the disruption of a skillful performance when for some reason or other we shift our attention to the golf club or the bat or the tennis racket from the game itself. The common complaint that the artist seemed to get stuck on technique rather than on the goal of the technique belongs to this class of disruptions and points to the importance of forgetting some of the things we have learned *as we have learned them.*

Further, Polanyi notes, the skillful use of the tool actually identifies it to an important extent with our own body.

The rower pulling an oar feels its blade tearing the water; when using a paperknife we feel its edges cutting the pages. The actual impact of the tool on our palm and fingers is unspecificable in the same sense in which the muscular acts composing a skillful performance are unspecificable; we are aware of them in terms of the action our tool performs on its object, that is, within the comprehensive entity into which we integrate the effective use of a tool. The same is true of a probe used for exploring a cavity or a stick by which a blind man feels his way. The impact made by a probe or a stick in our fingers is felt at the tip of the probe or stick, where it hits an object outside, and in this sense the probe or stick is integrated to our fingers that grasp it.[11]

This phenomenon Polanyi calls indwelling. By virtue of our bodies we dwell in the tools we use, and, as we shall see later, in an analogous way we dwell in the language we utter and the thoughts we conceive. For the moment, however, I would like to note the importance of the transposition in space of the sensations received through the probe or the tool. When inte-

[11] *Ibid.*

grated in the task, these sensations are felt as being where they originate rather than in our hands or our nervous system. Polanyi generalizes this into an explanation of the fact that we see colors and hear sounds as located in the objects that produce them. "Many of the clues of perception cannot be known in themselves at all; others can be traced only by acute experimental analysis; but all of them can serve the purpose of seeing, only if we make no attempt at attending to them in themselves. . . . The clues on which we rely for looking at an object will then appear to use in terms of shape, color, size, and position, and other visible features of the object. This is their meaning to us; and this meaning is considerably displaced away from our body, where many of its clues are situated."[12]

The relevance of indwelling for aesthetic experience and aesthetic education is obvious. One of the problems in aesthetic theory is to account for the phenomenal objectivity of tertiary or feeling qualities. The sadness is perceived as being *in* the music or *in* the picture or *in* the poem. "The picture is sad" is aesthetically a correct way of speaking. If this arouses the indignation of positivistic purists, it is not because of the deliverance of their experience, but rather because their theory of knowledge forces them to locate the sadness in the person who perceives the picture, the music, etc. Naively they perceive the music as sad and the sky as blue and not that their nervous systems are sad or blue.

Phenomenal objectivity is a problem for general epistemology because secondary qualities also appear to be in objects rather than where the physiologists say they must be. Polanyi comes to the conclusion that "Visual perception appears. . .as yet another instance of relying on a wide variety of clues, some inside, some outside of our body, for attending to their joint meaning, which in this case appears to us in terms of shape, color, size, position and other visible features of the object."[13]

Indwelling becomes even more generalized when language is

[12] *Ibid.*, p. 605. See also Maurice Merleau-Ponty, *Phenomenology of Perception* (London: Routledge, 1962).
[13] Polanyi, "Tacit Knowing," p. 607.

regarded as a tool for articulating thought. Thought then is an integrating activity which dwells in the acts of speech and writing, and it is their bearing on this thought that gives them their meaning.

Not only is empathy a form of indwelling for Polanyi, but all forms of knowing are: "The theory of tacit knowing establishes a continuous transition from the natural sciences to the study of the humanities. It bridges the gap between the I-It and the I-Thou, by rooting them both in the subject's I-Me awareness of his own body, which represents the highest degree of indwelling."[14]

Indwelling, therefore, would be the identification of ourselves with the multiplicity of meanings, isomorphisms of sense, feeling, and language that are the subsidiaries by which the aesthetic object is focally perceived. In other words, the work of art or the aesthetic object presents us with an image of feeling by means of subsidiaries that are related to feelings in ways that are not clearly apparent and of which at the moment we are not fully aware—in any case to which we do not directly attend.

What are some of the subsidiary elements that enter into and bear upon the focal awareness of the work of art?

1. Ducasse, among others, including Langer, has pointed out that the nameable emotions—fear, anger, joy, etc.—constitute but a small segment of the total spectrum of feeling. The other varieties occur too rarely or without sufficient strength, and their connection with standard situations are too tenuous to be named.[15]

If there is isomorphism of any kind between sensory qualities and affective ones, then it is quite conceivable that as we view a picture or listen to music or a poem, subsidiary and subliminal awareness of many nuances of feeling might be contributing to the focal awareness without our being able to tell just which subsidiaries are operating to produce this or that effect.

[14] *Ibid.*, p. 606.
[15] C. J. Ducasse, "Art and the Language of the Emotions," *Journal of Aesthetics and Art Criticism* XXIII (1964): 109–112.

2. Another type of subsidiary is represented by the observer's knowledge about the work of art. Knowledge about style, history, techniques, may contribute subsidiarily to the final phenomenal object.

3. Still other subsidiaries are the perceptual stereotypes of a culture. For example, in our culture we tend to organize the visual field in accordance with the rules of perspective and may expect paintings to do likewise. A culture in which the size of a represented object is determined by importance rather than distance from the viewer will endow the perceiver with a different perceptual a priori.[16]

4. Very important subsidiaries are provided by learning to work in some artistic medium. It is virtually impossible, one would suppose, to organize the perception of a visual field as an artist does without having tried to achieve certain pictorial effects. Conversely, it must be difficult for an experienced artist not to see and hear in patterns that emphasize the aesthetic impact of objects.

5. Of the same order, yet quite different in content, are the experiences with works of art in museums, schools, at home, and in public places.

6. Finally, there are the idiosyncratic subsidiaries of which there is no end. They range from random associations to the crucial episodes in the person's emotional life.

All four types of subsidiary elements are indeterminate, although they are not equally idiosyncratic. There is more likelihood that two observers chosen at random will share the perceptual stereotypes of their age than that they will be equally knowledgeable about Baroque music, and one would hardly expect similarity in their emotional histories. Accord-

16 See for example, Viktor Lowenfeld, *Creative and Mental Growth*, 3rd ed. (New York: Macmillan, 1957). Lowenfeld points out that in children's drawings that which is of apparently greatest concern is given visual prominence regardless of ordinary perspective. See also Donald T. Campbell, "Stereotypes and the Perception of Group Differences," *American Psychologist* XXII (1967): 817–30, which cites a cluster of such studies, including the classic one by D. Katz and K. Braly, "Racial Stereotypes of One Hundred College Students," *Journal of Abnormal and Social Psychology* XXVIII (1933): 280–90.

ingly, it is quite possible that aesthetic education would reduce the heterogeneity of response to a given work of art, but would not eliminate it. If after making sure that the person was not using subsidiary items that we knew were idiosyncratic (e.g., reveries of childhood episodes during a concert), a work of art still expressed "sadness" to that person, there is no way of logically gainsaying him. For not only is the apperceptive mass that he is bringing to the work unique, but the potential feeling differentiations in the work of art are indeterminate.

Are these indeterminables fatal to the claim that a work of art says something about life that is "true"? If we understand the sense in which it "says" anything, it is conceivable that it could say many different things, and that some or all of them could be true. The difficulty would lie in using agreement of observers as a criterion of truth. Clearly the truths expressed by works of art are not propositions about something other than themselves. Their truth is more akin to that of a witness whose being and action "speak" louder than words.

Truth as Existential

The acceptance of different kinds of articulate systems as mental dwelling places is arrived at by a process of gradual appreciation. Science as a system is tested by experience as verification, but the others are tested by what Polanyi calls validation. Our personal participation in validation is in general greater than in verification. But both verification and validation are everywhere an acknowledgment of a commitment. As distinct from both of these, subjective experiences can only be said to be authentic; and authenticity does not involve a commitment in the sense in which both verification and validation do.[17]

These comments illustrate Polanyi's stress on the person in knowledge, the highest as well as the most ordinary sort. The personal, however, is not the subjective or the capricious; it has to do rather with a faith in an objective reality that serves as the motivation for seeking knowledge and for keeping up the

---

[17] Polanyi, *Personal Knowledge*, p. 202.

search in the face of many obstacles. This is stressed in Polanyi's notion of the role of vision in discovery.

In a paper prepared for circulation among participants in the August, 1965, meeting of the Study Group on the Foundations of Cultural Unity, which appeared later in *Chemical and Engineering News* XLIV (1966), 17, Polanyi remarked: "Copernicus claimed that his system had unique harmonies which proved it to be real even though he could describe these harmonies only in a few vague emotional passages. He did not stop to consider how many assumptions he had to make in formulating his system nor how many difficulties he ignored in doing so. Since his vision showed him an outline of reality, he ignored all its complications and unanswered questions."

Polanyi refers also to a knowledge of hidden coherence in the kind of foreknowledge we call a problem. He likens it to a potential energy that is released when the weight slides down the slope. Our search for deeper coherence, he believes, is guided likewise by such a potentiality. Accordingly, even though we may not know what we are looking for, we can carry on scientific inquiry because the "gradient of deepening coherence tells us where to start and which way to turn, and eventually brings us to the point where we may stop and claim a discovery."

Scientific discovery reveals new knowledge, but the new vision which accompanies it is not knowledge. It is *less* than knowledge, for it is a guess; but it is more than knowledge, for it is a foreknowledge of things yet unknown and present perhaps inconceivable. Our vision of the general nature of things is our guide for the interpretation of all future experience. Any process of enquiry unguided by intellectual passions would inevitably spread out into a desert of trivialities . . . in fact without a scale of interest and plausibility based on a vision of reality, nothing can be discovered that is of value to science; and only our grasp of scientific beauty, responding to the evidence of our senses, can evoke this vision.[18]

The passages quoted from Polanyi remind one of certain remarks by Martin Heidegger: "Truth is no mark of the cor-

[18] *Ibid.*, p. 135.

rect sentence, expressed of an 'object' by a human 'subject'
and then somewhere—it is not known exactly where—holds as
valid; it is rather the disclosure of a being by means of which
an openness comes to be and endures. In this opening all
human conduct and behaviour is exposed. It is in this way,
therefore, that man is the ecstatic existent he is. *Truth in short
is a phenomenon of human existence transcending itself toward
a world and not strictly speaking the exclusive result of scientific or logical inquiry.*"[19]

Heidegger points out, moreover, that poets are our true
teachers in the sense of keeping us aware of the real powers
that shape our lives, and that they teach us to see more exactly
into the nature of things than scholars, scientists, or practical
men.

One gets a similar emphasis from Søren Kierkegaard's notion
of subjectivity as the truth, viz., that truth is a description of a
person's relation to the content of a belief rather than a correspondence between a belief and a state of affairs which it
purports to describe. But it is significant that for Kierkegaard
the aesthetic mode of experience is precisely what is *not*
existential truth, because it is a suspension of commitment
rather than an embodiment of it. It is only on the ethical and
the religious levels that the question of "being" the truth
arises, and it arises most unavoidably, Kierkegaard holds, in
the stark demands of Pauline Christianity.[20]

Doubtless both the Polanyi notion of indwelling and truth as
a state of being have something profound to say about the
human condition. To have the truth and to be the truth are
different existential states, I would grant, and I would agree
that other things being equal, to *be* the truth is more important
than merely to *have* it. There is also ground for believing that
those who think of the aesthetic experience as revelatory of

[19] Quoted by Eugene F. Kaelin in "Notes toward an Understanding of
Heidegger's Aesthetics," in Maurice Mandelbaum and Edward N. Lee, eds.
Phenomenology and Existentialism (Baltimore: Johns Hopkins Press, 1967),
p. 73.
[20] Søren Kierkegaard, *Stages on Life's Way*, trans. Walter Lowrie (Princeton:
Princeton University Press, 1945), p. 99.

the good and the true, as well as of the beautiful, also believe that the aesthetic knowing probes to a level of being that is deeper and perhaps more primordially significant than discursive forms of knowing.

Yet Kierkegaard, who had as much logic as passion—a balance he did not bequeath to all of his existentialist posterity—saw that life as passion was not the same as the image of passion presented by the artist, that the image of passion was conducive to an *understanding*, an objectification and depersonalization of feeling rather than an invitation to participate in it. In this sense, Croce was right in calling the aesthetic the intuitive mode of knowing, but knowing nevertheless and not necessarily a state of being that is better than or different from knowing.

This, I believe, is consistent with the well-nigh universal insistence among aestheticians on the phenomenal objectivity of the aesthetic object. Whatever the subsidiary elements that bear upon the focal target, to count aesthetically they must either be perceptible as images in the object or be excluded from it—regardless of their causal role and efficacy. Educationally, this distinction is of the utmost importance, because aesthetic education is to be regarded either as a means of converting the learner to some more or less mystical stage of grace fit to receive the aesthetic revelation of the real and thus leading to existential truth; or it is to be regarded as making the pupil more at home in the kind of aesthetic knowing that renders him receptive to images of feeling, to the *potentialities* of being as envisioned by the imagination of the artist. It is the latter conception, of course, that I am defending.

Tacit Knowing and Aesthetic Education

If a necessary condition for the genuine aesthetic experience is some form of tacit knowing, then in what sense can the subsidiary factors be made explicit objectives of instruction? Into what behaviors shall we translate them? The maneuvers referred to as aesthetic analysis can be thought of as potential subsidiaries. So can the teaching of art history and performance within some art medium. But how these inputs can be correlated with identifiable changes of sensitivity to aesthetic form or expressiveness is difficult to imagine. To postpone education until one can establish this correlation is to insure that it will never get under way. For although conceivably the component subsidiary motions involved in the final act of riding a bicycle can be analyzed out after the fact, we do not have the slighest notion—apart from extensive self-analyses and confessions of artists and critics—of the psychological causes of the image as it finally appears in the work of art. And one must reiterate that if this could be done, and if adequate causal laws about the process could be formulated, we would not have art as we understand the term. We would have another form of scientific technology.

Educationally, all schooling that is intended to function in interpretation of any sort accomplishes its goal by successful forgetting as well as selective retention. Categorical schemes used in interpretation function most efficiently as logical and psychological a priori—as stencils through which all experience is patterned; making them explicit is a task for philosophy and philosophers and not for men in their ordinary commerce with the world. Good general education imprints these "stencils" on the student so that in later life they function without his being any more aware of them than of his manners.[21]

Accordingly, to test the effectiveness of aesthetic education it is necessary to provide the student with opportunities to carry on aesthetic analysis of real works of art and listen to the dis-

[21] For a more detailed discussion of the various uses of schooling see H. S. Broudy, B. Othanel Smith, and Joe R. Burnett, *Democracy and Excellence in American Secondary Education* (Chicago: Rand McNally, 1964), chap. 3. Although I do not put too much importance on it so far as the thesis of tacit knowing is concerned, and although an adequate discussion would take us far afield, it might be of interest to note the hypotheses about transfer arrived at by Hendrix: (1) For generalization of transfer power, the unverbalized awareness method of learning a generalization is better than a method in which an authoritative statement of the generalization comes first. (2) Verbalizing a generalization immediately after discovery may actually decrease transfer power. Gertrude Hendrix, "A New Clue to Transfer of Training," *Elementary School Journal* XLVIII (1947): 198.

course that results. The instruction will have been successful if the categories he uses are appropriate to aesthetic analysis, if his judgments are genuinely his, albeit not unique to him, and if in talking like a critic, or at least in the manner of one, he gives evidence of habits of the enlightened cherishing found in the connoisseur.

Are these behavioral objectives? Loosely speaking they are, but more accurately they are manners of behaving rather than predetermined particular behaviors. To say that someone will talk like a critic is not to predict what he will say or how he will say it, just as to predict that a person will take a scientific view of something is not to tell us what he will say in particular. And yet these manners of "behaving," i.e., critically or scientifically, are identifiable. Is there any evidence for this?

There is perhaps no systematic way of providing the evidence, but there is a kind of indirect evidence that if not logically airtight is nevertheless impressive. If one compares a man who has had a liberal or general education, say through the sixteenth year of schooling, with one who has dropped out of school at any time before the twelfth year, the difference will be discernible. And the difference will reveal itself not so much in the amount of information each can recall on examinations in this or that academic discipline but rather in the manner of interpreting the phenomena that make up daily life, and this will be as true in humanistic interpretations as in scientific ones.

As an example of this, let me report a number of informal experiments with college students on the relation of the study of Latin to imagery. On a number of occasions I asked classes of college students, about equally divided into those who had had four years of high school Latin and those who had none, to set down the images (not the dictionary meaning) associated immediately with such words as transportation, object, transpire, conspire, predict, prejudice. The words obviously had Latin roots. I kept no statistics, partly because the results were almost without exception in one direction. Virtually no one without Latin study gave images associated with the Latin root meanings, e.g., transportation evoking the carrying-across image, and although not all who had studied Latin used Latin-root imagery, a great many of them did. Both groups did equally well on the dictionary meanings of the words.

Now the import of this observation is not that Latin should be studied for its transfer value to the learning of English vocabulary or to improve writing style. However, it so happens that a great deal of poetry written in English depends for its imagery on the understanding of Latin roots—Milton is only one of the most notable examples. These Latin images function tacitly in the aesthetic response to poetry, and if the poet had these in mind, the reader who has a good dictionary meaning of the term but not the appropriate image is simply not responding as the poet anticipated he would.

The interesting point about all this is that few if any of the Latinists could pass an examination in Latin to save their lives, and many of them did not realize that they were using imagery based on their long "forgotten" Latin lessons.

Now if Latin can function in this way, it is conceivable that many other studies do likewise. The study of the Bible, for example, furnishes a fund of stories and characters that make certain allusions well-nigh universally understandable in Christian countries. In the absence of this biblical background such allusions become useless to the poet or the author or the artist. I daresay that our school learnings in geometry and history in adult life function in the same subsidiary way rather than by recall of explicit details.

Accordingly, it is plausible to expect that much of what is taught about works of art, much of the school experience with works of art and their analysis, will continue to function long after the student has forgotten the details and circumstances of learning them. He would behave differently had he not at one time known them and studied them. Indeed his aesthetic education would have failed had not what had been taught focally in time come to function tacitly.

Another and more important consequence for aesthetic education, if the hypothesis about tacit knowing is tenable, is the support it gives to the common belief that art "says" or does something important about life and its values. If in all knowledge, and indeed in all experience, man is activated by a desire for coherence, if he dwells in a vision of reality by means of subsidiaries, then it can be argued that aesthetic perception functions subsidiarily in other modes of experience.

I am referring here to the power of aesthetic "rightness" to influence our cognition and our preference. For example, one often hears that scientists and mathematicians are attracted by the elegance of a theory or a solution. Then there is the notion that function and form are intimately related. That a beautiful woman can have serious faults of character always comes as a shock despite numerous confirming instances. Certainly among primitive peoples the appearance of things was an indication of their nature and potentialities. What a myth perceives, says Cassirer, are not objective but physiognomic characters. "Nature, in its empirical or scientific sense, may be defined as 'the existence of things as far as it is determined by general laws.' Such a nature does not exist for myths. The world of myth is a dramatic world—a world of actions, of forces, of conflicting powers. In every phenomenon of nature it sees the collision of these powers. Mythical perception is always impregnated with these emotional qualities . . . all objects are benignant or malignant, friendly or inimical, familiar or uncanny, alluring and fascinating or repellent and threatening."[22]

That aesthetic "rightness" can serve as a criterion for the acceptance of cognitive claims is illustrated by the reluctance of the public to accept the Warren Report as a true account of the assassination of John F. Kennedy. Despite repeated assurances, it is difficult for many intelligent people to accept the notion that so great an event could have been brought about by such trivial causes as the Warren Report adduces. Scientifically the Warren Report may be satisfactory but aesthetically or dramatically it is an outrage. Truth is often stranger

[22] Ernst Cassirer, *An Essay on Man* (New Haven: Yale University Press, 1944; New York: Doubleday Anchor Books, 1953), pp. 102–3.

than fiction because it lacks aesthetic plausibility. In the same vein all attempts to discourage people from making judgments about character from facial characteristics or to predict weather from the appearance of the sky are only partially successful. Despite the enormous advance in medical diagnostic instruments, the physician still relies on physiognomic qualities of the patient for important judgments.

The stubborn reliance on aesthetic clues to knowledge is a reverberation of the belief that the Platonic trinity of truth, goodness, and beauty is more than a way of speaking. If all knowledge is, in the Polanyi sense, personal, a matter of commitment as well as of inquiry and verification, then the demand for coherence of the aesthetic, cognitive, and moral aspects of experience makes sense.

The social value of art or the role of art in total economy of life, it would seem, depends on the possibility of such a coherence. Art for art's sake is a valid enough principle for the artist, and he has a right to be judged solely on the aesthetic quality of his work. But this means only that he is excused from making extra-aesthetic values the goal to which his work is an instrument or means. It is quite compatible with this doctrine for the educator to inquire about the other values a given work of art displays or presents in the manner of art. Of two works, both done with only artistic excellence as a motive, one such as *Guernica* may "say" something about other values; another, perhaps a still life or the mosaic in a temple, may say little about the human enterprise. The educator may justify the *Guernica* for curriculum purposes without sacrificing artistic merit or the autonomy of art.[23] But if the educator is to do this in good conscience, then he must be able to believe that art as art does serve as an exhibition or a nondiscursive statement of values of all sorts, and this presupposes some unity—formal or structural—among them.

[23] For the relation of aesthetic to extra-aesthetic values in art, see D. W. Gotshalk, *Art and the Social Order* (Chicago: University of Chicago Press, 1947), chaps. 9 and 10.

The final consequence of Polanyi's position for aesthetic education has to do with the role of standards. Although there is general agreement on the necessity of phenomenal objectivity of the aesthetic object, there is also virtual agreement that there can be no objective standards for aesthetic judgments. Such judgments, it is urged, are to be assimilated to the emotive theory of value judgments in general, and *de gustibus non est disputandum*. As we have already seen, this relativity of taste coupled with the "down with nonbehavioral objectives" slogan keeps aesthetic education in perennial jeopardy.

This is not the appropriate place to argue this issue in detail and certainly not in terms of philosophical principle, i.e., in terms of the grounds for making and validating value judgments. As a matter of fact, the schools, as well as most practitioners in virtually all fields, do use standards based on the authority of the expert. Scientists do not replicate all the experiments on which they rely for evidence, and apple-growers accept the judgments of experts who award the blue ribbons at the country fair.

The principle of authority in the arts is invoked in at least two ways. First, there is the quasi-official corps of critics who pass judgment on current works. Second, there is the tradition of such criticism which in each epoch assesses the work of the past.

In most fields of intellectual endeavor the legitimacy of the latter sort of authority—the sifted and resifted judgments of generations of critics—is taken for granted, just as the continuity of the work in a given intellectual domain is taken for granted. As Thomas Kuhn has pointed out, the induction of the new workers into a field is through "paradigm" science, which works on a pretty well-defined body of problems or puzzles by means of a generally accepted body of theory and principles.[24] The ferment at the frontier is reserved for the advanced creative workers, e.g., Galileo, Newton, Einstein, who

[24] Thomas Kuhn, *The Structure of Scientific Revolution* (Chicago: University of Chicago Press, 1962), p. 11.

may under certain circumstances force a revision of the paradigms themselves and thereby bring about a scientific revolution.

Almost the exact reverse of this situation obtains in the arts and in aesthetic education. Here the unspoiled spontaneity of childhood is more highly regarded than trained maturity. The latter presumably has been corrupted by tradition and conventionalized reverence for the masters. The critical tradition in the arts, therefore, is held suspect as the dead hand of the past that inhibits the creativity of the pupil. For this reason the remarks of Polanyi quoted above about the way in which each generation "dwells" in the tradition are of special importance.

Translating them into somewhat more prosaic language, we can say that in matters of value in general, and aesthetic values in particular, we have to see, listen, feel with the art of the past that has supplied the culture with forms of feeling. These are just as much a learned a priori as are the categories of the understanding used in science. The kind of knowing we have referred to as "aesthetic knowing" is a form of tacit knowing that uses these traditions as almost unconscious subsidiaries.

The problem of standards in art as far as education is concerned in principle, at least, is solved in the same way as it is solved in other fields of instruction. For the induction of the young the judgment of the experts—either their consensus or disagreement—is the only viable criterion. Authenticity of standards consists not in their originality or uniqueness, but rather that they are achieved by the same sort of aesthetic analysis and reflection as are used by the experts. The objectivity of aesthetic judgments lies not in the overwhelming agreement among the judges but rather in the agreement as to what in the work of art shall count as relevant evidence for such judgment and the means for finding in the work of art what is alleged to have been perceived in it.

In conclusion, I can perhaps repeat the initial argument, viz., that given the possibility of tacit knowing, one can assimilate aesthetic perception and judgment to it. If this can be done, as I believe it can, then aesthetic education need not be barred from the curriculum by its inability to formulate its goals and outcomes in behavioral terms and to demonstrate that such outcomes as it does claim can be correlated point for point with specific items of instruction.

F. E. Sparshott

I am not at all sure that the concept of play really belongs in this collection. It is true that writers on art and on education are alike in making much of play, but they use the concept in radically different ways, so that writers in one domain can hardly cite the importance of play in the other domain either as justifying their interest or as illuminating their own remarks.

Writers on the theory of art seldom or never think of the term "play" as singling out either a distinctive set of forms and methods in art to be distinguished from other forms and methods (for instance, the production of rhapsodies rather than sonatas, action painting rather than portraiture), or a special manner of performing artistic activities (for example, improvision rather than formal composition, sketching rather than building up glazes over a ground). They do not usually even think of "play" in this field as denoting a particular recommended attitude, one of lightheartedness or relaxation perhaps, that individual artists or members of the public might take toward art. Instead, "play" is used to characterize the supposed nature of all artistic activities as such, whatever their form, however they are thought of, and by whatever means they are carried out. Typical positions in this field are that "art" and "play" are synonymous terms, that art and play are coextensive, that all art is play, or that all play is art.

In the field of education things are very different. Few would hold that education and play are or might be coextensive, still less that "education" and "play" are synonyms. One might maintain that all play is or may be in some sense educational, or that all education is or could be taken as play, but the former of these positions would be more platitudinous and the latter more paradoxical than their aesthetic counterparts. More typically, the term "play" is reserved for specific educational activities, for certain educational methods that may be recommended either in general or for some special purpose, or for a particular attitude to schooling that may be suitable to certain phases in the educational process. In short, the role played by play in discourse about education is the exact converse of the one it plays in discourse about art.

The uses of "play" in these two fields of discourse being as I have described them, it is not surprising that although writers on art do not mix educational problems with problems about play, writers on education do sometimes fuse the question of the proper place of art in education with that of the proper place of play in education. But it is hard to make the fusion complete. Although art may be characterized as play, and an art program thought of as recreational, extracurricular, frillish, and so forth, the description of play as art is not likely to suggest itself in the context of a school's sports program.

With these prefatory warnings out of the way, we proceed to say some simple things about the notion of play itself.

The concept of play is not one of those, like "religious experience," that people have some practical difficulty in using. One seldom has to wonder whether to say of someone such things as that he is playing, or merely playing, or playing with something, or playing at what he is doing. Yet the difficulties of giving a theoretical account of how such expressions are

108 /

used are notorious to the point of scandal. Although "play" functions as a key term in theories of art and, to a lesser degree, of education, it seems irremediably ambiguous. So theoretically elusive is the concept that Wittgenstein used it to introduce his notion of "family likeness" concepts.[1] These concepts are those represented by words whose various uses have no single common feature, but each of which shares with some of the others one or more of a common stock of such features, as members of a family may be said to show a family likeness although some of them have only the family nose, some only a certain look about the eyes, and so on, and no one member has all of these marks. At the same time, Wittgenstein himself tacitly acknowledged not only the practical utility of such concepts but their suitability for making theoretical points, since his discussion of them arises out of his introduction of the concept of a game to elucidate his theories of the workings of language.[2]

Innumerable authors have quoted or paraphrased the passage in which Wittgenstein expounds family resemblances without doing much to elucidate the material they present. This reticence is not surprising. The passage is not only enigmatic through its inexplicit brevity, but even what it does say is somewhat deceptive, combining like so many of Wittgenstein's ploys an extreme originality and subtlety with a certain tricky naiveté. He adjures his readers not to take it for granted that all games have something in common, but to "look and see" whether they do.[3] The phrase "look and see" must be taken metaphorically, since Wittgenstein can hardly have meant us to get out our binoculars and watch a game of marbles, but he

---

[1] Ludwig Wittgenstein, *Philosophical Investigations*, trans. G. E. M. Anscombe (Oxford: Blackwell, 1953), §§65–77.

[2] *Ibid.*, §7 and *passim*. It should be noted that the claim that games have only a "family likeness" undercuts any objection that most "language games" have nothing gamelike about them, and thus enables him to exploit the association of games with arbitrariness without actually committing himself to the thesis that languages are arbitrarily used.

[3] *Ibid.*, §66. Even more explicitly he writes: "Don't think, but look" (*denk nicht, sondern schau!*).

seems to have meant his readers, for no apparent reason, to take it as literally as possible. Common features should be as visible as a nose on a face; a common social function, or a common relation to other activities, is not considered as a likely candidate. Yet in the elucidation of so manifestly social a concept as that of a game one would have thought that such functional aspects would have been the first to be looked for. Even stranger, having issued his challenge to "look and see" what common properties games may have, he shows no sign of having done any serious looking of his own, but merely assumed that there would be no common features; and the many writers who quote him have generally followed him in this assumption with a complacency equal to his own.[4] There is thus no real warrant for the common practice of quoting Wittgenstein's authority for the thesis that games have no theoretically significant properties in common. All he did, and no doubt all he meant to do, was provide a handy metaphor in case we found they had not.

The terminology we used in the preceding paragraphs will have shown the alert reader that the vagaries of the English language add to our difficulties. Philosophical and psychological theorizing about play has traditionally been the prerogative of European authors writing in French or (more often) German. But in these tongues the words for "play" and "game" are identical or closely related; the equation between play and games is made by the language itself and is taken for granted. In English it needs to be established by argument. But no argument is usually given; the influence of foreign theorizing is such that writers in English tend to assume that they too can take the equation for granted. The results are sometimes awkward.[5] Few people who say that art "is play" would be

---

[4] Cf. Maurice Mandelbaum, "Family Resemblances and Generalizations Concerning the Arts," *American Philosophical Quarterly* II (1965), 219–28.

[5] Thus Roger Caillois's *Les jeux et les hommes* (Paris: Gallimard, 1958) has to be translated as *Man, Play, and Games* (New York: Free Press of Glencoe, 1961). (Subsequent references are to the latter edition.)

happy about saying that art "is a game" or includes or involves games; few of those who say that games are art forms would be prepared to say that playing as such has anything artistic about it. Perhaps the reason English makes this extra differentiation has something to do with the prevalence in the English-speaking world of a passion for competitive sports (football, tennis, golf, cricket, baseball, hockey) which has come weaker and later to other lands. Perhaps the old English institution of "compulsory games" is less of a terminological paradox than "jeux obligatoires." However that may be, treatises on play in English usually have a gaping logical hiatus between the bits on playing and the bits on games.

People who talk about "play" in connection either with art or with education are not using the word casually but are deliberately making theoretical points. Our concern is therefore not with how the word is used in ordinary conversation, but with how it functions in theoretical contexts: that is, with the reasons people have and give for using the word to make descriptive or evaluative points about activities. The procedures of the "ordinary language" school of conceptual analysts are thus not likely to help us much, and I shall place no reliance on them.

There seem to be five distinguishable but connected reasons for calling something "play" in theoretical contexts. Three of these are the alleged possession of positive attributes, closely connected but logically distinct. These will be dealt with later. The other two are contrastive: activities are called "play" either because they are not work (or not worked at), or because they are not serious (or not taken seriously). With a little juggling, all five can be made to seem to mark out a single domain; but the juggling seems to be necessary, and I am inclined to agree with Wittgenstein that our reasons for calling activities "play" are after all fundamentally heterogeneous. Whether this is so may, however, be left to the reader's judgment; much depends on how liberally one interprets such phrases as "the same reason" or "a common feature."

First, then, play is whatever is not work.[6] A person is said to be playing when he is doing something, not sleeping and not slumping, but is not working. But what is work? This neglected concept, which occupies such a key position in our social thinking both practical and theoretical, needs far more attention than "play" does, but has never received it. Philosophers and even sociologists tend to fight shy of it. Perhaps we suspect that if we really became conscious of what we mean by "work," our society would collapse in anarchy and despair.

Basically, the notion of work seems tied to that of function.[7] Only what or who has a function can be said to be working or not working: a machine that is not working is one that is not doing what it was made for. To work or to be working is to be doing what one is meant to be doing, according to some warranted notion of where one fits into a tissue of purposes. As a machine works when it is doing what it was meant to do by its makers and users, so a person is working when what he is doing is what is prescribed by a social or economic role. The role may be one assigned him by his community or one taken up by him as his own way of forming a functioning part of his community. Not everyone who is acting in other ways than filling a social role is playing, however. He may be eating. But then, a person is not merely a part of a social organization, he is also a biological organism, and the maintenance of his biological system in working order is functional and not in any sense play. We regard as play only what makes no contribution to biological or economic survival or welfare, or what for the time being we consider as making no such contribution because we are attending to some other conspicuous nonfunctional aspect of the activity.

The concept of work as customarily applied to members of such societies as ours has further ambiguities. Work is not al-

[6] For a more elaborate account of this contrast, see F. E. Sparshott, *The Structure of Aesthetics* (Toronto: University of Toronto Press, 1963), pp. 207–18.

[7] This is not surprising: "function" is introduced as a philosophical term by Plato, and the word he uses is *ergon*, the ordinary Greek word for "work."

ways any kind of a function. Work may be a place. Is a man mowing his own lawn working? He is doing something defined as useful and expected of householders. But he is not at work, in the sense that he is not at his place of work. People go out to work and are at work all the time they are at their place of business, whatever they are doing there and even if they are doing nothing. Work is thus optionally defined as activity performed or time spent in an appropriate spatio-temporal context, from which activities regarded as play are excluded. Work may also be defined financially or in terms of power relations; a man mowing his own lawn is not working because he is not doing it for hire. So strong is the implication about power that a person who makes money on his own is said to be "self-employed."

The requirements of function and subordination come together in the notion that work is whatever one has to do; one may enjoy one's work, but that is not why one does it. Nothing done because one is compelled or coerced to do it, or that one does in a way in which one has to do it, counts as play, just as one cannot be successfully hired or ordered to play. And because one works whether one feels like it or not, there is an expectation that work will be irksome. Play is supposed to be delightful, because it is presumed that one would not be doing it if one did not feel like it.

All these facets of the notion of work are closely linked. If one goes away from one's home to a special place for long, regular periods, the likeliest reason is that some social function calls one there. And the converse view of a function fulfilled is a duty imposed. Such imposed duties are likely to be imposed, or to exist to be taken up, because of some social, economic, or biological need to be met. Remuneration makes imposition possible, and the meeting of the need makes remuneration possible. And so it may be that all the complexities of the notion of work reflect what happens when functions become institutionalized.

As noted, not everyone not commonly said to be working is playing, nor is "play" commonly used as a complementary term to "work" in even the most extended of the senses mentioned. In fact, the term "play" is seldom applied at all to persons mature enough to work. Adults are ordinarily said to be playing only when engaging in certain restricted activities: participating in games, interacting socially with small children or animals, making instrumental music. Similar restrictions even apply to children, to some extent. Although a small child may always be said to be playing when its activities seem to be to some extent organized, and it is neither asleep nor feeding nor (for instance) sucking its thumb, there is an expectation that it will be playing *at* or *with* something.[8] Either it will be interacting with a physical object (a toy), or it will be playing at some game with other children, or it will be engaged in a pretense (playing at being something). And, curiously enough, no one who is engaged in recreational reading is said to be playing: if a child is said to be playing with a book he will be manipulating it, building a house with it, or throwing it up and catching it. Nor is this all. He will not be said to be playing with a book if he is cutting it up for confetti. One might think that this is because to "play with" a thing designed for a function one must use it in the proper way, but that would not be right, for the proper use of a book is for reading and reading is not playing, while building card houses with playing cards is certainly playing with cards. One might think that playing with things involved manipulation but not destruction, but even this seems not to be right, since a child mashing its dolls would be said to be playing with them, though not very nicely. In fact, the colloquial use of the term "play" is as full of idiosyncracies as we expected, and it is fortunate that it is not this use that we have to clarify. It remains true that when theorists call art (for example) "play," they often do so, at least in part, explicitly to contrast it with "work" conceived very much as we have described it.

The contrast between work and play never seems to be more

8 R. F. Dearden, in R. S. Peters, ed., *The Concept of Education* (London: Routledge, 1967), p. 76.

than a very loose fit, as Mr. Dearden points out.[9] More generally, play is opposed to whatever is serious. One plays at whatever one does not take seriously; when one is being playful, one is not being serious. Like the concept of work, that of the serious is akin to that of function. A serious activity is one that people ought to be in earnest about, what may take precedence over other activities not so defined, what social and private provision may fittingly be made for: hence, what has an accepted place in the scheme of things, or in other words a function. It is appropriate to use words like "should" and "ought" in connection with the serious. The most notable difference between work and the serious is that the latter has no institutional overtones: it lacks the overpowering connection with jobs. For the rest, what counts as serious, as what counts as work, depends on attitudes and acceptances. There are apparently three ways in which the serious may be marked out. First, there is social acceptance: every society has its notions of priorities, hence its notion of what a person may be expected to take seriously and is remiss or to blame if he neglects. Second, people can and do set up their own individual standards of seriousness. They "take seriously" certain activities and not others, "play at" some things and not others, as they choose. To take something seriously, be serious about it, is simply to adopt toward it a certain attitude, to set oneself standards with regard to it, to take care about it, to be annoyed with oneself if one falls below whatever standards one has set. This may be either dispositional or occurrent; a man may be a serious chess-player, or he may just happen to be taking seriously a particular chess game he is playing. Finally, one may adopt absolutist notions of seriousness and establish that certain sorts of concern are serious matters whether or not anyone actually does take them seriously and whether or not they are treated as serious by one's own or any other society.

[9] *Ibid.*, pp. 83–84. The contrast is also made by Friedrich Schiller, *On the Aesthetic Education of Man* (London: Routledge, 1954), Letter 15, and by many others.

The contrast between the concepts of play and the serious is not wholly natural, as is evidenced by our serious chess-player. Insofar as play is contradistinguished from the serious, it seems to be downgraded. To play at something, not to take it seriously, is remiss if it is defined as a serious matter, and if it is not so defined it is dismissed from the start as unimportant. Yet play is sometimes said to be good and important. This seems paradoxical—how can what is not serious be important? But the answer lies ready to hand; perhaps it is important that not everything should be taken seriously. Perhaps there is a general function for nonfunctional activities, that of restoring a person's fitness for activities having a special function. In that case, no one such activity would be a serious matter, but it would be a matter for serious concern if there were no non-serious activities at all.[10] One might go further and say that only those things that most people and most societies do not take seriously are truly valuable or serious from some absolutist point of view, because they alone manifest the free play of creative intelligence when liberated from mundane concerns.[11] One would then expect that the term "serious" would appear in some contexts as a derogatory expression. And so it does. A person who is always serious, serious about everything, takes himself too seriously, is a sad sack. But Sartre and others have gone further and made *l'esprit de sérieux* itself a term of abuse.[12] To take anything, including oneself, seriously, is to regard it as imposed or necessary, and Sartre thinks that to regard anything thus is always to deceive oneself, since in fact man's existence precedes his essence and nothing in human affairs is necessary. To be serious is to deny the freedom that constitutes one's humanity. This doctrine does not mean that one should take nothing seriously in the more usual sense

10 Aristotle *Nicomachean Ethics* X.7.

11 Schiller, *On the Aesthetic Education of Man*, p. 79. The thesis that play is the only really important sort of activity goes back to Plato *Laws* 803e.

12 Jean-Paul Sartre, *Being and Nothingness* (London: Methuen, 1957), p. 626.

that one should not be in earnest about anything; only one should recognize that one chooses what to be earnest about by freely committing oneself to it, not by having it imposed on one.[13]

The notion that play is definable by contrast with the serious sorts ill with the fact that one can be a serious chess-player or take a particular game seriously. However, there is no real difficulty here. Insofar as I take it seriously, I do not merely play at it, and the designation of my activity as play depends on the social acceptance of what is serious rather than on mine. This possible duality of viewpoint is important, as Dearden points out, from a practical point of view: a community may accept the duty of providing for activities which the participants do not regard as serious, so that "play" properly so called may be an integral part of serious schooling.[14]

Whatever may be the merits of defining play as the antithesis of the serious, those who have spoken of play in theoretical contexts to shed light on art or education have not wished to suggest that either art or education is other than serious. On the contrary, their engaging in such theorizing is enough to show that they take art and education more seriously than most people do. Rather, they have thought of play as having certain positive characteristics that its opposition to work or to the serious may suggest but cannot adequately specify. There are three of these characteristics to which we now turn.

First, playful activity is an end in itself, neither directed toward the achievement of an end beyond the activity nor merely casual and aimless. Playful activity as such forms part of a self-contained system in which its own values are inherent. One may, of course, play for a nonplayful purpose, be paid to play, or play to please someone, but these are added purposes that are not necessary to make the activity playful; in fact, they

[13] Jean-Paul Sartre, "Existentialism Is a Humanism," in Walter Kaufmann, ed., *Existentialism from Dostoevsky to Sartre* (New York: Meridian Books, 1956), pp. 287–311.
[14] Dearden, in *The Concept of Education*, pp. 87–90.

detract from its status as play. Play is purposelessly purposeful, as Kant said of beauty,[15] in that whatever goals it may have are set up merely as objects for the sake of the activity that is to aim at them, rather than the activity taking place in order to secure the goals. One may play to win, but the winning is only defined in order to make playing possible. Insofar as winning a game or succeeding at it takes on a value of its own, the activity ceases to be play and becomes a business or something else.[16]

Second, playful activity is typically spontaneous. Playful activities are undertaken and continued for no other reason than that one feels like doing so, not called for by any sort of routine or demand. In the typical case, their course is determined by the free decision of the player in the light of the requirements of the game itself that his activities develop.

Spontaneity works against the structured, quasi-purposive character that play must have to be an end in itself. Thus a third note is added: the arbitrariness and spontaneity of playful activities take on patterned forms. Of games in the stricter sense it is even true that they are not merely rule-governed but rule-defined. To play a game is simply to follow certain rules that define a pattern of activity of definite but limited complexity. But what games thus show in a peculiarly determinate form is shown by all playful activities: that they are given a certain pattern for no other reason than to pattern them.[17]

The three characteristics named tend to work against each other. Perhaps we should say that in order to maintain purpose

---

[15] "Beauty is the form of finality in an object, so far as perceived in it apart from the representation of an end." Immanuel Kant, *Critique of Judgment* (Oxford: Oxford University Press, 1928), p. 80.

[16] Gambling offers an awkward counterexample to this thesis. But it is argued that although gamblers like their winnings, they are absorbed in their play and are not playing as a way of making an income, if only because the returns bear no relation to the activity undertaken. If a man really does "play the horses" for a living, or is hired or under contract to play cards, then we are inclined to say that what he is doing is working and not playing at all. Caillois, *Man, Play, and Games*, p. 5, adds that gambling, even if lucrative, is unproductive; play is pure waste.

[17] Johan Huizinga, *Homo Ludens* (Boston: Beacon, 1955), p. 10.

without losing freedom, play must balance spontaneity against rules, and that a certain tension must be maintained between them. However that may be, those who take these three characteristics as jointly defining play should not be taken as describing how the word "play" is used; rather, they are defining a mode of activity in which they see a certain ideal significance, whether or not things people actually do when said to be playing conform to this ideal.

Theorists often add other characteristics to those mentioned, but these others seem to me not to have the close mutual connection that those just mentioned show, but rather form the conditions in which they are realized or the reason for realizing them. I shall mention two of these.

Whoever plays, it is said, must be playing either *at* something or *with* something. His activity is thus marked off from the workaday world, and thus has its autonomy protected, either by a special set of material conditions or equipment or else by some inherent quality of the action. This latter must take the form either of a set of rules or of a role or similar set of guiding fictions.[18] A child may be playing *with* his toys (or, as a sort of limiting case, *in* his sandbox or *on* his jungle-gym, pieces of equipment too big to be played with as instruments but serving as instrumental environments); or *at* doctors and nurses; or playing dominoes—if he is playing *at* dominoes, the implication is that he is not playing dominoes at all but only making believe to do so, or else (another idiom) playing dominoes halfheartedly. Playful activities seem to need special environments, or special requirements (rules), or special equipment (toys), or special defining conditions (pretenses).

Another feature of play emphasized by its theorists, and sometimes even used as a defining term, is that it is self-expressive.[19] This, one would think, should apply only to the more spon-

[18] Caillois, *Man, Play, and Games*, p. 9.

[19] Elmer D. Mitchell and Bernard S. Mason, *The Theory of Play*, 2nd ed. (New York: A. S. Barnes, 1948), p. 81: "Play is explained by the fact that the individual seeks self-expression. Being what he is . . . *all that is necessary to explain play is the fact that he seeks to live, to use his abilities, to express his personality.*"

taneous and less rule-bound forms of play, but the distinction is not always observed. The reason for calling play self-expressive seems to be that if an activity is neither governed by accepted rules, as games are, nor imposed or taken up as a socially determined role, but is both chosen and carried on at the free choice of the agent, the choices thus made can reflect nothing other than the character and underlying preoccupations of the person playing. But this feature of play is one that it has, if it has it, only because it has the other features we assigned it. That an activity is self-expressive is never any part of what we mean by calling it play.

Wittgenstein seems to me right in implying that these alleged features of play cannot be reduced to a set of jointly necessary or sufficient conditions. Rather, activities termed playing, or play, or playful, or playlike, or games, tend to be those in which some of the above-named features are strikingly present or which in some other respects are strikingly like activities taken to be paradigms of play. However, the features, both positive and negative, that we have now cited do seem when taken together to suggest what we mean by calling something play. To single out some one of them, or some more esoteric feature such as make-believe, as the defining or characterizing feature of all games or all play is typical of theories about games rather than of accounts of the concept itself, what is meant by using the word. But it is worth noting how common these attempts to find a single definite and theoretically striking characterization of play are; obviously there is something about playing that strikes people as calling for explanation in a way that work does not. And it is not hard to see what this is. Anyone can see why people work—one might almost define work as what you can see why people do. But play activities are usually those that people do not have to do and yet insist on doing, make a point of doing, and become absorbed in doing. That there should be such activities seems to call not merely for a psychological, causal explanation, but a philosophical one; it looks as if it should be important in our attempts to come to terms with being human. Although we have all always been human, reflective people share the feeling that being human is somehow odd; and our addiction to play, or to other activities having the characteristic features we have chosen for play, seems a significant part of this oddness. Thus Schiller could say, "Man is only wholly Man while he is playing,"[20] even though on reflection we might think it less misleading to say that man is only man when he works, since any otter can play but it takes a reflective being to accept an obligation and to comprehend a function.

There is one vital ambiguity in the notion of play that we have not yet isolated for attention. It may function both as a sortal and as a characterizing concept. One may play at anything, or do it in play or playfully, by doing it nonseriously or treating it as a game, that is, by taking its requirements as self-imposed and affecting to ignore its serious or ulterior point. But certain kinds of activity are picked out as inherently playful or playlike in character: games among adults, for instance, and the spontaneously structured doings of small children. To engage in the latter is to play however one does it. Thus sometimes one uses "play" and related terms to indicate the sort of thing that is being done in whatever manner, sometimes to indicate the manner in which whatever is being done is being done. Theoretical discussions seldom keep these two senses distinct.

Now at last we are ready to say something about the role played by the concept of play in discussions of art and education.

Those who associate art with play generally hold that art is a form or forms of play, and very often hold it as part of a wider thesis about the nature of civilization. Civilization and culture, it is maintained, are fruits of leisure. They are what we do with our spare time after taking care of the necessities, food, shelter, warmth, procreation, and defense. The use of the term "play" to describe all such "superfluous" activities appears to go back

[20] Schiller, *On the Aesthetic Education of Man*, p. 8o.

to some remarks by Plato about his own philosophical activities,[21] and the thesis itself was made respectable by Aristotle.[22] But these progenitors did not give much time to the notion, and in its most developed form it is most familiar from Huizinga's *Homo Ludens*. According to this thesis, it is characteristic of men to give all their activities the sort of character we said typified play, so far as possible. Feeding becomes eating, the partaking of more or less ceremonious meals. Any activity can be made in some measure gamelike, but it can only be done completely for those which are in themselves biologically and economically unnecessary, to which class the arts preeminently belong. Cultural forms are thus ends in themselves, purposely developed into ritual and ceremony for their own sakes; socially spontaneous, in that nothing requires any society to elaborate them in one way rather than another; and rule-governed or rule-determined, in that right and wrong ways of doing things are arbitrarily established. Cultural activities also come to be segregated into isolated compartments (corresponding to playgrounds and play periods).

It is fair to say that on the above view of culture any cultural form that fully takes on the character of play, in being isolated and developed for its own sake, becomes an art form. "The Arts" are simply those activities in which this process is recognized. It is hardly even necessary to add the time-honored proviso that the arts are concerned with beauty, with exercise of eye and ear. Only the auditory and visual are susceptible of enough structure to bear the full play character; and the beautiful is just that whose enjoyment is divorced from economic use, so that the cultural-playful is already definable as taking its value from beauty.

The arts fit better into the positive side of the schema we established for play than into the negative. They are endotelic, their products taken as ends in themselves and enjoyed rather than used, and in many cases finding their value in the very process of production (as in dancing) rather than in the manu-

---

[21] Plato *Phaedrus* 276e. Cf. also Plato (or Philip of Opus) *Epinomis* 975c-d.
[22] Aristotle *Metaphysics* A.2 (982b20).

facture of a product.[23] The arts also form a segregated realm
or realms, marked off from the workaday world. As for spontaneity, one of our most cherished pieces of folklore about
artists is that they are inner-directed, to the extent that even if
they accept commissions they must follow an inner light in
their execution, and that to fulfill an order derogates from their
artistic status. The place of the rules that mitigate spontaneity
is taken by artistic conventions; it has always been obvious
that music, with its artificial scales and elaborately designed
instruments, is a rule-governed activity, and under the influence of Professor Gombrich we are coming to be more at home
with the notion that painting is so too.[24] It is even observed
that avant-garde attempts to make spontaneity the sole rule
have led only to the generation of instant conventions; the
word "happening" was scarcely coined before the genre settled
down to a routine repertoire of ladders, ballet clothes, and
toilet paper.[25] Finally, more than with cultural forms generally,
it is tempting to say of the arts that they play *at* or *with*. They
are traditionally thought of as essentially imitative (playing
at), and those who rejected this notion replaced it by the given
alternative, playing with, the manipulation of a medium.

On the negative side, contrasting play with work and the
serious, the fit with the arts is less good. Art is certainly not
nonserious. Both artists and their public and the community
at large are expected to take it very seriously indeed. In fact, to
have the concept of art at all is a sign that a society takes such
activities seriously. Nor is art easily contrasted with work, except in the sense that it is acknowledged to be biologically
nonfunctional,[26] and except in the sense that in mercantile

[23] C. J. Ducasse, *The Philosophy of Art* (New York: Dial Press, 1929), p. 99,
reserves the word "endotelic" for activities like art, which have a real end to
attain, even if only an internal one, in contrast with play, whose ends are
arbitrarily set up to provide something to pursue.

[24] E. H. Gombrich, *Art and Illusion* (New York: Pantheon, 1960).

[25] For the sameness of happenings, see the illustrations in Allan Kaprow,
Assemblages, Environments and Happenings (New York: Abrams, 1966).

[26] Roger Fry, *Vision and Design* (London: Chatto and Windus, 1920), p. 47:
"Biologically speaking, art is a blasphemy." But the opposite view is maintained

circles (especially in small towns) artists may be thought of as idle because they do not have jobs to go to—unless, of course, they have studios downtown in which they spend regular daily hours.

To say that an artist is playing while he is working is insulting. Since he is not playing a game, and since apart from games only what small children do is usually called play, to say that the artist is playing is to imply that what he is doing is unworthy of an adult as well as that he is neither working nor behaving in a serious fashion, nor doing the sort of thing that people take seriously. The descriptive sense of "play" turns out to be as derogatory as the straightforwardly evaluative, the sortal as depreciatory as the characterizing sense. And these implications cannot be negated simply by insisting that one means only to make a theoretical point. Yet, as we have seen, the implied evaluation is one that many reflective people reject. In their spontaneity playlike activities testify to freedom, in their following of rules they testify to rationality, to an orderly use of freedom as opposed to mere idleness or random movement, and being ends in themselves their value is intrinsic. The thesis of Plato and Schiller, that whatever is not play is bestial or slavish, seems well grounded. Yet our linguistic habits work inexorably against the recognition of this. It is therefore surely better to avoid saying that art is play unless one really means to decry it; instead, one should spell out every time what one would have meant by speaking of "play," or find some other term without these unfortunate associations. The positive theoretical characteristics covered by the concept do not outweigh the negative ones which fail to apply to art, and are overridden by the nontheoretical associations with childhood.

I said at the beginning that there is little carry-over from art to education in the way the term "play" is used. We shall now see that the theoretical characteristics which make an activity playlike, and which make art partly playlike and partly not,

by Charles Biederman, *Art as the Evolution of Visual Knowledge* (Red Wing, Minn.: Charles Biederman, 1948).

fit education less well. Education cannot be regarded as a form of play without absurdity. By "education" I suppose one means those learning processes, more or less systematically organized, whereby a person becomes one of the sorts of people regarded by his society (or the relevant subdivision of that society) as admirable or serviceable. Alternatively, more idealistically, and more intellectualistically, one may regard education as the acquisition of important knowledge organized according to its principles, together with a critical attitude toward such knowledge and an ability to apply it in practice.[27] On either interpretation, education is an eminently serious matter, and is so regarded by all. It is also very definitely, consciously, and deliberately functional. Thus it lacks both negative features of play. Nor does it have the positive ones. It is not an end in itself, since it must never lose sight of its aim as producing desired effects on mind and character, effects which are determined not by the moves of educational practice but by the needs and demands of the society within which the educational system operates. Education is rule-governed in the way any organized activity is, its procedures becoming formalized and practiced in their formality without consciousness of their original aim, but if they thereby cease to subserve that aim everyone regards it as a disaster and refuses to call the result education. However rule-governed, education is thus in no sense rule-determined. Nor is education spontaneous. The ages of beginning and ending, the lengths of terms and the hours of attendance each day are determined by the organizing authority, even if much of what is done while in attendance is left to individual initiative. And it seems to me that on the whole education is not so much self-expression as acquiring a self to express. Education does have the playlike quality of being set apart, segregated in an enclave of its own, but so do all specialized activities, including one's daily work.

Nothing, it seems, could well be less playlike than education, and this not because of arbitrary cultural preference but because of the functions that any process must fulfill in order

[27] Peters, *The Concept of Education*, pp. 3–19.

to be called education. But against this we have the ancient advice of Plato that the schooling of children should take the form of play.[28] In the light of what we have said, and assuming Plato's sanity, he cannot have meant that their education should actually be play in the full sense, only that it must be in some important respects playlike. Unfortunately, he did not say much about what respects these would be, except that what went on should not appear to be work and above all should not take the form of instruction. This suggests that he meant that the schooling of children should be playlike both in the sense that it should be free from a sense of coercion and in the sense that the activities of which it consisted should be of a sort recognizable as games or play.

Can education, then, be made to seem playlike? The self-education of adults surely cannot. One who chooses activities because they are educational will hardly think of himself as playing or amusing himself by engaging in them, however much he may delight in them. What a person does by way of teaching himself can be playlike only in the trivial sense that to learn golf one plays golf, or that the actions one finds useful in acquiring the vocabulary of a foreign tongue may happen to be like those performed in certain parlor games. What, then, of education submitted to, that is, schooling? It used to be argued that a child's play serves as an unconscious rehearsal that prepares him for serious adult life;[29] can we perhaps so arrange matters that children learn what we want to teach them by doing what seems to them to be playing, under the guidance of a discreetly directive adult? First, perhaps, one should ask why one would want to. Since they are not playing but engaging in a serious enterprise, why pretend that they are not? Since what they are doing has a purpose, why hide the purpose? The deception is unlikely to succeed, since even very young children are notoriously able to see through such insulting fictions; and if it does succeed the children may reasonably wonder why, if what they are doing has no serious

[28] Plato Republic 536–37.
[29] Karl Groos, *The Play of Men* (New York: Appleton, 1901), pp. 377ff.

point, they should be made to do it. However, what is surely meant is not that the children should be conned into thinking they are playing, but that what they do should be made more agreeable by being given the characteristics of the things they do for fun. Obviously this could not be completely successful, since nothing is wholly playlike except play, but one might introduce selected playlike features. This could not be done by pretending that the whole enterprise was jolly fun—this is the attitude to play not of the player but of the maiden aunt. But one could maximize spontaneity by trying to make the required concerns develop naturally or without strain from concerns either already present or spontaneously generated or at most (and most probably) suggested as if casually by the adult in charge. One could also try, as has traditionally been done, to make education like a set of games, by awarding scoring points ("marks"), giving prizes, and so on. This procedure is nowhere followed outside the classroom except in games, but seems to be currently out of favor as supposedly redolent of the "competitive," serious adult world—which, of course, uses no such procedures. Apparently the way to make education playlike is to stop it being gamelike, forgoing all structure in favor of a formless spontaneity.

The chief difficulty in making education playlike seems to be the one Plato put his finger on when he insisted that education was not instruction. Modern systems of schooling have assumed that young persons must be assiduously instructed in many things. The reason usually given for this is that modern civilization rests on complex technologies, but the connection between this truth and the actual procedures of schools is not explained. Whatever the reason, it is still usually taken for granted that during most of their childhood everyone must be incarcerated and plied with information. I am inclined to think that future ages will regard this practice with the same incredulous horror at human callousness with which we ourselves view the long continuance of chattel slavery. Meanwhile, so long as the system goes on, no matter how enjoyable what is done in schools may become, so long as children have to attend such places and so long as while there they have to assimilate a great deal of information, it is absurd to suppose that schooling can become significantly playlike.

In principle, the whole process of formal education can be treated as a game by anyone who is able to disregard the seriousness of its outcome—or who thinks its outcome is itself not serious, either because the values of society are no longer effectively embodied in its mechanisms or because those values themselves are from an absolutist point of view false or trivial. One can then take the whole business either as a game to be played seriously even though it is not taken seriously, or as something to be merely played at. But young children are in no position to do this effectively. Since they are in the process of learning the ways and values of their society, they can neither achieve detachment from, nor evaluate reliably, nor feel confidence in their evaluations of, those adult ways and values.

Education, then, cannot be play, and cannot as a whole be playlike except in certain limited respects. But that is not to say that play and playlike activities cannot be incorporated into the educational process, whether by way of play proper or by way of playlike techniques in carrying out serious activities.

First, when one has embarked on any activity that has a clearly defined objective and thus can take on a determinate structure, anyone can "make a game of it" by treating the activity as an end in itself and converting its structure into a ritual of rules. And there is an argument for doing this in schools. A child is shut in his school for several hours of most days all through his childhood. All this while, the child is as alive as he will ever be. He is not waiting for his life to begin, and cannot be expected to postpone indefinitely the time when his life will take on some value. It is therefore intolerable that what he does in school should be assigned no value of its own but should be regarded wholly as the preparation for adulthood that it also is. In addition, the use of actual games or gamelike episodes to enliven the classroom is standard pedagogy. Moreover, the earliest stages of formal schooling, nursery school and kindergarten, may be entirely given over to a playing that is only mildly directed. The rudiments of counting, dexterity in manipulating materials, sensitivity and grace in social interaction, are skills acquirable through play that are essential to education on either of our definitions. It may be objected that such skills and tacts are as well acquired out of school, in the home, or in a spontaneously formed peer environment, so that the first school years are really nothing but a glorified babysitting. But the babysitting is indeed glorified. No small part of education lies in keeping children out of impoverished environments and providing enriched ones. Plato's advocacy of play as schooling is closely linked with his conviction that a school's job is to make nourishment freely available and keep poison out of reach.[30] Where he differed from most modern practice was in his belief that this was good policy for older children too.[31]

Some interesting questions are raised by the insertion into more advanced schooling of activities formally defined as play. Outstanding among these are games or sports. Insofar as these are not voluntarily engaged in and extracurricular, their function is presumably to provide some physical exercise as antidote to the unnaturally sedentary norm of the school day. (I say "presumably" because school practices precede their rationalizations and outlive successive rationalizations.) As such, games are no more *playlike* than anything else in the curriculum, although they are, of course, inherently *gamelike* so far as their structure goes. But because of the association between games and playing they may be assigned some of the general characteristics of play. I have before me a high school "physical and health education" report form which begins: "This report is an attempt to give a complete picture of the student's total

---

[30] Plato *Republic* 401, 518.

[31] For Plato's advocacy of nursery schools, see *Laws* 794a–c. It must be emphasized that Plato's remarks on schooling consist almost entirely of fine-sounding principles, with no attempt to deal with even the most obvious difficulties. It is thus impossible to say what practices he did or would in fact advocate.

development as a contributing member of society." Now why should the poor girl who teaches basketball be supposed to be in a better position to fulfill this astonishing demand than any other teacher? Perhaps only because the things she teaches are defined as games and games are defined as play, and it is in play that the child expresses himself because his action is spontaneous. The fact that what the child actually does in her class has none of the relevant qualities makes no difference. The same incongruity may be observed between the beginning and the end of a textbook on play in education: the first part is all about self-expression and the like, a compilation of the standard theories about the nature and function of play; the end is all to do with the organization of games in an authoritarian context. The fact that the activities described at the end have none of the qualities postulated at the start is scarcely remarked by the authors.[32]

A similarly selective use of the concept of play is shown in the notion of "play therapy."[33] This is a technique for handling an emotionally disturbed child by confining him for a while in an environment containing toys and play materials in the presence of an adult who refuses to give him any hint as to what to do.[34] The idea is that what the child says and does in this predicament will express at least some of his preoccupations, which the adult can then bring to the child's consciousness by repeating the significant expressions back to him in a form that makes their meaning recognizable. In calling this

[32] Mitchell and Mason, *The Theory of Play*, Chaps. 19 and 20. Compare the remark cited in note 19 above with the following: "The impulse is natural but . . . the *forms* of play are not—they must be learned" (p. 514).

[33] Virginia Mae Axline, *Play Therapy* (New York: Houghton Mifflin, 1947).

[34] " 'I am tired,' said Miss Havisham. 'I want diversion, and I have done with men and women. Play.'

"I think it will be conceded by my most disputatious reader, that she could hardly have directed an unfortunate boy to do anything in the wide world more difficult to be done under the circumstances.

" 'I sometimes have sick fancies,' she went on, 'and I have a sick fancy that I want to see some play. There, there!' with an impatient movement of the fingers of her right hand; 'play, play, play!' " Charles Dickens, *Great Expectations*, chap. 8.

technique "play therapy" the term "play" is apparently used sortally, in that the child is given the opportunity to do some of the things that children often do when playing (manipulate clay, play with dolls, play in sandbox), although some of the equipment provided, such as a nursing bottle, is designed to elicit likely symptomatic behavior. But there is also some reliance on the dogma that play is self-expression, so that (by a logically illegitimate conversion) self-expression must be play. There is no pretense that the whole procedure is nonserious, however. On the contrary, the child must not leave the room except for an emergency because that would be "evading the therapy and attempting to *turn it into some sort of game.*"[35] The child's activities are spontaneous in that his choice of what to do is undetermined within wide limits, but unspontaneous in that his confinement in the unstructured environment is involuntary.

The technique of play therapy becomes relevant to our inquiry when its rationale is extended by some reformers to the nontherapeutic school situation, although its diagnostic and therapeutic uses would seem to have no place there. Presumably the diagnostic aspect is supposed to be superfluous, but the therapeutic side to be in place; all children are patients and all teachers therapists, however little they may have done to qualify them for their respective roles. It is taken for a matter of course that it is good for children to express themselves, and we are left to wonder how and why. Education and therapy are essentially different. The presumption of therapy is that the patient is sick and must be restored to a healthy condition before he can carry on with the normal activities of life. But education is itself one of those normal activities, and its presumption is that the student can function normally. To change an educational situation into a therapeutic one is to defraud the healthy student.[36]

[35]Axline, *Play Therapy*, p. 135 (my italics).

[36] For the danger of defining normal situations as occasions for therapeutic intervention, see Thomas S. Szasz, "The Mental Health Ethic," in Richard T. De George, ed., *Ethics and Society* (New York: Doubleday, 1966), pp. 85–110.

If it is in the area of physical education that the tension between the game aspect and the spontaneous aspect of the concept of play comes to the fore, it is in art education that a theoretically playlike activity finds a place in the schoolroom and the values of education and therapy are most intimately fused.

What is the function of the school art class? In the first place, involving as it does the manipulation of materials, it tends to be treated as occupational therapy, as a releasing form of self-expression whose product has no value other than its testimony to the mental health of its producer. Art is therapeutic "play."[37] In the second place, because at least some of the forms of activity indulged in are identical or continuous with those used in kindergarten, there is also a tendency, perhaps less in theory than in practice, to treat art classes as genuine play sessions, offering recreational relief from whatever rigors the rest of the school day may impose. But in the third place some practice and theory take the function of the art class to be the transmission of artistic skills, not playful or playlike in itself but doubtless affording the means to successful self-expression later on.[38] Here we note an ambiguity already hinted at in the notion of self-expression; in one sense a child is expressing himself if what he does shows what he feels like doing, but in another sense an inarticulate person is unable to express himself, and expression of anything demands expressive skills. Art classes that thus teach art are just like other classes, and even if art is really in some sense play, what one does in such a class would be playing only in the sense that one can only learn to play chess by playing it, although in another sense one is not yet playing because one is only learning to play.

The confusion about the function of art classes is deepened

[37] Rose H. Alschuler and LaBerta Weiss Hattwick, *Painting and Personality: A Study of Young Children* (Chicago: University of Chicago Press, 1947), I, 165: "Any suggestion about using his brush and paint to better advantage would be likely to frustrate his efforts and to diminish the value that the painting experience might otherwise have."

[38] Rudolf Arnheim, *Art and Visual Perception* (Berkeley: University of California Press, 1954), p. 168.

by the fact that, with the passing of generations, the values of art as therapy have infiltrated the adult art world through the notion of "action painting," painting whose value lies in the act of painting itself. The subsequent traffic in the by-products of this activity would be wholly mysterious if there were any reason to take the notion seriously.[39]

There used to be a notion that learning anything with no immediate commercial application must be learning to play, therefore must be nonserious and should be marginal in school programs. This notion we have seen to be a confusion and it is no longer theoretically respectable. It is becoming a cliché that automation and mechanization are making how to survive less of a problem than how to live the rest of the time; as work becomes less important, other pursuits must be socially elevated to the rank of the serious, and our notion of what a mature adult must be will explicitly involve a wider range of accomplishments than it did when men ate bread in the sweat of their brow and culture was for the gentry. Unfortunately, our educational institutions were framed when the task of mass schooling was to produce effective wage-earners, able to read and write and inured to long hours of sedentary boredom; and, as we have said, practice is slow to yield to theoretical change. Besides, the immediate determination of policy is often in the hands of school boards to whom every problem presents itself in terms of how the taxpayer's dollar is to be spent, and the best way to justify spending a dollar is always that it will earn $1.10. There are thus strong pressures in favor of retaining the old equation of the serious with work and of work with earning, which entails that while education is by definition serious only what is profitable can be real education.

The opposite tendency, however, which would convert school-

[39] Harold Rosenberg, *The Tradition of the New* (New York: Grove Press, 1961), chap. 2. Mr. Rosenberg's account of the transaction (p. 28) is much as follows. The action painter is quietly painting away to himself in his studio. A passing stranger smells the paint, batters at the studio door until the artist lets him in, and implores him to sell a canvas or two. "Some painters take advantage of this stranger" who does not understand about action painting and actually accept his offer.

ing into play, we have seen to reflect an equal confusion of concepts and values. Schooling becomes captive play, play therapy with no therapist, only because we dare not turn our children loose on the streets but are not prepared to commit ourselves or them to any view of what an educated person should be.

EPOCHÉ AND RELEVANCE

IN ÆSTHETIC DISCOURSE / 6

Eugene F. Kaelin

I

Thinking about art works or our experiences of them is not a prerogative of philosophers even when they are specialists in aesthetic theory or in the analysis of aesthetic discourse. Some art historians, for example, have been known to think about the primary subject of their discipline using concepts other than those of chronology and stylistics; and, as the cases of Berenson and Panofsky attest, some have actually succeeded in providing useful conceptual tools for the analyses of philosophical aestheticians. Critics, too, sometimes succeed in making sense at least in describing if less often in evaluating works of art. Thus when he coined the expression "action painting," Harold Rosenberg bequeathed to art historians a name for a whole school of American painters. His description was both apt and useful. And, along with museum habitués, artists themselves commonly talk to one another about their experiences of works of art and quite naturally expect to be understood. As long as there is a public object whose features may be pointed to or isolated by analysis and referred to within the context of intersubjective experience, communication is assured.

For ordinary purposes of communication, moreover, ordinary discourse suffices: experiences of art works are either had or not; and for those who care to do so, these experiences may be analyzed and described in terms of what we see, hear, understand, or feel. Indeed, so common is this habit and so widespread the interest in the valid use of aesthetic discourse that verbal communication of our first-order aesthetic experiences has itself become the object of a second-order, reflective concern. In essence this happens every time a critic or historian becomes critical of his own observations and principles.

Whether the critic is merely describing what he has seen or is engaged in a lengthy explanation of its supposed significance, questions about the adequacy of his results lead him out of one attitude or function into another: question his results and he is likely to appeal to the workability of his method; question his method and he should be willing to consider the methodological inquiry which led him to adopt it in the first place. Aesthetic educators face the same situation.

But here there is a difference. Although a critic or historian may proceed without regard to reflective, philosophical justification of their respective methods, the seriousness of pedagogical instruction necessitates an immediate appeal to methodological grounds.[1] For if teachers of teachers are to impart anything to their wards, it should be a workable method for instruction in the first-order discipline; and unless this is done in an authoritarian fashion, some justification for the proposed method must be given. Thus aesthetics, which is considered as a method of humanistic research, and meta-aesthetics, which is considered as its methodology, constitute an essential part of the pedagogical inquiry that has come to be called "aesthetic education."

My contention is that aesthetic theory must comprise suf-

[1] See my monograph, *An Existential-Phenomenological Account of Aesthetic Education*, in the *Penn State Papers in Art Education* (Fall, 1968).

ficient justifying grounds for the employment of specific educational procedures dedicated to instruction in the arts. Such principles as pedagogical autonomy, relevance, and completeness[2] are in particular extensions of aesthetic theorizing to the realm of educational theory and practice. I should like in what follows to clarify the expression "aesthetic relevance" in terms of phenomenological methodology. The need for such a clarification will be established by a review of the art teacher's daily predicament.

II

Teachers of art are inevitably called upon to justify the statements they make about works of art. Whether these are being created by the teacher or a student or merely being shown for the appreciation of a class of students, some minimal requirements are to be met before one would admit that education is in fact taking place in the situation. The interpreter's statements must first make sense, and second they must in some sense be true. But this dual criterion of intellectual inquiry is not always as clear and distinct as some philosophers would have us believe. I shall argue as usual that making sense is the primary concern of thinkers, and that the question of truth or falsity can arise only in a context in which sense has already been determined. But the case to be made is not so simple.

An example from the history of philosophy will serve as introduction to the argument. Applying the "hyperbolic doubt" as a methodical means of establishing certain truths, Descartes is led to an intuition of two distinct attributes: extension and thought, which, being totally unlike, are conceived as essential properties of distinct substances. The move from attribute to substance is taken as axiomatic in that nothing can come from nothing. Now human beings display both sorts of attributes. Their bodies are extended, and their souls or minds are capable of thought. Moreover, it is supposed that bodies are of themselves incapable of movement, so that the locomotion of

[2] *Ibid.*

human beings betrays an influence of the soul on the body. Interaction of the human body and mind is thus a fact, and closer examination of the structure of the body should reveal the mechanism of interaction. Under the force of passionate disturbance it is observed that the "animal spirits" move with increased rapidity. As these converge upon the brain to leave their traces, there must be a place (since the body is spatial) in which the convergence is felt: hence the pineal gland— which just happens to be located at the base of the brain.

No student of contemporary psychology is a victim of Descartes's error, but history is full of irony. We could, for example, claim that there is no interaction between bodies and minds, as Spinoza did; but in that eventuality we should be found in the embarrassing position of admitting that it makes sense to speak of minds as somehow distinct from bodily dispositions. The pineal gland hypothesis is not false—indeed it is neither true nor false, since hypotheses are neither—it is merely senseless. The first irony of history I shall note is that Descartes's interest in mental-bodily interaction led to a strict physiological psychology—and ultimately to behaviorism— which allows us to claim that the term "mind" as used by Descartes refers to nothing, and thus quite literally lacks a sense.

The point of this discourse is to show that outright inconsistency is not the only way of failing to make sense; it's just the most patent. As far as I know, Descartes's account of substantial relations did not become inconsistent until he began talking of finite substances (which need nothing else in order to exist) as dependent upon infinite substance or God. Spinoza's ethics was conceived in an effort to clear up this patent inconsistency. Psychologists today, it should be noted, do suppose the existence of entities or functions which are themselves not observable. Such concepts, called "intervening variables" or "hypothetical constructs," help us form or give structure to hypotheses which are tested for sense by the criterion of consistency as measured by relatedness to observations already made and other propositions already known; the "truth" of these hypotheses is then tested against a set

138 /

of predicted consequences, which again are of an order of direct observation.

Since to call a hypothesis "true" is to stretch the common-sense notion of that term as correctness or correspondence—the facts recorded in acceptable hypotheses are general and not individual and directly observable—various pragmatists have suggested other terms as epistemologically more suitable: "workability" or "success." Indeed, Charles Peirce generalized the patterns of thought in hypothesis formation and confirmation to express his "pragmatic maxim" as a general theory of meaning: "Consider what effects, that might conceivably have practical bearings [as inducement to habitual action], we conceive the object of our conception to have. Then, our conception of these effects is the whole of our conception of the object."[3] The example used by Peirce to illustrate his maxim is the Catholic belief in transubstantiation, the miracle of the Eucharist. He would have made fewer enemies and yet have registered the same point by using the Cartesian belief in the existence of substance itself. This, of course, was done by David Hume; and since Hume's time, science has become a study not of substances and their behavior but of observable data and their relations. It is my intention to apply Peirce's maxim to the concept of method in art criticism.

Since it is difficult to argue with success, and success in inquiry is one measure of "scientific truth," pragmatic theories of meaning and truth have had wide acceptance. But the consequences of such acceptance have not been an unmixed blessing to art educators who have attempted to apply these doctrines to the strictly aesthetic concerns of their discipline.

On the one hand, they have felt the traditional demand of making sense by adopting categories of common sense or the science of psychology to interpret the process of aesthetic communication: "intention" and "execution" for the artistic component, "substance" and "form" for the vehicular, and

[3] Charles S. Peirce, "How to Make Our Ideas Clear," in W. G. Muelder and L. Sears, eds., *The Development of American Philosophy* (New York: Houghton Mifflin, 1940), p. 346.

"reaction" or "effect" (sometimes "affect") for the appreciative, are prevalent examples.[4] When critical analyses of these categories are shown to make little effective sense or to produce few practical results, art educators are tempted to agree with the dismal pronouncement that aesthetics is a dull inquiry,[5] and tend to seek counsel in other disciplines.[6]

But, on the other hand, some art educators, like David W. Ecker, have accepted the pragmatic challenge to develop a theory of artistic creation in methodological terms.[7] The artistic process, like any other mode of thought, is a matter of practical problem-solving, the distinctive mark of the artist's thought being the qualitative nature of his problems. Ecker's step-by-step analysis of the process closely parallels Dewey's often formulated series of steps in a complete act of reflective thought. Although his account has the advantage of determining "meaning" in terms of the action and reactions of a painter to his work in progress, he has been criticized by Monroe Beardsley for having produced just another "finalistic'" interpretation of artistic creation.[8] Beardsley's reservations about such theories concern the sense of the means-ends categories implicit in Ecker's account, as well as the seemingly futile possibility of generalizing the description.

My own criticism of Ecker's argument[9] suggested only that it was incomplete, that to make sense of the distinctions made (such as presented relationship of component qualities, sub-

[4] For a summary analysis of these aesthetic concepts, see my monograph cited above.

[5] See J. A. Passmore, "The Dreariness of Aesthetics," *Mind*, N.S. LX (1951): 318–35.

[6] For two recent anthologies of literature collected for use in aesthetic education, see David W. Ecker and Elliot W. Eisner, eds., *Readings in Art Education* (Waltham, Mass.: Blaisdell, 1966); and Ralph A. Smith, ed., *Aesthetics and Criticism in Art Education* (Chicago: Rand McNally, 1966).

[7] David W. Ecker, "The Artistic Process as Qualitative Problem Solving," *Journal of Aesthetics and Art Criticism* XXI (1963): 283–90.

[8] Monroe C. Beardsley, "On the Creation of Art," *Journal of Aesthetics and Art Criticism* XXIII (1965): 291–304.

[9] Eugene F. Kaelin, "Aesthetics and the Teaching of Art," *Studies in Art Education* V (1964): 42–56.

stantive mediation, pervasive control, qualitative prescription, experimental exploration, and total quality), it is necessary to understand the structures of immediate experience in each act of artistic decision: in effect, that we must return to the facts of perception, to ourselves in the act of perceiving, if we are to understand the propriety of identifying any of the steps in his processual delineation, but especially if the last stage, that of total quality recognition, is to be counted as the solution to an artist's original problem. Ecker leaves that a mystery, as if a successful work must necessarily be recognized as such. I suggested then that it may be profitable to heed Husserl's advice and return *zu den Sachen selbst!* When the question of doubt arises we can only look again to see whether our perception is as lucid as we took it to be.

I shall save comments on the problematic character of artistic creation here and shall return to the subject after the phenomenological categories necessary for its elucidation have been made apparent.[10]

III

It has been suggested so far that art educators are in need of a workable method for justifying statements made about works of art, either in process or completed, and that the usual requirements of "consistency" and "truth" are too simple to serve even the minimal requirements of validity in verbal communications. Lack of contradiction does not suffice as a criterion of sense-making; and in cases of hypothesis formation and confirmation the question of whether a construct makes sense is answered, according to the pragmatic maxim, by both "truth" and consistency. Application of Dewey's pragmatic truth-test to the art educator's concern with creation calls for a further method of elucidating perceptual clarity. What the student needs is a set of aesthetic categories by which to establish the meaning of his empirically constituted data. Here the art educator–aesthetician has a choice of concepts: those of common sense, of practical psychology, or of traditional

---

[10] For Beardsley's discussion of Ecker's confusion of "problem" with "task," see "On the Creation of Art," p. 295.

aesthetics. However the choice is made, critical analysis of concepts is always in order, and the choice must be justified in terms of fittingness to the facts of aesthetic experiences. Husserlian phenomenology claims to be *the*—I should settle for *a*—method of performing the necessary critical analysis.[11]

The difficulty of expounding the Husserlian methodology is compounded by the various formulations the German master saw fit to give it. The clearest general exposition was first given in the three volumes of the *Ideen* (1913–30), only the first volume of which has been translated into English.[12] When the system became known, Husserl was criticized for "solipsism," and he reworked the substance of his Parisian lectures (1929), which acknowledge his debt to Descartes's attempt at radicalizing thought in the *Meditations*, into his own *Cartesianische Meditationen* (1930). These first made their appearance in French translation at Paris in 1931.[13] Although both treatises attempt to construct a ground for the certainty of human knowledge,[14] the first contains an exposition of the method, a description of the constitution of human experience, and a differentiation of "regional" ontologies (in which the dependency of psychology upon phenomenology is clarified), and the second seeks to correct the misinterpretation of the "constitution" thesis as a kind of transcendental solipsism.

What mattered for some of Husserl's disciples was the difference in the description of the method found in the two. *Ideas* sketched out a three-phased process of critical reduction:

[11] For examples of the method in application, see Roman Ingarden, *Das literarische Kunstwerk* (Halle: Niemeyer, 1931); Maurice Merleau-Ponty, *Phenomenology of Perception*, trans. C. Smith (New York: Humanities Press, 1962), and *Sens et non-sens*, 5th ed. (Paris Nagel, 1965), especially "Le doute de Cézanne," pp. 15–44; and my own *An Existentialist Aesthetic* (Madison: University of Wisconsin Press, 1962).

[12] Edmund Husserl, *Ideas*, trans. W. R. B. Gibson (New York: Collier Books, 1962).

[13] Edmund Husserl, *Cartesianische Meditationen und Pariser Vortraege*, *Husserliana*, Band I, ed. S. Strasser (The Hague: Nijhoff, 1963).

[14] See his independent treatment of the theme, *Philosophie als Strenge Wissenschaft*, in the series *Quellen der Philosophie*, ed. R. Berlinger (Frankfort-am-Main: Klostermann, 1965). Originally appeared in *Logos* (1910/11).

the phenomenological, which "puts brackets around" a conscious intention and the object intended; the eidetic, which reduces the intended object to a description of the meanings or meaning patterns by which it is known for what it is; and the transcendental, which limits attention to the immediate structures of the intending consciousness. In this last "reduction" the objects of inquiry are the "transcendences in immanence," i.e., the essential structures of consciousness implicit in any of its first-order acts of awareness. Reflection is the only method of access to these structures.

Consciousness itself is always of some object: its definition is the intending of "transcendent" objects (read: "other than consciousness itself") found in the conscious agent's world. In the *Cartesianische Meditationen,* however, the phenomenological reduction is called "transcendental," and eidetic description is declared to be the method of reflective self-conscious analysis. Any preference given to one or the other of these formulations is usually justified in terms of the objective of the inquiry. Since Husserl's own purpose was to explain the relationship between "transcendental phenomenology"—an eidetic science of possible conscious structures—and psychology—a summation of empirical facts—he felt the need to reformulate the method; his original formulation, however, is more useful for a critical (methodological) analysis of art-critical discourse.

According to Husserl, phenomenology is the one "critical" philosophical method which has succeeded in its aims; and either way we use it, it must begin with the suspension of the dogmatic attitudes of common-sense or prior philosophies. Indeed, common-sense and traditional philosophy were said to possess a common failure as explanations of our knowledge; each leave unexamined the belief that our worlds contain objects which cause within us psychological effects that come to be interpreted as (secondary or tertiary) properties of the objects themselves. Unless we take up an attitude (the phenomenological) which calls into question the validity of our beliefs established in the first (or natural) attitude, these beliefs are dogmatic indeed.

Descartes is praised by Husserl for being the first modern philosopher to call all his prior beliefs into question. And along with Descartes, Hume and Kant are noted to have glimpsed the import of a possible phenomenological method: Hume, for his tracing of ideas to their ultimate source in experience, which led to the denial of the significance of the substance concept, and his subjectivistic grounding of the concept of causality (ideas are traced to causes, and the grounds for our belief in causes turn out to be nothing but the subjective conditions of habit or custom); and Kant, for his transcendental deduction of the categories of the mind.[15] This historical account of the development of Husserl's method leads one to contemplate a second irony in the history of thought.

Lack of attention to the historical record has put American aestheticians in a poor position for appreciating the work of one of their most illustrous colleagues. The fact is that the Husserlian distinction between "intentional" and "real" or scientific objects once had wide currency in American aesthetics, owing to the earlier work of D. W. Prall.[16] In *Aesthetic Judgment* he describes an aesthetic object as "purely intentional," i.e., an intuition of the qualities that appear on the surface of objects and whose organization therefore has come to be called an "aesthetic surface." Beauty is a "supervenient quality" (nonnatural perhaps) which is what it is despite the flux, and our varying conscious experience, of nature. Thus, when he says "Discriminating perception focussed upon an object as it appears directly to sense, without ulterior interest to direct that perception inward to an understanding of the actual forces or underlying structure giving rise to this appearance, or forward to the purposes to which the object may be turned or the events its presence and movement may presage, or outward to its relations in the general structure and the moving flux—such free attentive activity may fairly be said

15 See Husserl, *Ideas*, p. 166.
16 For Husserl, see *ibid.*, pp. 240–41; and for Prall, *Aesthetic Judgment* (New York: Crowell Apollo Editions, 1967).

144 /

to mark the situation in which beauty is felt"[17] he is describing the phenomenological *epoché.* And this lesson in the reduction of the perceivable to the effect of its immediate presence is not lost in the second of Prall's treatises: "aesthetic content is not process at all. It is quality; color and sound, not physical wave motions; it is attracting, exciting quality; deep, rich color, moving emotional sound, not nerve currents or accelerated breathing or pulse."[18] By thus restricting his analyses to the properties of intentional objects, Prall meant to correct what he took to be the aberrant naturalism of Santayana.[19]

But his own attempts to find expressiveness controlled by "the order of elements intrinsic to sound, color and spatial form"[20] betrays a lack of confidence in the immediacy of aesthetic experiences. In spite of the separation of natural qualities from those of immediate perception, Prall thought it useful to search out the structural properties of sound (pitch, timbre, loudness) and color (hue, brightness, saturation) as if these were the natural causes of aesthetic quality perception, an understanding of which enables us to give an explanation of our experience of aesthetic expressiveness. In phenomenological terms, Prall considered the experience of aesthetic quality from the reduced, phenomenological standpoint; but the explanation he offered is couched in terms of categories composed from the natural standpoint. Since he violates the reduction, there is a corresponding confusion of aesthetic categories.

Besides offering a method to avoid such confusion, phenomenology must come up with an interpretation of aesthetic experiences in which the surface qualities of objects are observed to "deepen" into a recognition of objects and ideas represented in certain works of art.

Faced with natural or artificial objects remarkable for their

[17] Prall, *Aesthetic Judgment,* p. 57.
[18] D. W. Prall, *Aesthetic Analysis* (New York: Crowell Apollo Editions, 1967), p. 11.
[19] See George Santayana, *Sense of Beauty* (New York: Modern Library, 1955); 1st ed., Charles Scribner's Sons, 1896.
[20] Prall, *Aesthetic Judgment,* pp. 71–75.

aesthetic expressiveness, we are enjoined by Husserl to suspend our belief in all natural or causal explanations. If we follow the indication, we have an experience of the aesthetic (or surface) properties of the objects our consciousness intends. As art appreciators we have only to let the work happen. Failure to do so gives us some object other than that of our immediate, first-order experiences that should be elucidated in our art-critical discourse, just as Husserl claimed that failure to "disconnect the objects of consciousness" from the causal events of the world produced a corresponding failure in classical epistemology and logic. He calls the inquiry based upon this failure "psychologism."

When we consider that psychology is one of the empirical sciences itself in need of critical justification, we can understand Husserl's objections to psychologistic explanations of all human knowledge. The point has been made in recent aesthetics by Professor George Dickie, who posed the question "Is psychology relevant to aesthetics?"[21] Indeed, the question is rhetorical since the obvious answer is no.

If Professor Dickie is surprised to be thus associated with a phenomenological motive, the reason is simple to comprehend. His animadversions against claims of relevancy in responses to art works which are what they are because of a mysterious "aesthetic attitude" on the part of the subject are entirely sound.[22] But if they are thought of as a denial of our possibility to practice the phenomenological *epoché* (the suspension of the natural attitude for the adoption of the phenomenological), then his understanding of the methodological procedure is merely defective. For, as in pragmatic aesthetics, so in the

[21] George Dickie, "Is Psychology Relevant to Aesthetics?" *Philosophical Review* LXXI (1962): 285–302. See also his "The Myth of the Aesthetic Attitude," *American Philosophical Quarterly* I (1964): 56–65.

[22] Dickie's thesis runs parallel to that of Paul Ziff, who objects to characterizations of "aesthetic objects" as distinct from "physical objects." Ziff maintains that there are not two distinct objects, which might be known by the sort of response a viewer has, but only differing descriptions of the same object. See his "Art and the 'Object of Art,'" in W. Elton, ed. *Essays in Aesthetics and Language* (Oxford: Blackwell, 1954), pp. 170–86.

phenomenological, one either has or does not have an experience of the qualities of an art work, and only subsequently is judgment upon it pronounced. The reduction occurs after our experience of quality, not before, as a precondition to having the experience.

Thus, it is not claimed that one must first produce a certain psychological disposition or set in order to perceive the aesthetic qualities of objects; one might, as Prall maintained, merely be struck by the obtrusive qualities of a situation.[23] Moreover, one practices the phenomenological *epoché* precisely in order to avoid falling into a psychologistic interpretation of aesthetic experiences. In doing so, one merely suspends belief in the natural laws we know to have been effective at the time one had the experience in question. It was Prall's failure to practice the *epoché* that led him to seek the causal influence of the natural, intrinsic orders of sensory elements.

The result of suspending belief—or disconnecting an aesthetic experience from the context of "natural" events—is the opening of the possibility to find a categorial interpretation of the experience in its own terms. We merely describe what has happened. Ordinary language suffices to describe the objects of such experience as long as we do not lapse into the naive realism characteristic of most plain men and ordinary language philosophers,[24] for to do so would likewise be to violate the reduction. To practice the reduction, on the other hand, means that we must attend to those properties, and to those alone, of which we are aware at the moment of our aesthetic apprehension. And to be able to do this, we need nothing more than the capacity to concentrate, i.e., to focus attention and to re-

[23] Prall, *Aesthetic Judgment*, pp. 5–6.

[24] Ziff's thesis, apparently a denial of the relevance of metaphysical characterizations of art works, seeks a solution of the philosophical puzzle in language analysis. But his own claim that there are not two distinct objects, only differing descriptions of the same object, is itself metaphysical. It assumes that objects are what they are in spite of any interpretations made of them, and as such illustrates Husserl's claim that even some recent philosophies are dogmatic, i.e., noncritical in attitude.

flect. No, the pursuit of the psychological conditions under which attention-focusing and reflection take place add nothing relevant to our aesthetic knowledge. And our ability to attend and to reflect are amply proved by our decision to act in the proper way. Anyone can effectuate the reduction.

Knowledge of the facts of an aesthetic experience is gained first of all by acquaintance. Left uninterpreted, we should not even wish to call it cognitive; it is merely felt as the expressiveness of a given object or situation. Once we decided to bracket this act of becoming acquainted with aesthetic quality, however, we have constituted a "context of significance." It is this context that is analyzed and described by the art critic intent upon elucidating the content of his experience. And as long as each individual who calls into question the descriptions of a critic is willing to make the same reduction, i.e. place brackets around his consciousness of the same object, there is ground for arbitrating individual differences in reaction. The context of significance so created has been called by Stephen Pepper "the object of criticism."[25] When we reflect upon the content of the reduction, we find the scope of possible statements about the work of art to be strictly limited; physical descriptions of "the aesthetic object" are noted to be patently irrelevant, as by the way are the historical, biographical, psychological, sociological, and the like, usually made by the "critics" who have adopted one point of view or the other.

The first advantage of the phenomenological *epoché*, then, is the determination of the scope of relevant discourse about the expressiveness of art works which are enclosed in the bracketed experience. Whatever significance we find in the experience is bound to this context,[26] and what can be discriminated within the context are the referents of the words we use to describe the work in question. Primarily to guarantee a

25 Stephen Pepper, *The Basis of Criticism in the Arts* (Cambridge: Harvard University Press, 1949), pp. 168–69.
26 For a statement of the "postulates" of phenomenological criticism, see my "Method and Methodology in Literary Criticism," *School Review* LXXII (1964): 289–308.

value-free terminology, I call these contextual discriminations "counters."

If I perceive a yellow and a blue within the design of a painting, for example, it would be both meaningful and true to point out that such counters exist within the context of the painting's significance-structure. Such elementary descriptive statements allow me to call attention to the "local qualities"[27] of works of art. Indeed, as I continue to attend to these qualities, I may find that each of these counters affects the other, that the yellow and the blue perceived together constitute a "space tension" as the design begins to function as a unit in which a newly significant region of the painting becomes alive. The pull of the yellow against the blue may be stable, in which case a yellow plane or figure visually stands out off the picture plane while the blue recedes. Or the arrangement of other color values may reverse the progression and recession of the colored areas. And if the tension is only relatively stable, the painter may use this phenomenon for the representation of motion in the design. Cubist painters often used the stable type of spatial tension, while futurists tended to exploit the unstable relations for the purpose of depicting rhythmic or frenetic movement. In either way, the relations between perceptual counters themselves become counters of the significant context.

The question about the significance of the counters now becomes posable, and what's more, answerable. No individual counter bears an absolute significance. Blue does not mean "purity" or "repose" and yellow does not mean "gaiety" or "excitement." Since to attribute such absolute meanings to an individual counter is to violate the reduction—or the context, if you prefer—one would be guilty of importing meanings from a source other than an experience of the work in question. We must be careful, however, to distinguish "significance" from "signification." The former is the felt quality of the presentation—of the organized surface of the painting; the latter is the representation of an object or idea which, if discriminated

[27] See the categories employed by Monroe C. Beardsley, *Aesthetics: Problems in the Philosophy of Criticism* (New York: Harcourt, Brace, 1958), pp. 82–85.

within the context, may become another counter of the expressive vehicle. The significance of the surface is thus controlled by the perception of the relatedness of surface counters; and each individual counter has only that significance which its relations to other counters of a like kind create. The affective tone of the surface organization is nothing more or less than the state of the viewer's conscious-bodily states in the act of perception. And in nonobjective paintings there is no other significance.

Nonobjective paintings, then, are describable in terms of surface counters and their affective correlates; and the various kinds of sensorily discriminable counters go to make up the different media and intermedia that have become working materials for artistic exploitation, e.g. visual, aural, kinaesthetic, tactual, and the like.

An aesthetic surface thickens or deepens whenever depth counters make their appearance. The easiest way of imagining this process is to contemplate the motion of a line as it closes to form a figure. When the figure is that of a represented object, the context has become more complex. A simple portrait, a totally imaginary representation, and historical commemorative works may be structured in such a way as to be ultrarealistic (as in *trompe l'oeil*), realistic (as in Renaissance perspective painting), or in any degree of abstraction. Total abstraction, of course, is nonobjectivity; i.e., statements about any depth content of such a work are irrelevant, since there are no counters within the work to stand as referents for the words used in such statements. In successfully organized abstract contexts, moreover, any meaningful statement about the depth reveals an equally significant surface phenomenon, and vice versa.

Depth counters gain significance in context in the same way as any other counter: by a relation to other counters, be they surface or depth. One of the simplest cases of this phenomenon is the portrait. The significance of a portrait is not the subject who has served as model, nor even some abstract idea which may be associated with the object as depicted (posture,

150 /

attitude, social position, etc.); both of these are merely counters adding complexity to the context. The case of Van Gogh comes readily to mind. He recounts in his letters the difficulty of painting a bridge to be seen as the peasants who customarily use it see the object. The same struggle to capture the personality of his human models is apparent on the surface of his paintings. So plainly is this the case that we may conclude: the significance of a depth counter is the manner in which the surface is arranged to create the appearance of that object.

In more complicated cases, one depth counter is related to others of the same kind: between the representations of a woman and a child at the breast we are authorized to see a mother; but what motherhood means, as above, is determined by the qualitative feel of the surface organized to represent the idea. To use a logical analogy, the depth of a painting is like the subject of a proposition; its predicate is expressed nonverbally through the aesthetic surface. For this reason there are as many significances to (say) a crucifixion as there are ways of organizing a surface. A Grünewald and a Rembrandt express two different things, even when painting the execution of Christ; only the subject is the same. All the results of iconology and iconography are explicable in the same way. The depth of signification of the painting is readable from the relationship of represented objects, and the significance of that signification is felt as one perceives the surface through which it is expressed.

Surrealists have succeeded in increasing the surface-depth tensions by ambiguity in depth representations. As the dream object overlaps with the natural object, the original signification of the latter becomes modified but not confused; for the funding images suggest a third, "surreal" representation, whose significance once more is presented on a striking sensuous surface.

In summary, an expressive context is composed of counters, either surface only or both surface and depth. The significance of the context is experienced as the counters "fund" into perceptual closure: into the intentional "object" of our aesthetic awareness. Our critical statements are descriptive either of the counters or of the way in which they fund into a uniquely significant act. Thus, having bracketed our consciousness of a single object and described the structures involved in our experience of the object, we should have effectuated the "eidetic" reduction.

The result of this analysis is a set of categories which may be applied to any work of art.[28]

IV

Still another problem deserves consideration. We have examined some of the confusions surrounding the notion of an "aesthetic attitude" and have found them to be correlative to some corresponding confusions about an essential "aesthetic object." We have suggested that, since metaphysical speculation is out of order (as beyond the scope of aesthetic relevance), it is not pertinent to affirm or deny the existence of a peculiarly aesthetic object different in kind from physical objects. The work of art is the object of our awareness, and it was constructed by an artist in the physical medium of his art. Nor is there a peculiarly aesthetic attitude which would allow us to perceive the expressive qualities we may be blind to in another attitude. Aesthetic perception may take place in varying degrees of intensity; and when it has taken place, we need only bracket our consciousness of that object, hold it for contemplation, and reflect upon it. The next step is description.

But descriptions, even so-called phenomenological ones, are of different kinds. The critic attempts to describe the essence of an individual object, i.e., the structures of meaning implicit in the experience of that thing. When he succeeds, his language will permit us to enter into the process of creative communication, if for some reason the work itself failed to communicate with us in the first instance. Even should the reader not boggle at the expression "an individual essence," interpreted per Heidegger as the manner in which a thing

[28] For their application to the medium of painting, see my "The Visibility of Things Seen: A Phenomenological View of Painting," in J. Edie, ed., An Invitation to Phenomenology (Chicago: Quadrangle Books, 1965), pp. 30–58.

comes to be what it is and persists in that state, there is still the larger question of the relationship between such essences and the "meanings" elucidated in the eidetic descriptions of the last section of this article.

Have phenomenologists been over-hasty in their conclusion that such categories may be applied to any work of art? Roman Ingarden, in *Das literarische Kunstwerk*, does not hesitate to describe the essence of all literary works as a polyphonic harmony of surface and depth significance strata.[29] One counter-example would suffice to disprove his conclusion, and it is perhaps for this reason that he has left both the polyphony and the harmony unanalyzed; for to dispel their vagueness would be to invite criticism and easy refutation.[30]

The point is that, despite their own misleading language, phenomenologists need not fall victim to the essentialist fallacy. It is a fallacy to insist that essences exist in nature or in some transcendent metaphysical realm; but if the *eidos* is not a Platonic essence subsisting for all eternity, but a unity of meanings funding into a single significance or signification (depending upon whether our knowledge is aesthetic or conceptual), no ontological claims need be made at all. A critic describes objects phenomenologically reduced—separated from their context in the causal order of natural events. In his efforts to tell it like it is, he must merely refrain from all kinds of suppositions, be they physical or metaphysical, according to which the objects of their perception *must* be what they appear to be.

There may be as many such essences as there are ways of funding significance, as there are works of art or real, natural

---

[29] For a defense of his concept, see "Das Musikwerk," in *Untersuchungen zur Ontologie der Kunst* (Tübingen: Niemeyer, 1962), pp. 3–136, esp. pp. 33–35 and 107ff.

[30] The concept of a "polyphonic harmony," however, remains as open a concept as "art" (see Morris Weitz, "The Role of Theory in Aesthetics," *Journal of Aesthetics and Art Criticism* XV (1956): 27–35), and the specific nature of the harmony, which is determined by the actual qualities of the perceived context, does not go counter to the description of "essences" as "family resemblances" (see Ludwig Wittgenstein, *Philosophical Investigations*, trans. G. E. M. Anscombe (New York: Macmillan, 1953), p. 32). In each case, one should have to look and see how this harmony is managed.

objects. In both of these kinds of objects or "essences" it is the experience which stands warrant for the description. Art-critical language, of course, describes the structures of an actual work of art. Two faculties are therefore required to succeed at art criticism. Besides practicing the first stage of the phenomeno-logical reduction, critics must be perceptive of the structures inherent in individual works of art and endowed with enough verbal ability to describe what they perceive.

The aesthetician, however, works at the second phase of the reduction. Aiming at a general description of the conscious structures or meanings implicit in many works of art, he is at liberty to vary his examples, even to the point of extrapolating beyond his own narrow acquaintance with actual works of art. He may do this by modifying his consciousness to consider purely imaginary works of art, those which have never been executed in a physical medium. His descriptions then are of possible works of art. And if it were possible to imagine all of the conditions under which a work of art could appear to some consciousness, then aesthetics could become an a priori science (i.e., effective without regard to particular critical statements), much in the way that geometry is an a priori science and as, in presenting his general methodology, Husserl always claimed phenomenology to function. Whether the phenomenological aesthetician succeeds at describing all those structures involved in any possible work of art depends, of course, upon his skill at finding real examples or at conjuring imaginary cases which illustrate the possible ways human consciousness may be af-fected by artistic creations. It is best, no doubt, to leave "art" an open concept; as long as the context of significance governs whatever sense can be made and the contextuality of the con-text is open to some kind of eidetic description, there should be no insurmountable difficulties in making sense of particular works of art as yet uncreated.

Consciousness modification—the change from actual percep-tual cases to imaginary ones—is actually used in ordinary lan-guage analysis as well as in positivistic reasoning. When the linguistic analyst considers actual cases of word use, he refers the statements (or other expressions) to the conditions under which they are uttered. He can do this because it has already been established that the context of the use is indicative of the meaning. But this axiom itself has been established, as a methodological principle, by the consideration of many examples including all of those in which the analyst starts out by saying, "Suppose some one were to say. . . ." What he does is to call our attention to a possible use of the words in question and elucidates their meaning by referring to the conditions under which the words are supposedly uttered—to the context of possible use. It is for this reason, no doubt, that J. L. Austin referred to the method of ordinary language analysis as "linguistic phenomenology."[31] And aesthetic phenomenology shares his interest in therapeutic analysis.

On the side of logical empiricism, the technique of consciousness modification as a means of eidetic intuition is not without parallels to empirical generalization over a range of observational data.[32] In pointing out the parallels, Merleau-Ponty has shown that inductive generalizations produce the same results: the intuition of an essence—or generally applicable concept—even if the procedures differ. Thus, whether we start with a single example and describe the structures of meaning implicit in our consciousness of it or whether we begin by collecting many similar examples and abstract the similarities or family resemblances for naming as universals, the objects thus noted, described, or named are purely intentional: phenomena of meaning and not of physical or metaphysical existence.

However the knowledge of these intentions is arrived at, they may be arranged into regions, domains, or frames of reference. As a domain they constitute a range of relevant points of reference and delimit a corresponding range of discriminable acts

---

[31] J. L. Austin, "A Plea for Excuses," in *Philosophical Papers* (Oxford: Clarendon, 1961), p. 130.

[32] See Maurice Merleau-Ponty, "The Philosopher and Sociology," in *Signs*, trans. R. C. McCleary (Evanston, Ill.: Northwestern University Press, 1964), pp. 98–113.

of sense-making. Anything falling within the range of eidetic description makes some kind of sense, but whether a particular description of an individual essence is true or false must be decided on the basis of what appears in an experience of that object. For an applied aesthetics this means only that, given a set of meaningful aesthetic categories, a student may proceed to use them in the interpretation of individual works of art. This is what Husserl meant by getting back to the things themselves. And we could do worse than follow his advice in planning courses in aesthetic education.

For this reason also courses in aesthetics cannot be taught without first-order criticism. Although one could explain a set of aesthetic categories in terms of the levels of human experience from surface to depth, from sensory perception and affective tone to imagination or conception of real objects, ideas, and emotion, one could not demonstrate the sense of the explanation without considering individual works. In every case, as above, the context of analysis is what controls the limits of actual sense. A course in aesthetics conceived on this pattern is a course in the criticism of criticism; but for the purposes of economy in time it may be more profitable to begin with a derivation of the categories—by presentation of actual or imaginary cases. Once the student has learned what it makes sense to say, he can then be turned to the task of describing particular works of art. In the process he will have learned what kinds of statements are relevant to his analyses, and thus at the same time the kinds of statements he must avoid if his words are to make sense. In this way telling the truth comes after learning how to make sense, at least in the pedagogical situation.

We can do neither, of course, unless we are capable of "reading" the essence of a phenomenon as it is revealed in experience. In this sense, the truth of a phenemon lets itself be seen; and language analysis alone, unaccompanied by the revelation of phenomenal truth, can produce no aesthetic knowledge.[33] A correct interpretation of the sense revealed in the

33 For an account of the way in which works of art "let truth happen," see my

phenomenal occurrence, however, not only can but does. Again, this means only that whatever language we choose to use in the description of our aesthetic experiences must be tested for adequacy against the facts of that experience. It is the *epoché* which holds these facts for our continual reflective observation and thereby establishes the grounds for whatever truths we may state concerning them.[34]

V

It has been argued in the preceding sections that a modified form of the Husserlian *epoché* constitutes a workable method of aesthetic analysis—one called for in the work of D. W. Prall but not successfully worked out in either of his two treatises owing to his failure to abide by the conditions of the reduction. The strictly interpreted phenomenological phase of the *epoché* serves to isolate an aesthetic significance in its context, and thus helps to constitute the facts of the given discourse. The phenomenological aesthetician practices the *epoché* one degree further: he reduces the context of significance to its constituent structures such as "surface," "depth," and "total expressiveness." Each of these is given an interpretation in terms of conscious response to the art work as created by the "problem-solving" artist.[35] The aesthetic categories thus isolated may be used as criteria of meaningfulness, as practical guides of "the kinds of things to look for" in the appreciation of works of art. A pragmatic test of their usefulness is available in the degree to which students who apply them begin to find meaning in the confusing scene displayed in the history of art endeavor, as well as in the degree to which actual disagreements about the nature of particular art works are solved.

This latter result should come as no surprise, moreover, since qualified observers of aesthetic objects tend to agree, both in

"Notes toward an Understanding of Heidegger's Aesthetics," in Maurice Mandelbaum and Edward N. Lee, eds., *Phenomenology and Existentialism* (Baltimore: Johns Hopkins Press, 1967), pp. 59–92.

[34] For an illustration of first-order phenomenological criticism, see my "Visibility of Things Seen," pp. 43–54.

[35] See section II, above.

their first-order descriptions and their assessments of aesthetic value, and observers become qualified to the degree that they possess aesthetic knowledge. It is for this reason that panels of judges for art shows are picked from among experts—on the assumption that an expert knows at least what to look for in aesthetic expressions of a certain kind. The current concern for a methodical approach to aesthetic education bespeaks a similar motive for the production of informed teachers. To a certain extent, then, the final test must be found in these pragmatic realms. Can the method be taught to teachers, and can they produce students who are more knowledgeable than those who have been trained heretofore?

The method seems to work for appreciation. Can it be applied to those contexts in which "creation" is the subject of training? Descriptions of "the creative process" are notoriously vague, and many of them are undertaken with some kind of axe—psychological, metaphysical, or aesthetic—to grind.[36] One of them, however, the recent study of Professor David W. Ecker, seems to be relatively free from dogmatic presuppositions which have colored many of the preceding analyses. His approach is both empirical and methodological.[37]

In an effort to distinguish the part of creation which pertains to the imagination and the other which belongs to perception, Ecker has devised a scheme for photographing a painting as it can be said to exist at each stage of the development, with the later stage being inferred as an imagined future state with respect to the prior. Each stage is then given a description in terms of the relations between qualities revealed to perception. The account, which closely parallels Dewey's description of the stages in a complete act of reflective thought, has been criticized by Beardsley[38] and myself.[39]

Beardsley admits the subtlety of Ecker's case but discovers an error of intentionalism. Since Ecker claims that in one stage

[36] For one prominent example, see Brewster Ghiselin, *The Creative Process* (New York: Mentor Books, 1955).

[37] Ecker, "The Artistic Process as Qualitative Problem Solving," pp. 283–90.

[38] Beardsley, "On the Creation of Art," pp. 291–304.

[39] See my "Aesthetics and the Teaching of Art," pp. 42–56.

of a painting's development a pervasive quality of the problematic context becomes clear, and that this pervasive quality
then tends to serve for further decisions on the inclusion or
exclusion of certain possible moves until the final quality of
the work becomes apparent to perception, Beardsley's criticism has some point. For, from the moment a decision has
been made on the pervasive quality of the developing piece, the
rest of the artistic decisions become assigned and hence are
tasks rather than problems. The same criticism is possible for
Croce's doctrine of "the aesthetic object" which is said to
exist whole and entire in the imaginative activity of the artist,
such that whatever "externalization" of this intention is necessary to be performed consists in the task of finding the proper
physical and psychological materials for the construction of
the physical analogue to the purely intentional aesthetic object.

Ecker leaves himself open to this charge by citing examples
of teachers of art who assign classroom tasks of making (say)
a cubist painting. Since this style of painting is already known
and has been fully developed by earlier painters, the "problem" of the student is nothing more than the fulfillment of the
assigned task. In the creation of an actual work of art, the
student would discover the aesthetic object by manipulating
the materials of his medium. It was in this way that Collingwood modified Croce's intentionalism[40] without rejecting the
original thesis that the creation of an art object is an act of
original expression and a phenomenon of basic communication.

The question then arises whether appeals to an artist's imaginative intentions are always fallacious in aesthetic discourse.
And if not, then what kind of explanation can be given to the
imaginative component of the artist's activity.

It seems clear that appeals to the intention of the artist—as
to what the artist wanted to do—are always fallacious, if putative knowledge concerning this intention is erected into a
criterion for judging the value of the completed object. We

[40] For an account of the influence of Croce on Collingwood, see John Hospers,
"The Croce-Collingwood Theory of Art," *Philosophy* XXXI (1956): 291–308.

may safely assume that the artist did what he wanted to do, and in this case his purely subjective intention coincides with the structures of the work, which is the physical embodiment of that intention. Indeed, the work is the intention, objectively considered. Thus, any description of the work is also a description of the artist's intention. Yet, since the object as structured is the object to be judged, and by hypothesis the object and the intention are the same, it is obvious that the intention cannot be used as a criterion for judging the excellence of the object. As embodied, our judgment is upon the intention itself. And, alternatively, if for some reason there is a discrepancy between the subjective intention of the artist and the properties of the work, then by definition (using the intentional criterion) the work is a failure. In this case, moreover, one would have to give some sort of evidence that knowledge of an unexpressed intention was warranted. Then if it could be explained how the creator or the appreciator came to an awareness of the subjective intention, he would be in position to show how it became aborted in the context of the unsuccessful work. But to this day no such explanation has been forthcoming.

However, it is another thing to claim that some artists do as a matter of fact have a perfectly clear idea of what they wish to do in creating both surface and depth of their works of art. Some do, and some don't; and of those who do, not all of them formulate their intention prior to manipulating the "component qualities" placed at their disposal by the materials of the medium. Thus some artists seem perfectly capable of imagining colors as they themselves and others come to perceive them and of imagining sounds as they must be produced for anyone to hear music. To call all such appeals a fallacy of explanation is a piece of dogmatic condemnation without grounds in the empirical conditions of having the experience. What must be done is to find the explanation of these facts, when they are facts, which fails to do violence to either the demands for sense or the established relevance of the facts. How is it possible for one to imagine what has not yet been done in the medium, but which one knows must be done if a successful work is to be produced?

Ecker devised his method of photographic reproduction to this end. The later stage before its actual execution had to be imagined, if it was in fact, on the bases of the possibilities apparent in the prior stage. And to see a possibility is precisely what we usually mean by imagining the existence of the object to be created. We need not go as far as Croce and claim that the imagining is the creating; the intention must still be embodied. We say only that the artist sees what must be done; to use Sartrean language, he sees something, as it were, in absentia.[41]

Given the step-by-step development of a painting, one merely infers from what was done that the later stage was indeed a part of the prior context or one of its possibilities. Other decisions, of course, could have been made; but the fact that they were not is sufficient proof that they were no part of the artist's actual intention. How one picks out a given stage of a painting's development as the pervasive quality of the piece (which then is erected into a prescriptive control of further decision) remains a mystery in Ecker's account, however. This is not to claim that there are no pervasive qualities in aesthetic contexts. They correspond more clearly to the total expressiveness of the context itself and thus with the "total quality of the piece," or they change from stage to stage and thus correspond to the phenomenologically reduced quality of each stage of a painting's development, there to be perceived. The problem seems to be one of determining in just what stage the final quality of the piece becomes visible as a possibility in a preceding stage. Empirically this may happen at any stage following the first decisions, and, indeed, even before a single decision has been realized on canvas.

According to the testimony of some successful artists this happens as a matter of fact. How do such phenomena come to pass? The phenomenological description of them necessitates

[41] See Sartre, *L'Imaginaire* (translated as *Psychology of the Imagination*) (Paris: Gallimard, 1940), pp. 239–46.

the third and final stage of the reduction, the transcendental, which, it should be remembered, isolates the structures of consciousness—or of the intending bodily complex—immanent in the intentionality of the act itself.

To shorten a long story, within the stream of an artist's consciousness there are many acts, all intending some kind of object. The noematic correlate (the unity of eidetic meaning structures) of each noetic act (the intending) may remain constant while the object bracketed with them changes its ontological character. This is the effect of consciousness modification. The artist may look at what he has done (perception), and in this case the object is a real design on a real canvas and the noematic correlate of his act is the phenomenologically reduced qualities of that object considered as "meaningful" structures; or he may look at what he has done and see (imagination) what it is possible to do by projecting an imaginative design on the real canvas. The real canvas remains precisely what it is in both cases; but being phenomenologically reduced in aesthetic perception to the noematic correlate of an intending consciousness, that structure is modifiable by the addition or subtraction of other structures (by gobs of paints or lines, also phenomenologically reduced) in such a way that a new object has at least this kind of intentional existence. Whether the artist succeeds in changing the aesthetic character of the real canvas (as perceived in phenomenological reduction) depends upon the availability of physical materials, which, when reduced to their noematic structures, yield the qualities desired. Each of these "additions" or "subtractions" may be described in terms of the categories explained in section III of this article.

If this account is accurate, the creative painter continually modifies his consciousness from an act of perception to one of imagination and vice versa, without our being able to say which came first, as with the chicken and the egg. In creation consciousness is continually modified—it "flips" and it "flops"; but once more, to deny the possibility of such action is hardly consistent with the observation of creators in the act of making

162 /

a work of art.[42] And to insist upon an explanation at variance with the facts of our experience is precisely what we mean by "having an axe to grind."

To carry the explanation one step further, one could appeal to the existential concept of "temporality," the condition of human beings living in their privately significant worlds; but that would take my inquiry beyond its predesigned limits and, incidentally, change its phenomenological inspiration from the work of Husserl to that of Heidegger.[43] Suffice it to say here that, being simultaneously his past and a living project toward a significant future, the artist's decision is to create an environment consistent with his own creative desire.[44]

Thus, it is in watching their work that we perceive "where the students are." And this is still a viable starting point for aesthetic education.

[42] For my own account of the creative process, see "Art and Existence," *Humanitas* IV (1968): 188–210, and for its application to classroom instruction, "The Existential Ground for Aesthetic Education," *Studies in Art Education* VIII (1966): 3–12.

[43] See Heidegger, *Being and Time*, trans. J. Macquarrie and E. Robinson (London: SCM Press, 1962), pp. 383–423.

[44] How a teacher is to respond to this situation is the subject of my "The Existential Ground for Aesthetic Education."

ÆSTHETIC AND MORAL JUDGMENTS:

AGAINST COMPARTMENTALIZATION / 7

Joseph Margolis

One of the most strategic and difficult educational exercises is the detection and correction of conceptual prejudices. Fundamental and pervasive convictions, often demonstrably wrong, frequently control the investigation of focused issues in such a way that they are never or rarely called into question by the most strenuously opposed antagonists. Debate is unconsciously confined by the very process of inquiry, which tends to reinforce the acceptance of certain governing notions of great generality, by the precision with which it is addressed serially to controversies regarding detail. The pattern is inescapable, of course, but a mastery of a domain demands an ability to isolate and reconsider the principal, if unavowed, doctrines that provide a sense of system and competent scope to all or most accounts. In the discussion of values in moral and aesthetic discourse, in particular, it is regularly assumed that the relevant sorts of judgments fall into two neat bins, that moral and aesthetic judgments are distinguished by logically distinct properties, and that judgments within each set are themselves

164 /

logically uniform. It is clear that if these assumptions were not true, instruction regarding the relevant detailed issues would be seriously distorted to the extent to which they do play a controlling role; or to change the emphasis, instruction in a given domain cannot really afford to neglect the largest theoretical reflections on its own properties—but, in the nature of the case, it quite typically does. The following, then, is designed as a corrective both against particular distortions in the discussion of values and against the reinforced practice of disregarding the larger features of a given domain.

To reject a Kantian view of value judgments—that is, the view that sets of value judgments properly designated as moral or aesthetic judgments, or judgments of equally large denomination, are logically homogeneous within each set and logically distinct set by set—is not to deny that certain sorts of judgment within such sets have distinctive properties or that one may characterize particular judgments as moral or aesthetic or the like. I have,[1] for example, drawn attention to the fact that "ought" is *often* used in moral judgments in such a way that if I acknowledge that in given circumstances I ought to do X, then I cannot consistently not intend to do X in those circumstances. Merely to understand this sense of "ought" is to understand the sense in which one is bound categorically to act in accord with what it is one ought to do. I say bound *categorically*, to collect at one and the same time an essential part of Kant's insight about the unconditional obligation characteristic of many morally relevant situations and the sense in which, relevant to the use of "ought," it would be inconsistent both to affirm that one ought to do X and to intend not to do X. But to say this is not to hold either that the use of "ought" in nonmoral domains may not exhibit this same property or that, even in the moral domain, overriding *moral* considerations may not appear which, correctly grasped, relieve

---

[1] In a paper, "The Use and Syntax of Value Judgments," presented at the Second Conference on Value Inquiry, University of Akron, Akron, Ohio, April, 1968), subsequently published in *The Journal of Value Inquiry* II (1968): 31–40.

an agent of obligations to which he is *prima facie* categorically bound. The Old Testament injunction "Thou shalt have no other gods before me" suggests, for example, a sense in which to understand what God is, is to understand that given God's existence, we are categorically obliged to worship Him *and* that to acknowledge Him and not to intend to worship Him would be inconsistent. "One ought to worship God," then, may provide us with a categorical use of "ought" comparable to that use of "ought" which obtains in certain moral contexts. On the other hand, I may have wrongly supposed myself (or another) to be in given circumstances under a certain moral obligation; but to admit this is merely to acknowledge the compatibility of testing and correcting moral claims and of admitting the categorical nature of properly determined obligations. I may have supposed myself bound to keep certain information from another (supposing, for instance, that I am bound by a promise) and come to realize, by a proper weighing of the relevant considerations, that I was, in fact, obliged under the circumstances to reveal the information in question. Adjusting and correcting our beliefs about our obligations does not, in itself, count in any way against the unconditional force of obligations once correctly fixed.

Categorical obligation is prominently recognized, of course, as a marked and characteristic feature of the moral domain. It argues, as I have suggested, both that being a human being entails that one ought unconditionally to act in accord with those obligations properly designated as moral obligations and that one cannot consistently admit such obligations and not intend to act in accord with them. But to say this is to draw attention, in an extremely convenient way, to a central question concerning value judgments as a whole. We must be careful to distinguish between defending judgments and defending certain theories of judgment, between justifying particular value judgments by appealing to supporting reasons and proving particular theories of judgment by considering the recognized features of the domain of judgment in question.

It has relevantly been asked, for example by Kurt Baier, "Why should I be moral?" Evidently, the question asks for a *justification* for electing to act morally rather than immorally or, even, without regard to moral distinctions. In the moral domain, we normally justify actions, decisions, judgments by appealing to morally relevant and morally decisive reasons. But Baier's question—which is also implied in Plato's myth of Gyges—asks us to supply justifying reasons for preferring to appeal to morally relevant reasons rather than to reasons of any other sort. And this seems paradoxical. For one thing, if the justifying reasons are construed as *morally* relevant reasons, we shall merely be admitting a hierarchy (and, conceivably, an infinite hierarchy) of levels of moral justification; in that case, Baier's question might, schematically, be construed as, "Why should I be moral$_1$?" where the justifying reasons are (so to say) moral$_2$ but not moral$_1$ reasons. For another, if the justifying reasons are construed as not morally relevant reasons, one may, *in different contexts*, offer an indefinitely large number of alternative and possibly conflicting sorts of justifying reasons; for instance, in a financial context one may offer financial reasons; in a prudential context one may offer prudential reasons; in a political context one may offer political reasons; in a religious context one may offer religious reasons. The trouble is that, from the first point of view, one can never really get beyond moral considerations—which seems to be the intent of the question; and from the second, we can never tell *which* sort of justification decisively settles the superiority of preferring morally relevant reasons—the very ease with which we may provide an ulterior defense of acting in a moral way (and, correspondingly, of acting immorally or in a morally indifferent way) points to the irrelevance of such justification. To argue that *some* set of reasons would properly permit us to decide whether we ought to prefer morally relevant reasons or not is to suppose that the force of moral reasons is conditional upon the force of these ulterior reasons and that the force of these latter is itself categorical; but then we should, in context, take the latter reasons as moral reasons. Baier, it may be observed, appears to begin by asking for reasons by which to justify our preference for moral reasons, but he actually concludes (not without supposing that he *has* supplied compelling ulterior reasons) by positing what he takes to be "the very *raison d'être* of a morality," that is to say, by providing an analysis of what it is one is doing in offering moral reasons by which to justify particular actions and judgments.

We must be careful here. If a certain theory of morality is adopted—for instance Baier's, that moral reasons are "reasons which overrule the reasons of self-interest in those cases when everyone's following self-interest would be harmful to everyone"—then *reform* of existing moral rules and practices may be entertained and defended or defeated for relevant reasons. But all of this would occur within a suitably ramified moral context; it would not allow us to raise questions about whether we should prefer moral reasons and, if so, for what ulterior reasons. Baier's utilitarian account of morality does not supply *reasons* for being moral; it supplies a *principle* alleged to be embodied *in* morality and in morally relevant reasons and thus provides a basis for formulating reasons for preserving or changing what may count as moral conduct and morally appropriate reasons. Whether and on what grounds an alleged moral principle (say Baier's utilitarianism) can be defended is an entirely independent issue. But to accept a utilitarian account is to accept a view of what it is that constitutes the superiority of moral reasons; it is not to supply a superior set of reasons that moral reasons supremely serve in some instrumental capacity. One may, alternatively, speak of reasons for holding a certain theory of moral values, but this is merely another way of registering that such reasons are not moral reasons.

It is, of course, possible (as we have seen) to hold that adherence to apparent moral reasons may be assessed by appeal to ulterior reasons, but these (if they were alleged to accord with some moral principle) would simply lead us to admit the superiority of $moral_2$ reasons over $moral_1$ reasons. The advocates of such a view are bound to favor some reform of values and are bound to suppose that they themselves are favored with privileged access to "true" or "higher" values. Nor is it by any means peculiar to moral dispute that such pretensions arise. In the aesthetic domain, for instance, if one supposes that beauty is a transcendental attribute of God and that art seeks to produce things of maximal beauty (rather as in the view of Jacques Maritain), one may, similarly, argue the need for a reform in the reasons by which we justify our aesthetic preferences. We might conceivably begin with the question, "Why should we prefer aesthetic values?" (in the relevant sense) and end by detailing—in a manner quite analogous to Baier's—our theory that the very *raison d'être* of art (aesthetically considered) is to maximize beauty, a divine attribute that manifests itself in degrees and may be measured and produced. Ignoring moral considerations, we may argue that our aesthetically relevant reasons for judging works of art are superior reasons because they serve, in some suitable way, to realize values marked along the scale assigned to the divine attribute of beauty. But once again we should have confused a theory of beauty (or a principle of beauty) with aesthetically relevant reasons by which to assess particular works of art. Or we should have subscribed to aesthetic$_2$ reasons that, it could be claimed, take precedence over aesthetic$_1$ reasons. To seize the parallel is, in effect, to admit that the bearing of theory on judgment is essentially the same whether we speak of the aesthetic or the moral domain; reference to categorical obligation does not affect that issue in the least.

In any event, when we wish to justify a moral judgment we appeal to morally relevant reasons, and when we wish to justify an aesthetic judgment we appeal to aesthetically relevant reasons. But when we wish to defend a moral theory or a theory of aesthetic values, or when we wish to defend a *principle* of values of one sort or another, our defending considerations are not moral reasons or aesthetic reasons or reasons of a similar sort. Here we address ourselves to considerations of systematic coherence and comprehensiveness and the like *with respect to an admitted body of valuational practices.* Here we concern ourselves with the congruence and adequacy of our conception of a domain of values with the characteristic practices that obtain within the domain itself. We suppose the field to be relatively constant, with a view to assessing competing theories: the possibility of radical reform and change of values, even when dependent on the adoption of alternative theories and principles, misleads us about the distinction between the defense of value judgments and the defense of theories of value. For the reasoned adoption of a theory of value is very likely to have consequences bearing on the subsequent defense of relevant judgments, but its defense presupposes a set of judgments and practices whose own defense is relatively independent *of the theory in question.* The relationship is not at all unlike that which holds between observational statements and theories about the nature of physical reality in the sciences; the very notion that competing theories are about a certain domain and that relevant grounds must be mustered by which to assess their relative force and adequacy is itself coherent only on the assumption that the provision of defending reasons for given judgments is, in principle, relatively independent of the theories *under examination* regarding the domains of such sets of judgments. And, of course, to say this much is to say absolutely nothing about any substantive claims regarding particular practices *via* value judgments or about any substantive claims regarding particular sets of value judgments and practices *via* first principles or suitable theories. Still, it suggests, by exhibition, that the relationship between value judgments and value theory is relatively uniform from one domain of values to another.

It needs also to be said, returning to our original illustration, that the categorical force of certain morally relevant "ought" judgments does not, as such, require any significant adjustment in our account of the logical features of the justification of value judgments in general or of the construction of valid arguments—for example, of the so-called practical syllogism. If an "ought" judgment is a judgment that someone is under an obligation, it is, I should say, a finding and may be said to be concerned with a matter of fact. (I shall explain this concept

170 /

further below). The categorical force of such a judgment relates to a certain kind of consistency between conduct and
judgment (at least as far as the practical syllogism is concerned) and, precisely by bearing on conduct as it does, entirely obviates the need for positing a distinctive kind of
syllogistic form for the usual paradigm arguments. R. M. Hare,
it may be remembered, had concerned himself with the distinctive logical properties of moral arguments because he had
held that moral judgments are action-guiding and that value
judgments that are action-guiding "must be held to entail
imperatives." It may be readily shown that moral judgments
need not be action-guiding and that, even if they are action-
guiding (in the way in which certain "ought" judgments are),
their force may be brought out without (what on independent
grounds is implausible) assuming that they either are or entail
imperatives. For consider that moral judgments said to be
action-guiding are said also to be *justified* on some grounds or
other; if this is so, then the judgment that such and such an
action is morally justified may, logically, be entirely freed from
an action-guiding judgment. And consider that the impera-
tivist thesis cannot possibly go forward without the assumption
(in order to provide parity with the actual range of moral discourse) of past-tense imperatives and parallel imperatives for
first-, second-, and third-person contexts; but, obviously, first-
person and past-tense imperatives are anomalous. And consider
that there are moral judgments regarding character, that is,
patterns that depend to a large extent on gifts and talents that
different people have but that cannot be entirely open to
analysis in terms of deliberate action or of what people may
choose to do. And consider that moral judgments may be made
without the intention of directing anyone to act in this or that
way but merely to register one's appreciation of a certain relevant property that someone's conduct exhibits. The upshot,
to return to Hare's challenge, is that the practical syllogism
(or other appropriate logical models) conforms to the logical
form of normal syllogisms (or other normal models), except
that (what is practically but not, in the narrow sense, logically

/ 171

relevant) the conclusion, having a certain categorical force, bears on the ulterior question of the consistency of judgment and conduct. To say this, however, is of course not to say that formal arguments involving imperatives will not exhibit logically distinctive properties.

What we have thus far seen, then, is that we are able to provide for the distinction of certain subsets of value judgments without subscribing to what I am calling the Kantian view. However characteristic certain sorts of judgment may be in this or that large domain, there do not seem to be any features of a logical sort that uniquely mark all admissible judgments within that domain or mark all members of a subset of such judgments as distinct from the membership of some subset of another similarly large domain. Categorical "ought" judgments would appear to be the most likely candidate for the Kantian view; but, as we have seen, similar categorical judgments may appear in the religious domain, the categorical feature of such judgments does not require distinctive forms of argument, and even questions regarding our justification for subscribing to the kinds of justifying reasons that obtain for such judgments may be readily generated (if they may be generated at all) in the same way for judgments of other domains.

That there are striking (and often denied) parallels between prominent subsets of judgments from quite different value domains may be further demonstrated by considering characteristic arguments in these domains. Aesthetic judgments, or judgments of beauty, have, certainly since Kant, been taken to be fundamentally and necessarily different in logical respects from moral judgments, or judgments of categorical obligation. We must of course concede that judgments of the form "X is beautiful" may well deserve to be analyzed as exhibiting a considerable variety of relevant logical forms, some of which at least *are* quite different in nature from the form of categorical "ought" judgments.

Here I must enter an important distinction between two basically different sorts of value judgments, that may appear

172 /

in any well-defined domain such as the moral or the aesthetic. The distinction intended lies in there being a range of judgments ("findings") that behave logically like factual judgments, except that we say their predicates are valuational predicates, and there being a range of judgments ("appreciative judgments") that logically depend on one's taste and preference (which cannot, therefore, be said to be true or false or correct or incorrect, in the manner of factual statements and judgments). Thus, the judgments that John murdered Mary (the "finding") and that John had dinner with Mary are both factual judgments, in spite of the fact that "murdered ——" is a valuational predicate and "had dinner with ——" is not. Correspondingly, the judgment (in typical contexts) that Lily is lovely and the judgment that Metaxas brandy is a fine after-dinner drink are appreciative judgments, judgments that depend on one's taste and preference, judgments that cannot be simply true or false. Disputes of different sorts may arise for the two sorts of judgments: justifying reasons may be demanded for each, although with respect to the second pair the apparent denial of either appreciative judgment is not the contradictory as the corresponding negative judgment would be, with respect to the first pair.[2]

If "X is beautiful" is essentially connected with personal taste, then either it functions in some way other than as a value judgment (perhaps as a mere expression of personal preference) or it may serve as an appreciative judgment of some sort. But since appreciative judgments also occur within the moral domain, this merely demonstrates that it is false to hold that the member judgments of distinct value domains do not, or cannot, share logical properties thought to be essential to, or characteristic of, judgments of either sort. What I am interested in proposing, further, is that, precisely for the ranges of judgment historically thought to be most fundamentally opposed in essential logical respects, it is quite easy to demonstrate that the closest possible parallels obtain. That

[2] I have explored this further in "Value Judgments and Value Predicates," *The Journal of Value Inquiry* I (1967–68): 161–70.

is, it is a relevant, but somewhat soft, argument to hold that judgments logically weaker than, and different from, findings may occur in the moral domain. But it would be a very decisive argument against the prejudices of the Kantian view to show that aesthetic judgments may exhibit the objectivity of findings and that disputes with respect to them may proceed in precisely the same way as do disputes with respect to categorical "ought" judgments.

Consider, to this end, typical rules in both the moral and the aesthetic domains, for instance, "Lying is wrong" and (adopting Monroe Beardsley's specimen of a "General Canon") "Disunity is always a defect in aesthetic objects." To these rules correspond counterpart "ought" judgments. To the moral rule, "One ought not to lie," which is a judgment of categorical obligation; to the aesthetic (what, admittedly, is not altogether familiar usage), "One ought not to assign merit to aesthetic objects on the grounds of disunity," which is not a judgment of categorical obligation (which fact explains why, not having practical consequences in the same way as does the moral judgment, it does not characteristically occur). In any case, the practical consequences of admitting moral "ought" judgments (as we have seen) do not affect the logical properties of such judgments; correspondingly, the aesthetic "ought" judgment is merely a recasting of the rule itself, that stresses that the primary use of aesthetic categories concerns judging things rather than securing a preferred conformity of conduct. In spite of such differences—which are in themselves logically negligible—relevant moral and aesthetic disputes behave in precisely the same way.

Now the interesting thing about such would-be rules (or, rather, the universal judgments corresponding to such rules) as "Lying is wrong" and "Disunity is always a defect in aesthetic objects" is that one wants to say both that the judgments are analytically true and that one can find exceptions to the rules without self-contradiction. And this is a paradox. But we *do* want to say that lying is not always wrong and we *do* want to say that disunity sometimes contributes to the aesthetic merit or interst of a work of art. I may argue that lying to save a life in particular circumstances is the morally advisable (and even obligatory) thing to do, and I may argue that a certain departure from the requirements of unity, in a particular painting (for instance, in a good many of the paintings of James Ensor), positively enhances the aesthetic merit of that painting. It makes no difference whether, for either issue, it is the case or not: the fact is that the claim is an entirely admissible one and can be *debated*—which shows that it is simply not construed as self-contradictory. Of course, if "Lying is wrong" and "Disunity is always a defect in aesthetic objects" are construed as analytically true (or as tautologies), there can be no dispute at all of the sort mentioned. What I wish to emphasize is that precisely the same paradox may occur for both moral and aesthetic judgments and is resolved in precisely the same way; for in showing that this is so, I mean to show that a subset of aesthetic judgments behaves in the same way logically as the most prominent subset of moral judgments—and in the same way with respect to every conceivably relevant detail.

In order to escape paradox, a suitable distinction must be made. We must, in considering whether lying is wrong and whether disunity is always a defect in aesthetic objects, be construing such remarks in two quite different but equally pertinent ways. It is a perfectly fair paraphrase of the first precept to say, "Saying in a morally reprehensible way what one believes to be false is morally reprehensible"; and it is a perfectly fair paraphrase of the second precept to say, "Objects that are aesthetically defective with respect to their unity are aesthetically defective." To offer such paraphrases is to indicate not only the necessary truth of these precepts but also their vacuity. They have, as one may concede, extremely restricted uses in discourse, being largely confined to instructional contexts in which the very terms of moral and aesthetic judgment are actually introduced; the moral precept has, typically, an additional use of importance, since it serves as a reminder of the practical implications of acknowledging a moral obligation.

On the other hand, if one says "Lying is not always wrong," one very likely means to be saying that some conduct, usually characterized as lying, ought not properly to be so characterized, or that, although it is wrong insofar as it is lying, some conduct cannot be merely characterized as lying and, characterized in morally more decisive respects, it is not actually wrong. Correspondingly, if one says, "Disunity sometimes contributes aesthetic merit to objects," one very likely means to be saying that some arrangements, usually characterized as exhibiting disunity, ought not properly to be so characterized, or that, although it is aesthetically defective insofar as it does exhibit disunity, some arrangements cannot be merely characterized as exhibiting disunity and, characterized in aesthetically more decisive respects, it is not actually aesthetically defective.

I find both of these sorts of paraphrases (for both moral and aesthetic contexts) to be entirely plausible; but to admit them, of course, is to dissolve the paradox. Paraphrasing along the lines of securing analytic truths relates primarily to initial instruction and reminder; paraphrasing along the lines of exception and qualification relates primarily to actual disputes about values. The second, more important, option draws attention to two quite distinct ways in which counterconsiderations are advanced in the usual disputes—always, I must insist again, equally open in aesthetic and moral contexts. According to the one sort of maneuver, we dispute about whether the instance before us is properly to be subsumed under a given category—since to be thus subsumed (according to the tautological rule) is tantamount to being assigned the value corresponding to the relevant value predicate. According to the other, we dispute about whether, having properly subsumed the instance before us under a given category, it may be subsumed as well under another which will affect the assignment of the relevant value predicate. The first consideration concerns the classification of items, antecedently identifiable in value-neutral terms, under categories that invite appropriate value judgments; the second concerns the relative weight with respect to the ascription of value predicates, for items thus classifiable, of different classifications. With regard to the first, we may query whether an alleged instance of lying or disunity is properly so characterized; and whether it is or is not determines the propriety (according to the rule) of ascribing the assignable value. With regard to the second, we may query whether to characterize correctly something as an instance of lying or disunity suffices, in view of other possible and relevant ways of characterizing things, for the ascription of the assignable value; whether it does or does not depends on the relative importance of different classifications for the value in question. If something lacks unity, it lacks beauty (we may say), but whether something may yet be beautiful though it lacks unity is an altogether distinct and admissible question. Correspondingly, if something is an instance of lying, it is *pro tanto* an instance of conduct that is morally wrong; but whether what is an instance of lying may yet be morally right is, once again, an entirely distinct and admissible question.

We see, therefore, that to admit that "Lying is wrong" and "Disunity is always a defect in aesthetic objects" is entirely consistent with either or both of the strategies of dispute just posited. This shows at a glance that the usual moral and aesthetic rules are, in a sense, not very intimately connected with arguments supporting particular moral and aesthetic judgments. The vacuity of the rules, with respect to the first strategy, is clear from the fact that we may always dispute about whether the instances before us, to be subsumed under a given rule, are correctly so subsumed; the grounds on which this must be decided have nothing whatsoever to do with the bare rule itself. Alternatively put, the rule may not unreasonably be construed as a mnemonic device by which to recall the relevant criteria in terms of which things are actually judged. And again, with respect to the second strategy, what we may call the competence of the rules, even buttressed by detailed criteria for classification, may be challenged in the sense that to judge something to be wrong or aesthetically ugly is to render a comprehensive judgment—one in which a great many considerations may converge toward a single verdict—and that, on the strength of particular, enumerated rules, it is only possible to concede the verdict conditionally. We do not allow such moral or aesthetic predicates as "wrong" or "ugly" to apply to anything solely on the strength of such restricted moral categories as lying, contract-breaking, cheating, murder, promise-breaking, or on the strength of such restricted aesthetic categories as disunity, disharmony, simplicity, monotony. Here, then, the analytic truths, "Lying is wrong" and "Disunity is always a defect in aesthetic objects," may be conceded compatibily with holding that the relevant predicates, "wrong" and "ugly," are, ideally, applied to actions and objects on the combined weight of all relevant moral or aesthetic considerations and, in practice, applied only conditionally on the weight of particular considerations however relevant. The same action may be an instance of lying—in which respect it may be judged wrong—and an instance of saving another person's life—in which respect it may be judged right; what the moral sum of such considerations may be can never be foretold merely from an application of a fractional, though relevant, rule. Similarly, the same painting may exhibit disunity—in which respect it may be judged ugly—and may exhibit a certain expressiveness through its very disunity—in which respect it may be judged beautiful; what the aesthetic sum of such considerations may be once again cannot be foretold by the application of a single canon. We may provide for this conditional use of the relevant predicates graphically by writing our specimen rules as ellipses: "Lying is wrong . . ."; "Disunity is always a defect in aesthetic objects . . . ." We shall understand by this that our conduct is never judged in a morally appropriate way solely in terms of lying, even when lying is a consideration, and that aesthetic objects are never judged in an aesthetically appropriate way solely in terms of disunity, even when disunity is a consideration.

The parallels between moral and aesthetic judgments already exhibited are the decisive ones. But we may usefully amplify the account in a number of ways. For one thing, the argument does not depend on selecting tautological rules. For example, in the moral context, we might have considered a version of a Kantian duty that is not tautologically formulated—"One ought to will that all his faculties should be developed" (the duty of self-development or self-realization). Correspondingly, we might have considered a version of a nontautological aesthetic canon, for instance, one based on G. D. Birkhoff's empirical speculations—"Aesthetic value varies directly with aesthetic measure" (or one based on Jay Hambidge's "dynamic symmetry"). Obviously the two strategies of dispute already noted would still obtain. Another consideration is this: even if the moral or aesthetic rule, whether tautological or not, were construed as the major premise of an appropriate syllogism, we should find that we are not ordinarily prepared to formulate necessary and sufficient conditions for the subject of the rule, for instance for occurrences of lying or for occurrences of disunity. We appear, in disputes about values, to argue more by analogy from case to case than from antecedently formulated conditions. And this suggests that, in effect, we should be hiding the logical informality of moral and aesthetic arguments if we held that open concepts like lying or disunity provide the major premises of practical or aesthetic syllogisms. If we can be said to be able to formulate necessary and sufficient conditions for morally relevant concepts, there can be no objection to according the same rigor to aesthetic concepts (for example, as in academic or highly formalized art traditions); and if the logical informality mentioned is ascribed to either the moral or the aesthetic domain, it will be impossible to deny that a corresponding informality obtains in the other. Another consideration is this: the global designations "moral" and "aesthetic" are themselves open concepts, a substantial part of whose use is primarily designed to allow the *stipulation* of approximate boundaries to distinct domains of value, in order, precisely, to facilitate philosophical description; it is an irony, therefore, to reverse the order of inquiry and to attempt to sort out logical distinctions among sets of value judgments designated as "moral" or "aesthetic" by a close examination of the meaning, or the conditions of use, of these terms themselves. Needless to say, any effort to extend the catalogue of distinct domains of value (for example to the prudential, the religious, the legal, the medical) will be affected by the same difficulty.

I can find no other relevant respects in which to challenge the parallel posited for the logical properties of certain subsets of moral and aesthetic judgments. We have seen that to reject the Kantian view is not to deny distinctive subsets of value judgments within distinct domains of value or the ability to identify particular judgments as moral or aesthetic or of another comparable sort. We have seen that the categorical force of moral judgments does not affect the logical properties of such judgments but only the relationship between conduct and judgment, that practical syllogisms need not have any logical properties distinct from those that hold for comparable formal arguments elsewhere, that questions of justifying our adherence to moral or aesthetic considerations or of the relationship between theories of value and of actual moral and aesthetic judgment are identical for the two domains. We have also seen that the principal strategies for conducting disputes about values are equally available in both domains, that rules or would-be rules exhibit the same variety in both domains, that reliance on informal or analogical arguments or on formulable necessary and sufficient conditions characterizes both domains equally, and that the global category terms "moral" and "aesthetic" are themselves primarily designed to register systematically useful stipulations regarding the uniformities noted among given sets of judgments and practices. But if all these considerations be admitted, the Kantian view of value judgments must be seen to be decisively defeated.

I have, in effect then, been arguing for a fundamental revision in the characterization of the moral and aesthetic domains, at least as far as value judgments are concerned. I have claimed that there are no logically distinguishing features of such judgments as such, although there are indeed logically distinct kinds of value judgments that may appear in either domain.

If the claim is allowed, there are no distinctive kinds of disputes that arise in one domain or the other, however characteristic certain sorts of disputes may be. There is simply no reason to investigate moral and aesthetic judgments and arguments about values separately. They go hand in hand and a competent grasp of one, apart from familiarity with stock cases and the like, is tantamount to a competent grasp of the other.

"SEEING AS" AND "KNOWING THAT"

IN ÆSTHETIC EDUCATION / 8

Walter H. Clark, Jr.

I

In our less benevolent moods we might say of a student, col-
league, or critic, "Jones *knows* literature (music, painting), but
he has no *feeling* for it." Whatever such statements may reveal
of our personal attitudes toward Jones, they rest upon a logical
distinction which it is the purpose of this paper to examine.
Roughly this is a distinction between knowledge and experience. More specifically it is a distinction between the kind of
knowledge that can be put into words ("Jones knows the
themes in *A Portrait of the Artist as a Young Man*") and the
experience appropriate to our most comprehensive engagement
with works of art, an experience customarily referred to by
philosophers as "aesthetic." Of course it must be understood
that "knowledge" and "experience" do not designate mutually
exclusive categories. It is almost always the case that there are
certain things one must know beforehand in order to experience a particular work of art; and conversely, once having experienced a work of art one may be said to have a knowledge
of it dependent upon that experience. On the other hand it is

important to point out that the knowledge necessary to such an experience is not necessarily sufficient to produce it. Nor is it the case that a demonstration of the sort of knowledge that is usually consequent upon experience of a given work of art is proof that such an experience has taken place for the person who gives it. One may arrive at such knowledge through other means, as by a word-of-mouth report from another experiencer.

The first task that confronts us in this investigation is one of finding more specific language in terms of which to deal with the concepts of knowledge and aesthetic experience. For the former I have chosen to make use of a term introduced by Gilbert Ryle. He talks of *knowing how* and *knowing that,* and it is the latter that I propose to pick up and turn to my own purposes.[1] In contrast to this I shall place the notion of *seeing as,* which will be elaborated into a rough model for aesthetic experience itself. In what follows I shall be more concerned with questions than with answers, more concerned with *seeing as* than with *knowing that,* more concerned to establish the nature of aesthetic experience than to deal with problems of pedagogy. Nevertheless, it is through comparison with *knowing that* that I hope to illumine the notion of *seeing as;* and it is through consideration of pedagogical problems that I shall try to expand the model proposed for aesthetic experience. The concluding portion of the paper will pose some very difficult questions with which such an account must deal, but for which I see no clear answers at present. This paper, then, invites the reader to follow for a certain distance one theory as to the nature of aesthetic experience and its implications for education and to join the author in contemplation of the difficulties encountered by it.

II[2]

In the eleventh chapter of the second book of his *Philosophical Investigations,* Ludwig Wittgenstein distinguishes two

[1] Gilbert Ryle, *The Concept of Mind* (New York: Barnes and Noble, 1949), Chap. 2.

[2] The treatment of aspect in this section owes much to an argument developed

uses of the word "see." These he terms, on the one hand, *seeing*, and on the other, *seeing as*. The importance of this distinction, he says, "lies in the categorical difference between the two objects of sight."[3] Those things which are objects of *seeing* are publicly verifiable as such. Thus we may describe someone as *seeing* a Rorschach blot, a cloud, a diagram, or any of the myriad objects whose existence is ultimately to be established according to the methods and criteria of physical science. *Seeing as* is quite a different matter. An ink blot may be *seen as* a head, a cloud may be *seen as* a camel, a diagram of the Schroeder Reversible Staircase may be *seen as* right side up or inverted, the duck-rabbit diagram may be *seen as* a duck or a rabbit, etc. In none of these cases, however, would an onlooker describe an observer as *seeing* what he is *seeing as*. The object of *seeing as* is no less real than the object of seeing, but it is different. The difference, moreover, is not in the quality of the experience of the observer. When I *see* a cloud *as* a camel the experience is as vivid as when I *see* the cloud itself (when I *see* the cloud *as* a cloud?).[4] In the words of N. R. Hanson, " 'Seeing as' and 'seeing that' . . . are not psychological components of seeing. They are logically distinguishable elements in seeing-talk, in our concept of seeing."[5]

What relevance has this distinction to aesthetics? I shall maintain that talk of aesthetic experience can be translated into talk of *seeing as*. The advantage of such a translation is that it enables us to give greater specificity to the concept of aesthetic experience and to make distinctions which could not otherwise be made. What can be seen—the painting—is, as it were, a carrier of what it can be seen as, termed by Wittgen-

by the author in an unpublished Ph.D dissertation, "Ascriptions of Good in Ethical and Aesthetic Contexts" (Harvard University, 1965), pp. 77–107.

[3] Ludwig Wittgenstein, *Philosophical Investigations*, trans. G. E. M. Anscombe (New York: Macmillan, 1953), p. 193. See also Ingrid Stadler, "On Seeing As," *Philosophical Review* LXVII (1958): 91–94.

[4] There is a good discussion of this and related points by Jonas F. Soltis in *Seeing, Knowing and Believing* (Reading, Mass.: Addison-Wesley, 1966), p. 40.

[5] Hanson, *Patterns of Discovery* (Cambridge: Cambridge University Press, 1961), p. 21.

stein the *aspect.* I shall be maintaining that aesthetic experience is characterized by apprehension of certain *aspects* of aesthetic objects. Since this use of the *seeing as* distinction is quite different from that of Wittgenstein, and since the connection between *seeing as* and aesthetic experience is novel, some elucidation is called for at this point.

Although I shall maintain that all cases of aesthetic experience of a work of art involve *seeing as,* I do not maintain the converse of this position; that all cases of seeing an aspect of a work of art involve having an aesthetic experience. Perhaps the simplest way to make this clear is with respect to Wittgenstein's duck-rabbit diagram.[6] Suppose that we are considering this diagram as a work of art. Merely to be seeing either the duck aspect or the rabbit aspect is not necessarily to be having an aesthetic experience. Having an aesthetic experience involves a different kind of aspect; something on the order of *seeing* the work of art *as* balanced or complex or unified. We may, however, have an aesthetic experience of the diagram while seeing either the duck aspect or the rabbit aspect. In seeing the duck aspect or the rabbit aspect of the diagram we might be said (among other things) to be seeing what the diagram represents. But works of art need not be ambiguous in what they represent. We can say, for example, that a particular painting from Van Gogh's Arles period represents a room with a bed and a chair, etc., etc. Let us term what we *see* the Van Gogh painting *as* (when we *see* it *as* a painting of a room with a bed, a chair, etc., etc.) its *representational* aspect. I am claiming, then, that to see the representational aspect of a work of art is not to have an aesthetic experience of the work of art; or, more correctly, that one can see the representational aspect of a work of art and yet not have an aesthetic experience of it. But it is difficult to imagine that one might have an aesthetic experience of the Van Gogh painting without seeing its representational aspect; possible, I think, but not likely. Perhaps, therefore, we should say that seeing

6 Wittgenstein, *Philosophical Investigations,* pp. 193ff.

the representational aspect is either a preliminary stage necessary to having an aesthetic experience, or else a phenomenon which is customarily attendant upon it. The relation of representational aspect to aesthetic experience poses interesting questions, but they are tangential to the purposes of this discussion. What is important to note, I believe, is that we may see aspects of a work of art without having an aesthetic experience of it. Yet I claim that the seeing of an aspect is always associated with having an aesthetic experience (that it is always possible to talk of aesthetic experience in terms of *seeing as*). This argument, therefore, as it proceeds, must provide an account of the nature of those aspects which are characteristic of aesthetic experience.

Let us now consider *nonrepresentational* aspects of works of art. Suppose we are examining the picture of a room at Arles by Van Gogh; specifically we are paying attention to the colors of the picture. Suppose that one of us wants to point out certain features of the colors in this picture. He might say, for example, "Notice the red and orange here and here, and this yellow. Notice how the colors complement one another. This is a very warm picture." There are several things we can say about what is going on here that lead up to a point I wish to make. First, we may say that it is a fact that the picture contains such and such reds, oranges, and yellows. The speaker draws our attention to something which is objectively *there*, something we can *see* when he says, "Notice the red." But when he says, "Notice how the colors complement one another," he invites us to *see as*. If we ask him, "What do you mean, 'complement'?" he may do one of two things. He may say, "By 'complement' I mean 'go together.' These colors harmonize." Or he may isolate some of the reds and oranges of the picture and show them to us in paired swatches ("Don't you *feel* the complementarity?"). We may agree or disagree that the colors go together. We may or may not feel something when the paired swatches are shown to us, and if we do feel something, we may or may not agree that our feeling is to be associated with complementarity of the two colors. Again, as with the case of pointing to the colors red, orange, yellow, it is a fact that the speaker is asking us to notice something in the painting, in this case a qualitative relationship, not a color. But is the qualitative relationship itself a fact? Is the relationship "there" in the sense that the red, yellow, and orange are "there"? (Are the duck and the rabbit "there" in the sense that the diagram is "there"?) Yes and no. Everybody sees the red. Not everybody sees the colors as complementary. But stop. Not everyone sees the red. Some people are color blind. It may be for some as if they were blind to the quality of complementarity.[7] Perhaps we should say, "More people seem 'as if' blind to the complementarity of colors than are blind to the color red." If we go on to consider the statement "This is a very warm picture," we find that it may be treated in much the same way as "the colors complement one another." Asked whether warmth is "there" in the picture we should have to admit that some people feel warmth in it and some do not. Some are "as if" blind to the warmth. Perhaps we should say, "There is something there in the picture; and some people respond to this whatever-it-is by feeling that there is warmth in the picture, and some do not."

The remark that "The colors complement one another" differs from "This is a very warm picture" in at least two respects. The first statement is about a part or parts of the picture, whereas the second is about its entirety. Further, we are likely to find more people "as if" blind to the quality mentioned in the second than to that in the first. How might we compare these statements to one about the *colors* in the painting? Or how would we compare the qualities to the colors? First, we can say that if someone does not see a certain color in a painting, he is blind to it. One is not blind to these qualities in the same way. One is, rather, "as if" blind to them. If one fails to see these aspects, the failure is not to be explained in physiological terms, or at least not in the same way as a

[7] *Ibid.*, pp. 213ff.

failure to see colors. To be "as if" blind to the complementary qualities of colors in the picture, or with respect to its warmth, is to be in much the same situation vis-à-vis the picture that we are with respect to the duck if we cannot see it in the diagram. If we cannot see the duck aspect we are "as if" blind to it. One difference between these cases that I have labeled "as if" blind and real blindness is that the latter is, by and large, not susceptible to correction, whereas the former are highly susceptible to change. We may be "as if" blind to the duck aspect one moment, and see it the next. It is so with the complementary quality of the colors or the warmth of the picture as well. We may be blind to them when someone first speaks of them, and we suddenly come into possession of them as his account continues (or we may not). In the same way we may be in possession of the warmth of the picture at one time (or over a period of time) and suddenly lose it. The state of "as if" blindness with respect to aspect is, finally, subject to change by social processes, whereas physiological blindness is not.

Thus far we have completed two stages of our argument. We first introduced the concept of aspect in terms of Wittgenstein's distinction between *seeing* and *seeing as*, and then made a further distinction between representational aspect and qualitative aspect. The task that remains is to trace a connection between qualitative aspect and aesthetic experience. It is at this point that I propose to turn to the language of critical evaluation. The reasons for doing so are two. In the first place we need to do the best job we can of isolating criteria that are generally acceptable as aesthetic. In the second place we want to distinguish among qualitative aspects those which are peculiar to the aesthetic experience. I am assuming that criteria used in judgments of aesthetic value will serve to identify these aspects. The model to which I shall have recourse here is that of Monroe Beardsley.[8] I do not wish to be

8 Monroe C. Beardsley, *Aesthetics: Problems in the Philosophy of Criticism* (New York: Harcourt, Brace, 1958), chap. 10.

held to a defense of his particular scheme. It is, rather, the general notion of a connection between the criteria of aesthetic evaluation and aspect which concerns me. Beardsley's scheme is useful because of the care with which it is worked out, and because of its formalist orientation. Other schema, however, might easily be substituted for Beardsley's without damage to the argument.[9]

Beardsley commences his account of aesthetic evaluation by offering a formula: "X is good because. . . ."[10] What is of interest to him and to us is what will follow "because"; that is to say, the sorts of reasons offered in support of an ascription of goodness. On grounds which need not concern us here, but which he discusses at length, Beardsley argues that a valid reason in support of an ascription such as "This is good" must refer "to some characteristic—that is, some quality or internal relation, or set of qualities and relations—within the work itself, or to some meaning-relation between the work and the world."[11] It is Beardsley's contention that reasons of this sort, various as they may be, can be divided into three main groups: those which attribute *unity* to the work of art (it is well organized); those which attribute *complexity* (it is rich in contrasts; it is subtle and imaginative); and those which attribute characteristics of *intensity* (it is vivid, forceful, beautiful, tender, tragic, graceful, etc.). Reasons which attribute goodness to a work of art by virtue of its having such qualities are regarded by Beardsley as referring to what he calls "General Canons." The three General Canons, or criteria, of unity, complexity, and intensity identify qualities of works of art, one or more of which are always to be cited in support of ascriptions of goodness. Other qualities, which may be subsumed under

---

[9] Frederick Copleston, A *History of Philosophy* (Westminster, Md.: The Newman Press, 1960–62), II, 422. See his note on the aesthetic theory of Thomas Aquinas, whose criteria for beauty (integrity, proper proportion, and clarity) show an interesting similarity to Beardsley's criteria for aesthetic value.

[10] Beardsley, *Aesthetics*, p. 456.

[11] *Ibid.*, p. 462. For an account of the terms which follow below see pp. 462–65.

one or another of these General Canons, may also be cited as reasons. These Beardsley terms "Specific Canons." Where an ascription of good is supported by an appeal to a General Canon it will often be possible, according to Beardsley, to be more specific by citing a Specific Canon which may be subsumed under it. Thus, if someone says "This is a good painting because it has unity" and is challenged, he may go on to point out features of balance, claiming that the balance contributes to the unity of the painting. On the other hand, it need not be the case that a quality cited as satisfying a Specific Canon in one situation will so serve in another. Delicacy, for example, may be subsumed under intensity with respect to one work and not with respect to another. We may summarize Beardsley, then, by saying that the qualities denominated by the General Canons are always good-making where present in a work of art, but that this is not the case with respect to qualities denominated by the Specific Canons, for such qualities may be good-making in the context of one work of art but not in that of another.

Two things distinguish Beardsley's account from the one we are developing. In the first place, his General and Specific Canons occur in the context of a model for the justification of ascriptions of good. They identify the sorts of criteria to which one might appeal in justifying ascriptions of good. We are concerned with value judgments only insofar as they point the direction to aesthetic experience. A second and crucial distinction between Beardsley's account and the one we are developing here has to do with verification. The criteria to which his Canons refer point to features in the work of art which are assumed to be objectively *there*. It is essential to his view that the features of the work of art to which reasons (why the work of art is good) point as satisfying criteria included under one or another of the Canons, should be verifiable as *there* in some way approximating as nearly as possible the ways in which the scientist verifies the existence of the phenomena of physics. But we have already pointed out the categorical nature of Wittgenstein's distinction between *seeing* and *seeing as*. The objects of *seeing* are subject to the processes of verification. The objects of *seeing as*, on the other hand, are peculiarly personal and are not subject to verification. To talk about the distinguishing characteristics of aesthetic experience as involving the perception of *aspect* is to talk of our experiencing a work of art for the sake of something which a third party cannot truly describe us as perceiving. The educational consequences of this are considerable.

Why then use Beardsley or any other such model? I am maintaining that the Canons under which are subsumed the criteria for calling a work of art good serve to identify the characteristic aspects of the aesthetic experience of works of art. What Beardsley offers as criteria and rules I treat as identifiers of goals. Consider unity. Beardsley says that an ascription of good with respect to a particular work of art, X, may be justified by pointing out that features in X satisfy the Canon of Unity (i.e., that the work of art is unified). I say that if we are concerned with having an aesthetic experience of X (where X and all other works of art exist primarily to this end, and where our commerce with X and all other works of art is fundamentally for the sake of having aesthetic experiences of them) then to mention that it is unified is to identify an aspect of it (to say that it may be *seen as* unified) and further, that having an aesthetic experience involves seeing this and/or other aspects.[12]

III

In order to bring out the significance for education of such an account of aesthetic experience as that described above, we turn to a distinction made by Gilbert Ryle in *The Concept of Mind*. Wishing to deny that all minded activity can be ex-

---

[12] It will be seen that by the logic of this argument the aesthetic function of ascriptions of value is simply to indicate that there are aspects to be seen in connection with a work of art. The citation of criteria identifies the pertinent aspects. Evaluation is thus much less important with respect to art than in the arena of morality, or wherever else it serves to guide choice.

plained by reference to prior mental acts of some *anima* or mental executive (in his phrase, "the ghost in the machine"), Ryle first distinguishes between disposition and occurrence.[13] To talk of the fragility of glass, for example, is to speak of its disposition to break. The shattering of a particular glass, in contrast, is an occurrence. The distinction here exemplified in natural terms Ryle applies to certain mental phenomena. In so doing he is, in fact, removing them from the domain of his "mental executive," since, by definition, dispositions are not doings. To talk of the fragility of a glass is to make a hypothetical prediction, not to attribute any action to the glass. In the same way Ryle separates mental acts and events from mental dispositions. Arriving at the solution of a problem, finding a needle in a haystack, seeing a diagram as a duck— these are all occurrences (acts, happenings, successes). The case of *knowing*, on the other hand, is quite different. *Knowing* is not an occurrence. It is not something that we *do* or that happens to us. In Ryle's analysis *knowing how* (to do something) and *knowing that* (something is the case) are both amenable to treatment in dispositional terms. Thus it is that for Ryle, *learning*, in the sense of coming to know that or know how, involves the acquisition of a disposition to tell or otherwise act in a suitable way under the appropriate circumstances. The student who knows that one theme of *A Portrait of the Artist* relates to the myth of Daedalus and Icarus has acquired the disposition to expound in an appropriate manner on the subject when queried in examination. The student who knows how to swim has acquired various dispositions which are cashed in the act of swimming. Acquiring a disposition in Ryle's terms means to have learned and not forgotten. Knowing something need not imply consciousness of or attention to the thing known. It follows that there is a clear difference between knowing something and thinking about the thing known. We know many things of which we are not at the moment aware. Knowing does, however, imply a retention of the thing known

[13] Ryle, *The Concept of Mind*, Chap. 5.

over a period of time (i.e., ability to respond in a particular way under the appropriate circumstances over a period of time). It does not seem that we could properly speak of someone's knowing something for five minutes, then not knowing it for another five minutes, then knowing it once more.[14] In these respects we mark a difference between *knowing that* and *seeing,* or *seeing as.*

By now the reader will have become aware of this paper's tendency. In announcing the dichotomy of knowledge and experience as its main focus, and then reducing the terms of the dichotomy to perceptual occurrences of a particular sort on the one hand, and mental dispositions on the other, we have been preparing the ground for a consideration of *knowing that* and *seeing as* with reference to aesthetic education. In what follows, the differences between them will be discussed under three main headings. First we shall consider *seeing as* and *knowing that* as goals of the teaching process. This will lead to consideration of differences in teaching methods which might follow from differences in what the teacher is trying to achieve. Finally we will discuss testing and the particular problems created for the teacher who has been trying to get students to see a work of art as having aesthetic characteristics. The overall purpose of this discussion is to try to bring out the peculiar characteristics and problems which distinguish aesthetic education from what might be thought of as the more usual kind—where the end of teaching has to do with the inculcation of knowledge or of skills, and to do this in such a way as to throw light on a theory as to the nature of aesthetic experience.

The outlines of differences to be traced between *seeing as* and *knowing that* are already clear. The distinction between occurrence and disposition is susceptible of much more careful analysis than present space allows, yet to bring out some of its more obvious implications will help to point the educa-

---

[14] See, for example, Israel Scheffler, *The Language of Education* (Springfield, Ill.: Charles Thomas, 1960), chap. 5.

tional significance of the distinction. We can, first of all, distinguish between disposition itself and the process (activity) of acquiring it. The period of active acquisition (learning period) is one which involves trying on the part of the learner, trying which may issue in success or failure. We can speak of the student as trying to learn (memorize, puzzle out, etc.) the themes in A *Portrait of the Artist*. Once learned, once the disposition has been acquired, such descriptions are irrelevant. One does not try to know what one knows, though it is true that one may forget. When we talk of knowing in terms of having a disposition we are talking in part about reliability (predictability), something to which behaviorists refer in terms of stimulus and response. This is not to say that the notion of occurrence is completely apart from the notion of disposition, since dispositions are cashed in occurrences (the fragility of the glass, a disposition to break, is made manifest in terms of its breaking, an occurrence). Nevertheless, it does not follow from the existence of this relationship that all occurrences are to be regarded as the cashing of dispositions. It is, in fact, theoretically possible to distinguish a continuum between occurrences which cash dispositions and those which are *sui generis*. The criterion for placement along this continuum (given the circumstances) is reliability of prediction. We can talk with considerable confidence of the fragility of glass because of the frequency with which our expectations of what will befall a dropped glass are satisfied. This example represents a solid disposition. Such is the case to a lesser degree with respect to knowing the themes of A *Portrait of the Artist*. Where someone is unable to provide us with an answer when asked about the themes in A *Portrait of the Artist* we conclude that he does not know them; either he has not been taught them or his teacher has failed in the attempt to teach him the themes of the book. In contrast to these examples, consider the athletic coach whose intent is to have his team win games. He engages in various activities with the idea of influencing his charges in certain ways just as does the teacher

194 /

of literature. Among other things he teaches certain *knowings that* and *knowings how* and requires his players-to-be to give evidence of having learned what he has taught them. The final end of his instruction, however, the winning of games, is not to be interpreted as the cashing of a disposition by his players in the same sense that a student giving the correct answer on a test can be thought of as cashing a disposition. "To get the winning habit," though it may occupy a favored place in the coaches' jargon, does not make sense from a logical point of view because winning is simply not the sort of thing that can be brought under an agent's voluntary control (if indeed it were, the concept of "game" as it exists today would cease to exist). A difference between *teaching that* and teaching football, then, runs along the following lines. What is required of the learner in the first instance is a period of *trying*. Once the student has learned X, considerations of effort, of success or failure, cease to be relevant, for the very definition of *knowing that* carries with it the implication that the knower be able to recall the thing known under appropriate circumstances. The teaching of a sport also requires a period of trying on the part of the learner. He will be required to *learn that* and *learn how*, and thus we are entitled to say that the preliminary phase of getting athletes to win games involves the successful acquisition of dispositions. However, it does not necessarily follow from the fact that the player-to-be acquires such dispositions as are required of him by his coach, or that he tries to his fullest extent in the game itself, that he will be successful in winning the game. Teaching football, therefore, cannot mean teaching to win, though winning may be thought of as the ultimate end of the coach's instruction, as well, perhaps, as a long-run indication of its effectiveness. I am suggesting that the analogy between teaching aesthetics and teaching games is much closer than the analogy between teaching aesthetics and the kind of teaching which consists mainly of the passing on of information. All three kinds of teaching call upon the student to acquire certain dispositions. In the case of *teaching that* such dispositions constitute the end of teaching. They define success in teaching. In the case of *teaching to see as* or teaching games, *learning how* or *learning that* are preliminary (usually necessary) steps—a part of the trying process. But in these latter cases the end of teaching consists of occurrences not subject to dispositional incorporation. The acquisition of skills and knowledge, even those necessary to success, do not amount to winning games on the one hand, or having aesthetic experiences on the other. N repetitions of aesthetic experience in the presence of art objects give us much less license to predict an aesthetic experience upon presentation N plus one, than N demonstrations of *knowing that* X give us license to predict a demonstration in situation N plus one. It is only in the feeblest of senses, if at all, that the teaching of aesthetic content can be said to involve the acquisition of a disposition as its end.

In considering problems of method insofar as they relate to teaching to *see as* we must start from this point. *Knowing that* a work of art is unified is not equivalent to *seeing* it *as* unified. Under the circumstances it makes sense to ask what else is necessary or what else the teacher can do besides inform the student. At the outset it should be remarked that on one hand it *may* happen that *telling that* will be followed by the student's *seeing as* (as when we show someone an ambiguous diagram and tell him that it can be seen as a duck and as a rabbit—for most people the information is sufficient), and on the other hand that it is theoretically possible to teach *seeing as* without any recourse whatsover to *telling that*. (The duck aspect of Wittgenstein's diagram comes through more readily if the diagram is shown in conjunction with other, more obviously ducklike, representations. Teaching the student to *see* a diagram *as* representing both duck and rabbit might consist merely of a judicious display of other diagrams along with the ambiguous one. In getting students to *see* a painting *as* unified it might be possible to display a set of reproductions from

which the nonunifying elements would be increasingly ex-
punged.)

In talking about methods, as in talking about testing, a major
problem arises as a consequence of the privacy of aesthetic
experience. Here the analogy between teaching sports and
teaching to *see as* breaks down, for the end toward which
the coach orients his teaching is one that is clearly defined and
easily measurable. There is no need for him to teach his charges
to recognize when they have won, since "to win" a game is not
an experience but another sort of occurrence, one that is public, context-bound, and fully described in any precise definition
of the game itself. The same point deserves to be made in
comparing *seeing as* and *knowing that,* for the latter is fully
susceptible of verification, and indeed can be defined in terms
of the methods of verification. The relevance of Ryle's arguments to the present discussion, in fact, derives in large part
from his determination to describe *knowing that* in terms
of behavior.

What methods might be prescribed for teaching which strives
to achieve such an invisible, indescribable, unmeasurable goal?
Avoiding specific recommendations for the most part, I should
like to suggest two strategies for approaching this problem.
One strategy involves reducing it to simplest possible terms
and attempting to extrapolate from the solutions developed
at such a level. In the argument of this paper ambiguous diagrams have served as vastly simplified models of works of art.
I am suggesting that difficulty in seeing representational aspect in an ambiguous diagram parallels the difficulty we can
have in seeing qualitative aspect in a work of art. One place
to look for solutions to the problems involved in teaching
aesthetic contents, then, would be the psychology of perception.[15] What is the role of *attention* (the alternation of duck

[15] See, for example, Charles E. Osgood, *Method and Theory in Experimental Psychology* (New York: Oxford University Press, 1953), p. 220ff. Also Noel Fleming, "Recognizing and Seeing As," *Philosophical Review* LXVI (1957): 161–79.

and rabbit in the diagram can be controlled to some extent through the alternation of fixation points)? What is the role of *context* (the rabbit aspect of the diagram is more apt to appear if we have just been looking at pictures of rabbits)? What is the role of the development of a hypothesis on the part of the perceiver as to what it is that he is seeing (Norwood Hanson comments, "There is a sense in which seeing is a 'theory-laden' undertaking.")?[16] Attention, context, hypothesis, and other such variables have their equivalents in the teaching of literature and are susceptible of control by the teacher. A hard look at the psychology of perception may well suggest other such possibilities for investigation.

Another strategy would involve searching out established educational programs whose goals are similar to those of aesthetic education and subject to some of the same caveats. An investigation of the methods of such programs might well suggest new leads in the methods of aesthetic education. Two examples will suffice to illustrate the sort of thing I have in mind. The group approach to problems (often known as brainstorming), regarded as a specifiable technique with principles and rules capable of being taught, is a relatively new phenomenon in the world of business.[17] Although it might appear that the goals of a psychologist teaching brainstorming to a group of businessmen must differ greatly from those of an instructor teaching a poem to an English class, there are certain similarities. In neither case can it be assumed that mastery of information or techniques will guarantee results. Both students and businessmen need to be taught to attend to themselves in certain ways, to recognize certain sorts of experiences; in the case of the brainstormers these might be called "aha" sensations, in the case of the students, aesthetic experiences. In any case the methods of brainstorming have much to suggest to the teacher of aesthetic matter. The em-

---

[16] Hanson, *Patterns of Discovery*, p. 19.

[17] See, for example, W. J. J. Gordon, *Synectics* (New York: Harper and Brothers, 1961).

phasis on emotional and personal involvement which is a distinguishing mark of these techniques amounts to a deliberate move away from the passivity of *knowing that* toward an experimental and active engagement with the problem. It is just this sort of engagement which is needed in the teaching of aesthetic content.

Another area where established educational programs exist is that of education of the religious (i.e., education for the religious life). The similarity of goals is striking, as is the similarity of problems. It must be fully as difficult to describe or define "sanctity" as it is to give an account of the nature of aesthetic experience. Certainly one cannot directly teach religious aspirants to be holy any more than one can teach football teams to win games or students to have aesthetic experiences. I do not doubt, however, that an examination of writings on the congregational life in Christianity (see for example the *Rule of St. Benedict,* or the *Spiritual Exercises* of St. Ignatius), or of the writings of the early Fathers, or of guides to the mystical life, would suggest methods of teaching students to *see as* which would go beyond *teaching that* or *teaching how.*[18]

A few words on testing are in order here. The usual test for *knowing that* involves a demonstration in words, as the test of *knowing how* involves a demonstration of skill. But where the student *knows that* he is supposed to *see* something *as,* a verbal demonstration must leave the teacher in ignorance as to whether the student has actually *seen* the object *as,* or whether he merely *knows that* the object is to be *seen as.* This problem can be avoided by deliberately not telling the student what we are trying to get him to *see* the work of art *as.* In so doing, however, the teacher deprives himself of a most useful method, i.e., *telling that.* Another kind of test, showing the student a similar work of art and asking him to describe how he sees it, avoids this problem but raises another.

---

18 See, for example, Robert Ulich, *Three Thousand Years of Educational Wisdom* (Cambridge: Harvard University Press, 1954), pp. 3–201.

It rests on the assumption that success in *seeing as* is subject to transfer. To the extent that this is so *seeing as* can be treated as a skill, and I should want to be wary of such a claim (just as one would not wish to claim, for example, that sanctity is a skill, though the acquisition of certain skills may be relevant to the attainment of sanctity). Finally one may claim that the proper experience of art (*seeing* it *as* having unity, complexity, and intensity—or something on this order) will have a subtle and pervasive influence on the experiencer, and furthermore that such influence can be assessed over a period of time by the onlooker. This is analogous to saying that while we cannot give tests for sanctity, as we *can* give tests for knowing the themes of A *Portrait of the Artist* or for knowing how to swim, we can assess its presence in a person over a period of time (perhaps the phrase "the odor of sanctity" gives testimony to the peculiar nature of this apprehension). This is not very satisfactory from the point of view of speed and efficiency, but does perhaps leave room in teaching for greater variety and efficiency of method. In the last analysis, if something has to go by the board, this writer would prefer to see efficiency of testing sacrificed for the sake of improvement in methods of teaching aesthetic contents.

IV

Let us devote this final section to a brief assessment of what has gone before. I hope to point out once again the advantages of what I have been trying to do, but I should be less than candid if I did not indicate some unavoidable problems. Perhaps it can be shown by someone else that these problems are not as difficult as they appear to me to be.

In this paper I have attempted to develop a model or account of aesthetic experience which would lend itself readily to analysis of problems of teaching and learning. The decision to take over Wittgenstein's distinction between *seeing* and *seeing as* was motivated by three main considerations. First, I wanted to avoid an excessive emphasis on verification and the problems engendered by it. If the critic's job (as also the teacher's —the two roles are closely intertwined) is seen exclusively as the utterance of true statements about the work of art, then our attention is directed toward matters of verification, and it is simply taken for granted that a statement properly verified is a piece of successful communication. I have desired to show that this need not be the case; that the measure of the usefulness of critical activity must come in terms of the reader's experience. This seems to me to make for a more just appraisal of success in teaching, while still allowing the teacher a reasonable scope for the utterance of true statements. The introduction of the concept of *seeing as* strikes me as a singularly apt device for avoiding this problem. The second reason for adopting Wittgenstein's distinction stems from considerations of simplicity. Of the various modes of perception, vision is the most direct and phenomenally the simplest. Casting an account of aesthetic experience in terms of visual perception was a calculated risk. I stood to gain in economy and ease of developing the model. I stood to lose if the notion could not be generalized for consideration of music and literature. It seems to me that in fact there *are* problems of generalization, and I give an account of the most serious one a bit further on. The third main reason for adopting Wittgenstein's distinction was that it enabled me to set up a comparison of teaching methods and problems of testing in cases where the end of teaching involves the acquisition of a disposition on the one hand (*knowing that*), and having experiences not subject to dispositional incorporation on the other (*seeing as*). We all know in our bones that *teaching appreciation* is different from *teaching that*. What I was looking for was a way of making these differences explicit with some degree of logical rigor.

So much for the intent of this essay. It now remains to describe briefly two difficulties which I have not been able to resolve. I think it significant that both arise in connection with the claim that aesthetic experience can be explained in terms of *seeing as.* They are as follows: (1) Are we really entitled to talk about *seeing* a painting *as unified?* May not such concepts as unity, complexity, and intensity be too abstract for us to talk of perceiving them? (2) Suppose that *seeing as* is an adequate model for aesthetic experience with respect to the visual arts, will it do for music and literature? Can we talk of *hearing as* and *taking as,* or some variation of these terms?

I do not feel that I can give an adequate answer to either of these questions, though I feel that both are important. The distinction between representational aspect and qualitative aspect seems sound to me. I think it makes sense to talk either of *seeing* a diagram *as* a duck or to talk about *seeing* two colors *as* complementary. The difficulty appears to arise when one attempts to move up the scale of generality, for it should be clear that not every property of an object is a quality (is directly perceivable), and it would appear that the more general and abstract the property we are attributing to a work of art the less likely it is that an object can be *seen as* having it. Still, the injunction "*See* it *as* unified" does not sound nonsensical on the face of it. Furthermore, unity and complexity are clearly more defensible in conjunction with admonitions to "See it as——" than is intensity, for the former point to formal properties of the work, whereas the latter is directed less to the work in isolation than to its relations with the world around. Is such a relationship a proper object of perception? I doubt that this is always the case.

As for the applicability of our model for the nonvisual arts, let us consider only literature, as it offers the greatest difficulty. Again, the question is one of how we are to interpret the injunction "*See* it *as* unified." Two options appear to be open. One would be to translate *seeing as* into some phrase more appropriate to our commerce with literature, for instance *taking as.* Clearly this step moves away from perception and toward conception. Frankly I would prefer a term which placed more emphasis on perceptual experience. An alternative would be to retain the phrase *seeing as* and to interpret it as a metaphor.

This I regard as a rather desperate remedy, and only to be resorted to if it should turn out to be impossible to put the case in straightforward terms. Nevertheless, it is the position I now find myself in, and I regard it as less than satisfactory.

Iredell Jenkins

There is a widely current adage to the effect that a successful teacher must be a good deal of an actor. There is an equally familiar adage that holds that students can learn only by doing. I am inclined to believe that each of these old saws contains a large measure of truth. But when we take them seriously and consider them together, they constitute something of a paradox. The first treats the teacher as a performer, and so makes of his students an audience, and the second insists that the students are performers, which would make the teacher their director. All of which leads one to think that an examination of the nature of performance might well throw some light on education. At all events, the possibility seems worth testing, and that is what I mean to do in this paper.

I

The performer starts with an artistic artifact, or first-order work of art. This is his script, score, choreography, or the like —what in general can be called his *text*: it is Shakespeare's *King Lear*, Beethoven's Quartet Opus 132, or a Balanchine ballet.

204 /

The challenge of the performer is to bring this text to full realization. For as it stands it is only a potential work of art, waiting to be made actual in performance and to be realized in the lived experience of an audience. The performer's text is an abbreviated and abstract version of the real work of art, as this has been felt by the artist who created it, and the performer must give it the finished and concrete form in which it can be felt by an audience.

The performance that effects this transformation is complex: if it is to be understood, its elements must be unraveled and its structure analyzed. As in similar operations, this vivisection threatens to kill the subject. But that risk must be taken, and it can be minimized by recognizing what is being done; something that is coherent and dynamic in its occurrence is being broken down into separate and static moments.

A performance is evidently a process; it has pattern, development, and direction. This process has two significant features. First, it consists primarily of a movement through which meanings that are only implicit in the performer's text are made explicit in his performance. Within this process we can distinguish three phases, or moments, which I shall arbitrarily call apprehension, expression, and embodiment. Second, this process as a whole, and each of its moments, is characterized by a double necessity: the performer must respect and realize the unique content and meaning of his text—of the work of art he is performing—but at the same time he must translate and embody this uniqueness in terms that are general and familiar, in order to make it publicly accessible and meaningful. In sum, in the course of a performance a work of art is being explicated, and this explication requires that the work be both exhibited and interpreted.

I am sadly aware that this brief statement of the elements and structure of performance must have little power of illumination or persuasion. But we need to start with a general and comprehensive view of the subject, for without such a framework the details now to be discussed would be isolated and unintelligible. Throughout the following discussion, it must be remembered that the moments and aspects identified above are not sharply distinct in their occurrence. They are always present from the inception of the process, they act reciprocally upon one another, and they merge gradually and cumulatively into a finished performance. Though these moments can legitimately be discriminated by analysis, they only actually exist as elements in a synthesis.

A performance is rooted in its text, and its success depends upon a clear and coherent apprehension of this. The performer's first acquaintance with his script or score is necessarily hurried and superficial: he is anxious to grasp the whole of this at once—to see not only how it begins but also how it develops and ends—and this impatience entails that much of its meaning remains vague and implicit. The performer's excitement about the possibilities of a text is the driving force of his performance, but this excitement must be disciplined and kept faithful to the actual meanings that its text imposes, not allowed to run wild with the possibilities it affords. In this latter case, performance degenerates into "free" or "impressionistic" interpretation, or into a mere exhibition of virtuosity. So the performer must set out to master his text. As indicated above, this effort confronts a double necessity and entails two distinct but integrated undertakings. One of these, very obviously, is a meticulous study of the text itself. The performer must read his script or score closely and repeatedly; he must elicit its latent meanings, explore its subtleties, clarify its intentions, and resolve any passages that are ambiguous or enigmatic. The attention of the performer is here focused sharply on his text, as he seeks to gather everything that this has to say for itself. But this very effort to be faithful to the text he is performing requires that the performer go beyond this and bring to bear upon it the body of his own experience and skill. No work of art is autonomous and self-explanatory. What it has to say must be couched in a language that is already understood and must appeal to a familiarity that is prepared for it.

That is, a work of art has no meaning in isolation, but only as part of an experiential context. So the performer must expand and fill in his text out of his own familiarity with the material it presents. He brings to his text the full weight of his knowledge, perception, emotion, and imagination. And if his experience seems inadequate to the demands imposed upon it, he purposely sets out to repair his deficiencies. It is not at all unusual—indeed, rather the contrary—for a performer either to discover for himself or to have it impressed upon him that he is too immature, naive, or inexperienced to understand properly the work he is trying to perform. Perhaps less obviously, but probably no more rarely, the performer's success will be impeded because his reading and treatment of his text are overly subtle, sophisticated, and cynical. This is to say that apprehension is a transaction between the performer and his text—with the author always looming behind this text, and often actually present to protect and interpret it. This transaction requires a delicate balance of innocence and worldly wisdom, of sympathy and guile. The performer must be sensitive and faithful to his text, but he must also supply to this the context of meanings that it assumes and requires in order to be itself. To the extent that this double effort succeeds, the performer moves toward a grasp of what the artist is talking about and what he is saying about this.

Concurrently with this effort to apprehend his text, the performer anticipates the finished form that he will give to this in his performance. This is the act of embodiment. As the performer first scans his text to get an overview of it, he simultaneously projects an idea (a design or draft) of the performance through which his apprehension is to be externalized and consummated. He envisages the characterization or rendition that he hopes to achieve and the devices by which this is to be realized. In a strict analytical sense, what the performer apprehends is a set of intangible and transient meanings, conveyed by the abstract symbols of his script or score; but in this very act of apprehension, these meanings are embodied in a medium, given a concrete and stable form, and so made publicly available. This embodiment again has a double character. On one hand it is highly individuated, being this performer's interpretation and projection of what his text says and intends. As such, it is a unique concretion of matter, form, and meaning. To realize this uniqueness, we need only compare different performances of the same play, sonata, or ballet. But on the other hand this unique embodiment must be realized in a medium that is already well established and highly organized. Every artist and performer necessarily works with what I shall call an artistic cosmos, which consists of a vast complex of themes, styles, idioms, symbols, techniques, manners of treatment, and so forth. This artistic cosmos defines the familiarities and the expectations of the public, and so imposes itself upon the performer—as upon the artist—as a condition of intelligibility. It is only in the terms set by this public domain that the performer can clarify and communicate his private vision. Of course, this cosmos is neither rigid nor permanent: it leaves room for artistic initiative and innovation, and it offers itself to be exploited in various ways. It is a bestowal and a blessing, in that it makes possible performance, as well as every other refined mode of communication; but it is also an imposition and confinement, in that it limits the reach and the manner of performance. The performer must accommodate himself to his artistic cosmos at the same time that he exploits it, for it is the only vehicle through which he can project and realize the meanings he has found in his text.

Apprehension and embodiment are the two poles between which performance moves. Looked at abstractly, in static and structural terms, these initial elements have a sort of independence and objectivity. Each of them is somehow "there" in consciousness; the apprehension is "given," the embodiment is "demanded," and between them they constitute the material with which the performer works. But this material is at first extremely raw, requiring much refinement and finishing. Looked at concretely, performance is the full expression—the making explicit and public—of what is originally only incipient. This work is a process of synthesis, consisting in the elaboration and fusion of the original apprehension and embodiment. Since each of these elements has the double character noted above, this synthesis requires the weaving together of four distinct strands. The performer must explicate his text fully and faithfully; he must elucidate and enrich this out of his own resources and experience; he must project his own interpretation of his text; and he must embody it through the medium of the current artistic cosmos. This process of expression constitutes the public performance that we encounter at the theater and concert hall.

This is not the place to enter into more detail concerning the problems the performer confronts, the skills he employs, and the procedures he follows in achieving this synthesis that is a finished performance. Indeed, there is not a great deal that can be said about these matters without leaving the realm of general analysis and entering into the specific performing arts. But there is one point that must be touched on briefly, not only for the direct light it throws on the nature of performance but even more for the illumination it reflects on the character and the challenge of education. This point concerns the ways in which a performance can go astray or be perverted.

It is extremely difficult to say with any precision just what makes a good performance. But it is child's play to put your finger on the flaws in a bad performance. To corroborate these claims, one need only compare a few favorable and unfavorable reviews of plays and concerts: the former are usually little more than rhetorical and impressionistic eulogies; the latter are painfully exact dissections. These adverse criticisms are normally found to fasten on one or more of four failures, which correspond to the double challenges posed by the apprehension and the embodiment with which the performer works. That is, his performance is judged to fail because it does not do justice to some of these elements it deals with and so does not achieve the fusion that it seeks. Of course, since a performance aims at a synthesis, a failure in one of its aspects entails failure in another: the performance fails as a whole, as a living creature dies. But this failure can be analyzed and its cause identified.

Critics often accuse performers of neglecting or abusing their text. Either the performer does not take the trouble to study his text closely and see what it says and intends, or he willfully distorts or abandons it, using it as a mere vehicle for the exploitation of his own personality. Even where a performer makes a sincere effort to master his text, he may fail because his resources of intellect and experience are not adequate to understand it. He may lack the sensitivity, the depth of feeling, the quick imagination to follow the clues the author provides; or his acquaintance, either direct or vicarious, with the subject his text treats and the manner of treatment it employs (the symbols, style, idiom, and so forth) may be deficient. In sum, apprehension fails either because it does not bring its text into focus or because it cannot supply the context that this requires. Analogous failures haunt the other pole around which a performance revolves. We often hear a performance criticized on the ground that it is not sufficiently distinctive and individuated: it is characterized as "routine," "uninspired," "mechanical," or "shallow." It is felt that the actor has not successfully "captured" or "realized" his character, or that the concert musician has not "entered into" the concerto and "made it his own." The performer here stands accused of having no definite idea of how his text should be embodied; he merely applies acquired skills and inherited techniques and follows direction without any conception of what he is trying to create. In short, he handles his artistic cosmos quite expertly, but he has no idea what to do with it. But a performer is equally apt to fail if he neglects to master his artistic cosmos or tries to escape its grip and operate independently of it. If the vision (the interpretation of his text) that a performer seeks to embody is highly personal and novel, he may feel his artistic cosmos as a confinement he must shatter or an encumbrance he must

210 /

throw off. In such a case, a performance may be highly stimulating and challenging, but it will also be largely unintelligible. We sense that the performer is trying desperately to say something significant but in a language that he has not yet mastered and that we do not anyway understand. This collapse of communication leads finally to frustration on both parts: the performer feels rejected and we feel betrayed.

Running through all of these modes of failure is the disintegration of performance into its constituent elements; these become isolated and compete with one another instead of fusing into a coherent whole. The performer's text, his interpretation, the embodiment he projects, and the techniques he employs clamor separately for our attention, which shifts erratically from one to the other of these and never achieves more than a partial and temporary synthesis. What was meant to be a vibrant and unified whole is decomposed into dead and scattered parts.

In brief conclusion of this phase of my inquiry, I would urge that both artist and audience are in essentially the same situation as the performer. They confront a similar challenge, pursue a similar end, and encounter similar difficulties. All begin with a text—a concretion of matter, form, and symbol—that is enigmatic and fragmentary, and they have to discover and realize for themselves the meanings implicit in it. The performer's text is a script or score that he must apprehend, express, and embody. The artist's text is seemingly nature itself (the book of life and the furniture of the world) as illuminated by his own sensitivity. But it is interesting to note that artists often take their point of departure from already existent artistic artifacts; they transform novels into plays, operas, and ballets; they make songs from poems and poetry for melodies; tales inspire paintings, and vice versa; historical personages and episodes are a rich mine of artistic raw material; and in our fascination with the "free spirit" of artists, we forget how much of their work has always been done on commission, with its conditions set quite closely. The audience's text is an artistic artifact, but no matter how carefully this is contrived to control and guide response, it is still no more than a collection of clues that must be interpreted individually and followed successively if they are to lead anywhere and issue in anything. So the artist's text is not as raw as it first appears, nor is that of the audience as finished. And both artist and audience transform their text into something it was not originally; that is, they assume the role of performers, and perform before themselves. It is only through performance, in the sense here given to that term, that aesthetic values can be clearly and firmly grasped.

II

Now what is the meaning of this for education? Everything, I think. For I would argue that education is itself a mode of performance—that it is, indeed, at once the protean form and the apotheosis of performance. To pursue an education is to engage in the art of performing. We become educated just to the degree that we become accomplished performers of ourselves.

If this analogy is to be fruitful and persuasive, we must take seriously the etymology of the word "education." It derives from the Latin *educere*, which means "to lead forth," "to draw out," "to bring up." *Educere* carries the meaning of an act that frees something that has been in captivity or confinement, that discloses what was hitherto hidden, that removes hindrances and brings things to their proper condition. Put more abstractly, *educere* refers to a process which leads from the implicit to the explicit, from the inarticulate to the expressed, from the incipient to the fully realized.

To point this out is certainly not to announce a startling discovery. This derivation and meaning are known to every educated person and acknowledged by every educator. But in our practice we largely contradict what we proclaim. We construct monolithic "educational systems," with tables of organizations, curricula, programs, and so forth; we speak of "giving an education" to people, and we refer to a person as "educated" when

212 /

he has gone through a prescribed course of study; we think of "educational requirements" rather from the point of view of society than of individuals. In sum, we treat education as a formalized routine that is more or less the same for everyone and is altogether external to those who take part in it. People "enter upon" and "finish" their educations rather like contestants in an obstacle race. All of this being the case, it should not only refresh but even refine our understanding of education if we follow out carefully the analogy with performance.

This analogy tells us, in general terms, that education is a process that involves the apprehension, expression, and embodiment of the person himself who is becoming educated. In this process, the text with which we work is the self. This text is given to us, just as is the script or score of the artistic performer. It consists of the whole bundle of characteristics with which we are born: physical size, structure, and type; physiological and neurological morphology; and the various psychic qualities that we refer to as talents, capabilities, abilities, weaknesses, limitations, predispositions, tastes, tendencies, and so forth. From the most primitive times, it has been recognized that every man bore within him this element of individuation, which gave him life and a manner of life, made him a unique person, and controlled his destiny. After a long career full of vicissitudes and shifting identities—such as vital spirit, soul, telos, essence, ego, hereditary endowment—this has become for us the highly respectable scientific concept of the genotype. There is unquestionably an enormous gain in precision and power from the earliest to the latest of these interpretations. But they all convey a common central doctrine: that the nature and meaning of human existence are found in the unfolding, development, and realization of a nature given to man at his beginning. This is the text that we perform in education.

The first necessity that confronts this performance, as any other, is to apprehend its text. Socrates acknowledged this fact in his dictum "know thyself"; we pay homage to it in the elaborate batteries of tests that we give to young people to measure their intelligence, aptitudes, skills, interests, preferences, and anything else that we think might be helpful in exposing a person's potential. Self-awareness is both the driving spur and the guiding rein of education in the true sense; without its constant presence, the process degenerates into the acquisition of miscellaneous facts and skills and conformity to extraneous models, all of which may be quite irrelevant, or even alien, to the person being educated. This text that is the self has two important general characteristics that must be borne in mind in our reading of it. In the first place, it has both specific and individual aspects: it represents at once the replication of a type and the genesis of a unique person. Every human being has much in common with all other human beings, especially as regards basic physical, physiological, and psychic structures and functions. It is this fact that justifies our formal and routine educational procedures, such as curricula, programs, courses of study, and so forth. But every person is also unique, and this requires that our educational system allow this uniqueness to assert and express itself and to find the substance it needs. This dualism is responsible for much of the tension and disruption that characterize formal education, such as the failures, the dropouts, the disillusioned, and the contemporary student rebels. The educator is naturally apt to center attention on the common and typical characteristics and needs of students; it is in this way that he can most easily know them and deal with them. And it is a legitimate and important part of the educator's task to transform his students into normal mature human beings. So as he reads the text of his students' personalities, he looks for common traits, he expects to find common abilities, and he seeks to secure a standard performance. On the other hand, those who are being educated are strongly aware of their individualities. Each is reading a private text, and is intent on performing this in a way to give it the fullest expression. Both his awareness of his self and his aspirations for this point him along a unique line toward a unique goal. So in the context of formal education he is looking for

214 /

what will help him to play the role and assume the character that he envisages for himself. In sum, the teacher tends to see himself as training a chorus, while each student asks to be treated as the star of the piece.

The second important characteristic of the self is its extraordinary plasticity. Far more even than any artistic text, it permits of various interpretations. Of course, the form or genotype that we carry within us does define certain patterns, courses, and norms of development. As it is now often put, the genotype is a complex code that transmits information, "telling" the organism what to do and when and how to do it. But all of this constitutes only a general framework—the outline of a plot and a sketchy characterization—and within the limits it sets the human endowment is highly plastic. This plasticity has two significant aspects. First, it means that every person is capable of various becomings and outcomes. The human potential is rich and flexible, permitting of different developments toward different ends. Men are not foredoomed to a rigid life sequence but face large alternatives as to what they are to do and be. Second, this plasticity means that the potentialities of the self are not realized automatically and spontaneously. Rather, they must be carefully trained and nurtured. Man must decide what alternatives to follow and must pursue these with discipline and cultivation. If a person does not choose to be something, he will be nothing, for a mature and realized human being is less a product of nature than of art—or, more exactly, of education. When we first acquire a sharp self-consciousness and become aware of the text it is our happy lot to interpret, it is the first of these aspects that most vividly impresses us. We have an enormous sense of our possibilities and powers and of what we can do with them: we are going to be a fireman, a cowboy, a locomotive engineer, a farmer, a deep-sea diver, a soldier, and hundreds of other things. And even much later in life we see ourselves as writing the great American novel, making vast scientific discoveries, devising a plan for perpetual peace, dominating the stock market, sitting on the Supreme Court, or being a renowned scholar. It is a long and painful path to the realization that though all of these outcomes may be abstractly possible, very few of them can be made concretely actual. Possibilities are mutually exclusive, our own time and energy are finite, and the world imposes its harsh conditions. We now come to the tragic recognition that we must make hard choices and must eliminate far more than we select out of the text we are given. That is, we learn that every "yes" we give to life entails an infinity of "no's." With this, apprehension is well on its way to embodiment, and our interpretation of the text that is the self begins to take on a definite objective form. But before dealing explicitly with this phase of the educational performance, there is something else to be noted of the text that is originally given us.

For this text, like any other, is not autonomous and does not exist in isolation: the self has its full being and meaning only in a social and cultural context. Every person is born not only with a genotype but in a situation. He is precipitated into a complex environment and set of relationships which are antecedent to him; and so he finds himself occupying various places and playing various roles that have been arbitrarily assigned to him. His situation makes him an older or younger sibling, rich or poor, of the upper or middle or lower class, white or black or yellow, with cultured or illiterate parents, in a happy family or a broken one, Protestant or Catholic or atheist, and so on through a multitude of dimensions. The text that a person apprehends—the self that he is to educate—is largely molded by this situation, both in fact and in his interpretation of it. Men are not the hapless victims of fate. We are ineluctably born into situations. But we can succumb to them or exploit them. And this exploitation can itself take many forms. Still, the situation in which the self is placed has a great deal to do with its manner of development, just as the environment of soil, water, and sun has with a seed. And this relationship is greatly complicated for man by the fact that he not only has a situation, but is conscious of it. Indeed, the way in which a person feels and experiences his situation—its advantages and disadvantages, its opportunities and demands, its possibilities and frustrations—is probably more important than the situation itself. Different individuals will respond to the same situation in radically different terms: one will feel deprivations where another finds challenges, and one will claim privileges where another acknowledges responsibilities.

From the point of view of education, the most significant point about genotype and situation is that they are open structures. If human development were as automatic and predetermined as the transition from acorn to oak, and if the social milieu were as rigid and as uncompromising as the natural ecology, then education—as the term is here used—would be both unnecessary and impossible. All that would be required would be a minimal amount of training and indoctrination to prepare men for the places they were to occupy and the parts they were to play. But since the self is plastic and its surroundings are fluid, man is educable and must be educated. And this education can be relevant and meaningful only if it is based on a sound apprehension of the self. Every person needs to explore his talents and interests, to measure his powers and limitations, to assess his situation and what it offers him. In becoming educated, as in other modes of performance, we can do a great deal to enrich and expand our text; but if we too much disregard or distort it, we destroy it. This is not too serious in the case of an artistic text, as it survives to await a happier performance. The self gets performed only once; so if we seriously misread its text, correction is impossible.

Here as elsewhere, embodiment proceeds concurrently with apprehension. As self-awareness comes, with its sense of our diverse powers and the possibilities the world offers these, we begin to create careers and personalities for ourselves. From the start these exhibit the double character that we would expect: they express and envisage an absolutely unique person, an individual who stands alone, who is to be and do what no one has been or done before; they also reflect very largely the ideals, images, and models that are current in the social milieu. Every man, to a greater or lesser degree, feels his uniqueness and integrity and seeks to preserve them in the personality he projects; but he can embody this only in the vocabulary of purposes, standards, and accomplishments that his society recommends to him.

At first these projections tend to be highly incomplete and transient. They do not take any precise shape but remain vague and general: they are types or patterns that we mean to embody, guises that we intend to assume. Further, they lead only a brief existence, succeeding one another rapidly, not taking a firm hold upon the self and not generating any programs for their accomplishment: they are ends of which we briefly dream but for which we plan no means. They reflect various facets of the self as this develops and various social models that we encounter as the range of our experience increases.

In time, the embodiment that we envisage assumes a more definite and stable form. We discard a good many of the outcomes we earlier cherished, rejecting them as "childish fancies," "youthful follies," or "impossible dreams." We assess our abilities and skills, take account of our background and position, and come to what we call a "realistic" appraisal of ourselves. Simultaneously, society influences the terms and manner of this embodiment in many ways, some grossly obvious and objectionable, some so subtle as to be subliminal. It inculcates certain norms, ideals, and values that it hopes—with little faith and less justification—we will incorporate in the selves we embody. More practically and effectively, we are given a quite clear idea of what is socially accepted, approved, and rewarded. We learn that there are stereotypes to which we must conform and patterns of success that we must follow. To some extent, all of this occurs quite naturally and unconsciously, without real purpose or planning on our part; it is a function of personal development and social pressure, of genotype and situation. We mature, as both individual and social beings. And the necessities of life compel us to narrow our choices and accept the accommodations that are offered. But if this process is left to the play of only these forces, it is fatally vulnerable to accident and ignorance. So maturation must be supplemented by education.

The function of education is to help men to perform the texts they are given, that is, to realize their own best potentialities. Success in this effort depends upon the refinement and fusion of the four strands with which it deals. The process starts with a self in a situation and moves toward a unique personality pursuing a career that is socially adjusted and effective. As with any performance, each of these must receive the proper attention, and they must be brought into a satisfactory synthesis. So the task and problems, as well as the failures, that confront education follow from its character as performance; they repeat the pattern traced in the preceding section, and a detailed discussion of them would be redundant. However, there are three salient points that distinguish education from other modes of performance. These rest on differences of degree, not of kind. But these differences are sufficiently large to have a significant effect, and a consideration of them will bring out some of the crucial features and difficulties of education.

The most obvious of these differences lies in the fact that the educational performance revolves around those who are directing it rather than those who are performing it. The structure and content of education, as well as the manner in which it is conducted, are all defined and controlled a great deal more by teachers than by students; and both of these, even, are overshadowed by the vast and impersonal pressure of "the educational system." Of course, this difference is not absolute. By the time an artistic performer begins his public career he has undergone a long period of training and formation, and he is never far removed from the influence of directors, coaches, and conductors. But the difference is still important, for this closely defined and controlled performance constitutes the student's education, while it merely prepares the artistic performer for his career. A second distinguishing feature of education is the incompleteness and inaccessibility of the text with which it works. The scripts and scores that artists have to perform are often pretty messy affairs, full of deletions, interlinings, and last-minute additions; and they may undergo further change while the performance is being prepared and even presented. But at least they are relatively finished, stable, and open to inspection. The case is quite otherwise with the self that is to be educated. This is certainly given, and is effectively present, whether we acknowledge it as genotype, endowment, essence, or telos. But its presence is potential, or implicit; its being, so to speak, lies in its becoming; and it makes itself fully known only in the course of its history and realization. So the performance that is education takes its start from a text that is largely inscrutable and whose various possibilities justify divergent interpretations. We can read the text of the self only as we perform it, and as we correct our reading it is often too late to incorporate this in our performance. This leads directly to the third distinctive feature of education: we can perform the self only once. This performance is not repeatable, which means that we cannot, in the light of later developments, go back, wipe the slate clean, and modify our reading of earlier portions of the text. The interpretation of an artistic text grows and changes in the course of performance. In education the text itself is modified and can never be restored to its original state. A script or score endures with its meaning intact. A self ages and can never recover its innocence.

If we consider these three features in conjunction, which is the way they always occur, we can get a clearer idea of the pitfalls that particularly threaten education and the steps by which these can be avoided—or at least our fall into them can be broken. We have noted the utterly obvious fact that teachers and institutions exert a pervasive influence over the educational performance. We have also noted that the texts that are being performed—the unique selves of individual students

—are largely incomplete and inaccessible. This being the case, there is a strong tendency for a single generalized text to be substituted for the many and multifarious texts that the students carry within them. Since these texts are private and inscrutable, neither teacher nor students can really know before the event what sort of performance best suits them. Teachers generalize from past experience: they plan curricula, organize courses, classify students, set examinations, and devise grading systems. Students confirm or disconfirm by future experience: they discover unsuspected facets of their personalities, they develop novel interests, the meanings they find in life and the world become wider and more coherent; or, on the other hand, they find themselves on a forced march through a dull and barren landscape. It is a revealing fact that if you ask a teacher what he teaches, in at least ninety-nine cases out of a hundred he will tell you the titles of his courses, not the names of his students. It is equally revealing that when students prepare for examination, they pay more attention to the character of the teacher—his opinions, interests, prejudices, interpretations, and so forth—than to the content of the course. Admittedly, this picture is to some extent an exaggeration. Any good educational system tries to allow for individual differences and to offer programs that will accommodate a variety of abilities and interests. And any good teacher tries to take account of the personalities of his students and to get them involved as active participants. But this picture is not, I think, a caricature. And to the extent that the shoe fits, it indicates that the educational process is badly subverted. For now the teacher is transformed into the sole performer, while the students are relegated to the passive role of members of the audience.

This danger of substitution is cushioned by the fact that its threat is widely recognized. But unfortunately it is reinforced by the intrusion into education of the alien ideals of democratic egalitarianism and libertarianism. Democracy is essentially a political creed. It stipulates that for its purposes, and in special and limited respects, men are to be regarded as free and equal. For government and for law, men are taken as identical; each is to count for one, regardless of personal merits or demerits, situation, status, or past history. Furthermore, each man has the right to think, speak, and act as he sees fit, so long as he does not impinge on the similar rights of others or violate the rules that serve the common good. Politically and legally, it is as though life had a gigantic eraser that wiped the slate clean every instant and everyone started naked and fresh. There is no need either to challenge or defend the value of these ideas in their original sphere; they have long proved their worth. But there is serious need to question their applicability in the field of education. There is no doubt of the influence of these ideas; they have penetrated the attitudes, the purposes, and the procedures of education. Educators are led to believe that all students must somehow be equal, and certainly ought to be, even if they don't seem to be. So they are reluctant to acknowledge, and even more to act upon, the inequalities that they inevitably discover. They assume that all selves have the same potential and occupy the same situation. They then devise an educational system that is geared to a generalized idea of the text to be performed and of the situation of the performers, with this generalized idea being itself the joint product of statistics and self-projection. But however much educators may deplore and deny inequalities, they are forced to accept individual differences and the right of individuals to express these differences. So they provide for the libertarian cult by installing a wide variety of generalized programs, among which students are free to exercise the rights of choice, change, and manipulation in any way they like. In short, education stipulates that for its purposes students are to be regarded as free and equal. And this is a travesty of the educational performance; it ignores the texts to be performed, it neglects the background that gives these much of their meaning, it treats the members of the cast as though they were collectively a chorus and individually star performers, and it supplies no plot at all but only a series of disjointed scenes. What this issues in is not a performance but a "happening."

The motivation behind these procedures is laudable: it seeks to protect the student against arbitrary assignment to a role and strict direction in its performance. It is based on the recognition of the double truth that the self—the text we perform in becoming educated—only becomes accessible in the course of its performance, and that this performance is itself unique and unrepeatable. From this there follows a double obligation. First, education should provide a setting for performance—an intellectual milieu—that is relevant to the real interests of students and the actual situation they confront. Second, the educational process, or performance, should be such that the reading of the text of the self—the student's embodiment of his personality and career—can be kept flexible and tentative. In short, education should prepare students to play many roles, but should commit them to none.

The egalitarian and libertarian manner of discharging this obligation is to provide a smorgasbord where students can sample at will and then help themselves to what they prefer. The failure of this technique has been suspected for some time and has now been abundantly proved by widespread student unrest, culminating in the familiar rebellions and riots. But such failure could have been predicted all along, for this technique rests upon the mistaken assumption that we can discover ourselves and fulfill our destinies by blind trial and error; that is, it exemplifies the application to education of the Baconian method of inductive generalization. This method has long been discredited in scientific circles, and it is high time that education followed suit.

For it is not enough for education merely to expose students to various accumulations of facts, ideas, and skills. It must transmit a tradition, which is the analogue, on a far larger scale, of an artistic cosmos. For our present purposes, the significant fact about a tradition is that it has no real present. It summarizes the past and anticipates the future, but it undergoes perpetual change through a specious present. This fact naturally gives rise to different manners of treatment. The school of thought I have just discussed seeks to guarantee change and the openness of the future, but in doing this it sacrifices continuity with the past and coherence in the present. It is so fearful of indoctrinating students that it fails even to initiate them. The opposite approach is equally prevalent: it is so impressed with the achievement of the past, embodied in history, literature, doctrines, and techniques, that it comes to regard this as an end in itself, quite apart from its relevance or irrelevance for the present and future. Overcome by inertia, it denies any necessity to adapt to change.

Life challenges education to secure a synthesis of these views. I obviously—and fortunately—cannot deal with that vast matter here. But I think that the analogy with performance might suggest one final clue that points toward an answer. The focus of education should be shifted from subject matters to problems. The advantages that this promises are simple and straightforward. Subject matters are antecedent and extraneous to the self. They are closed systems, containing within themselves the answers to the questions they pose. They ask nothing of us, merely offering themselves for our acquisition. We learn subject matters by acceptance and repetition. Our relation to them and their expounders is that of an audience. Given these characteristics, it is highly improbable that our encounter with a subject matter will give rise to a performance, in even the most attenuated metaphorical sense of the term. In order for this to occur, we must become dissatisfied with certain elements of the subject matter and so transform these into problems.

For a problem confronts us in a very different manner, and the response that it solicits from us is quite literally a performance. Problems are open and incomplete, with their solutions lying ahead of them. Their very uncertainty—their undisclosed balance of threat and promise—makes them personally rele-

224 /

vant; however remote and hypothetical they may at first appear, we realize that they may engulf us, so they arouse our concern. Problems issue from the past, they exist in the present, and they point toward the future. Since they are unsolved, they draw us into themselves, and the movement toward their solution involves us as participants and even contributors. Finally, problems serve as double foci of synthesis: various disciplines must be brought to bear to solve any of them, and every problem leads beyond itself to others.

Problems confront us with difficulties and challenges, whether these be near or remote, actual or hypothetical. So they immediately turn our attention to the self and its situation. To measure their impingement upon us, we must measure ourselves: we take stock of our resources and abilities, our purposes and standards are called into play, our prejudices and opinions are brought into the open, our background, status, and prospects come under consideration. Any problem, to a greater or lesser degree, incites us to the effort of self-apprehension. But furthermore, problems demand that we take a position with regard to them: we must consider various possible solutions, weigh their relative practicality and merit, estimate their outcomes, and take a stand. To deal with a problem, either in theory or practice, is to become involved in change; both we and the world are to become different. So we are called to a fresh consideration of our own values and goals, as well as of the avowed standards and the actual practices that are current in society. When we become seriously concerned about any problem, we necessarily challenge the framework of our lives, both personal and public. And when we commit ourselves to a particular resolution of a problem, we necessarily project a new embodiment based on a new apprehension.

A subject-matter approach tends to turn problems into dead issues. When we put the problem itself at the center of attention, it becomes vital and urgent. To deal with problems under the vicarious conditions of the classroom, in relative leisure and detachment, with constant exposure to other points of view and with our own under intense criticism, and without the awful finality of irrevocable commitment—this is to perform the self under the happiest of conditions. It is to become educated.

PERSUASION: ÆSTHETIC ARGUMENT

AND THE LANGUAGE OF TEACHING / 10

Brian S. Crittenden

Teaching and Persuading

Persuading is an important speech activity in which a teacher frequently engages. It is not as though a certain amount of persuasion insinuates itself into didactic language despite the teacher's effort. On the contrary, even if it were possible for him to eliminate persuasion entirely, he should not try to do so. For the teacher is not in the position of an anthropologist attempting as nearly as possible simply to describe the beliefs and values, the ways of thinking and so on, which characterize some primitive society. The teacher does not merely report to his class that a line of reasoning in algebra is considered valid by expert mathematicians or that scientists commonly believe that a certain hypothesis provides a satisfactory explanation for certain phenomena, and why they believe this way. If the activity is to be *education* in mathematics or science it is necessary to consider directly whether the argument is really valid and whether the evidence in support of the hypothesis is really adequate. Moreover, unless we are dealing only with a pretence of teaching and learning, the mathematics teacher must himself see the conclusion as entailed by the premises and be trying to bring his students to see it in the same way. The students, for their part, must also be trying to grasp the connection. If they are content simply to commit the argument to memory or to acquire the information that this argument is commonly believed to be valid by expert mathematicians, they are not strictly learning mathematics.

In any episode within the total process of education the teacher is engaged in making many truth or other value claims: X is true, probable, valid, doubtful, false, desirable, etc. A distinguishing feature of his making these claims as a teacher is that he is attempting to persuade others to see X in the same way. It should also be noticed that apart from persuasion in reference to particular procedures, arguments, theories, and the like, the teacher must be presumed to believe that the total effort of becoming educated, to which he deliberately contributes, is worthwhile. Although the teacher may judge that details in the process are irrelevant or antithetical to the ideal of being educated, his work may be characterized as being in a general way an attempt not simply to describe and explain the ideal but to persuade his students that it is worthwhile.

At this level even if the teacher were playing the role of a purely descriptive anthropologist, he would at least be committed to persuading his students that this was the appropriate and worthwhile way to learn. The teacher's notion of education may be more or less true and adequate but, whatever it is, once he engages seriously in the task of teaching he undertakes to persuade systematically.

If persuasion is—or should be—so significant a part of a teacher's task, it is obvious that the concept deserves to be closely examined. This task is made more pressing because persuasion is one of those terms whose reputation has been rather tarnished in recent years. We have been made uncomfortably aware of the hidden variety of persuaders, and we have hardly needed anyone to point out the less subtle practitioners who cajole us every day in print and on radio and television. I believe that a careful analysis of the logic of aesthetic argument will provide a clearer understanding of the form of persuasion that is appropriate to the process of teaching and learning.

Observing an Object Aesthetically

When a person in a context of critical evaluation seriously claims that a certain group of novels, for example, has great artistic merit while another (say detective stories) has scarcely any, we expect him to be able to furnish some justification for his preference. In such a context we do not assume that the speaker is talking about the present state of his feelings; it is quite consistent with his judgment of the novels that he might sometimes feel more like reading a detective story. Nor do we suppose that he is merely reporting on his attitude to the two groups of books. We would not find an appeal to his pro and con attitudes as being a satisfactory reason, in the circumstances, for his claim. Precisely because these attitudes are at least contextually implied by the critic's claim, they are part of what we expect him to justify.[1]

In attempting to examine the basic features of an aesthetic argument, I think it is first necessary to consider what constitutes an *aesthetic* claim (or judgment) and the kind of evidence which is relevant to its support. In order to avoid difficulties which do not bear on this discussion I will refer only to the appreciation of human productions which are unhesitatingly recognized as being examples of some form of art. It is true of course that the question of whether an object is a work of art of a particular kind is sometimes a crucial part of the evaluation. Still, there are many occasions when critics are agreed that an object is a play or a painting or a piece of sculpture and the question to be answered is just how good a one it is.[2]

---

[1] See P. H. Nowell-Smith, *Ethics* (London: Penguin Books, 1964), for discussion of pro and con attitudes (pp. 112–21 *passim*) and for contextual implication (pp. 80–83).

[2] Of course some theorists, such as R. G. Collingwood and Susanne Langer, use "work of art" only for objects with positive aesthetic value.

It should also be observed that the mere classification of an object as an example of an art form does not imply any conscious awareness of its distinctively aesthetic aspects. Most people, including those of minimal education, can accurately recognize paintings and statues among the things they see, detect certain sounds as music, and tell when someone is reciting a poem. That is, they may correctly name an object of art without necessarily attending to the features which distinguish it as art. It follows that when people go beyond naming a work of art and respond affectively to it, or express their opinion of its value, the experience or judgment may not be (at least predominantly) aesthetic. A group of people who have just seen the performance of a play may be excitedly assessing it in terms of high praise. They are all delighted and think it an excellent play. However, we will probably not gain any clue about the aesthetic character of their assessments simply by examining the language in which they are expressed. Even the term "beautiful" can be used ambiguously in this context. Nor can anything be gained by directly attending to the kinds of feelings the observers have. There is no pattern of feelings which we can immediately identify as "aesthetic." When a person believes he is responding to an object specifically as a work of art, he naturally describes any definite feelings he has on such an occasion as aesthetic. Whether the judgment and experience of the object are aesthetic depends on how the object is seen and this will only be revealed in the kind of reasons one gives for his appraisals and in the explanation of his affective response. The play may be thought to be excellent because it is a financial success, or has made the author into a celebrity, or its characters and the action are historically accurate, or it presents an enlightened view on homosexuality, or it is motivating people to engage in demonstrations against the government. One person is seeing the play primarily as a business venture, another as a moral tract, another as an instrument of social reform, and so on.

What, then, is involved in seeing a play or other work of

230 /

art *aesthetically?* In a predominantly aesthetic appreciation (as distinct from one that is economic, intellectual, moral, etc.) the focus of attention is on the perceptual features of the object as they relate to one another in the pattern of the whole.[3] The perceptual may be extended here to include the recognition of features in terms of human emotions since these are typically, although not necessarily, depicted or evoked in works of art. One can recognize this close involvement of the emotions in all forms of art without having to espouse the theory of expressionism. In a work of art various materials are put together so that in the perceptual experience human beings are affected in a certain way. Works of art draw on the large store of associations, either "natural" or conventional, between sensations, feelings, and attitudes. Music may be sad, a shape may suggest speed, in one context the color red may be a symbol of life and in another of purification.

To offset any false impression of a sharp division among raw sensations, emotions, and thoughts, and as a basis for a correct understanding of aesthetic argument, I must here comment at least briefly on the logical aspects of observation. In the first place, seeing (which I will use as the example) is not simply a physical and physiological process—involving light waves, the sense organ, and nervous system—in which the viewer has a perceptual experience, and to which, if he desires, he may give an interpretation by drawing on his store of concepts and theories. As Hanson points out, there is more in seeing than meets the eye.[4] Along with the notion of visual sensation, the concept of seeing includes that of cognition. The two aspects are tied together from the very beginning in our learning of language (ostension and naming) and even before language de-

---

[3] This also applies to the aesthetic appreciation of objects which are not works of art, although in these cases particular perceptual features are more likely to be detached from the object as a whole: e.g., the scent or odor of a rose appreciated quite independently of its shape.

[4] See N. R. Hanson, *Patterns of Discovery* (Cambridge: Cambridge University Press, 1958), chap. I.

velops, in the infant's deliberate, purposeful discrimination of his perceptual field.

On innumerable occasions every day our acts of seeing occur without involving a judgment or any kind of conscious reflective process. I see a tree and I see that the tree is green without argument or inference. However, it is clear that when we visually experience even the common and familiar objects of our environment, theories and other cognitive elements inevitably enter in. In a sense, even these acts of seeing are really "seeing as." But because the knowledge involved is so generally possessed and our descriptions of such objects so confirmed, we do not say "I see it as a tree" or "It looks like a tree to me." Of course such an expression would be used even here if, for any reason, we believed that we were not seeing a real tree or that the physical and physiological conditions were abnormal.

When specialized knowledge and affective associations are involved they may be relevant to "seeing" in two basic ways. First, one may simply see the same object as before but describe it in a different way: I see a tree, a willow, a symbol of hope; I see an old man, I see one of the greatest living musicians, I see Stravinsky. It should be noticed that in such cases, although the observers may be presumed to see the same features in the objects to which the different descriptions refer, one would expect their total experience in seeing the objects to vary. Two observers seeing the same person walking along the street can both give exact descriptions of his appearance, clothing, and so on; however, one sees a stranger while the other sees a friend.

Second, because of special knowledge an observer may in fact be seeing a different object, or at least different perceptual features, from anyone who lacks the knowledge. In relatively simple cases the informed observer would no doubt argree that the object he saw could be described or classified in layman's terms. A forestry expert and a layman both see trees, and these are the objects to which the expert refers. However, he would emphasize that in the light of his knowledge, his attention is drawn not only to expected features but also to surprising ones which would otherwise not even be noticed. This difference in what is seen should be distinguished from the situation in which two people agree fully on the description of what they see, but one of them knows how it is connected with other things and perhaps infers from it the presence of something else which is not observed. It could be said that he sees the object as a symptom, but in this it is simply an instance of the first way, discussed above, in which special knowledge influences seeing.

We often employ models and metaphors to help us think about and explain what we see. Sometimes these do influence what we actually see. More often, I think, we employ "see" itself in these contexts metaphorically. A philosopher who accounts for all reality in terms of process still literally sees rocks and mountains like the rest of us—although his affective response to them may well be different.

We may also speak of how the cognitive and affective enter into seeing in terms of the attention we focus on some aspect. Again, two observers may agree that they are talking about the same object while differing over the features which visually predominate. This kind of "seeing as" is not to be confused with what happens when we respond to questions like "What does that cloud or ink blot remind you of (or look like)?"

In these comments on observation I have tried to stress that our acts of seeing, hearing, and so on involve highly complex mutual interactions among our thoughts, emotions, and organic sensations. When I claim therefore that the *aesthetic* point of view is the one which gives primary attention to the perceptual features of the object as they relate to one another in the pattern of the whole, I do not wish to suggest that intellectual, moral, and other considerations are irrelevant. What one hears in listening to a Beethoven symphony, for example, and one's enjoyment of it, clearly depend on the extent of one's technical training. The crucial point, however, is that if one is attending *aesthetically* to the music, this training is ancillary to the appreciation of the sound itself. Thus, a person is judging an art object and reacting to it aesthetically when the reasons and explanations he gives are either immediately about, or directed to, the pattern of relationship between the features to be observed in the object. In other words, aesthetic reasons, "responses," and judgments are those which concentrate on the "formal" qualities of an object. I don't think one has to have any clearly defined theory of art to know that some reasons, such as reference to the weight of a painting or the box-office success of a play, are not even candidates for an aesthetic argument.

The Nature of Aesthetic Argument

We must now examine how statements about the formal qualities of an object logically support an evaluation of it as a work of art. It might be supposed that the transition from the description of the object to a judgment of its aesthetic value is effected by a general principle which is self-evidently true or accepted as the ultimate general premise by agreement or is an established empirical generalization. In other words it is supposed that if the conclusion is to be valid the argument must be either deductive or inductive in form. I wish first to argue that both these forms fail to account for the logic of an aesthetic argument, then to examine more positively what seem to be the distinctive characteristics of this kind of argument.

(1.) *Deduction.* The theories which claim a special discernible quality called "beauty" or treat art as the symbolic expression of human feelings commonly employ a deductive form of argument. However, on close analysis it becomes clear that they are not deductive arguments at all. In fact, since they assert that we have a direct intuition of what constitutes the aesthetic value of an object, it is not really necessary to engage in any form of argument. The theoretical superstructure is not part of a reasoning process culminating in an evaluation but simply states the a priori conditions which make it possible for such an intuition to occur.

234 /

Arguments which invoke a metaphysical principle or rulelike statement as the major premise clearly have a deductive form. The critical question here is the way in which the truth of the major premise is established. If it were self-evidently true, the argument would be both deductive and analytic. But there seems to be no candidate of this kind available. The alternatives therefore are that (1) an ultimate premise is arbitrarily decided upon as the starting point in the chain of deductive argument, or (2) the major premise is established inductively, or (3) it is supported by another form of argument which is neither deductive nor inductive.

The adequacy of induction, through which general rules or rulelike statements are most likely to be established, will be examined shortly. I will argue later that if metaphysical principles of the kind which Coleridge,[5] for example, invoked are to have any chance of being justified, it must be through an argument that is not strictly deductive or inductive, one which focuses on ends and formal qualities—in effect, an aesthetic argument. Such a form of argument may also render the device of making a decision about the first principle an unnecessary expedient.

In summary, if we attend to the strictly deductive form of argument—one in which the universal premise is not an empirical generalization—the principle which warrants the transition from the description of the perceptual features of an aesthetic object to aesthetic evaluation must itself be justified in some nondeductive way or else arbitrarily adopted.

(2.) *Induction.* One characteristic form of an inductive argument involves an inference, on the basis of what has been observed, that something else not observed is the case. The implicit generalization is of the form "whenever A, B, C, it is reasonable to expect (or assert) X." So if we can point out certain characteristics of a painting, we are justified in inferring that it is also aesthetically excellent—provided experi-

[5] In effect, Coleridge's principle may be stated as follows: unity in complexity and complexity in unity is the criterion of value in all realms of being and value.

ence has shown that objects which possess these properties also typically have aesthetic excellence.

Another version of the inductive argument is more sensitive to the logical differences between describing and evaluating. It attempts to insure the connection between the properties cited and the evaluation inferred by marking out those properties which are "good-making." These are taken to be the features an object needs if it is to do efficiently the task for which it was designed.

The limitations on a strictly inductive approach to aesthetic argument can only be brought out by shifting the emphasis to a more direct inquiry into the character of the latter. In anticipation of this, I would point out cursorily that the first kind of inductive approach fails because in an aesthetic argument we are not finally collecting data on the basis of which we may justifiably assert some *new* fact about the object. Even when all the "facts" are agreed on, it is an attempt to show that one way of seeing the facts is correct or preferable in comparison to others; and since seeing in this way necessarily involves taking a more or less favorable or unfavorable attitude to the object, the argument also attempts to show that the taking of such an attitude is reasonable.

The second kind of inductive approach is inapplicable precisely because questions of aesthetic value are not about the efficiency of means to an agreed end. It might be argued that art objects are made for the purpose of producing a distinctive type of experience called "aesthetic," and thus the means-end model and the concept of efficiency can be applied. The problem here is that there is no unique set of psychophysiological characteristics by which an aesthetic experience can be independently identified. Whether there is an aesthetic experience depends on the aspect under which we react to an object, and its intensity may be disproportionate to the aesthetic quality which the object possesses. The justification of the aesthetic response depends on a direct assessment of the object. Of course, even if we could shift the whole discussion to a special kind of human experience called "aesthetic," questions of relative quality would still arise.

(3.) *Aesthetic Argument.* In one of its most fundamental aspects, the logic of an aesthetic argument involves the activity of appropriately naming and describing. Here, I believe, is the clue to the mode of transition from description to evaluation in aesthetic arguments and to the kind of persuasion they exert. The business of naming and describing is closely related to that of observing which was discussed earlier. Sometimes a difference over correctly naming or describing what we see (or hear, etc.) depends on a more careful attention to the features of the object or event. When we notice the additional aspects, the problem of correct description is resolved. Frequently, however, the difficulty does not arise from a failure to attend to all the perceptual features. Instead, one may be ignorant of, or have forgotten, some context of experience which is relevant to the object. Two people see a man get out of a car, snatch a child from the sidewalk, and drive off. Both agree on this description; one however sees it as an act of kidnapping, the other (who knows the man and the child) sees it as a father impatiently retrieving his errant son. In such cases, the different ways of describing the object or event do not produce differences in what is *literally* seen. But obviously they may significantly influence the total response of the observer.[6]

A more complicated situation exists when there is a question of how to describe correctly a combination of observed particular items or the details of what we usually take to be a single unit. Just as all seeing is, in a way, seeing as, so all description involves some element of interpretation. We have only to think of the familiar difference between describing an object in terms of its properties and in terms of what it does: is the grass green or does it green? At this level, our interpretation is a common, fundamental feature of the language and

---

[6] For a good discussion of this point see John Wisdom, "Gods," in Antony Flew, ed., *Logic and Language*, 1st and 2nd series (New York: Doubleday Anchor Books, 1965), pp. 202–4.

constitutes, for practical purposes, a "neutral" description. However, in everyday experience we are constantly introducing much stronger interpretative notes into our descriptions. We say, for example, that a person we observe is sneering or driving recklessly, or acting prudently, or is ashamed. Another observer might describe the person as smiling, as driving skillfully, as acting in a cowardly way, or as being embarrassed. If the observers are asked to describe, in the "neutrally" descriptive level of language, the details of what they literally see, it is likely that they will be in full agreement. In this case, the difference is not settled by pointing to some detail which had not previously been seen.

The situation may, of course, be similar to the earlier one in which the observer lacks some pertinent information. For some reason, it always happens that X's facial expression looks like a sneer even when he is really smiling. Once we know this we can adjust our reaction, but we are still correct in saying "When X smiles his face has the expression of a sneer." Apart from this possibility, however, a real difference often exists over the correctness of a particular characterization or description of what the observers agree, at one level of description, they have seen. Now the argument is an attempt by one observer to convince the other to see the elements on which they are agreed as fitting together in one pattern rather than another. It is this kind of subtle shift in interpretative content from one level of description to another which, I believe, is essentially involved in aesthetic argument.

Before illustrating it directly in such argument and examining in particular the aspect of persuasion, I wish to emphasize one further important feature of what has just been discussed. Convincing a person to see something differently will, in some circumstances, involve no change in what he literally sees, while in other circumstances the argument can hardly be described as successful unless there is a change in what he literally sees. If we change our mind and agree that someone's driving is reckless it doesn't mean that on the next film replay we literally see his recklessness as, all along, we have noticed that his car is red. But if we are now convinced that someone is smiling rather than sneering, I think it must be said that, apart from the exception already noted, we now literally see a smiling face—even though we don't see any new component elements. It is obvious that this latter claim is particularly germane to aesthetic contexts. Of course, both are to be distinguished from what happens when a person is convinced that, despite what we all see, things are really different. We still see the sun rising and setting and straight sticks bending in water despite what we know about the solar system and the law of refraction.

In an aesthetic argument the crucial issue turns on what we perceive and how we describe it. Primarily, it consists of a movement in the identification, classification, and description of the perceptual features of the art object from relatively neutral to strongly interpretative language. In a complex work of art this movement may be traced through several aspects. Each redescription has the character of an evaluation. The judgment eventually passed on the work of art is the final redescription and its appropriateness depends on the "cumulative effect" of all the intermediate interpretative descriptions. These do not fit together in a deductive form which logically entails the conclusion and any one alone would not save it from being arbitrary.

This whole pattern is well illustrated in F. R. Leavis's method of criticism.[7] In his discussion of D. H. Lawrence's "Piano," for example, he begins by considering the claim that the poem deserves to be called sentimental. He points to the features which amount to this kind of description: the appeal is directly emotional; the "swelling and lapsing" rhythm suggests that free rein has been given to the release of feelings; there are, at least at first sight, the *banal* phrases: "vista of years," "the

[7] Here I am primarily interested in the form rather than the substance of Leavis's argument. The example is taken from " 'Thought' and Emotional Quality," *Scrutiny* XIII (1945): 53–71.

heart of me weeps," "the insidious mastery of song," and so on.

Leavis argues, however, against this impression by drawing our attention more closely to the poem's features. There is, he suggests, a general rather subtle movement which is anything but a "simply plangent flow." It derives principally from the poet's stress on particulars. In this way the poem escapes "banal romantic generality" and the remembered events are stripped of unreal glamor. We become aware that the poet is presenting the swell of emotion in a somewhat critical fashion; feeling is not divorced from intelligence.

Through such interpretative description Leavis is building up the case for an overall positive evaluation of the poem. He points to the aspects of the poem in which are manifested the critical, intelligent treatment of the emotions evoked and thus its general complexity. For example, the "insidious mastery of song" does not sweep the poet, as one might expect, into a great, vague emotional state. In contrast to the "black piano appassionato" and the clamor of the present singer he recalls "hymns" on a Sunday evening and a "tinkling piano." The poet observes that he is "betrayed" by the song and carried back "in spite of myself." In this context we see particular phrases differently: "the heart of me" is not really banal but an expression of the dissension between the poet and his emotion. By carefully analyzing and displaying the details of the poem, relating them to one another and to the poem as a whole, Leavis argues against a general description in terms of vague romantic sentimentality and in favor of one which speaks of the poem as a complex, critical, intelligent achievement of a strong emotional effect.

Leavis's discussion of Shelley's poetry in *Revaluation* provides a vivid example of the shift from relatively neutral to evaluative description on a large scale. Elsewhere, he summarizes his final redescription in this way: "Shelley's poetry is repetitive, vaporous, monotonously self-regarding and often emotionally cheap, and so, in no very long run, boring."[8]

[8] F. R. Leavis, *The Common Pursuit* (Edinburgh: Penguin Books, 1963), p. 221.

In relation to this form of argument it is natural enough to ask how the critic knows what aspects of the work to choose. In principle, I think this is the same problem that arises over classification and description in many other areas of experience. How does one learn, for example, to be a judge of character, to decide that someone is being sincere rather than hypocritical?[9] Certainly there is no set of clear-cut rules which admits of precise application. Among the various forms of art there are, of course, plenty of rules about techniques. A knowledge of these may be helpful to the critic, but matters of technique have to be clearly distinguished from the formal qualities which are the object of aesthetic criticism and evaluation. Leavis gives a good account of what is involved for the literary critic and it applies, I believe, to other forms of art as well.

The business of the literary critic is to attain a peculiar completeness of response and to observe a peculiarly strict relevance in developing his response into commentary; he must be on his guard against abstracting improperly from what is in front of him and against any premature or irrelevant generalizing—of it or from it. His first concern is to enter into possession of the given poem (let us say) in its concrete fulness, and his constant concern is never to lose his completeness of possession, but rather to increase it. In making value-judgments (and judgments as to significance), implicitly or explicitly, he does so out of that completeness of possession and with that fulness of response. He doesn't ask, "How does this accord with these specifications of goodness in poetry?", he aims to make fully conscious and articulate the immediate sense of value that "places" the poem.

Of course, the process of "making fully conscious and articulate" is a process of relating and organizing, and the "immediate sense of value" should, as the critic matures with experience, represent a growing stability of organization (the problem is to combine stability with growth). What, on testing and re-testing and wider experience, turn out to be my more constant preferences, what the relative permanencies in my response, and what structure begins to assert itself in the

[9] See Ludwig Wittgenstein, *Philosophical Investigations*, trans. G. E. M. Anscombe (Oxford: Blackwell, 1967), p. 227.

field of poetry with which I am familiar? What map or chart of English poetry as a whole represents my utmost consistency and most inclusive coherence of response?[10]

A question which may still persist about aesthetic argument as I have depicted it is this: granted the interpretative description, what authorizes us to conclude that the art object is thus aesthetically good or bad? I would have to say that a central purpose of the foregoing discussion was to show that no additional logical bridge is needed precisely because the redescriptions constitute an accumulated evaluation. Suppose someone agrees that a poem evokes emotions with banal romantic generality. Can he seriously deny, or even wonder, whether in this respect the poem is aesthetically weak? Compare this with the situation in which two people agree that someone is cruel and insincere. If one of them then questions what bearing these have on an assessment of the man's moral character, or says "and his cruelty and insincerity contribute to his moral greatness," it must be concluded that he has not really seen him as cruel and insincere or that he does not understand the terms. For acceptance of this description involves a recognition of the person as morally reprehensible.

The Aspect of Persuasion in Aesthetic Argument

In response to the questions which have just been raised we are brought back to the crucial and integral part which persuasion has in aesthetic argument. The effort to persuade is central at every phase of the argument, for the persuasive force of the conclusion depends entirely on a cumulative effect. Ideally, the critic is mediating between the observer and the work of art. He is trying to bring the observer to experience the object in a certain way. So the nature of his appeal to the observer reflects the complexity that is involved, as we have seen, in acts of perception. His task may be set out, with artificial detachment, in this way:

10 Leavis, *The Common Pursuit*, pp. 213–14. Cf. Roger Fry, *Vision and Design* (London: Penguin Books, 1961), pp. 222–24.

1. To assemble the knowledge which is necessary for an adequate understanding of the work of art.

2. To make explicit the spontaneous and conventional associations assumed in the work of art and which influence our affective responses. Of course, if we do not share some common ground of experience with the artist, what we learn about these associations will belong to 1.

3. To propose an interpretative description of the perceptual features of the object by pointing to their relationship with one another and to the work as a whole. In order to convince the observer both to see that the work is thus correctly described and actually to see it that way, the critic frequently makes explicit comparison between the work and others of its kind and appeals to our experience in any other sphere (intellectual, moral, religious, etc.).

In an actual critical argument, the effort at persuasion is directed to what we think about, how we feel toward, and what literally we see in an object as these mutually interact and determine our enjoyment (or otherwise) of its formal qualities.

It must be stressed that the persuasive nature of an aesthetic argument is not incompatible with its objectivity. On the contrary, the critic is answerable to the real perceptual conditions of the object which he discusses. That is, the object must have those properties and belong to that context of conceptual and other elements which make it perceptible in the way which the critic claims. It thus makes sense to wonder whether an evaluation of a work of art is true or false. Is Shelley's poetry *really* repetitive, vaporous, and so on, as Leavis maintains? The practice of judging a work of art aesthetically and seeing it in the way we judge it is of course a highly complicated matter. We cannot expect the precision of a mathematical deduction or the virtual consensus we have for the truth of many classifications and descriptions which we make with such immediacy and ease in our everyday experience.[11] But even should the

[11] Among the latter, the expression of even a simple evaluative description introduces complications in deciding the truth or falsehood of the claim. Com-

terms "true" and "false" be restricted in their application on this account, we may still speak about the reasonableness of an aesthetic argument and the adequacy or appropriateness of the evaluation.

It follows that success in persuasion cannot be the sole criterion in our assessment of a critical argument. A critic may succeed in convincing a large number of people to see a work of art in a certain way. But unless he is directing them fundamentally to an appreciation of the object in its formal qualities and unless the discernible features of the object do support his claims about it, he is not presenting a genuine and valid aesthetic argument. Bringing someone to see a work of art differently is thus no guarantee that the argument is correct or even that it is aesthetic.

On the other hand, I have tried to argue that if the nature of aesthetic argument and evaluation are properly understood, it is not possible for someone to admit the correctness of the conclusion without reflecting this in the way he sees the object. This dichotomy can exist only when one tries to force aesthetic argument into a strictly deductive or inductive mold. There it is possible to be preoccupied exclusively with questions about the truth of the premises, whether the conclusion is logically entailed by them, and whether the inferences we draw about the quality of a work of art are guided by sufficiently well-established generalizations. The burden of much of the foregoing discussion has been to show that aesthetic argument has distinct features which do not fit these molds. F. R. Leavis, whom I have quoted on the role of the critic, does not deny that one might distill a set of principles and abstract norms from his writings. It is clear, however, that if they were simply used as major premises and inference warrants, together with specific observation of the work of art, the nature of the argument would be quite different from what he actually employs. In reference to this possibility of formulating general prin-

pare, for example, the following: this is a tree, the tree is white, . . . is a eucalyptus, . . . is tall, . . . is graceful.

ciples, he makes the following comment on his own method: "The cogency I hoped to achieve was to be for other readers of poetry—readers of poetry as such. I hoped, by putting in front of them, in a criticism that should keep as close to the concrete as possible, my own developed 'coherence of response', to get them to agree (with, no doubt, critical qualifications) that the map, the essential order, of English poetry seen as a whole did, when they interrogated their experience, look like that to them also."[12]

When due weight is given to the persuasive intent of an aesthetic argument, the conclusion cannot be treated simply, or even primarily, as a verdict or an award or a "grading." Verdicts, awards, and gradings can be made by applying a set of definite rules. We may agree that X is not guilty (technically) while believing that he really is, or that a certain wine is excellent while being unable to endure its taste. This sort of thing can happen in the assessment of art if we attend only to the technical aspects. But when we are concerned directly with the aesthetic, the formal qualities, we come to grasp the correctness of the evaluation by coming to see the object according to the evaluation.

To set in a clearer light the aspect of persuasion in aesthetic argument, it is useful to compare it with persuasion in other kinds of argument. If a logician, for example, sets out to demonstrate that there is a logical fallacy in a certain argument, we must suppose that he is convinced about the fallaciousness of the argument and is trying to bring others to see it in the same way. Let us suppose the argument criticized is mistaken and that the logician correctly and clearly presents his case. He will no doubt persuade most of his readers that the argument they thought was sound is really invalid. This means they are now aware that at least one logical rule is being broken in the argument and so agree that the logician's claim about it is true. It seems that this is the limit of his persuasive intent as such—although it may in fact go further since the

---

[12] Leavis, *The Common Pursuit*, p. 214.

terms "true," "false," "valid," "invalid" involve a valuing of propositions and arguments. However, the logician as such is not trying to persuade anyone not to employ the argument and it is enough for his purpose if people know, through his demonstration, that the argument is invalid, even though they continue to "experience" it as valid.

In a scientific argument, there is also a persuasive aspect. It is concerned with demonstrating the correctness of claims about the explanatory and predictive power of a given hypothesis or theory. Although the adoption of a theory, before and after experimentation, does affect our way of understanding and observing the world, scientific argument as such is not directed to changing our attitudes to the objects about which the theories and hypotheses are developed, or to affecting a different kind of experience of these objects. A scientist who offers evidence for a statistical claim about the connection between cigarette smoking and lung cancer is, qua scientist, trying to convince us of the accuracy of his claims—not that smoking is a bad thing or that we should give it up.

How does the persuasive aspect of moral argument compare with that of the aesthetic? Although the nature of moral argument is itself widely disputed, I think it would be agreed that the moralist is not simply trying to persuade us that "X is what you ought to do" is a correct conclusion. As a moralist, it is even more to his purpose to persuade us to agree that we ought to do X. This is the immediate object of the argument. Ultimately, of course, he is attempting to bring us to do X. But this depends on many other factors, such as our having the acquired dispositions to act virtuously and with self-control, in addition to the argument on a given occasion.

If moral argument is construed as either deductive or inductive in form, it can persuade in both the ways mentioned and, granted various acquired dispositions, can move one to action. But on the strength of being deductive or inductive, moral argument can only lead someone to an intellectual conviction that X is the goal he ought to pursue or that A is what he ought to do because it is necessary for the achievement of X. He may not find X desirable and may detest doing A. As far as moral argument in the forms being discussed is concerned what the agent feels like doing is irrelevant and thus it differs sharply from aesthetic argument in the scope of its persuasion.

If we break with the strictly "deductive or inductive" alternative, a different and probably more satisfactory view of moral argument can be taken. Here the persuasive intent is more comprehensive: not simply to convince us that X is the goal we ought to pursue but to bring us really to desire it for what it is. Of course, in this account, the style of moral argument is ultimately assimilated to that of the aesthetic. Even in a specific instance, the introduction of a moral principle is an effort to redescribe some action or goal so that it will be seen as desirable (or undesirable). But when we come to making decisions about the overriding set of end values and the whole style of life which they mark out for us as moral agents the aesthetic characteristics of moral argument are evident. At this point the logic of its persuasive effort is that of an aesthetic argument.[13]

Language and Aesthetic Experience

I have argued that in an aesthetic argument the effort of persuading someone that a certain judgment about a work of art is correct also involves bringing him to experience the object according to the judgment. He not only agrees that the conclusion "Shelley's poetry is boring" is correct but finds himself being bored in reading Shelley's poetry. An adequate account of the power of language to effect such a change in our experience of an object's formal qualities would involve an examination of how we acquire and use language as members of human society. This task is beyond the scope of the present discussion. However, I would like to emphasize some features which are immediately relevant to an appreciation of the persuasive force of aesthetic argument.

---

[13] I will return to this point in illustrating the application of aesthetic argument to the language of teaching.

In the first place, whatever native capacities are involved, children acquire the use of language as an integral component in their total development as social beings. Although this process of acquisition is modified by many other aspects of socialization, the possession of language is not simply another social skill like all the rest. From the time a child understands that words refer to things and develops internal speech, language exercises a crucial influence on every aspect of his experience. Thus, for example, it determines to a large extent the form of his thought; some verbalized thought is involved in most of the self-awareness he has of his intentions, feelings, and desires; his development in logic and general intellectual growth depends on the mastery of language. I would stress, in particular, the special unifying bond which language provides between the various activities of our mental life (many of which involve overt behavior), between these and actions we perform, in some sense, as a consequence, and between human beings as they deal with one another and their social and physical environment. We have to resist the tendency to divide thought and action too sharply or to identify the cognitive, affective, and conative (and so on) as rigidly separate compartments in our mental life. Earlier, I drew attention to the place of theory in perception. There is, of course, a complex web of connections—some logical, some depending on contingent associations—not only of our verbal thoughts or the intelligible speech of others with what we perceive, but also with what we feel, will, want, do, etc. A person hears a noise outside and thinks it is a prowler; he experiences a sinking feeling of fear and rushes to the phone to call the police.

It is obvious that the impact of what I say on another person depends on how he understands it—and this may be affected in a number of ways. To illustrate: (1) He may grasp the meaning of the words as I do, but the sentence may be ambiguous. (2) He may not know the meaning of some of the key terms or not realize they can be applied in the way I use them. (3) He may have a different interpretation of the context in which my "speech act" occurs. Accurate communication depends on grasping the speaker's purpose as well as knowing the meaning of words and sentences. One has to detect irony, for example, and the clue may be in the inflection of the speaker's voice or his gestures. (4) Probably most important for aesthetic argument, his knowledge of the meaning may not be appropriate for the kind of word being used. If a person grasps the meaning of the interpretative descriptive terms characteristic of aesthetic argument, like "tragic," "sentimental," "boring," exactly as he does that of "π" or "molecule," it would be futile to engage with him in aesthetic argument. And if he knows the meaning of "good," "right," "ought," "duty," etc. in the same way, a moral argument with him would be similarly futile.

Short of this extreme case, the sense of the interpretative descriptive terms (i.e. the complex of mental events they arouse) will inevitably reflect differences in experiences from one individual to another. Between the typical members of one social class, for example, and another the sense may be really quite different. The extent of the difference should not, however, be overstressed. It is true that in the learning of language there are features unique to each individual and that the process goes on throughout one's life. At the same time, apart from the probability of like innate mental structures in human beings for the learning of language, it would simply not exercise its vast social function of communicating and influencing thoughts, feelings, desires, intentions, and actions unless the broad characteristics were the same for all its users.[14] If it were otherwise we could not speak meaningfully of the common language. Moreover, even where special conditions produce radical diversity it should not be supposed that the differences are irremediable. If aesthetic argument fails because the people to whom it is addressed have not had the kinds of experience which enable them to appreciate the terms being employed,

[14] See W. V. O. Quine, *Word and Object* (Cambridge: M. I. T. Press, 1964), pp. 7–8.

it means that the educational process in this sphere has to be moved back to a more rudimentary level. Again there is a clear analogy with the use of moral argument.[15]

To avoid misunderstanding I explicitly recognize that people have profound aesthetic experiences of various forms of art without knowing how to describe their experience clearly or to speak with any precision about what it is that makes the object so aesthetically satisfying. On a more general level, we frequently know what we or others want or feel or are doing even though we can't find the right words for it. Complex thinking occurs in many situations with only fragments of inner speech—and perhaps with no speech at all. But throughout this paper I am focusing on the use of argument in relation to objects of art: giving descriptions at various levels, stating reasons, evaluations, judgments; an intricate linguistic exchange between people who are presumed to have had sufficient experience to make such an exchange meaningful.

I have argued for the view that in an aesthetic argument the critic tries to persuade his audience to think about and experience the work of art in its formal qualities as he does. In these brief comments on the influence of language on experience and doing, I wish finally to refer directly to the relation between understanding the aesthetic argument and experiencing the

[15] A brief reference will be made shortly in the text to the ideological rhetoric about indoctrinating children into "middle-class" values. Just because so-called middle-class children happen to possess certain desirable human values, this is no reason for withholding them from others. In any case, it is doubtful whether members of the middle class are equipped, without special educational effort, to appreciate the language of aesthetic argument. I am doubtful also about the value of crash programs in language when dealing with the crucial terms of moral and aesthetic discourse. It seems to me that a much more sophisticated and complex approach has to be taken to the learning of language in these areas: that children need the experiences in which they not only learn the meaning of the language in a dictionary fashion but also in a way that is appropriate to their appreciation of it in moral and aesthetic contexts. If it is *educationally* desirable to appreciate certain forms of art, and this depends, at least for its full achievement, on grasping a sense of certain terms, then it is educationally desirable to provide all children with the experiences in which the language of aesthetic argument becomes meaningful—even when these experiences have historically been distinctive of this or that social group.

object. There are two extremes to be avoided. The first is the assumption that the critical argument can, in some way, convey the experience of the object itself; that is, substitute for it. The opposite extreme assumes that talking about the aesthetic qualities of a work of art is irrelevant, that the only valid argument is the immediate presentation of the object itself. In this view if someone asks about the quality of, say, a Chopin prelude the appropriate response is simply to have him listen to it being played: the argument is the performance.

I will comment briefly on each of these positions. In reference to the first, it is evident that language from its most mundane uses to the highest reaches of literary art can dramatically effect changes in every aspect of human mental life and action. Although sentences do not possess the properties of the things they are about—unlike maps in relation to a terrain—their sense is acquired in human experiences in which all the conceptually distinguishable facets are complexly interacting. People are hurt, excited, depressed, encouraged, stirred to action, and so on by what others say. From a great novelist's descriptions we can imagine people and events with as much, if not more, vividness as any we have actually known. Incidentally, despite individual differences in the possession of language, literary artists usually manage to communicate much of what they write to a vast number of people in essentially the same way. For example, people frequently agree that a film has portrayed the characters and incidents of a novel as they had imagined them. The description of an ancient lost work of art by a contemporary could evoke a mental picture of a very beautiful object. If we had the skill we might reproduce it and then find, if the original were recovered, a striking similarity. Artists produce very accurate pictures from verbal descriptions. But none of this is to attend in a literal act of perception to an object in its formal qualities. It only shows how the aesthetic argument, like relevant factual knowledge, can enter into the aesthetic experience. We may, of course, appreciate the brilliant literary qualities and acuity of the critic. But if we stop here and are not led through the argument to appreciate the object differently, we are preoccupied with the critic in another role—as artist, not as critic.

In reference to the second extreme—that the argument is in the performance—it can be pointed out that it ignores the crucial role of theory in our perception of objects and fails to take account of how much is involved in the full appreciation of even moderately sophisticated works of art. It overlooks the complex function of an aesthetic argument: not simply to bring about an aesthetic enjoyment of the object, but to evaluate it and to build up a case for why it is correct to appreciate it in such and such a way. And finally, the performance of a work (in those forms of art which lend themselves to it) is hardly an argument even in the metaphorical sense, but is an artistic achievement to be critically evaluated and, as in listening to music, part of the total complex of art to be enjoyed.

In summary, if we accept (1) the previously discussed influence of theory (typically expressed in language) on perception, feeling, and other kinds of human experience and (2) the capacity of linguistic utterances, in appropriate circumstances, to effect changes in what one believes, feels, desires, does, etc., we at least have the raw material to account for the power of aesthetic argument to convince a person that a certain judgment about the formal qualities of an object is correct by leading him to experience them in the way that the judgment expresses it.

Persuasive Aesthetic Argument and Teaching Discourse

To what extent does all this discussion of the persuasive character of aesthetic argument bear on the teacher? It is, of course, immediately relevant to his discourse about works of art in all their varied forms. I will not examine this aspect directly any further because, in the present context, we are more interested in exploring the extension of persuasive aesthetic argument to the teacher's role more generally. Since I have been talking about the use of argument (setting out reasons and conclusions), our attention will necessarily be limited even in this wider view to the "speech acts" of the teacher. It is evident that these do not exhaust the didactic instruments at his disposal; I do not even wish to imply that they are necessarily the most important. The question, put more specifically then, is how the aesthetic type of argument, with its distinctive persuasive character, enters into teaching discourse generally. In proposing my answer, I will only have in mind the teacher who is contributing to a process of general education. What I say may not necessarily apply, therefore, to teaching and learning which is strictly vocational or professional or otherwise narrowly specialized. I will give most of my attention to the way in which, as it seems to me, the persuasion of an aesthetic-type argument pervades the total educational enterprise. Of specific aspects within the general process of education, I will discuss only moral argument in any detail.

THE TOTAL EDUCATIONAL ENTERPRISE

It is quite inadequate to reduce the process of education to the sum of the transactions by which one person instructs another in a set of closely related skills and theories (as in mathematics, physics, history, etc.). As an *educator*, the teacher's role in, say, mathematics is not restricted to helping students understand the theory of number and acquire the skills necessary for solving mathematical problems or for applying the knowledge to other fields. As an educator, he is assumed to believe in the value of mathematics, that it is one of the great human achievements in knowledge—not just a tool to use but something to be possessed by—that what goes into learning mathematics involves an enlargement of the quality of human life in a way that is unique and cannot be achieved by any other means. As an educator, he has to take concern for how the learner is assimilating mathematics into the unique pattern of his conscious human life. He is not programming a machine (in which his only interest is that, given input of a certain kind, there should be a corresponding output) but engaging in a personal human relationship with a thinking, feeling, willing, desiring, self-conscious agent. As an educator, he also sees that mathematics (for example) is not being integrated in isolation into the life of the learner, but as part of a total process called education. So the teacher as an educator is dealing with "whole patterns": both the elements of the educational process cohering to form an object which he must believe, if he is to practice as a teacher with any sincerity, as worthy of attainment, and these elements, whether taken together or separately, as they fit into the life of a living human person. In its ideal form, education includes not merely the integration of knowledge, but the integration of knowledge in the learner.

All this amounts to saying that the educator is involved in initiating others into a distinctive style of life characterized by specific values, attitudes, and ways of proceeding. Because he is convinced that this style of life is worthwhile and because one of its distinguishing preferences is for reasonable rather than arbitrary choice, part of his task as an educator is to persuade rationally those being initiated to see the whole life style of the educated man as inherently valuable for human beings and to choose it as such. No doubt an educator may use various kinds of argument in this process of rational persuasion, such as examining the consequences of being or not being educated. In the end, however, I believe he is forced back to depicting as fully as possible the characteristic features of the life style of the educated man and to comparing and contrasting it with alternative styles. It is thus finally a form of aesthetic or critical argument—a judgment not about means but about the total pattern which the component elements form. At this most fundamental level, the norms of rational persuasion for the educator are essentially those of aesthetic argument discussed in the earlier sections. We could say that the form of persuasion distinctive of aesthetic argument pervades the teacher's discourse because it is brought into play whenever he offers a defense of the specifically educational value of schooling.

To avoid possible misunderstanding, I will make some brief

observations on the style of life which I have here referred to as that of the educated man. First, it is an ideal which is only more or less adequately embodied in actual curricula. The schools at a given time may only be partially or peripherally concerned with the development of its distinctive characteristics, and in some instances may be working in a direction that is clearly antithetical. Second, the dynamic nature of inquiry and human life more generally are such that the substantive details of the life style of an educated man can never be stated once and for all. Third, it is a general life style that is compatible with a variety of more specific forms.

Over the centuries, schools have typically presented it embedded in the context of some more specific style of life: for example, "the agonistic ideal of life" variously interpreted in the educational programs of ancient Greece, the Augustinian version of a Christian humanistic culture in the schools of the Middle Ages, the seventeenth-century English gentleman of the landed aristocracy in John Locke's educational program, and so on. Apart from the occasions in which the latter has compromised or conflicted with educational values, there has also been a tendency to suppose that the acquisition of some very specific style of life was identical with, or a necessary condition for, becoming genuinely educated. At the present time this tendency takes the form of confusing educational values with characteristics which de facto distinguish a certain social class or racial group. For example, from a strictly educational viewpoint it is irrelevant that a logically sophisticated form of speech happens to be possessed by only one of the subgroups within a society. Sociologists might use it as a criterion of a certain class, but because it is an instrument of logically sophisticated thought it is really a general human and educational value and not one that is intrinsic to a particular group. In this situation, the educator has to disengage it from the special life style of the social class (or racial group) of which, by historical accident, it has come to form a distinguishing part.

I have argued that ideally the role of the teacher as he is concerned with the whole pattern of knowledge and inquiry and with its integral assimilation by other human beings (particularly during their period of most rapid general development) can usefully be compared to that of the critic. Of course the points of similarity are only partial—for example, from some aspects the teacher's role is more like that of an artist.[16] But insofar as the teacher is arguing in favor of the general style of life involved in becoming and being an educated man, the appropriate procedure available to him is essentially that of the critic. For as we have seen the critic mediates between the work of art and the "public" and typically tries to persuade the latter to see the work in a certain way, a way of seeing which includes an evaluation. So the teacher (as educator) mediates between the life style of the educated man and his students and presents its features not simply as a set of skills and dispositions useful, in given circumstances, for certain extrinsic ends, but as determining a characteristic way of living that is humanly perfecting and worthwhile in itself. Persuading his "public" to perceive as inherently valuable the total pattern of elements which comprise being educated is an essential function of the educator. Basically, then, he is in the same position as a critic attempting to persuade someone to take a certain evaluative view of the formal properties of a work of art as they cohere in a single pattern. Hence, to the extent that he persuades by way of explicit discourse and does so according to a method that is consistent with educational values, he must employ a form of critical or aesthetic argument.

In presenting an aesthetic argument, the critic himself is obviously engaging in a specific form of teaching. He sometimes extends his teaching function to the provision of background knowledge and experience upon which the force of the

[16] Max Black has drawn out similarities to the artist in the process of education. However, he concentrates exclusively on the student and does not apply the analogy to the teacher. "Education as Art and Discipline," in Israel Scheffler, ed., *Philosophy and Education*, 2nd ed. (Boston: Allyn and Bacon, 1966), pp. 39–46.

aesthetic argument may depend. More often he assumes that these have been acquired already. Even in the former case, however, his teaching effort is strictly instrumental to the main business of critical argument. When the teacher, engaged in general education, uses the critical style of argument in favor of educational values he is in a rather different position. Not only must he be sensitive to the limitations of his students in grasping this argument, but it falls directly within his responsibility as an educator to provide much of the background knowledge and experience on which the appreciation of the argument depends. Of course this is not the work of any one individual. The impact of the argument in its final form derives from the cumulative preparatory work of many teachers. At the same time, it should be stressed that this other teaching and learning is not merely instrumental to the persuasive critical argument about the value of being educated. It is an integral part of the process itself and the presentation of the critical argument, although pervasive and fundamental, is only one of the teacher's tasks as an educator. To gain an adequate understanding of mathematics or literature, for example, is to possess already some of the elements which form the critical argument itself.

MORAL EDUCATION

In moral reasoning we typically resolve the question of what we ought to do on the basis of some general moral prescription which we believe applies in the present circumstances. An important part of moral education consists in learning how to apply such principles accurately and with moral sensitivity. Even more important, it also includes an examination of the principles themselves—not only the general formal characteristics of moral rules, but the justification of this substantive principle (or set of principles) rather than some other. For fundamentally the same reasons we have already discussed in reference to aesthetic argument, I would claim that a teacher cannot provide an adequate justification of a set of moral principles (or indicate how such a justification might be undertaken) if he adheres to either a strictly deductive or inductive approach. The former involves a regress in which each moral precept is shown to be entailed by a more general one until we come to the principle which is taken to be the foundation and starting point of the whole series. Since there are no satisfactory candidates for such a principle—whose truth is self-evident or intuitively grasped—the whole effort at deductive justification comes finally to rest on an arbitrary decision to accept some principle as unquestionably true.

The inductive approach treats moral principles as shorthand generalizations of experience. If one probes beyond the surface of the argument, it becomes clear that crucial questions about determining what features of an act shall count as morally good-making or the criteria for deciding which consequences of human actions are satisfactory, desirable, good, and so on have still to be answered.

Within the framework of an accepted set of principles we do, of course, use both deductive and inductive argument in reaching moral judgments. What I am claiming, however, is that the effort to give an adequate argument for the total moral framework itself cannot conform to the deductive or inductive model but must be of an aesthetic kind. The ultimate justifying argument is not directly for this or that set of principles (still less for one ultimate principle against another) but for a whole style of life whose essential features are believed to constitute the most morally worthwhile way for a human being to live. The argument directly examines these features as they fit together to form an ideal picture of the moral life. As with critical argument, it involves close comparison and contrast with alternative arrangements of the same details and with other entirely different pictures of the moral life, and in this it attempts to convince us that the evaluation of the various alternatives is correct by bringing us to see the alternatives in just such a way. As we noticed earlier in comparing moral and aesthetic arguments, when the former is assimilated to the latter there is no longer any room for a gap between an intellectual conviction that X ought to be done and one's feeling toward the doing of X. If the moral argument is in an aesthetic-like form one can only be convinced by it if he really comes to see X as a morally desirable way of acting. When someone is not convinced by the argument about a whole pattern of moral life the onus is on him to point out the features which demand a different interpretative view or which constitute the superiority of some other pattern. Of course as often happens in disputes over the relative merits of works of art, it may not be possible to reach a definitive conclusion about the superiority of competing moral life styles or of claims concerning the morality of particular kinds of human acts. But even in unresolved disputes the ultimate preference for one style over another need never be merely a decision of the will. One can always expect that a person who has chosen a given general moral ideal should be able to point out those aspects in virtue of which he sees it as he does.

Although this account of ethical argument contrasts sharply with one in which the consequences of action constitute the central focus, there is a sense in which consequences are relevant. The aesthetic-like moral argument is primarily about a concrete reality, a life lived in a certain way. It tries to persuade us that living in such and such a way is humanly most worthwhile. Now if people commonly found that the actual experience of living according to the ideal was dismal or even intolerable, that would be evidence to suggest that in the critical analysis of the ideal some aspects had been overlooked or misunderstood. Granting this, it is still the case that when the teacher is directly engaged in presenting an ultimate reasoned defense of the life style of the educated man and the more comprehensive life style of man as a moral agent (or in examining the kind of reasoning that would be appropriate for such a defense), he must take up the inherently persuasive aesthetic mode of argument. It should be noticed in passing that as an educator he can not consistently advocate any theory of the morally good life which conflicts with educational values.

Aside from the direct evaluation of works of art, moral education is by no means the only specific part of the general process in which the teacher's discourse essentially involves an aesthetic-like persuasive argument. In mathematics it enters into the choice between alternative solutions to a problem, and in science it is a factor in determining the acceptability of a theory or the use of one explanatory model rather than another. Its presence is, in fact, pervasive because it is employed whenever a classification is made which is in the nature of an evaluation. Thus its influence is particularly strong in the construction (and teaching) of history, the interpretation and evaluation of current events, social scientific studies, and in developing the skills of practical judgment and decision-making (although unfortunately this last is usually not an explicit part of general education curricula).

To a certain extent we can use relatively neutral terms in our descriptions of individuals and groups and of their actions. If this were not so, it would be impossible to talk about different interpretations of the same event or even to understand, much less evaluate, the adequacy of any interpretation of an event, contemporary or historical. However, neither a historian's account nor the description which a person gives of a situation in which he has to make an important decision is ever simply, or even predominantly, in relatively neutral terms. The "raw material" is always seen under a particular aspect or as making a certain pattern and the terms of its redescription already have the form of an interpretation or evaluation. Analogous to the critic and the work of art, the historian or the individual justifying a practical decision is frequently trying to persuade us that what he describes really amounts to being irresponsible, aggressive, intelligent, progressive, or whatever other interpretative classification he employs. If a teacher is to be fully effective in these areas (either to teach or teach about history and so on) he needs to be aware of the role this aesthetic-like persuasive argument plays and know how to employ it.

The Appropriateness of Aesthetic-like Persuasion in Education

Throughout this discussion I have attended only to persuasion exercised by the teacher directly through his "speech acts." Obviously, he also can and does persuade deliberately through many other means; for example, by manipulating a situation so that a student comes to experience what it is like to be discriminated against. Moreover, he often unconsciously influences the attitudes of his students, and his effectiveness as a teacher, particularly when he is attempting to change or form attitudes, is inevitably to some extent a function of how they perceive him as a person. With reference to persuasion that is exercised predominantly through the use of language, I have argued that it ought to be a part of a teacher's role if he is acting genuinely as an educator. To the extent that neutrality means never committing oneself favorably or unfavorably about anything, it would seem that to be neutral and to teach are logically incompatible. But even if such an extraordinary exercise of neutrality in this sense is possible, it is certainly not desirable. The important question is *how* the teacher persuades. Clearly, as an educator he is bound to limit himself to rational methods. This of course does not settle the matter because, although certain uses of language can immediately be placed as either rational or irrational, there are a number of border disputes. C. L. Stevenson in *Ethics and Language* goes so far as to treat all persuasion as irrational (or, as he prefers, nonrational). He makes a contrast between persuasive and rational methods for changing attitudes.[17] I argued earlier that any kind of argument (whether it is demonstrating a logical fallacy, or solving a mathematical problem, or justifying a scientific theory) has a persuasive aspect—at least when used by a teacher. An argument is rationally persuasive when the

[17] C. L. Stevenson, *Ethics and Language* (New Haven: Yale University Press, 1962), chap. 6.

conclusion is accepted because of reasons, evidence, and methods of procedure and when these are relevant to establishing such a conclusion.[18]

Throughout we have been exploring the characteristics of a rational mode of argument, critical or aesthetic, which is neither directly deductive nor inductive. In critical argument, unlike the others, persuasion cannot be restricted in its psychological effect to an isolated intellectual assent. It is of the essence of critical argument that one accepts the judgment as justified as one comes to experience the object in just that way. Hence, rather than separating the cognitive and affective, as Stevenson does in his treatment of persuasion,[19] we should accept their complex interaction in the process of critical argument. The mode of aesthetic argument is thus both a rational procedure and one in which the persuasive influence is psychologically extensive (involving a person as he feels, desires, wills, acts, etc., as well as thinks). Because an educator should be concerned for the integral development of a person in the acquisition of knowledge, it would seem that this mode of argument is not simply another rational procedure at his disposal, but one of special significance. I have tried to show how it enters into many particular aspects of teaching and learning and is finally the only effective way in which an educator can rationally persuade on behalf of the values which are distinctive of becoming and being educated.

[18] Cf. J. N. Garver, "On the Rationality of Persuading," *Mind* LXIX (1960): 170; Stanley I. Benn, "Freedom and Persuasion," *Australasian Journal of Philosophy* XLV (1967): 265–67.

[19] According to Stevenson, we can change attitudes either by changing beliefs or by "the sheer, direct emotional impact of words" (*Ethics and Language*, p. 139). Cf. Nowell-Smith's comments on advising and exhorting in *Ethics*, chap. 2.

THE CONCEPT OF MEDIUM

IN EDUCATION / 11

Michael J. Parsons

I

Probably everyone is familiar with the phrase "educational media" and with the kinds of items it refers to. For the sake of clarity, however, it may be worthwhile to set down a short list of these. Among the devices sometimes called "educational media" are: films, of all kinds; television, both open and closed-circuit; programmed texts, with and without "teaching machines"; computer-based information banks; records and tapes, in various forms of sophistication, such as "language laboratories"; books, blackboards, microphones, and overhead projectors.

It has long been clear that the old term "visual aids" is inadequate for such a list. This is not so much because many of these devices are wholly or partially nonvisual, an inadequacy taken care of by the simple change of the adjective to "audio-visual," as in the title of the journal in this area, *The Audio-Visual Communications Review*. It is rather that we have come to realize that there is more to their role in the educational process than is suggested by the word "aids." They are not merely ancillary to, or illustrative of, teaching in the classroom, nor does the teacher have a choice whether or not to use them in his teaching. Instead, we now tend to think, there is a sense in which they are ever present in teaching, and inescapably so; if we are to teach we must choose among these devices, if only by default. Education, it seems, can proceed only through the offices of some medium: no medium, no education. Though the study of what used to be called "visual aids" is now properly assuming a large place in colleges of education, there is no universally agreed upon term for the subject of that study. The most frequently suggested are couched in terms either of "technology" or of "media," though there are others (e.g., "communications"); and, since these are coupled with characteristic teaching-learning options, they give rise to at least the following alternatives in the literature: instructional technology, instructional media, teaching technology (rare), teaching media, learning technology (rare), learning media (rare), and, most frequent, educational technology and educational media. I have also seen "media technology."

It is apparent that behind these terminological difficulties lie conceptual ones. If education is the kind of activity that is dependent upon a medium, then what kind of activity is that? More concretely, what is and is not to be counted as a case of a medium in education? Consider, for example, the difficulty of setting limits to the list of devices given above. I have seen it urged that teacher-talking should be counted an item on this list, and I suppose that in some circumstances one might urge also teacher-being-silent. Similarly the person and the dress of the teacher, the architecture of the school, and the social interaction of the students each have their advocates of inclusion. Even among the items on my list there are different kinds of distinctions. For example, the difference between a lecture given by a teacher in person and on television is not of the same kind as the difference between a verbal account of an incident and a film of that incident; and neither of these is of the same kind as the difference between reading a book silently and hearing it read aloud, or as that between talking about engines and working on engines. Which of these distinctions, if any, provide ground for distinguishing one medium in education from another? It may be worth remarking that the word "media" is in educational circles almost always found in the plural. I suspect that one reason for this is that it is more vague, for to name some particular as a medium goes partway to committing oneself to a view of what an educational medium is. Similarly, the adjective "educational" remains noncommittal between "teaching" and "learning," either of which, as I hope to show, would be clearer. This noncommittal character of the phrase "educational media" is not necessarily to be deplored, of course, since it reflects a genuine uncertainty as to the nature of the various devices we have invented. Nevertheless, there is a value in having the implications and alternatives spelled out, and one way to do this is to discuss the appropriateness of the use of the notion of a medium in education.

This I propose to do here by comparing the use of "medium" in education with its use in aesthetics, where it has a long history. Its range, however, is wider than this. Indeed, Beardsley, arguing that it "has so many different, and yet easily confused, senses, that it is now almost useless," gives this list of extra-aesthetic examples: "the newspaper as a mass medium, air as a medium for the transmission of sound, Mrs. Beauchamp as a spiritualistic medium, the United States mail as a medium of communication."[1] It is true that on occasion it may refer to almost anything between a means to an end and a container for a thing contained. McLuhan, for instance, calls a light bulb a medium of artificial light. Nevertheless, I think that in its extra-aesthetic uses it usually refers to a special kind of means, a means of what might be called "transport." That

[1] Monroe C. Beardsley, *Aesthetics: Problems in the Philosophy of Criticism* (New York: Harcourt, Brace, 1958), p. 82.

is to say, even in popular use being a medium is associated with being a vehicle for the transmission of something; and a vehicle is a species of means.

For this reason, it seems to me that the central uses of "medium" are in connection with two kinds of activity, art and communication, and that its use in other cases is peripheral or derivative. Of course the notion of "communication" may itself be considerably extended by metaphor; here I intend it in a fairly narrow, certainly nonmetaphorical, sense. Some examples of what are usually accounted "communications media" are: telephone, semaphore, messages in bottles. I think the "mass media" are also to be interpreted largely as media of communication: television, cinema, newspapers, magazines, radio.

I shall therefore compare "medium" in art with "medium" in communication and speculate as to which use is appropriate in education. For it happens that education has some points of similarity with both art and communication, and it may be that the plausibility of "educational media" rests on these similarities. The question of the appropriateness or the implications of this phrase is therefore largely a question of how far and how importantly education is to be thought of as like art or like communication.

It might be objected against this procedure that the use of "medium" in aesthetics is only a special case of its use in communications, but this evidently depends on conceiving art itself as a form of communication. This is one of the metaphorical extensions of the notion of "communication" which I have already disclaimed. The metaphor may have its value, but many things might be said against it. Some of these will be said in the course of my argument.

II

How has "medium" been used in talking about art? It is true, as Beardsley once again remarks, that its uses have been many and not clearly distinguished. But this is the case with many terms in aesthetics and does not seem, in itself, sufficient reason for giving it up. There is a sense for which "medium" is an appropriate and even perhaps traditional term and it can be carefully stated, as it has been recently by Aldrich.[2] In this sense the "medium" is what the artist works with to achieve his total aesthetic effect; it is what he changes and arranges and is guided by in making the work of art. For a painter, it is the appearance of his paint; not, strictly speaking, the paint itself— the pigment and its ground—but its appearance; this is what the painter is sensitive to and what, when arranged by him, constitutes his painting. Similarly, in music the medium is sound; in literature, the appearance of words and of meanings and so on. The notion that what the artist works with is the appearance (*der Schein*) of things has been important in aesthetics at least since Schiller, and it is fundamental to the work of such diverse figures as D. W. Prall and Susanne Langer. It seems reasonable to suppose, therefore, that it is not a notion likely to be relinquished.

It is not my purpose to attempt a full account of this notion. Instead I shall ask the subsidiary question: what are the important differences between it and the notion of a medium of communication, since, as I have claimed, the use of the term in education seems to borrow something from both?

One might start by observing that a medium in art is commonly said to be opaque rather than transparent.

Whenever an artist sets out to "imitate" something, as a writer may set out to write a war story, or a painter to paint a landscape, he may be said to start with some "subject matter": events in the war, objects in the landscape. However, this subject matter is transformed as it finds a place in the work of art; it is not simply transmitted or arranged, but is changed into something quite different, which for clarity (following Aldrich) may be called the "content" of the work. In such cases the difference between subject matter and content is radical; they exist, as Plato insisted, on different planes of

---

[2] Virgil C. Aldrich, *Philosophy of Art* (Englewood Cliffs, N.J.: Prentice-Hall, 1963), pp. 35ff.

reality. The subject matter exists as natural objects exist; the content of the work of art exists only as images, verbal, or visual. The landscape, for example, is reduced to two dimensions; what was capable of being touched and smelled is now accessible only to sight (the paint may be touched and smelled, of course, but not the appearance of the paint). The point here is that the landscape as "content" is wholly dependent on the artist's use of the medium: change the appearance of the paint and you change the landscape. The landscape-as-content is not something which conceivably could have been represented by some other painting, or in some other medium, though the landscape-as-subject matter is. The same is true of the war story; change the words and you change the war-as-content, though the war that is being written about (if there is one) remains the same. Art, in short, is not a simple and direct reflection of reality, for "subject matter" and "content" are not the same. Of course they are related in some way, for unless there are similarities between them, there is no sense in speaking of subject matter at all. And "nonrepresentational" art differs from communication even more clearly since communication cannot be without subject matter. It is the medium of art, then, that determines the character of the content and obliges us to distinguish this from the subject matter, where this latter is relevant.

This may be thought of as another way of saying that a medium in art is not, as it is in communication, a means to an end. For means-end reasoning is appropriate only where the character of the end is not necessarily connected with the character of the means. A means is something which, when it has brought about the desired end, is discarded, and therefore in principle (though not always in practice) it would be possible for a different means to have brought about the same end. Means are in principle substitutable one for another.[3] This is not the case

[3] See R. G. Collingwood, *The Principles of Art* (New York: Oxford University Press, 1958), pp. 15–17, for a discussion of what it is to be a means to an end.

with a medium in art. The appearance of the paint is not irrelevant when the painting is finished; the words cannot be ignored
and the story retained. Rather the medium is the work of art,
and if it is removed there is nothing left. If it is substituted
for, a different work of art (at best) is obtained.

On the other hand, a medium of communication is, ideally,
transparent. I mean by this simply that its function is to reproduce its original material as faithfully as possible. And this
original material, the subject matter or what the medium deals
with, is not to be distinguished from its content, the message,
except perhaps where mistakes have been made. A magazine,
for example, may begin with the account of a battle or the
photographs of a landscape that we have been discussing.
Communication, which is the object of the magazine, is the
faithful reproduction and dissemination of these products of
art; which is to say that the magazine is most successfully used
as communication when it prints what the writer wrote with
no distortions, and when it reproduces the photographs as
much like the original as possible. That this is so, and that we
do not often regard the magazine as a medium for creative art,
is supported by the fact that minor changes in technique are
felt to affect not the character of the subject matter itself but
the success with which the subject matter is reproduced. They
are thought of as technical rather than artistic changes, better
or worse means to the same end rather than as alternative ends.
Furthermore, if one were to exchange one medium of communication for another, one would not be thought of as changing the content. If the account of the war is recorded on tape,
or read over the radio, if the photographs are reproduced on
TV, we are inclined to think that the content remains the
same, though we may debate the technical success of the new
presentation.

Of course it may be that a magazine editor thinks of himself
as an artist; and it may also be that his handling of the visual
appearance of the pages justifies this claim. If this is so, then
the editor is both an artist and a communicator (unless being

an artist hinders his success as a communicator), and the magazine is a medium in both senses at the same time. But this is an accidental combination of both of the things I am discussing, one which is not conceptually necessary.

It will be evident that film and TV also may be either aesthetic media or media in the communications sense. They are both staples on the list of "mass media," and both are sometimes used as a communications medium is used: to record and distribute interviews with important people, for example. On the other hand both may be aesthetic media, which is to say that in the hands of an artist they may transform their subject matter into a unique content. For this reason we habitually mark the distinction between reruns of movies on TV, where TV is a medium of communication only, and original plays written for TV, where it is also an aesthetic medium. And there are gray areas where we are uncertain which way to describe what is going on, as when a film is made of a play performed in a theater. To transform a play from the aesthetic medium of the theater to the aesthetic medium of the film requires, as Sir Lawrence Olivier has demonstrated, original creative ability of the director; and in less successful cases we are uncertain whether to say that the aesthetic medium is that of the theater or of the cinema, though we are in no doubt as to which medium of communication is being used.

It is also true that if one were to work frequently with a particular medium of communication, such as TV or film, one might find one's modes of thinking shaped by it. The effect on one's imagination might well be an effect which no other medium would have had. In this sense we may say that Gutenberg man differs from Hollywood man, and that the medium is the message.[4] But there is a difference between this and the sense in which the content of a work of art is not translatable from one medium to another. For there is a difference between the content of a work of art and the long-range effect of work-

[4] The reference is to Marshall McLuhan, *The Medium Is the Message* (New York: Bantam Books, 1967).

ing with a medium of art, and, similarly, between the content and the effect of a medium of communication. It is true that in some cases, perhaps in many, the effect is more important educationally than the content. *Time* magazine, for example, notoriously has a style that makes one item of news very like another, the motives and characters of great men indistinguishable except in detail, the surface of life one-dimensional.[5] This is of great importance to the educator, and in many ways we have not made enough of it.

But this does not mean that *Time* magazine is after all a medium of art rather than of communication. It means that it is the latter only to a limited degree (the limits set by its style) and that everything to which we pay attention has some effect upon us.

My first distinction, then, between a medium in art and a medium in communication is in terms of their opacity and transparency. One traditional image of transparency is the mirror, and in this sense we may say that communication, and not art, is a mirror. Aldrich, speaking of a medium in the aesthetic sense, says:

A mirror is not a medium. When you see something in a good mirror, you are seeing *that thing* via the mirror. What is seen thus remains pure subject matter. . . . There is no content in the mirror because there is no visible material and medium; thus there is no work of art, for nothing has been formulated in a medium as the content. Art is most certainly not a mirror held up to nature for the sake of the mirror-image. A mirror-image is not embodied in a medium that has certain opacities in its own right. One does not look into or through the medium of a work of art at the subject matter as one does indeed look through or into a glass. In art, the subject matter undergoes some sort of transfiguration when it is realized as the content in the medium. . . . Thus the notion of transparency of the medium is misleading; vehicle of transfiguration is better.[6]

[5] Herbert Marcuse writes of *Time* magazine style and the dimension of thought it allows in *One Dimensional Man* (Boston: Beacon, 1964), pp. 92ff.
[6] Aldrich, *Philosophy of Art*, pp. 47–48.

Another common image for a medium in communication is that of a channel. The phrase "communications channel" is widely used, minor opacities being referred to as "noise." Now a channel is clearly a means to an end; it is a conduit which is calculated to conduct subject matter from one place to another without changing its character. Making, maintaining, and using a channel are technical matters which may be guided, in principle, by calculation and experiment. Moreover, it is easy to see how, in the case of communication, experiments in the form of comparisons of efficiency are to be instituted, for we can easily measure how much information is transmitted and with how little noise. It may be noted that this justifies thinking of the senses as media of communication. So one may compare the ear and the eye for efficiency in this respect; for example, by having one class read a piece from a book to themselves, reading the same piece aloud to another, similar class, and having a third follow it visually on the page while hearing it read aloud, and comparing the results. In such a case one is comparing communication channels; the medium in the aesthetic sense remains the same throughout, for it is all in words. When the senses are thought of in this way, it is the nature of the case that they can be used as channels only in conjunction with at least one other medium, in either the communications or the aesthetic sense. When one watches TV, for example, the TV is one medium, the eyes and ears another. It is a part of the notion of a medium in communication that one may be subordinated to another, in just the way that one means may be subordinated to another. One might with ingenuity construct a long chain of such dependencies: the eyes may be the medium for watching the TV screen which is the medium for a documentary film in which there appears a photograph. . . . Nevertheless such a chain depends on there being something to be transmitted. There is never, *pace* McLuhan, a medium without something mediated, any more than there can be a means without an end, for the two notions are conceptually related. On the other hand,

272 /

there can be no such hierarchy of dependencies among aesthetic media. If we put together mime and the spoken word, we have not two distinct media but one new one; if we use elaborately painted backdrops on the stage, there is still only one aesthetic medium. It follows that the phrase "mixed media," which is heard in talk about both art and education, properly refers to media of communication. Yet all cases are cases of mixed media in the sense that one must always use a sense channel plus something else.

It is of interest to note that in the brief history of the systematic study of "educational media" a theory flourished (though it was short-lived) which regarded the devices available to the teacher as ideally transparent in the sense I have been describing; which is to say it was a theory which ranked such devices in terms of their capacity for faithful reproduction. I shall call this the Reality-Substitute theory of educational media, for reasons that will become obvious. The child, it was assumed (no doubt this theory was linked with wider ideological movements), learned best from contact with reality. If chickens or mountains were to be studied, the teacher did best to bring chickens to the child, and the child to the mountains. Pictures, maps, movies, models were to be used only because they were more accessible than chickens or mountains, being better than nothing, but less good than the real thing. And among these devices one was better than another insofar as it reproduced the original more faithfully. Thus one might say that a model can reproduce a mountain better than a picture, since it can preserve the three dimensions; that a picture is better than a map, since it preserves much of the mountain's visual character; and that the map is better than a purely verbal description because it retains in two dimensions the spatial character of the original. One could safely predict, I think, that with this method of argument, words ("verbal learning") would usually come at the bottom of the list.

Evidently the Reality-Substitute theory regarded educational media as channels of communication, in that any distortion that is due to the medium is to be regretted. The passing of this theory may be attributed to the naiveté of its conception of reality, according to which it appears that reality is anything not normally found in a classroom. This is not a useful conception of reality for a schoolmaster. For example, the Reality-Substitute theory would have us declare that it is better, because more realistic, to watch a scientific experiment carried out in a laboratory than to watch a film of it. Yet it may well be that one can learn more from the film than from the experiment in the flesh. It is an accidental virtue of the camera that it may give the child a better viewpoint from which to watch the experiment than he got in the laboratory. More important, the film-maker does not have to try to reproduce as much as possible of the "reality"; instead, he may do better by simplifying. For the richness of actuality may confuse the beginner. What is most significant for the particular experiment—the color of a litmus, a pointer on a dial—may have to compete for his attention with many unfamiliar sights, sounds, smells. A film may omit these distractions, and direct attention to what is of greatest significance. Nor is it tied to the visual surface of the experiment if that is not of great explanatory value: it could use diagrams or animated cartoons.[7] In much the same way, we may learn more of Thomas à Becket in the theater than we would from being present at his death in the cathedral. To generalize, educational media may be better regarded as instruments of Reality-Simplification than Reality-Substitution.

Another way of putting this point is in terms of the subject matter to be communicated. One may say that educational media set out to transmit not reality but theories about reality. What is to be studied is not so much a set of objects as of theoretical relationships, which may be more or less clearly exemplified in particular cases. This way of putting it is in line with a tendency in education today with which we are all

<hr/>

[7] See G. Holton, "Conveying Science by Visual Presentation," in G. Kepes, ed., *The Education of Vision* (New York: Braziller, 1965), pp. 50–77.

familiar. When milk comes to us not from a cow but through complex economic channels, and when no one accepts responsibility for the ravages of the automobile, we need theories to interpret the world for us. General Motors is not a person, and the milkman is not a cow, and only theory will enable us to understand why not. Schools today, therefore, are increasingly concerned with the promotion of theoretical understanding, rather than the observation of objects, and educational media, according to the Reality-Simplification theory, are for the transmission of theories. Both the Reality-Substitute and the Reality-Simplification theories implicitly take the media of communication as an analogy for educational media, it seems, though the latter is clearer about the nature of the "message." This conception of the message brings me to the second major distinction I wish to mark between the notion of a medium in art and a medium in communication. This is that in communication the content may be distinguished from the medium, in art not.

We say that communication takes place when some content has been transmitted, some messages passed on: no message, no communication. In uncertain cases we try to isolate the message. Suppose someone claims that the smile on the teacher's face is a means of communication. Well then, we ask, what is the message it conveys? We might say, it is as if the teacher said, "It's another lovely Monday morning and I'm happy to be with you." If that is what the teacher means by it and also what the child understands it to mean, we may agree that the smile was a means of communication. We will not agree if the child was puzzled by it or thought it meant, "I've discovered your guilty secret and you won't get away with it." Either way, what the smile cannot be said to communicate is itself; the message that we look for must be something other than the smile itself. Therefore, it must be distinguishable from the medium. And, it is evident, for it to be distinguishable in this way it must be formulable also in some other medium, as, in the example above, in words. A message

/ 275

is something which in principle may be communicated through alternative media, though not always with equal success. One may therefore conceive it independently of any particular medium and consider which would be the most suitable medium for it. We may ask: does this message lend itself to visual treatment? If so, we will use photographs or simplified diagrams. Is it more economical to use mathematical symbols? and so on. This kind of question, which is typical of the communications engineer, assumes that the message is in some sense already determined, that it is of a certain character to begin with, and that the task of the communications engineer is to choose a medium that accords with that character, will distort least, and be most economical. Such choices no doubt leave large areas for disagreement and individual judgment. Nevertheless they are technical choices, in which only a lack of the relevant information leaves room for disagreement. For where the end is determined (in this case, where the message is fixed), disagreement over means can be settled by an increase in knowledge.

In art, on the other hand (to make the contrast explicit), the end is not known in advance, except in the most general sense. If it were known in advance, then the specifically artistic work would be already done. The rest, we would say, is copying or transcribing. For it is common to say that art consists in the activity of discovering the character or significance of something, of formulating content for the first time; that it is the perception of form, the crystallization of significance out of chaos. This I take to be part of our common notion of what art is. It follows from this that in art the "content" is not separable from the medium as a message is separable from the medium of communication, for to separate content from its medium would necessitate formulating it in another. Such a formulation would have to be either the creation of another work of art, or a reduction of the content of the work of art to a message. Either way no equivalence could be claimed. Art and communication are therefore distinct in this way also, and

276 /

if one insists on saying that a work of art has a message, then one has at least to recognize that it is a peculiar kind of message, one which is unique to that work of art. One cannot ask of it the question that I have said distinguishes the communications engineer: which formulation is most efficient? Similarly, to say that art is communication is to use the notion of communication in a hazy and rather unusual way, and not in the sense which I am discussing in this paper. For what art can be said to communicate is only the character of its own medium; thus Edman, summarizing Dewey: ". . . the communication of art is something far different than conveying practical information or stating general and abstract ideas. Art communicates by celebrating the qualities of human experience. Its celebration is through the delight, at once perspicuous and vivid, of patterned energies, ordered experience. Art communicates because it renders available in clear and heightened unities the qualities of experience that are seen with absorption and heard as direct and as delightful."[8]

III

What light, then, does this contrast of a medium in art with a medium in communication throw on the interpretation of "educational media?" It clarifies, I think, two models that we use to conceptualize the situation in which the phrase is used. It remains not to choose between these models but to suggest how they affect our thinking about education and "educational media."

In education today we increasingly distinguish among the kinds of questions educators should ask about the curriculum. Two kinds commonly distinguished relate to two topics: (1) what subject matter to teach the child, and (2) which media to use. Thus, in a representative analysis of the components of a program of curriculum revision, we find, as two of four items, "(b) the process of identifying the subject-matter which is to be dealt with within [an] educational unit; (c) the embodi-

[8] Irwin Edman, "Dewey and Art," in Sidney Hook, ed., *John Dewey: Philosopher of Science and Freedom* (New York: Dial Press, 1950), p. 62.

ment of that subject-matter in material form, as text, laboratory or classroom materials, and other learning aids."[9] It is clear that the second of these is modeled on the kind of question that I have said is peculiar to the communications engineer. These questions are analogous, not identical, since the situation of the communications engineer and of the teacher are actually different. They will differ in that the engineer must ask: what representation of this message can be transmitted most economically and with least distortion? The teacher must ask: what representation of this message offers the best chance of being understood and learned? The criteria of success will differ because the purposes of the two differ. For example, some principles of math are commonly presented in schools for the first time in graphic form because they are more easily understood that way, whereas merely as communication algebraic systems of notation may be more efficient.

These differences, however, are likely to be swamped by the similarities which lie in what the questions presuppose. There are at least two common presuppositions, and they correspond with the differences I have marked between art and communication: they are that there is a message already formulated and hence determined, and that the character of this message governs the choice of the medium. This last means that the character of the medium being considered is not important in itself, but only as it affects success as measured by the relevant criteria. The medium, that is, is a means, ideally transparent. There may be other similarities, but the strength of the analogy seems to me to lie in these two; the communications model of "educational media" is appropriate insofar as it is appropriate to conceive education as the learning of a set of messages known in advance to the teacher, through whatever means seems most efficient. Evidently this goes a long way. Education has always had to do with the learning of messages and is hardly conceivable without them. Moreover, this is a useful

[9] J. R. Zacharias and S. White, "The Requirements for Major Curriculum Revision," *School and Society* XCII (1964): 66.

way of conceiving the teacher's business. It simplifies his task, emphasizes his power, and focuses attention on his choice. By making this choice a technical one, that is, by turning it into a means-end question, it encourages research, the accumulation of knowledge, and technological invention. The teacher becomes a specialist and can hope for systematic improvement as knowledge increases. One might suppose that a clearer name for "educational media" conceived this way would be "teaching technology"; a phrase that I will use for this purpose in the latter part of this paper.

Similarly the weaknesses of the analogy are related to these assumptions. It is not always transparent that in education the message can be formulated in advance. Sometimes it is more important to teach skills than information, such as the skill of asking questions; or appreciations, such as the appreciation of the problematic character of a situation. The nature of learning outcomes of these kinds is much debated, but few assimilate them finally with messages. If anything, it is the other way around.[10] Another way of saying this is to observe that education is also importantly a matter of acquiring dispositions and changing habits and in this respect may lie outside the range of the communications analogy. Some habits it does lie within the power of the teaching technologist to foster, notably the habit of receiving and remembering messages. With ingenuity others can be made to fit, such as the habit of thinking scientifically about certain kinds of problems. And there are some, such as "creativity," of which it may seem doubtful that they would ever be brought into such a framework. The issue here seems to revolve around the question whether the content of such habits can be reduced to a set of messages known in advance. In the same way the second assumption may not always be justified. For example, I have said that using certain media constantly may very well affect

---

[10] For a brief summary of the current literature on this topic see Jonas F. Soltis, *An Introduction to the Analysis of Educational Concepts* (Reading, Mass.: Addison-Wesley, 1968), pp. 36ff.

one's imagination in various ways. We can try to state this in the terms of the teaching technologist by saying: constantly communicating via a particular kind of channel can be shown empirically to produce certain side effects, as constant use of books leads to linear thinking. Since some of these effects may be valuable and some not, the teaching technologist will modify the second assumption, agreeing that the medium may be important in this way as well as for its suitability for particular messages. The difficulty here is in deciding how much and in what way the various effects of the media are valuable. What are the advantages and disadvantages of "linear thinking," for example? How does it compare with "visual thinking," which Arnheim thinks has been undervalued in education?[11] How can such a question be answered? Not simply in terms of the greater communicative efficiency of linear thinking. Herbert Read has suggested that certain important ideas are particularly suited to statement in particular media and that to be unacquainted with the medium is to be at a disadvantage in understanding the relevant idea.[12] It seems not impossible that some ideas can be articulated in words but not in music, in algebraic symbols but not in words, in paint but not in prose. It may also be that the reverse relation holds: that if one is too much in the habit of linear thinking, some other modes of thinking are inaccessible. If any of this is plausible, then the question becomes: how valuable are these ideas or modes of thinking? At this point we have circled, it seems, from the analogy with communication back to the analogy with art. Such a question is certainly not a technical one, and the necessity of bearing it in mind cannot but embarrass the teaching technologist.

A third kind of difficulty arises from the fact that communicating is a process that requires motivating, rather than one that provides motivation. It may happen that children are

[11] Rudolph Arnheim, "Visual Thinking," in G. Kepes, ed., *The Education of Vision*, pp. 1–14.

[12] Most notably in *Icon and Idea* (New York: Schocken Books, 1965).

interested in certain messages that the teacher is going to communicate; but if they are not, then, since the message is predetermined, the problem arises of providing that interest. Considered as a technical problem, this tends to be assimilated to the problems of salesmanship, the latter being more and more in our society a matter of finding means to the end of provoking interest in messages. Thus we find in the language of teachers the units of the new curricula referred to as "packages," and the classroom teacher's job (not that of the media specialist) as "selling" these units to the children. This is a common image; I have heard students in class suggest that most teachers would benefit from a course in salesmanship. It is evident that this mixing of the images of communication and salesmanship reflects developments in society at large, where the communications media are usually advertising media as well, concerned with the manipulation of interests and attitudes as well as with the transmission of information. The supermarket imagery of the school may not yet be at a very sophisticated level, but it points to one of the weaknesses of the communications analogy: overemphasis on the activity of the teacher and underemphasis on the activity of the learner, with a consequent easy descent into exploitive and manipulative attitudes which, while we tolerate them in magazines, have in the past been thought out of place in the schools.

What of the analogy of media in education with media in art? Here one turns up straightaway ancient metaphors that cannot be properly disinterred in the available space. I shall therefore be brief with them. Both the teacher and the learner have often been thought of as artists; that is, as being concerned with media in education in the way that artists are concerned with media. Of these, however, the metaphor of the teacher as artist, though it may be the more common in rhetoric, seems the less plausible in practice. Its frequency may be due more to a conviction of the importance of teachers than to a sense of its appropriateness; and it is often used to mean no more than the practice of teaching requires judgments about particulars. Any greater significance of the image seems to me to founder on the fact that the "significant forms" that the teacher must strive to produce are newly significant to the student and not to the teacher. That is to say that the teacher, though he may learn something as he teaches, cannot guide his teaching by what he is learning but by what the student is learning. Otherwise, we should have to say that he is "teaching himself" and not others, which is a less direct way of saying that he is learning and not really teaching at all.

With the companion metaphor of the child as artist I must be equally perfunctory. It is perhaps arbitrary to say that it seems more plausible; it may only be that it has been discussed in the literature in more detail. Black, for example, pictures the learner as struggling with different kinds of material (such as mathematical relationships) to arrange them into comprehensive and significant form. Such a conception throws emphasis on the conception of the subject matter as indistinguishable from the medium. The outcome of the child's struggle, guided by his intuition, is determined in large part by the particular character of the material struggled with, as the artist's is.[13] The outcome of this activity of the child is whatever the learner manages to formulate; it is not to be construed as a message, for it cannot necessarily be known to others in advance. The medium also is "opaque," important in its own character, since the outcome depends in large part on that character. These two features, it will be seen, are the obverse of the two assumptions just discussed in connection with the communications analogy.

The strengths of the analogy with art, then, it will be expected, are the obverse of those already discussed. They lie, in the first place, in the fact that the child does have to work at making sense of the lesson, that what finally counts is the significant pattern he apprehends, and that the content of learning, so to say, is as important as the subject-matter of

[13] Max Black, "Education as Art and Discipline," in Israel Scheffler, ed., *Philosophy and Education* (Boston: Allyn and Bacon, 1966), pp. 32–38.

teaching. Another way of saying this is that the learner must come to have a feeling for the subject if he is to be said to have learned it: unless a man has at some time appreciated the elegance of a proof or the wit of a poem he cannot be said to know geometry or poetry. The kind of knowledge that is important to education is not reducible to information or simple kinds of messages.[14] The complementary weakness of this lies in the plain fact that a child may get a problem wrong even though it seems to him that he has it right, and that this is also important in education. The aesthetic medium, to follow the analogy strictly, might be said to be not geometrical relationships but the appearance of geometrical relationships, what Susanne Langer might have called Virtual Reasoning, reasoning that has the appearance of validity. But evidently Virtual Reasoning may be invalid reasoning, as validity is defined by the consensus of the relevant experts. Indeed, as the history of mathematics demonstrates, it is often a hard thing to learn that what seems obviously right is not so in fact, and this may be especially the case in a society where, as I have remarked, the surface of life is no longer self-explanatory. Many a child starts by finding that, for example, deficit financing is obviously wrong, or that segregation is obviously right, and certainly today education includes coming to understand that one's intuitions of certainty may be mistaken. One strength of the analogy, then, is that it is true that in the end the child must rely on his intuitions, but this fails to take account of the complementary fact that the artist's imagination, unlike the learner's, has been shaped by a long discipline in the art.

With regard to the second assumption about the medium, if the learner is thought of as an artist, then he will decide which medium he will work with, for the medium is simply what he finds to be relevant. There is an obvious point in insisting on this. If the learner is more interested in the shapes and smells

14 See R. S. Peters, *Ethics and Education* (Glenview, Ill.: Scott, Foresman, 1967), p. 73.

of the laboratory than in the color of the litmus, he is not doing chemistry, no matter what the lesson is called; if he does not consistently abstract mathematical relationships it is pointless insisting that he attend to mathematics. This brings up the difficulties in justifying forcing a medium on the learner. For if he works better with music than with math, with literature than with philosophy, why should we foist unsympathetic media on him? Do we ask poets to paint, or musicians to make statues? Evidently these questions do not call for technical answers. Yet we can justify, presumably, obliging children to learn at least some of the things that we oblige them to learn; there are some messages that everyone needs if he is to be educated. The question can be asked, within the framework of the communications analogy, about the "learning style" of the individual learner. That is to say, if it is the case that people can articulate ideas better in some media than in others, that is an important fact about them, and one which will affect the teacher's choice of communications medium. It seems that we are not, on the whole, sensitive enough to such variations among people, and that their investigation might well be one of the central topics in the systematic study of "educational media."

IV

One might summarize the results of this discussion as follows. There are at least two different ways of construing "educational media," both of them important, neither adequate by itself. One of these focuses largely on the teacher's problems, making them technical in character, and construing "media" as a particular kind of means. It implies a predetermined curriculum, and offers to settle the choice of media by measurement and comparison. Such a model suits many elements of our technological society. A good name for this conception of "media" might be "teaching technology." The second model throws emphasis on the activity of the learner, and on what he can discover and create. His results cannot easily be compared with one another, or with those of other children. The choice of medium is necessarily the learner's. The teacher may offer only opportunity and criticism, though this is of great importance. This model is somewhat out of fashion. A suitable name for this conception of "media" might be "learning media." The phrase "educational media" is systematically ambiguous between these two models, covering both teaching and learning, and the channels of communication and the media of art. This may be a practical advantage, since neither conception seems sufficient.

I have adumbrated the inadequacies of these models of "educational media" which turn out to be complementary, but I have not discussed the possibility of combining both models in the same situation. It might be possible to conceive of the teacher as a communications engineer at the same time as thinking of the learner as an artist, though at first sight this seems implausible. However, whether these two frameworks are incompatible or not, and whether they can be made to be compatible with minor adjustments, are questions not to be attempted at this time.

CREATIVITY / 12

D. W. Gotshalk

The Meaning of Creativity

Creativity is a very general concept. Indeed, process philoso-phers, following a modern tradition extending from Fichte to Whitehead, make it the essence of cosmic actuality.[1] In this sense, every event is creative: the explosion of a star, the birth of a new animal species. Each is, like "the creative process which we term our lives,"[2] an advance into novelty. I shall not discuss creativity in this broad cosmic sense, only crea-tivity in the fine arts. But I shall follow the process philoso-phers in one respect. In ordinary language, to be "creative" is to be exceptionally virtuous. There is something elevated and very special about the "creative" person. On the other hand, for the process philosopher all actual occasions are creative. As Whitehead remarks, it is as creative to knock your neighbor down as to perform any expressive act.[3] Both are advances into novelty.

[1] See Charles Hartshorne, *The Logic of Perfection* (LaSalle, Ill.: Open Court, 1962).
[2] Alfred North Whitehead, *Modes of Thought* (New York: Macmillan, 1938; G. P. Putnam's Sons, Capricorn Books, 1958), p. 103.
[3] *Ibid.*, p. 40.

In what follows I shall use the process philosopher's neutral sense of creativity rather than the honorific sense of ordinary language. To be creative in the fine arts will mean simply to produce something novel. It may be something solemn and grand, or something outrageous and trivial. But if it is something new, the production will be creative. As just indicated, this does not mean that all creative acts in the arts will have the same value. Their results at least may have a vast range of values. It means rather that the creative process in the arts will be treated as a matter-of-fact occurrence, and described, so far as possible, as any matter-of-fact occurrence.

If this creative process always occurred in a simple sequential order, as many matter-of-fact occurrences do, describing it would be comparatively easy. But no such order seems to exist. To be sure, the process has a beginning, a middle, and an end. But its beginning may be a fully self-articulating inspiration, a scarcely perceptible urging, a chance sight or sound, or any number of other things. Middles and ends are equally various. In these circumstances, instead of setting up a sequential model and trying to fit the diverse instances of artistic creativity into it, I propose merely to describe the factors that seem to me necessary for the occurrence of the process as it is most commonly known, noticing the temporal position of the factors only incidentally. I shall indeed consider two major questions: What are the chief components of the creative process in the fine arts? What contribution, if any, can a knowledge of these components make to aesthetic education and to education generally?

The chief factors or components of the creative process in the fine arts seem to be at least five: background, aims, structure, limitations, and values.

Background

By background I shall mean the total inheritance of the artist that functions pertinently in the creative process. I say "pertinently" to disencumber the process of unilluminating detail. In a sense, the whole universe is the background of every creative act. "Each task of creation is a social effort, employing the whole universe."[4] In the background of a creative artist are his spatial, temporal, gravitational, and similar world relations to every molecule and atom in the universe. And these enter into his nature. Change any one of them ever so slightly and you change a relational property of his nature. Still, I think we can abstract from this complex background in our discussion. The reason is that it does not appear in any distinctive role in an artist's creative endeavors. It is a uniform background for all of his acts and is not especially influential in his artistic acts. On the other hand, the talent an artist is born with, the formal and informal training in an art he has received, the understanding he has absorbed from his physical, social, and cultural milieu—such elements are likely to have a special determinate influence on his creative activity in an art, and it is these, along with similar detail including any from his world-wide relations, that shall be meant by "background" in the present discussion.

This pertinent variety must be available in the creative process to be important. To have a rich experience which you are not able to tap, for example, is not much help in creation. But ordinarily "creative persons," it is said, "have an unusual capacity to record and retain and have readily available the experiences of their life history."[5] Also, a good deal of this pertinent background is not merely a function of the artist's memory. If his society knows only the quarter-tone musical scale, a composer is unlikely to write diatonic, chromatic, or serial music. If only religious institutions employ painters, the pictorial artist of the day is most likely to devote his major attention to religious painting. The background of an artist's work is supplied as much by the conditions under which he lives as by his private memories and present possessions, and

[4] Alfred North Whitehead, *Process and Reality* (New York: Macmillan, 1929), p. 340.
[5] Donald W. MacKinnon, "What Makes a Person Creative," in E. Kronovet and E. Shirk, eds., *The Pursuit of Awareness* (New York: Appleton-Century-Crofts, 1967), p. 337.

anything in the external world that affects his style, "cramps" it or inspires it, is part of this background.

Although the immensity of this background makes it impossible to describe its innumerable detail, several useful generalizations can be made about it. First, this background is what the artist works *from* in the creative process. It is the "data," the given stubborn accepted fact, against which the novel or nongiven that he creates will contrast. Second, it is what the artist works *with*, for it includes his talent trained or untrained and the medium he has accepted for his work. In creation, the artist addresses his powers to a field of possibilities. The powers are his own, the possibilities are in his medium, but at the moment of creation both lie in the background from which his work will emerge.

More comprehensively, the background of artistic creativity can be divided into two great sectors: internal and external. The internal sector includes the artist's inborn gift and temperament, his character and personality. It also includes all of his experiences in the home, school, neighborhood, and society beyond, and all the memories he has stocked in his being— verbal, symbolic, sensorimotor, kinaesthetic—as these bear on his work. The external sector consists of all that the environment contributes to his creative activity: the training, the occasions for creative activity, the chance inspirational stimuli, the climate of opinion, the prospect of artistic survival. These two sectors fuse into one great whole, but their elements are usually distinguishable, as the training an artist was given is distinguishable from his memory of it. Also, it is useful to distinguish them because the internal sector has more special relevance to aims and structure, while the external sector has more special relevance to limitations and values.

Aims

The human being is a self-guided creature, and creativity in the arts is infused with self-guidance. In the creative process the powers of the artist are on the move directed toward a detailed outcome. This is the aim. But of its full specific nature in a given case the artist may be only dimly aware. Indeed, in some cases the aim may be no more than a seeking to discover what will turn up by letting brush, fingers, or pen roam at random in a medium. At the other extreme, it may be a methodical effort to produce a previsioned professional commodity. Usually it is more than an overarching intention. During creation the artist is ordinarily a veritable mass of aims, many of them emerging only in the shaping process.

This is not surprising. Creation in the arts, like many other human actions, is a quest for value realization. It is an effort to imbed in a work features producing intrinsic satisfactions. In its full tide, the whole personality, conscious and unconscious, is involved. This means that the slant of the artist's value inclinations will enter into his activity. The affinity of Matisse for long lines, thin shapes, exotic colors, or of Rouault for large round shapes and dense textures, denotes directions of their sensibility that result in features of their paintings. Nor is the presence of these features in the paintings related only to the terminal satisfactions of the artist but also to the fact that instrumentally he can use them effectively. Thus, the aim in the creative process is always more than any large overall goal, however definite. It includes a multitude of tiny directions, often unconscious, that spring from the artist's inclinations and insight as he strives to produce a satisfying result.

Throughout the creative process this aim factor induces some assessment of what is being done. It is not always clear to the creator that his aims are being satisfied or that the aims in operation are the aims he wants. Back-tracking, correction of detail, even total redirection sometimes result. I have argued elsewhere that a critical element—at times no more than mere approval or disapproval it is true—customarily mingles with the surges of artistic creativity, and exerts an influence upon it.[6] In more categorical terms, this appears to be the position of Beardsley who in his account of artistic creation accepts and defends Vincent Tomas's theory "that creation is a self-

[6] D. W. Gotshalk, *Art and the Social Order* (Chicago: University of Chicago Press, 1947; New York: Dover, 1963), pp. 65–68.

correcting process, in which the artist constantly redirects its aims."[7] Incidentally, this view seems compatible with having a very definite end in view or having no such end at all. But its chief reference is to all of the aims in the creative process, and to the constant estimating of their effectiveness and repairing their ineffectiveness where the artist discerns it and can make such repair.

Let me extend a little our point about the density of the aim factor. The creative person is said to be relatively free of repression.[8] Consequently, in his self-guided acts, such as creation, he is likely to give full rein to his deepest value tendencies. In previous epochs, when the artist was the servant of a royal patron or religious institution or worked in a school under a master craftsman, his main aims were usually specified for him. He did what he was told. But even within such restrictions many artists saturated their works with their individual qualities, as Giotto and Mozart did, and their artistic aims cannot be realistically described or appraised without consideration of the fine detail. To tell a religious story, to write a lively operatic comedy—such aims give only the faintest intimation of the multitude of intentions that guided such creators as they wrought the fabric of their works. A color is placed in a certain area of a fresco, a musical figure is inserted in a certain passage of a score. Each carries forward in its own little way the ostensible overall project. But each does it with delicacy, ease, and enhancement of pattern, that is, with qualities that bespeak artistic intention and personal care, aims within the larger aim, shaping the detailed result. Every main region of a masterpiece is sometimes of this sort.

Structure

The creative person has been described as relatively free of repression. This means that he tends not only to welcome ex-

---

[7] Monroe C. Beardsley, "On the Creation of Art," in Ralph A. Smith, ed., *Aesthetics and Criticism in Art Education* (Chicago: Rand McNally, 1966), p. 160. See Vincent Tomas, *Creativity in the Arts* (Englewood Cliffs, N.J.: Prentice-Hall, 1964).

[8] MacKinnon, "What Makes a Person Creative," p. 338.

periences but also to combine them. Repression dissociates items of experience which therefore cannot be combined. This combining of accumulated items, which introduces the third component of structure, is close to the essence of artistic creativity. Background, aims, and all the other components including value affinities, function as creative only as they enter into and shape a novel artistic structure.

Combining is unifying, a mode of coordination. It is unifying a multiplicity. Some emergent from the nonconscious appears in the artist's consciousness. It may be a rhythm, a phrase or sentence, a vision of a line or shape. If a creative aim is in motion, the artist may reject the emergent. Or he may accept or modify it, and rebegin or continue on this basis. If no creative activity is in progress, the emergent may initiate one. In any case, throughout a creative process a number of such emergents may appear, suggesting, even demanding, what should be combined with them. These interior configurations, which may become the gems of the creative outcome, are commonly considered a mystery. And in some sense they are. But it is notable that they usually come most profusely to persons who have had some experience of artistic creation, and who are energetically devoted to artistic achievement, and they customarily reflect the value slant of this person. Unconscious in origin they may be, but self-expressive they usually are, being reformations of items into reflections of the artist's personality.

Yet this account of the structuring of the multiplicity in terms of emergent inspirations and personal expression is far too simple. With or without an overall design to guide it, a process proceeding in these terms is only one mode of creative coordination. There are others. One is an assembling of merely external fragments, bits and pieces, valued by the artist. David Jones, the Anglo-Welsh poet-painter, gives this general model for *modern* modern art: "A series of fragments, fragmented bits, chance scraps, really, of records of things, vestiges of sorts and kinds of *disciplinae*, that have come my way by this chan-

292 /

nel or that influence. Pieces of stuffs that happen to mean something to me."[9] At the other extreme is a multiplicity flowing from a single sustained internal eruption, a lyrical outpouring that seems to come in one piece.

If the structuring of items is, as I have said, close to the essence of the creative process in the arts, what is needed for its finer achievements? Eagerness, ambition, industry certainly may help. Being steeped in a subject, "loaded" so to speak, gives imagination a large field in which to work. Facility is not always inborn, and training can nurture it. Yet to acquire facility is not to achieve felicity. Something more is required. In the best cases, where the structuring is subtle and comprehensive, a good deal of the credit commonly must go to the underground. The artist himself is often surprised and amazed at what comes forth, frequently discovering from it for the first time precisely what he wants to say in the work in progress. Intelligence may intervene to judge aptness and establish coherence. But the primary job is the work of the extraordinary deep-level combinatory power called genius, which sends forth from the depths rich, integral, and novel structures.

In the next section I shall say a little more about the nature of high artistic achievement. But in the foregoing discussions I have probably emphasized too much the role of the personal qualities of the artist. Let me briefly redress the balance. In the arts of the West, especially since the Renaissance, the personal quality has been very prominent. The artist has sought more and more to create a work that satisfied him, that is, that embodied his values. Even when he was copying nature or following the wishes of a patron, he was selecting and underlining, and, instead of a cold traditional stereotype, was producing an authentic if sometimes attentuated personal disclosure. But the structuring of items is ordinarily controlled by more than the value affinities of the artist. There is also the subject being treated. Whatever it is—an event, landscape, people, an emo-

[9] Harold Rosenberg, "The Concept of Action in Painting," *New Yorker*, May 25, 1968, p. 118. Italics in text.

tion, idea, or other nonobject, the structuring must unify items so that the subject is shown. The structuring must be subject-expressive as well as self-expressive, and must be geared to this goal. Thus, in building an artistic structure, we might say that besides background, aims, and all they imply there is a twofold limitation. The artist with his individual value affinities and genius or lack of it is one limitation. The subject of a work is another.

Limitations

There is, however, another major limitation of artistic creativity, which gives this fourth component added complexity. This is the medium in which the artist works. You can do many things with words, colors, people before a camera. But there are also many things you cannot do. These limitations springing from externals with which an artist works are augmented by limitations of his larger environment. In certain environments you cannot get a certain type of stone or clay, and you can work in it only if you change residence or otherwise overcome this limitation. Similarly, as I have said, certain societies present cultural limitations. Living in ancient Greece and using its available resources, it would be impossible even for a musical genius to compose a modern symphony.

These numerous external limitations of artistic creativity, however, are not unmitigated hardships. They may irritate. As in anti-art, they may even lead the artist to show in scorn the weakness and poverty of his medium: to "paint" a bare canvas or in music to contrive absurd instrumental sequences. But these limitations can be stimulants as well as irritants. After all, value is possible only within limitation. Unless an entity meets a need, a want, a wish, an end, or overcomes the limitation projecting them, it has no value to a human being. The problem of creativity presented by medial limitation is not the negation of value but the execution of aims within the medial possibilities. These possibilities are the opportunities for aim-realization, and the use of them is the way to value-realization.

Indeed, the great triumphs of artistic creativity are works in which all sense of medial limitation has disappeared. The medium seems to be completely used up, expressive in all detail of subject and artist alike, in a result of surpassing interest. This may be accomplished in two ways, perhaps in others. Whitehead writes: "It is one function of great literature to evoke a vivid feeling of what lies beyond words."[10] This is one way. But it is one function of great literature, I think it can also be said, to evoke a vivid feeling of what is *in* words. Classical perfection in the use of a medium is as stunning a realization of its possibilities as romantic suggestion, and there is as much reason to give the palm to a Racine or Molière as to a Shakespeare or Marlowe. Like Mozart and Beethoven, Poussin and Rubens, each has produced some results in which the medium seems used to the full, and you can delight equally in the perfect finish of the one or in the surge of unlimited strength in the other, marking the triumph of aim over limitations.

Values

Value, the fifth component of creativity, has already been mentioned at several points. Creativity is an advance into novelty. But in the arts it is an advance to a prized or despised novelty. The novelty is infused with value or disvalue. Perhaps the primary value in a work of art is the quality of the whole: the rough clumsy character of a Beethoven scherzo, the studied melancholy of a Haydn slow movement. But the value of a work is always more than its general beauty or ugliness. In structuring, as I have remarked, aims play a role in each detail. Of any region of a work you may ask: What does it say? What does it add? Each question is a request for value, the value of the region. Not merely the work as a whole but its multiplicity in pattern is an example of aim projection and value (or disvalue) realization.

Elsewhere I have argued that a work of fine art may be said

[10] Whitehead, *Modes of Thought*, p. 7.

to have sixteen different types of aesthetic value.[11] Such a work is a four-dimensional whole composed of materials with form, expression, and functions. It is an array of materials: sounds, colors, lines, shapes, bodily movements, words, or some other material. It has a form or system of relations pervading and organizing these materials. It expresses many things from abstract qualities such as zest, verve, hilarity, and melancholy to concrete characters and scenes such as Innocent X and Guernica. It is a unit with a function, performing or shaped to perform a certain task: to satisfy its creator, to be aesthetically exciting, to pass time, to make money. Furthermore, each of these four dimensions can have not only its own intrinsic aesthetic interest. It can contribute to the aesthetic value and interest of the other three. The granite of a statue, besides being of interest in its own right, can contribute an impression of solidity and strength to the noble figure being expressed in the statue, whereas another material such as soap or porcelain would not. And this instrumental relation of material to expression illustrates a relation that can be found between any two dimensions of a work of art. Accordingly, statues, poems, paintings, musical compositions, etc., can exhibit as many as sixteen different types of aesthetic values (or disvalues): the four intrinsic to the four dimensions, and the twelve between the four dimensions, three from each.

To be sure, the overall approach—the detachment of the pervading quality of a work—remains the most frequent and direct way to get at its value or disvalue. The essence of artistic creativity is a novel structuring of items into an original whole. The dimensions are to flesh out this novel creation, detailed features of the imaginative construction. What does the total effort yield in satisfaction? This is the question most naturally asked before scanning the details to discover how they perform.

The components of artistic creativity, then, are at least five: background, aims, structure, limitations, and values. The crowning feature of the process is the production from a com-

[11] Gotshalk, *Art and the Social Order*, Part II, pp. 87–169.

plex background of a novel structure embodying in its details and in its whole a realization of aims that imbues the work with a variety of values (or disvalues). Let me add here a few words about this crowning feature, the production of the novel structure. In the "Aims" section of this essay I described it as consisting of combining diverse items, and I believe this is overwhelmingly the case. But sometimes it consists more of de-combining, of simplifying, of isolating from an encumbering mass a form already there. The plot of a story may be a thin thread imbedded in a multiplicity of actual incidents. The layout of a junk sculpture or of street-noise "music" recorded on tape may have been obtained by stripping down a massive whole of which they were a part. Usually, it is true, some combining with other things is used to "touch up" the structure. Still, the main activity is a stripping away of diversity rather than combining diversity. The genius of discernment competes with the genius of synthesis for the honor of creative center by its role in such cases.

Aesthetic Education

I turn now to our second major question which concerns education, and first, aesthetic education. What can a knowledge of artistic creativity contribute to aesthetic education? If you know about this process in general or in a specific case—Giotto decorating the Arena Chapel, Beethoven composing the *Third Symphony*, Joyce writing *Ulysses* or *Finnegans Wake*—can it add anything to your aesthetic education in the fine arts?

Clearly the answer to this question depends first of all on the meaning of "aesthetic education" and "the fine arts." Adopting a suggestion I have made elsewhere,[12] you might mean by "aesthetic education" in the fine arts the "developing of sensitivity to the aesthetic values" there. The question then would be what you will mean by "the fine arts." If you mean by fine art the act of creation, as action painters are said to do, then knowledge of the creative process, either by direct experience

[12] D. W. Gotshalk, "Aesthetic Education as a Domain," *The Journal of Aesthetic Education* II (1968): 44.

or from description of it, would be the only enlightenment available for developing sensitivity to the aesthetic values in fine art. It would be the whole cognitive basis of aesthetic education in the area. But you may mean by fine art what is usually meant: the production of works of aesthetic import. This would shift the emphasis to the products of the creative process: works of art. Some have argued that a knowledge of artistic creativity can contribute nothing to the appreciation of the aesthetic values in works of art. These values are independent of their mode of production. They are there for us to respond to, however they were produced.[13] I think this position overlooks several important considerations.

The aesthetic values of a work of art are indeed in the work and to be determined for what they are there. But to respond to them in this way requires that we understand them correctly. Here accurate genetic information can sometimes be very helpful. Some works of art are transparent and self-evident. Others are full of darkness and obscurity. To know how or why they were put together as they are often removes the puzzles they generate. This illumination may be very elementary. Thus, when a person sees that certain qualities of a fresco arise not from the naiveté of the artist but from the limitations of his medium, or that certain qualities of a piece of music arise from the demands of its subject rather than the perversity of its composer, he may get a clearer and truer perspective on the values in the work. Learned exegesis of subterranean detail, important as it is in this respect, is not the only way to illumine these values. Doubtless some knowledge provided by the genetic approach is useless. But much is not. Even a date may suggest a whole cultural environment in which a work was produced, explaining certain characteristics of its theme or function. Also, while some of the clarification provided by genetic information might have been gained by direct study of a work, it is usually more easily gained by a

[13] Beardsley, "On the Creation of Art," p. 167.

person who is aided in this study by some knowledge of creative circumstances.

An important distinction should be recognized here. This is between genetic information about a work and genetic standards for judging a work. Genetic standards, such as judging a work by the intention of the artist, are generally inadequate, and have been severely criticized.[14] The proper standard is one that judges a work by the requirements of art, not, for example, by what the creator intended the work to be.[15] On the other hand, genetic information frequently can show us better what we are dealing with in a work of art, and thereby improve our position for responding to and appreciating the aesthetic values that are there. It is not itself a mode of judgment. Knowledge of the creative process rather gives information on why this feature of a work is as it is, what this feature was supposed to do or not do, etc. In this way, the information sharpens sensitivity to the values that are there, and by helping to reveal them aright can promote an education in these aesthetic values.

Another View

There is, however, another meaning to aesthetic education in the arts besides "developing sensitivity to the aesthetic values" there. This is that aesthetic education is education in artistic production, or developing creative talent. Perhaps this second meaning confuses "aesthetic" and "artistic." What is being described is art education rather than aesthetic education. But let us suppose it is a valid meaning of aesthetic education.

Obviously, in this sense of aesthetic education a knowledge of creativity in the arts could be of great value in it. Knowing the ins and outs of an activity you yourself are repeatedly trying to perform could clarify what you are up against, what you can do, and what you may not be able to do. The danger in such education is the temptation of the instructor to stand-

14 Gotshalk, *Art and the Social Order*, pp. 196–97.
15 *Ibid.*, chap. 8.

ardize the process, to reduce it to a stereotype, to say this fixed way is *the* method, this is what you have to do. Nothing could be farther from an enlightening education in artistic creativity, whose patterns are so various. Still, an analysis of artistic creativity, describing the character and variety of its components, illustrating each with apt and numerous examples, can give the learner a better conception of its possibilities and uncertainties, and enable him to shape better his competence for the task. A sophistication of this sort, an awareness of the opportunities and hardships of the artistic undertaking, is perhaps the most significant fruit of education in the area, and to the person whose life's task is artistic creation, knowledge of creative practice is I think the most effective way of acquiring this sophistication when it is combined with practice itself.

Education

Does creativity in the fine arts, as we have described it, have implications for education generally? I think it does. In both teaching and learning I believe we can find the same factors that we have found in the creative process in the arts: background, aims, structure, limitations, and values; and an illuminating account of these factors in the arts can shed light on their character and role in education. To be sure, the similarity between fine art and education in this regard is generic, not specific. Between the two there is an analogy only, not an identity. But there is a genuine parallelism.

Thus, the teacher brings to his performance a diversified background: all he has learned, all the pedagogic talent he has developed, all he has prepared for the occasion; and the learner comes with his characteristic background. The teacher has an aim: to convey the knowledge he has of the subject. Indeed, he has a multitude of aims, usually including the selection and emphasis of the details of his subject that he thinks are of central importance and value. The learner has a different aim: to acquire what knowledge he recognizes as significant for him. But his activity will be (or should be) as purposive as the teacher's in its different way. Further, to perform his task, the teacher will organize the variety of his knowledge that he believes to be germane to his presentation, even though it may be merely into a collage of notes. The learner will also try to order his acquisitions into some intelligible form. Each will seek to impose a structure on the multiplicity of items, and this structure will bear the imprint of its author with such novel accents as his personality has. Obviously there will be limitations. The teacher will be confronted by the limitations of his students, his subject, his pedagogical apparatus. He will also perform under the limitations of his own knowledge, teaching talent, and personality. The learner, in the classroom at least, will be confronted by some of these limitations, and will have limitations of his own due to such ignorance or incompetence in the field as he may have. Finally, where the teacher is able to make his performance convey genuine insight into his subject and the learner is able to acquire this insight, and the efforts of both seem to absorb all means at hand in the realization of this insight, you have probably the supreme value possible in education.

If teaching and learning are so parallel to artistic creativity, what is the difference? Why not call teaching and learning fine arts, as we do music and painting? There is a difference, and this difference is particularly clear in the aim. The aim of teaching and learning is cognitive: to impart and/or acquire knowledge. Where knowledge is the aim, the structure created or assimilated has a transstructural reference. It refers to a world of action and fact beyond the cognitive structure as the basis of its validity. In contrast, the aim in the fine arts is to create a structure that is valuable in itself, just to see or hear, apart from what may lie beyond it. The aim is an experience excellent in intrinsic nature. Such experience may give you knowledge and truth about other things, or, as Socrates thought, complete deception. That is another matter. The important point is that it give you something valid and valuable in its immediate being rather than in its mediating or mediate being, as knowledge structures do.

/ 301

This difference in aim makes a difference in every other aspect of fine art and education: in the specific background relevant, in the specific structure created, in the specific limitations to be overcome, and in the specific values to be realized. Nevertheless, a genuine parallelism remains. The generic components of the processes of the two are the same. This means, as I have said, that an illuminating account of the components of the one could shed much light on the components of the other. In sum, the creative process in the fine arts affords a generic model for both teaching and learning, and can give that kind of nonliteral or imaginative enlightenment of the components of these processes that analogy used properly can always give.

IMAGINATION / 13

Maxine Greene

"The imagination," writes Wallace Stevens, "is the power that enables us to perceive the normal in the abnormal, the opposite of chaos in chaos."[1] Expressed poetically, it becomes the "Blessed rage for order,"[2] the source of meaningfulness. A world absolutely and finally understood becomes "blank cold"[3]

[1] Wallace Stevens, *The Necessary Angel* (New York: Vintage Books, 1965), p. 153.

[2] Wallace Stevens, "The Idea of Order at Key West," in *The Collected Poems of Wallace Stevens* (New York: Alfred A. Knopf, 1964), p. 130.

[3] Wallace Stevens, "The Plain Sense of Things," in *ibid.*, pp. 502–3. Copyright 1952 by Wallace Stevens. Reprinted by permission of Alfred A. Knopf, Inc.

> After the leaves have fallen, we return
> To a plain sense of things. It is as if
> We had come to an end of the imagination,
> Inanimate in an inert savoir.
>
> It is difficult even to choose the adjective
> For this blank cold, this sadness without cause.
> The great structure has become a minor house.
> No turban walks across the lessened floors.

because it is resistant to imagination. Such a world is separated by a "great pond" from the ego, a pond lacking all "reflections" of the human self. The positivists prize this kind of objectivity, "the plain sense of things." The poet knows that truth is to be found there; but he says that imagination must effect some vital connection between the self and "things" if people are to live their lives in wholeness, in vitality. Bridging the gap, the "great pond," imagination cannot alter or distort reality. It can, however, impart value and significance; it can create new integral wholes; it can overcome man's alienation from his world.

Stevens's renderings touch at several points on the concept of imagination as it functions in contemporary aesthetic contexts. Imagination is generally conceived to be an active rather than a passive affair. It is thought of as a formative or constructive activity of the mind, going beyond cognitive resolutions and rule-governed unifications. It has to do with the discovery of what Stevens calls "resemblances," with symbol-making, synthesis, and transmutation. Although it is a process of mediation between man and his world, it is often equated with "fictionality,"[4] signifying the distinction between its products and those of "plain" or empirical sense. It implies (as it did for John Dewey)[5] something other than the habitual, the hum-

---

The greenhouse never so badly needed paint.
The chimney is fifty years old and slants to one side.
A fantastic effort has failed, a repetition
Is a repetitiousness of men and flies.

Yet the absence of the imagination had
Itself to be imagined. The great pond,
The plain sense of it, without reflections, leaves,
Mud, water like dirty glass, expressing silence

Of a sort, silence of a rat come out to see,
The great pond and its waste of lilies, all this
Had to be imagined as an inevitable knowledge,
Required, as a necessity requires.

[4] René Wellek and Austin Warren, *Theory of Literature* (New York: Harcourt, Brace, Harvest Books, 1956), p. 14.

[5] John Dewey, *Art as Experience* (New York: Minton, Balch, 1934), pp. 269–70.

drum, the mechanical; and it may suggest, as for Jean-Paul Sartre, "a negation of mundane existence."[6] But it involves more than "pretending" in Gilbert Ryle's sense;[7] and it is not merely an affair of the interior life, since (where talk about the arts is concerned) it culminates in some formal and sensuous embodiment,[8] in the creation of realms of possibility.[9]

For the ancients, imagination had a more limited meaning. It was considered the opposite of imitation (signifying any sort of reproduction or copying). Breaking through boundaries of time and space, generated by expanding "admiration," imagination was presumed to reach outward toward the Ideal—perhaps the really Real in the Platonic mode, perhaps something fictive, an analogue of the Real.[10] As I. A. Richards points out, there was ambiguity in treatments of the subject: an opposition between "a projective outlook, which treats imagination's products as a figment, and a realist outlook, which takes the imagination to be a means of apprehending reality."[11]

In the seventeenth century, imagination was used to mean invention, especially when invention was "inspired" or when it possessed the atttribute John Dryden (following Renaissance thinkers) called "grace."[12] Occasionally it was used to mean "imaging," the construction of pictures in the mind or the thinking of "unreal" things.

The empiricists of the eighteenth century developed a mechanical model to explain the activities of imagination—or "fancy," treated as synonymous. Concerned with breaking

[6] Maurice Natanson, *Literature, Philosophy and the Social Sciences* (The Hague: Nijhoff, 1962), pp. 111–12.

[7] Gilbert Ryle, *The Concept of Mind* (New York: Barnes and Noble, 1949), pp. 256–59.

[8] Margaret Macdonald, "The Work of Art as Physical," in Melvin Rader, ed., *A Modern Book of Esthetics*, 3rd ed. (New York: Holt, Rinehart and Winston, 1965), p. 219.

[9] See, e.g., Victorino Tejera, *Art and Human Intelligence* (New York: Appleton-Century-Crofts, 1965), p. 215.

[10] I. A. Richards, *Coleridge on Imagination* (Bloomington: Indiana University Press, 1960), pp. 25–26.

[11] *Ibid.*, p. 26.

[12] Samuel H. Monk, "A Grace Beyond the Reach of Art," *Journal of the History of Ideas* V (1944): 131, 150.

down the contents of the mind into its component parts, they saw those parts—or "ideas"—as nothing but faint replicas of sense perceptions. Poetry was composed of largely visual images, replicas of things seen, combined by fancy in more or less ingenious ways.[13] Images of nonexistent things (unicorns, for instance, or dragons) were thought to be fabricated out of ideas of sight, which might be divided up and recombined. A construct which *seemed* to be novel or creative was understood to be nothing more than a rearrangement of materials originally conveyed by the senses. The form or design of a work of art was explained in terms of some anticipated effect on the reader or spectator, or (as David Hume put it) in terms of some "aim or intention" in the mind of the artist which could not always be defined.[14]

It was Samuel Taylor Coleridge who effected the break with the mechanist or associationist approach and opened the way for a consideration of imagination as active and formative. He found his inspiration in Immanuel Kant's *Critique of Judgment* with its emphasis upon the synthesizing, ordering power associated with the "transcendental faculty of imagination."[15] For Kant, aesthetic creation was a special instance of the use of that power; and Coleridge, developing his own view of the "shaping spirit of the imagination," was much influenced by the Kantian emphasis on the autonomy of the aesthetic and the possibilities to be found in what was called the "beautiful representation of a thing" which could not be encompassed by concepts.

The poet coined the term "esemplastic" to describe the unifying function of the imagination. He spoke of knowing as a product of an "intimate coalition" of subject and object, or the mind and the natural world. This conception of the "coalescence" of subject and object enabled him to think in terms of

[13] See, e.g., Morris H. Abrams, *The Mirror and the Lamp: Romantic Theory and the Critical Tradition* (New York: Norton, 1958), pp. 162–64.

[14] *Ibid.*, p. 165.

[15] Immanuel Kant, *Critique of Judgment* (Critique of the Aesthetical Judgment), in Albert Hofstadter and Richard Kuhns, eds., *Philosophies of Art and Beauty* (New York: Modern Library, 1964), pp. 280–343.

what would later be called "empathy," or the projection of the self into the object; it enabled him to write, "we receive but what we give."[16] He began speaking of the imagination as a power with the capacity to fuse feelings and images, to transmute experiences and ideas into symbols which could be harmonized within a work of art.

Coleridge also made an important distinction between fancy and imagination. Fancy he saw as "a mode of Memory emancipated from the order of space and time" (as had the associationists) playing passively with "fixities and definities."[17] He saw imagination in two dimensions:

The primary *Imagination* I hold to be the living Power and prime Agent of all human Perception, and as a repetition in the finite mind of the eternal act of creation in the infinite *I Am*. The secondary Imagination I consider as an echo of the former, co-existing with the conscious will, yet still as identical with the primary in the *kind* of its operation. It dissolves, diffuses, dissipates, in order to recreate; or where this process is rendered impossible, yet still at all events it struggles to idealize and to unify. It is essentially vital, even as all objects (as objects) are essentially fixed and dead.[18]

William Wordsworth, similarly concerned with the constructive and illuminating function of imagination, distinguished between its creative and abstracting virtues. When the imagination made many into one, however, or when it made one into many, it retained the capacity to achieve a truth of comparisons, to suggest relationships and resemblances in a manner which presumably fulfilled desire.[19] Presenting "the growth of a poet's mind" in his long poem, "The Prelude," Wordsworth showed how new worlds may be imaginatively created

[16] Samuel T. Coleridge, "Dejection: An Ode," in Ernest H. Coleridge, ed., *The Complete Poetical Works of Samuel Taylor Coleridge* (Oxford: Oxford University Press, 1912), I, 362–68.

[17] Samuel T. Coleridge, *Biographia Literaria* (Oxford: Oxford University Press, 1907), I, 189–90.

[18] *Ibid.*

[19] William Wordsworth, "Essay Supplementary to 1815 Preface to *The Lyrical Ballads*," in Carlos Baker, ed. *The Prelude—Selected Poems and Sonnets* (New York: Holt, Rinehart and Winston, 1962), p. 38.

when the poet's mind, engaging with things in their specificity and concreteness, projects flavor and emotional quality into nature. New meanings are created as likenesses and continuities are revealed. The work of imagination enables the poet to render in time a clarified vision of the earth, sometimes in a moment of apocalypse, as in Book VI of "The Prelude":

> Imagination—here the Power so called
> Through sad incompetence of human speech,
> That awful Power rose from the mind's abyss
> Like an unfathered vapour that enwraps,
> At once, some lonely traveller. I was lost;
> Halted without an effort to break through;
> But to my conscious soul I now can say—
> "I recognize thy glory;" in such strength
> Of usurpation, when the light of sense
> Goes out, but with a flash that has revealed
> The invisible world. . . .[20]

In spite of positivist and associationist challenges (by Bentham, for instance, and Mill), the approach to the imagination as "esemplastic," autonomous, and creative persisted among artists and those interested in the arts. John Keats spoke of it as an independent activity, the veritable center of "poetic sensibility." Like Coleridge and Wordsworth both, he saw that it was part of imagination's visionary power to encompass contraries (like fire and ice, life and death) without destroying logical contradictions and without attempting rational solutions. Charles Baudelaire turned to imagination as the governing principle when he rendered the universe as a "forest of symbols," a web of "correspondences" between natural forms and states of the human soul.[21] The angels in Rainer Maria Rilke's *Duino Elegies* represent imagination in their primal, transforming role. It was imagination, for Rilke, which permitted the artist to penetrate "into the confidence of things,"[22] to assimilate them for the sake of artistic expression.

[20] William Wordsworth, "The Prelude," Book VI, in *ibid.*, pp. 304–5.

[21] Charles Baudelaire, "Correspondances," in Edna St. Vincent Millay, ed., *Flowers of Evil* (New York: Harper and Brothers, 1936), p. 196.

[22] Rainer Maria Rilke, *Letters to Merline*, trans. Violet M. MacDonald (London: Methuen, 1952), pp. 273–75.

Stephen Spender says that the basically romantic view of imagination as "Verb" is still central to modern views of literature. "The reinstating of imagination as primary, central, the verb, was perhaps the attitude responsible for the greatest modern achievements: works like the last novels of Henry James (particularly *The Golden Bowl*), *Finnegans Wake*, Yeats's Byzantium poems, the *Duineser Elegien*, put these writers in the God-like position of being isolated within their own creations, of having to reinvent the world and all its values within their art."[23]

Somewhat the same thing may be said about painters, although they seldom use the term "imagination" when describing what they do. Henri Matisse, however, distinguishes literal representation from artistic evocation by talking about a process notably akin to Coleridge's "Secondary Imagination":

If upon a white canvas I jot down some sensations of blue, of green, of red—every new brushstroke diminishes the importance of the preceding ones. Suppose I set out to paint an interior: I have before me a cupboard; it gives me a sensation of bright red—and I put down a red which satisfies me; immediately a relation is established between this red and the white of the canvas. If I put a green near the red, if I paint a yellow floor, there must still be between this green, this yellow and the white of the canvas a relation that will be satisfactory to me. . . . I must organize my ideas; the relation between tones must be so established that they will sustain one another. A new combination of colors will succeed the first one and will give more completely my interpretation. I am forced to transpose until finally my picture may seem completely changed when, after successive modifications, the red has succeeded the green as the dominant color. I cannot copy nature in a servile way, I must interpret nature and submit it to the spirit of the picture—when I have found the relationship of all the tones the result must be a living harmony of tones, a harmony not unlike that of a musical composition.[24]

[23] Stephen Spender, *The Struggle of the Modern* (Berkeley: University of California Press, 1965), p. 17.

[24] Henri Matisse, "Notes of a Painter," in Morris Weitz, ed., *Problems in Aesthetics* (New York: Macmillan, 1959), pp. 347–48.

He is describing an activity, an ordering process. As his work proceeds, he dissolves, diffuses, then recombines and re-creates, always for the sake of more complex relationships and a richer, more unified whole. Like the poet, he begins with sensation, with a concrete cupboard which he "penetrates," possesses with his eye, and which he then transmutes into colors on the canvas. The activity of changing and modifying the colors (according to the painter's "conscious will") so that they will sustain one another and eventually create a "harmony" is an imaginative activity in the Coleridgean and the modern senses.

Viewed in this way, Matisse's painting may be understood as "the creative imagination at work." This, says Stephen C. Pepper,[25] "consists in following through faithfully the demands of feeling in esthetic materials, bringing into the work materials called for by other materials till a complete organic unity is established." In a sense, the work of art completes itself; since, as Pepper puts it, "the esthetic materials seek their own satisfying structure and equilibrium through the artist, who does not dictate but follows their guidance."

This implies, of course, that the work of art is far more than the inner creation of the imagination Croce thought it was.[26] We are, in fact, proposing that the concept of the imagination as it functions today—and, indeed, as it has developed over time—signifies a formative activity which culminates in the formulation of an art object. Margaret Macdonald says that there might be an excuse for affirming that some composition or creation occurs "in the mind" or "in the imagination"; but she insists that what is done "in the head" could be done as well on canvas or through the medium of words.[27] Like Gilbert Ryle, she is objecting to the notion of the mind as a kind of theater or picture gallery in which "ghostly likenesses"[28] can

[25] Stephen Pepper, "Organistic Criticism," in Rader, ed., A Modern Book of Esthetics, pp. 471–72.

[26] Benedetto Croce, "Selections from Aesthetics," in Hofstadter and Kuhns, eds., Philosophies of Art and Beauty, pp. 556–76.

[27] Margaret Macdonald, "The Work of Art as Physical," p. 219.

[28] Gilbert Ryle, The Concept of Mind, p. 265.

be seen. Unlike Ryle, however, she is not subsuming imagination under "pretending," which has to do with what Dewey called the "rehearsal" of plans of action, the anticipation of consequences, and so on. Nor is she treating the concept of imagination (or "fancying") as "those activities of make-believe into which people casually and even involuntarily drift."[29]

We would emphasize again the "conscious will" associated with the formative imagination. As Vincent Tomas makes clear, one of the differences between passive imagination and creative activity is that "critical judgment and fastidiousness" are essential to the latter.[30] Matisse's account of his own processes of creation makes clear enough that what he does is subject to critical control, even as it makes clear that he has not foreseen his final product in advance. The control has largely to do with effecting appropriate relations among the colors or tones, those considered necessary because of the "spirit of the picture." Much the same thing happens in the writing of a poem, a story, or a novel. James Joyce's *Portrait of the Artist as a Young Man* is judged to be a work of art largely because of the way its symbols and images are interrelated and unified—because, in other words, of the imaginative control maintained over a continually expanding network of relationships. There seems, as Tomas says, to be an "aesthetic necessity" perceived by the artist as he plays with, diffuses, relates, and forms the materials with which he works. It is a "necessity" imaginatively perceived and imaginatively obeyed.

Obviously, it is quite different from "logical necessity," as the creative process is different from the deductive process. The fruits of both processes differ significantly as well. In an essay challenging idealist aesthetics and illustrating what he calls his "journeyman's" aesthetics,[31] W. B. Gallie makes a point

[29] *Ibid.*, p. 264.
[30] Vincent Tomas, "Creativity in Art," in Francis J. Coleman, ed., *Contemporary Studies in Aesthetics* (New York: McGraw-Hill, 1968), p. 347.
[31] W. B. Gallie, "The Function of Philosophical Aesthetics," in *ibid.*, pp. 407–8.

that is relevant here. His concern is to clarify one of Wordsworth's discussions of the "abstracting virtue" of the imagination and to set right some of Wordsworth's self-contradictions.
Contrasting the explicit and definable abstractions of mathematics to the vague and indefinite abstractions of the poet,
Gallie concludes (as Wordsworth did) that the very vagueness
of poetic abstractions may account for "the peculiar, 'pleasure
of the imagination' to which they give rise." He goes on to
say that such "pleasure requires, first, that the comparisons
framed by imagination shall be so new that the object they
start from shall come to 're-act upon the mind . . . like a new
existence,' and second, that such comparisons shall not be too
explicit: otherwise it would be impossible for a sense of their
truth 'to grow—and continue to grow.' "

The crucial point has to do with complexity of relationship
and with the perspectives opened up by comparison. When an
object (or an idea, an event, a feeling) is perceived in "the
vast range of unexplored relations" in which it stands to other
phenomena, the imagination itself is enlarged, and the "great
pond" of which Stevens speaks is bridged at several points. Or,
to use the language of the painter Max Ernst,[32] an "intensification of the visionary faculties" may occur when a great
variety of elements are imaginatively brought together in relationship. People who cannot perceive relationships between
"a drum and a street lamp—via the unmentioned throbbing of
the heart and nerves in a distraught man," Hart Crane once
wrote,[33] are people "who have never accumulated a sufficient
series of reflections." The poet said that artists had to count
on the existence of such bases, such reflections:

In the minds of people who have sensitively read, seen and
experienced a great deal, isn't there a terminology something
like shorthand as compared to usual description and dialectics,
which the artist ought to be right in trusting as a reasonable
connective agent toward fresh concepts, more inclusive evalu-

[32] Max Ernst, *Beyond Painting* (New York: George Wittenborn, 1948), p.
14.
[33] Hart Crane, *Poetry* XXIX (October, 1926): 34–35.

ations? The question is more important to me than it perhaps ought to be; but as long as poetry is written, an audience, however small, is implied, and there remains the question of an active or an inactive imagination as its characteristic.

Crane was talking about metaphor and symbolism; and, like many others, he was perceiving the "active imagination" to be the crucial factor. According to Wallace Stevens, "Poetry is a satisfying of the desire for resemblance. . . . Its singularity is that in the act of satisfying the desire for resemblance, it touches the sense of reality, it enhances the sense of reality. . . ."[34] The imaginative creation of ever-widening patterns of wholeness, does not, it appears, diminish or distort "reality," even if it is the case that the activity of imagination serves "to reinvent the world."

Reinventing, imagination makes it possible to look, as Thomas Mann said, "both ways." It does this through the creation of symbols, which arise out of the search for continuity and resemblance.The contemporary artist, deprived of the *consensus gentium* of past eras, has had to devise a language of symbols and apply them to the open, mysterious world of the present. William York Tindall has written:

Symbol, as we know it today, emerged during the romantic movement, which is best understood perhaps as an attempt to recover the upper half of the broken chain and, uniting it with the lower, to create something like the lost world of the Middle Ages and the Renaissance. The upper half of this restoration, however, required new meanings. Not only the place of spirit, it came to mean the imaginative, the subjective, the unconscious, or sensibility, separated by that famous dissociation from fact and reason, which continued to occupy the lower half of the chain.[35]

A symbol, of course, is an object—a red letter A, a wild duck, a white rose, a courtroom, a tuberculosis sanitarium—which refers to something beyond itself. In the context of art works, a symbol is interesting in and of itself even as it points beyond

[34] Wallace Stevens, *The Necessary Angel*, p. 77.
[35] William York Tindall, *The Literary Symbol* (Bloomington: Indiana University Press, 1955), p. 38.

itself. "By uniting the separate," writes Tindall, "it can organize experience into a kind of order and, revealing the complex relationships among seemingly divided things, confer peace."[36] But the peace conferred will depend upon the degree of awareness, perhaps upon the degree of active imagination, possessed by the one who reads or looks or hears. The analogues of the cows and bats and roses may be limited to an extent by the context of Joyce's *Portrait*; but there is a sense in which they remain analogues for something wholly mysterious, something that escapes definition—like the "dumb blankness" evoked by Melville's whale.

The ambiguity noted by Richards with respect to the ancients' view of imagination is not very evident today. Imagination, in contemporary aesthetics, is not a pathway to the absolute or to some pre-existent Ideal. The ineffable, the indefinable—sometimes summed up in what Susanne Langer calls a sense of "import"[37]—are generally accounted for by the involvement of subjectivity in the creation and appreciation of works of art. Langer herself, of course, sees works of art as "constructed symbols, made in the mode of imagination, because imagination reflects the forms of feeling from which it springs, and the principles of representation by which human sensibility records itself."[38] There is considerable disagreement with her conception of "feeling," "sentiency," and even "subjectivity"; but there is considerable unanimity with respect to the fusion of the inner and outer visions which imagination makes possible.

John Dewey, describing imagination as "a *way* of seeing and feeling things as they compose an integral whole," emphasized its role in "the large and generous blending of interests at the point where the mind comes in contact with the world."[39] He found "some measure of adventure" in this meeting of mind

---

[36] *Ibid.*, p. 16.

[37] See Susanne K. Langer, *Problems of Art* (New York: Charles Scribner's Sons, 1957), chaps. 1, 9, 10.

[38] Susanne K. Langer, *Mind: An Essay on Human Feeling* (Baltimore: The Johns Hopkins Press, 1967), I, 99.

[39] John Dewey, *Art as Experience*, p. 267.

and the world; and he called the adventure imagination. The inner vision and the outer vision, he said, have been opposed to each other in the history of art. "But the inner vision is not cast out. It remains as the organ by which outer vision is controlled, and it takes on structure as the latter is absorbed within it. The interaction of the two modes of vision is imagination; as imagination takes form the work of art is born."[40]

Using Emily Dickinson's phrase, we might say that an artist sends a personal "letter to the world." The origin of the letter is in the inner vision, which is probably inchoate, inarticulate, self-complete. In Emily Dickinson's case, it was a vision much affected by Calvinism, scorn of orthodoxy, alternations of ecstasy and despair. Something—the fascination of language, the need for release, the desire to propitiate indifferent nature, the loss of love—moved her to the point where her innerness converged with her particular "world." It was at that point that her imagination began actively to work. The town of Amherst, the Old Testament, Shakespeare's plays, the English language, her father, fields, flowers, snakes, schools, people in the streets, blue umbrellas, graveyards, all the aspects and appurtenances of the "outer" offered both resistances and raw materials. The poet became imaginatively engaged; she began finding "old and familiar things . . . made new in experience," as Dewey put it. She began embodying possibilities in poems which were works of art, embodiments which were, according to Dewey, "the best evidence that can be found of the true nature of imagination."

This dramatic convergence of inner with outer is not only evident in literature. Merleau-Ponty wrote of Cézanne:

Heredity may well have given him rich sensations, strong emotions, and a vague feeling of anguish or mystery which upset the life he might have wished for himself and which cut him off from men; but these qualities cannot create a work of art without the expressive act, and they can no more account for the difficulties than for the virtues of that act. Cézanne's difficulties are those of the first word. He con-

[40] *Ibid.*, p. 268.

sidered himself powerless because he was not omnipotent, because he was not God and wanted nevertheless to portray the world, to change it completely into a spectacle, to make *visible* how the world *touches* us.[41]

It was at the point of Cézanne's "difficulties," as well as his doubt, that the interaction between mind (or his "qualities") and the world took place. It was in the changing, in the making visible that imagination in its active sense went to work.

Ben Shahn renders the work of imagination in the essay called "The Biography of a Painting."[42] Perceiving himself as artist and "inner critic," he writes of the "two-way communication" which constitutes the painting process, of the tension between idea and image, artist and medium. And then: "It is not a spoken idea alone, nor a legend, nor a simple use or intention that forms what I have called the biography of a painting. It is rather the wholeness of thinking and feeling within an individual; it is partly his time and place; it is partly his childhood or even his adult fears and pleasures, and it is very greatly his thinking what he wants to think." (Significantly, Shahn concludes his chapter with a quotation from Rilke's *The Notebooks of Malte Laurids Brigge*, in which the poet explains how many varied experiences an artist needs to have had and assimilated in order to write even a few lines. The passage concludes with a remarkable account of the active imagination as we have conceived it here: "For it is not yet the memories themselves. Not until they have turned to blood within us, to glance, to gesture, nameless and no longer to be distinguished from ourselves—not until then can it happen that in a most rare hour the first word of a verse arises in their midst and goes forth from them.") The old and the familiar are transmuted, as mind interacts with the world; and suddenly, after long and secret preparation, "the work of art is born."

[41] Maurice Merleau-Ponty, "Cézanne's Doubt," in *Sense and Non-Sense*, trans. Hubert L. and Patricia Allen Dreyfus (Evanston, Ill.: Northwestern University Press, 1964), p. 19.

[42] Ben Shahn, *The Shape of Content* (New York: Vintage Books, 1957), pp. 59–60.

What, precisely, *is* born? The artist often aspires, as Cézanne did, to create a complete world, to be Godlike in his transmutation of materials. The work of art, however, is a function of a particular artistic tradition and at once a particular moment in cultural history. Cézanne's *Mont Sainte Victoire* would probably never have existed if it were not for the Impressionist movement and Cézanne's rebellious decision to restore solidity to painting through study of the architectonics of space. Dürer's *Melancolia I,* as Erwin Panofsky makes clear,[43] would not have been what it was were it not for the imaginative fusion and transformation of "two great representational and literary traditions." T. S. Eliot's "Ash Wednesday" is a consequence of the poet's encounter with Dante and the religious tradition, as much as it is a function of the interaction between Eliot's mind and the contemporary world. One of the functions of the imagination, in fact, is to make uniqueness and originality possible within the limits set by the culture, the artist's own personality, and the medium through which he works.

But works of art have a strangely dual existence. On the one hand, they are in the world as actualities to be read, heard, seen. On the other hand, they are what Sartre calls "unreal objects," analogues,[44] open possibilities. They are separated from the domain of "plain sense" and from all other works of art. Dorothy Walsh explains this phenomenon by talking of the importance of an art object's "boundary":

Such an object may appear to possess an indefinite richness of internal depth and range, but it always has a boundary which isolates it from all other entities including other works of art. . . . Every musical composition and every poem begins and ends and so returns upon itself. It never just commences and ceases. When it is thoroughly understood, every part is heard in the totality of the whole. It is surrounded by silence or at least by irrelevancy as pictures are surrounded by their frames. Thus works of art, present as physical things and

[43] Erwin Panofsky, *The Life and Art of Albrecht Dürer* (Princeton: Princeton University Press, 1955), p. 171.

[44] Jean-Paul Sartre, *The Psychology of the Imagination* (New York: Citadel Press, 1963), pp. 265–67.

present as cultural products, are, nevertheless, as works of art, imaginative vistas out of the actual. To enter into the contemplation of a work of art is to pass through the context of the actual to the appreciation of a unique, discontinuous possibility.[45]

"Undifferentiated art and intelligence have often been and are well called imagination," writes Victorino Tejera, "the imaging, probing, relating, and sympathetic power . . . which creates the 'realm' of possibility."[46]

To enter that realm, to become perceptive enough to enjoy an aesthetic experience, the individual must break with the routine and habitual. He must be able, first of all, to recognize—at least in the case of literature—that he is entering a "fictional" or imaginary domain when he opens a novel, a short story, a play, or a poem. The work in question—*Ulysses, Farewell to Arms, Paul's Case, Franny, Oedipus Rex, Hamlet, Death of a Salesman, Paradise Lost,* or *The Death of the Hired Man*—must be understood to have been created according to certain artistic conventions. "The center of literary art," write Wellek and Warren, "is obviously to be found in the traditional genres of the lyric, the epic, the drama. In all of them, the reference is to a world of fiction, of imagination."[47] If a reader takes literally Balzac's claim to have been "the secretary of society" and goes on to read *Père Goriot* or *Eugenie Grandet* as a secretary's report on what actually happened, he is not only deceiving himself; he is giving up the possibility of having an aesthetic experience.

The same thing may be said of the person who perceives a painting as a mere representation of something in the outer world, an "imitation" to be judged solely in terms of its fidelity to reality. This would mean that the painter went to work with a prior idea of what was to be rendered on his canvas, and

[45] Dorothy Walsh, "The Cognitive Content of Art," in Eliseo Vivas and Murray Krieger, eds., *The Problems of Aesthetics* (New York: Holt, Rinehart and Winston, 1965), p. 610.

[46] Victorino Tejera, *Art and Human Intelligence,* p. 215.

[47] Wellek and Warren, *Theory of Literature,* p. 14.

that his creative activity involved no more than a realization of some image he had in mind when he began. But this is denied by everything we have said about the imagination, about the shaping of raw materials, about "making" itself. Unless it is possible for an individual to perceive a painting in such a way as to perceive the "aesthetic space" of what he is looking at, he will be unable to realize the painting as an aesthetic object; he will be unable to appreciate it as a work of art. Virgil Aldrich calls the necessary mode of perception "prehension" and writes that "the aesthetic space of things perceived thus is determined by such characteristics as intensities or values of colors and sounds, which . . . comprise the medium presented by the material things in question."[48] On the basis of what we have said about the constitutive, formative, *active* functions of imagination, we propose calling this way of looking imaginative rather than (in Aldrich's language) "impressionistic."

For Dewey, the perception required is "an act of reconstructive doing" in which "consciousness becomes fresh and alive." His description of it comes close to his description of imagination: "*This* act of seeing involves the cooperation of motor elements even though they remain implicit and do not become overt, as well as cooperation of all funded ideas that may serve to complete the new picture that is forming."[49] For this to be possible, slackness, conventionality, and automatism must be overcome. The aesthetic experience demands a free, formative surge of activity—which, in effect, is imaginative activity.

Sartre treats imagination as a process of wrenching oneself from everyday reality. "In order to imagine, consciousness must be free from all specific reality and this freedom must be able to define itself by a 'being-in-the-world' which is at once the constitution and the negation of the world; the concrete situation of the consciousness in the world must at each mo-

---

[48] Virgil C. Aldrich, *Philosophy of Art* (Englewood Cliffs, N.J.: Prentice-Hall, 1963), p. 22.
[49] John Dewey, *Art as Experience*, p. 53.

ment serve as the singular motivation for the constitution of the unreal."[50] The work of art is "unreal"; but it exists in relationship to the reader's or the observer's consciousness, and its referent is the individual's subjectivity. Imagination creates the relationship and enables the reader, for instance, to posit a literary work as an aesthetic object. An "imaginative consciousness," in fact, is the necessary condition for *Hamlet* or *Moby Dick* or any art object to be constituted as an aesthetic object. Once so constituted, it enables a reader to confront his own consciousness in the most authentic fashion. Breaking with the mundane, "bracketing out" the stereotyped, the reader lends his own life to the Prince of Denmark, takes responsibility for Ishmael in search of himself. Shakespeare or Melville guides his participation in the particular work; but the reader's subjectivity becomes the subject of the work. He may "see," therefore, as he has never seen before; he may be made aware of himself as "being-in-the-world" as never before. By means of imagination, says Sartre, the individual equipped to engage with works of art may discover his own reality.

This relates closely to what Wallace Stevens has said about the relationship between imagination and reality. And it does not exclude a conception of the art object as "possibility." Stevens wrote: "The imagination is the power of the mind over the possibilities of things; but if this constitutes a certain single characteristic, it is the source not of a certain single value but of as many values as reside in the possibilities of things."[51] How is the individual to realize such possibilities unless he defines his own vantage point by confronting himself? Imagination may help him do this, even as it helps him bridge the "great pond" that may be separating him not only from the world but from the available ways of forming it. Imagination, conceived as a formative activity, and as one that unites the inner and the outer visions, may open the way to expanding meaningfulness and to expanding control.

The implications for educational theory, then, are manifold.

[50] Jean-Paul Sartre, *The Psychology of the Imagination*, p. 269.
[51] Wallace Stevens, *The Necessary Angel*, p. 31.

Our time is generally considered to be one of fragmentation and confusion; and much of the current curriculum discussion has to do with ordering and organizing experience; with creating larger and more coherent constructs through which to "know" the world. Philosophers and curriculum theorists both speak of widening young people's views of life, deepening their insights into relationships, providing what Philip Phenix calls an "integral perspective" on the world.[52]

Learning is conceived to be a distinctively active process, and the materials chosen from the various subject-matter disciplines are to be not only representative of those disciplines but the kinds of materials capable of arousing imagination. Materials of this sort have the potentiality for involving individual students as actively concerned inquirers, capable of "discovering" the structures of various subjects and of using the basic elements of knowledge to interpret the impinging world.[53] The kinds of activity asked of such students are akin to imaginative activity. Their own observations, particular "facts," diverse concerns and commitments become, as it were, their raw material. The learning they do requires classification, interpretation, ordering and reordering according to relevant norms and rules.

Now it is probably the case that the creative activity resulting in works of art is not rule-governed in this fashion. In fact, as we have suggested, the norms involved may be defined as a work of art takes shape. Where the mastery of disciplinary content is concerned, certain prescriptive principles become the principles of organization: indeed, they provide the context for the insight and understanding desired. But, as Thomas F. Green suggests, "when behavior becomes principled, i.e., when it becomes norm-regarding, then it is possible to entertain the prospect that there may be alternative ways of doing the same

---

[52] Philip H. Phenix, *Realms of Meaning* (New York: McGraw-Hill, 1964), pp. 1–8.

[53] Cf. H. S. Broudy, B. Othanel Smith, and Joe R. Burnett, *Democracy and Excellence in American Secondary Education* (Chcago: Rand McNally, 1964); Solon T. Kimball and James E. McClellan, Jr., *Education and the New America* (New York: Random House, 1962), chap. 13.

thing. . . ."[54] Moreover, a choice is involved when a person understands the principles he is adopting and the reasons why. If he has freely accepted them as binding upon him, he can choose to embody them in action—or not. Green says that part of what is involved "is participation in some human activity to which the principles are germane." If a student participates, say, in the activity of learning physics, and if he accepts—and then acts upon—certain principles because they are, in effect, the rules of the physics game which he wants to play, he may be said to be creating his own norms. "Which is to say simply," comments Green, "that every human action makes concrete in the world the norm to which it points."[55]

If this is the case, the connection between principled activity and imaginative activity may be closer than it first seemed. George Santayana often stressed the possibility that rational choice follows upon primary creative impulses which are entirely legitimate even in scientific and mathematical thinking. "Aesthetic values," he wrote, "everywhere precede and accompany rational activity, and life is, in one aspect, always a fine art; not by introducing inaptly aesthetic vetoes or aesthetic flourishes, but by giving to everything a form which, implying a structure, implies also an ideal and a possible perfection."[56] Learning *does* involve forming and structuring, made possible by the acceptance and incarnation of particular kinds of norms. "It is for want of education and discipline," said Santayana, "that a man so often insists petulantly on his random tastes. . . ." The concept of imagination, as it now functions in aesthetic discourse, holds a number of implications for those concerned with combatting the "random" and effecting a qualitative transformation of children's impulses and wants into "norm-regarding" action. Whether rational activity begins in the indeterminate, in vague feelings of curiosity and wonder,

[54] Thomas F. Green, "Teaching, Acting, and Behaving," in B. Paul Komisar and C. B. J. Macmillan, eds., *Psychological Concepts* in Education (Chicago: Rand McNally, 1967), p. 205.

[55] *Ibid.*, p. 208.

[56] George Santayana, "Justification of Art," in Vivas and Krieger, eds., *The Problems of Aesthetics*, p. 525.

or in the kind of "aesthetic values" which signify a cherishing of form, it seems likely that learning too begins when the "inner" (impulses, want, interest) engages actively with the "outer" (in this case, the structures of knowledge made available, or the inherited traditions conceived to be valuable). "To have a mind," writes R. S. Peters, "is not to enjoy a private picture-show or to exercise some inner diaphanous organ; it is to have an awareness differentiated in accordance with the canons implicit in all these inherited traditions."[57] This is not unlike some of the renderings of imaginative activity we have seen: to engage in such activity is not merely to form an internal image; it is to have the kind of awareness that enables one to respond to the demands of the medium being used, consciously (and critically) to recombine and re-create until a new order, a new wholeness is achieved and embodied in a work of art.

The idea that imagination involves not only forming but embodying also holds implications for education. Today education tends to be discussed in "task" or "achievement" terms. When a child learns something, he learns how to *do* certain kinds of intellectual things. He learns the reasons for believing certain things. Effective teaching is no longer considered to be merely a matter of training children in a variety of skills, of "telling," "showing," or indoctrinating. It is considered to be an intentional process of liberating people to think for themselves and form their experience for themselves. This involves categorizing, patterning, and various kinds of conceptual ordering. One of Coleridge's descriptions of poetic imagination might well serve as analogue. The "synthetic and magical power" called imagination, he wrote,

reveals itself in the balance of reconciliation of opposite or discordant qualities; of sameness with difference; of the general with the concrete; the idea with the image; the individual with the representative; the sense of novelty and freshness, with old and familiar objects; a more than usual state of emo-

[57] R. S. Peters, *Ethics and Education* (Glenview, Ill.: Scott, Foresman, 1966), pp. 16–17.

tion, with more than usual order; a judgement ever awake and steady self-possession, with enthusiasm of feeling profound or vehement. . . .[58]

A fusing takes place; a "blending of interests" occurs: the child's experience, once he has achieved some mastery in a particular dimension, is reconstructed, reordered, renewed.

Obviously this cannot happen if he remains passive, or if he clings to the habitual, stereotyped ways of seeing his world. The linking of imagination to "adventure," to awareness, to authenticity also has meaning for those interested in educational theory. Too frequently the aesthetic—and even the imaginative—are associated with a notion of passivity or some mystical identification with an encompassing "All." As we have seen, imagination now tends to be associated with critical judgment as well as with "conscious will" when the creative process is discussed. When the appreciative process is discussed, a distinctive kind of perceptiveness is linked to imaginative activity, a clarity of vision requiring a full (albeit "disinterested") engagement of the one who reads, looks, or hears.

None of this is intended to obscure the important differences between cognition—or discursive knowing—and the nondiscursive awarenesses made possible by the arts. "The sensory elements in scientific and practical perception are used as clues to achieving knowledge and action, respectively," writes Harry Broudy in a pithy summary statement.[59] The disinterestedness and the distancing required for aesthetic appreciation make the qualities of a work of art valuable for their own sakes and for the contributions they make to the emerging totality, the work itself. The reader is not expected to abstract the sections on the sperm whale from Moby Dick and treat them as additions to his body of knowledge or guides to some action with respect to whaling. The viewer is expected to gain pleasure from the modulating effects of color in Cézanne's presentation

[58] Quoted in Kathleen Raine, Coleridge (London: Longmans, Green, 1958), p. 24.
[59] H. S. Broudy, "The Structure of Knowledge in the Arts," in Ralph A. Smith, ed., Aesthetics and Criticism in Art Education (Chicago: Rand McNally, 1966), p. 27.

of a plate of apples and to permit his imagination to work in constructing a painting out of Cézanne's colors, planes, and thrusting forms. Imaginative activity culminates in new patternings, in integral orders, not in pointers to specific kinds of behavior, not in conclusions, not in "truths."

It is nevertheless true, as Joseph Margolis points out in a discussion of critical interpretation, that "Whatever the scientific description of objects and events may be, things appear in the imaginative dimension of our experience to be loaded with emotional associations and symbolic import and even to suffer distortions in characteristic ways."[60] He has in mind the imaginative schema called myths, which are "capable of effectively organizing our way of viewing portions of the external world," no matter what the scientific status "of the propositions it may subtend."

The exemplary definition of myth appears in Mark Schorer's *William Blake*.[61] As Schorer sees it, a myth is "a large controlling image" discerned in human experience, to be understood as the basis of ideas rather than their contraries. Mythic images are the elements by which thought is sustained and propelled. As Richard Chase sees it, myth is an "esthetic device" for bringing the imaginary world into harmony with the empirical or experienced facts of life so as "to excite a sense of reality amenable to both the unconscious passions and the conscious mind."[62] It follows that myth may be a prototype of the work done by imagination; it may be a mode of expression (usually dramatic expression) of the patternings of human impulse, a crucial way of ordering experience for the sake of communion with others and for the sake of identifying the self with respect to the world. "Rational belief is secondary," says Schorer. "We habitually tend to overlook the fact that as human beings we are rational creatures not first of all

[60] Joseph Margolis, "The Logic of Interpretation," in Margolis, *Philosophy Looks at the Arts* (New York: Charles Scribner's Sons, 1962), pp. 113–14.

[61] Mark Schorer, *William Blake: The Politics of Vision* (New York: Vintage Books, 1959), p. 25.

[62] Richard Chase, *The American Novel and Its Tradition* (New York: Doubleday Anchor Books, 1957), pp. 53, 245.

but last of all. . . . Belief organizes experience not because it is rational but because all belief depends on a controlling imagery, and rational belief is the intellectual formalization of that imagery. . . ."[63] He writes of fundamental sets of images like Christianity, socialism, and the American Dream, about the waxing and waning myths of modern civilization in the midst of which we live, and about the importance of myth in literature perceived as art.

The relevance of this has several facets. First, it reinforces the claim that imaginative ordering plays a focal role not simply in aesthetic experiences but in the various ways in which human beings deal with and interpret the world. Second, it suggests that the differences between discursive knowing and imaginative apprehending are not so great as they are sometimes thought to be, since both involve ordering by means of concept, principle, or schema. Third, it illuminates the importance of paying heed both to the inner and the outer vision in the process of educating; and it indicates once more the way in which the inner takes on structure when it is externalized, or when (as Dewey put it) the outer vision "is absorbed within it."

Finally, there is the question of possibilities. In a sense, a student stands against a world of possibilities, a world of possible forms. In a sense, it is imagination that puts him in relationship to these possibilities, just as it is imagination which enables him to order the indeterminate situations in which his inquiries begin. As in the case of works of art, possibilities signify richer and richer orders, more and more complex relationships. And this means, perhaps paradoxically, that a proper regard for imagination may intensify the sense of reality.

Wallace Stevens, as usual, says this best. In his poem, "The Latest Freed Man," he presents a man tired "of the old descriptions of the world." He is a man who sees an ordinary banal landscape, landscape that has not been imaginatively described. Then, suddenly, his imagination goes to work; the landscape becomes personally meaningful to him; it becomes

[63] Schorer, *William Blake*, p. 26.

relevant because there has been an encounter between his inner self and the world. Dramatically, reality seems vivid; it appears to become more real:

> It was how he was free. It was how his freedom came.
> It was being without description, being an ox.
> It was the importance of the trees outdoors,
> The freshness of the oak-leaves, not so much
> That they were oak-leaves, as the way they looked.
> It was everything being more real, himself
> At the centre of reality, seeing it.
> It was everything bulging and blazing and big in itself,
> The blue of the rug, the portrait of Vidal,
> Qui fait fi des joliesses banales, the
>   chairs.[64]

[64] Wallace Stevens, "The Latest Freed Man," in *Collected Poems*, pp. 204–5. Copyright 1942 by Wallace Stevens. Reprinted by permission of Alfred A. Knopf, Inc.

INTENTION IN LITERATURE:

ITS PEDAGOGICAL IMPLICATIONS / 14

Peter F. Neumeyer

I

INTENTION IN LITERATURE

What if LeRoi Jones were discovered to be a monumental hoax? What if there were no Negro poet shaping his outrage into the art of poetry, but instead there was living on Long Island a clever and cynical young white man determined to pull our collective leg and to cash in on the current sympathy for civil rights by inventing for himself the fictitious character LeRoi Jones, in whose name he sent out scathing poems about racial oppression, and about whom he flooded the newspapers with invented stories of the fictitious poet's increasing militancy, arrests, and encounters with the white establishment? What then would we think of the poems of LeRoi Jones? Would Hill and Wang still publish them? Would students at the Harvard Graduate School of Education have come to my office insisting that, given our times, the School has the obligation to offer courses in the poems of Jones and his like? And —most simply—would the poems themselves still move and excite us?

What if Eskimo sculpture—those sleek bears and seals the cost of which has skyrocketed in the last five years—were not produced by Eskimos at all, but were manufactured in Detroit, in a small factory owned largely by the Ford Motor Company, by a process in which a new, stone-resembling compound were poured into molds, and the products shipped to different parts of the country so that a suspicious number of polar bears would not end up in any one corner of the country? Would the market for Eskimo art collapse? Would the molded seals and bears be ugly, not beautiful?

And what if John Bunyan, author of *The Pilgrim's Progress*, instead of having been an unsophisticated and obscure Bedfordshire brazier, had been an eloquent, wealthy, and recognized Protestant preacher in his own time—would then some of the luster of *The Pilgrim's Progress* be illusory, created by our democratic prejudices?

Analogous cases are not unheard of in the history of the arts. Classical sculptures and, if my memory serves me, a most startling and stark Greek helmet at the New York Metropolitan Museum were not long ago shown to be something other than what they had been presented as. (Note, I do not say "fakes.") Literary hoaxes are numerous: *The Rowley Poems* —supposedly medieval ballads, actually written by an eighteen-year-old genius two hundred years ago—and the eighteenth-century "epics," *Fingal, an Ancient Epic*, and *Temora, an Epic Poem*, purporting to be heroic poems by Ossian, a primitive Highland bard thought to rival Homer—but being really the work of James Macpherson, who died in 1796—moved and stirred their readers, and in turn fed the primitivistic-Romantic sentiment which gave them birth in the first place.

Put simply and directly, I am asking how much what we know of the origins of an art work should affect our opinion of it.

Stated still more specifically, and in pedagogical terms, is it helpful, harmful, or meaningless for students to have their impression of a literary work directed by knowing something of its genesis, or might there be different answers for students of different ages or for students from varying backgrounds, some of whom might, perhaps, be "motivated" if they know that Hemingway's stories came from hunter and boxer Hemingway, rather than from an Oscar Wilde, or that a given poem was written by a Negro like themselves? Is the purpose of getting youngsters to read well served by a teacher who draws on special information that may be, properly speaking, outside or beyond the work itself?

As a refinement of that question, consider the propriety of extraliterary "motivating devices" employed in textbooks. In a junior high school text,[1] is any justifiable literary purpose served by announcing before Whitman's "I Hear America Singing" that Whitman "has been called the poet of democracy," and that "he expressed in new ways the growth and vigor of the young nation"? What if he had been called "the poet of parliamentarianism," and if he were deemed to have synthesized all the *old* ways of expressing "growth and vigor of the young nation"? Would anyone care? And what of the fact that this poem about mechanics, carpenters, boatmen, etc., is superimposed on a photograph of what seem to be builders, with a crane swinging some beams into place? Is that an addition to the poem, or a subtraction from it? Is it a perversion of what this poem was meant to be? *Or does anyone give a hoot what the poem was meant to be, considering what (say, in the junior high text) it turned out to be?*

There we are at the real crux—at the point where we must consider the words of perhaps the most eloquent spokesmen against what is frequently called the intentional fallacy: ". . . the meaning of a work resides within the work; no judgment of intention has relevancy unless corroborated by the work itself, in which case it is supererogatory. It is therefore circular and misleading to speak of judging the work with respect to its success in carrying out the author's intention." So speak Monroe C. Beardsley and W. K. Wimsatt in their article on intention in *The Dictionary of World Literature*.[2]

[1] Mary Agnella Gunn, Thomas G. Devine, Ralph C. Staiger, and David H. Russell, eds., *Exploration Through Reading* (Boston: Ginn, 1964), p. 279.

[2] Joseph T. Shipley, ed. (New York: Philosophical Library, 1943), p. 329.

The philosophical discussion of intention in literature is by no means new. In the journals we may find eloquent argument, such as the 1921 article by Oskar Walzel, titled "Künstlerische Absicht" (Artistic Intention),[3] in which the author emphasizes that what writers have said about their own creative endeavors is frequently questionable, citing the instance of Richard Wagner's view that it was often only during the process of actually creating that the creator's intention evolved. Walzel maintained that much comes from an artist's unconscious and that the perceiver's knowledge of which of the given ingredients stem from the artist's conscious and which from his unconscious would, in fact, merely obfuscate and get in the way of the proper reception of the art work.

Walzel reminds us that the degree of cultivated, as against intuitive, genius evidenced in the plays of Shakespeare had been argued in Germany by the Schlegels (his outstanding translators) and by Novalis—just as that argument is of course implicit in all the tedious discussion in the English-speaking world regarding whether works manifesting the universality of Shakespeare's must not have come from a sophisticated Lord Bacon, or even a committee of scholars, rather than from the son of a respectable but untitled Stratford glover. Specifically, too, Walzel deals with the works of Emile Zola, and those of Goethe, marshaling evidence of the divergence in significant works from the authors' publicly stated purpose.

Not totally unlike I. A. Richards in England, Walzel insists that a work becomes complete, as it were, only in the eyes of the beholder, and that therefore it is to be judged largely by the responses it arouses in us, rather than by what we think we know of the artist's purpose. To this not unfamiliar argument, Walzel adds the one idea, which may strike us as rather typically teutonic, of the *Formwille* of an artist, an era, or a

---

[3] Oskar Walzel, "Künstlerische Absicht," *Germanisch-Romanische Monatsschrift* IX (Heidelberg, 1921): 321–30. I perhaps give more space to Walzel's views than they would otherwise warrant, first, because being in a somewhat obscure German journal, they may not be quite as accessible or familiar to the general reader as they would otherwise be, and second, to make the point that the discussion of intention did not begin with Wimsatt and Beardsley.

nation (*Volk*).[4] The notion of such a *Formwille* is piquant, if untranslatable—signifying something like *an internal, perhaps organic, urge to assume a certain shape*. That, maintains Walzel, does indeed exist, but it is not to be confused with the artist's conscious intent.

The argument in English as to the relevance of intention (specifically in literature) has evolved its *Formwille* mainly in the previously cited statement by Wimsatt and Beardsley in *The Dictionary of World Literature*. This statement was then rebutted in an article by Ananda K. Coomaraswamy, in *The American Bookman*.[5] And Coomaraswamy's argument, in turn, was answered in the now well-known essay by Wimsatt, titled "The Intentional Fallacy."[6]

Coomaraswamy reminds us of the classical authorities, represented by Plato and others, who maintained that one is "unable to judge whether a poem is good or bad" unless one knows whether its intention "has or has not found its mark."[7] As Coomaraswamy puts it, "The only possible literary criticism of an already existing and extant work is one in terms of the ratio of intention and result." No other measure of a work is as objective; there are no other absolutes by which a work may be judged at all, as there are no degrees of perfection in art. Wimsatt, argues Coomaraswamy, was in fact saying that an author should or should not have intended what he intended, and is not really speaking significantly about the art work itself.

"How," one would then ask, "could you know really what the author intended?" And especially one would ask this if one is impressed by the often-stated contention that one *cannot* know what an author intended, either because the author does not tell (except in the work itself, as it *is*), or—perhaps more in keeping with a skepticism birthed by developments in psy-

[4] *Ibid.*, p. 327.

[5] Ananda K. Coomaraswamy, "Intention," *The American Bookman* I (1944): 41–48.

[6] "The Intentional Fallacy" appeared first in *Sewanee Review* LIV (1946), but is now most easily available in Wimsatt's collection of essays, *The Verbal Icon* (Lexington: University of Kentucky Press, 1967), pp. 3–18.

[7] Coomaraswamy, "Intention," p. 42.

chology in the last fifty years—because the author *does not* know what he intended—does not know, even if he thinks he knows. And to this question Coomaraswamy answers, as I read him, that one empathizes with the author, and so identifies with his point of view that one does indeed forsee what that author will (can? should?) say next. Largely, it is a matter of common sense too, Coomaraswamy suggests, for, after all, if a man is shooting at a target with a bow and arrow, we may assume with reasonable assurance that he is probably meaning to hit the target.[8]

Coomaraswamy's argument was answered in the previously mentioned expansion and restatement of the Beardsley-Wimsatt position, Wimsatt's well-known article "The Intentional Fallacy." Fully realizing that I am not improving Professor Wimsatt's essay by doing so, I will enumerate below what seem to me to be its main points. First, however, since we will speak of judging literary works, let me warn that there are implications in the word "judging." In using that word, we may or may not have in mind "evaluating." Possibly all we mean is "explicating," though even in explication there must needs be implied value judgments. Whether we mean *explication* or *evaluation* has pedagogical implications which are important but which are only tangent to the main point of this essay, and so I stop short of considering the problem. Second, it will help

---

[8] Coomaraswamy's view found qualified support in Charles Child Walcutt's "Critic's Taste or Artist's Intention?" *The University of Kansas City Review* XII (1946): 278–83. Walcutt suggests that Mr. Coomaraswamy's confidence in his own ability to know authors' intentions may derive from "his wide knowledge of great art and of various literary traditions," but that, in fact, Mr. Coomaraswamy confuses this knowledge "with his ability to see what was in the artist's mind before he wrote." There is a distinction, then, between an "intention" we can impute simply on the basis of our knowledge of literary history and tradition, and the very personal intention of the author, of which the author himself might or might not have been aware, and which, conceivably, might have been quite counter to the tradition of his time. Curiously, Professor Walcutt seems to retract his criticism of Coomaraswamy (and allow criticism on the basis of imputed, personal intention) when he writes that a "good critic" would arrive at an accurate understanding of what the poet would have described in a prose statement as having been his intent even "if he had not had access to the prose statement." (p. 283).

in clarifying Professor Wimsatt's view if we say at the outset what he has developed inductively and subtly in his essay—namely that there are essentially two kinds of evidence by which we may judge (comprehend) a work. First, there are indicators of intention that are external to the work, such as the author's biography, his psychology, his historical era, and the like. These, maintains Wimsatt, are outside of the work, and therefore are not relevant to its evaluation. Second, there is internal evidence. In this category falls the syntax, the diction, all the material actually there on the printed page. That is the work; and that, says Wimsatt, comprises the evidence for our appraisal of the work. Wimsatt speaks also of a third category, "an intermediate kind of evidence," which straddles the narrow line between the relevant and the irrelevant, and which might include an epigraph attached to the work, notes appended to the work, or allusions in the work. Keeping in mind the distinction between internal, external, and border-line evidence, let me summarize below the main points of Wimsatt's essay. The points may overlap. And most of them I will refer to again in the second part of this essay—the part dealing with the implications for pedagogy. Wimsatt, then, says:

1. For the reader of a work, knowledge of the author's intent is neither available nor desirable "for judging the success of a work of literary art." (Note again the slippery word "judging.")

2. "Intention" could be imputed to an author only if the author succeeded in carrying out his intention. And that we cannot know.

3. A poem simply *is*; it goes into the world alone. One must judge it independently from other factors, just as one would a scientific statement. Poetry is of a different order of communication from other types of verbal messages.

4. The "thoughts" in a poem are to be imputed to a *dramatic speaker*; they can be given the author only by biographical inference.

5. In reply to Coomaraswamy's criticism that poetry can be judged solely by the ratio of accomplishment to intention,

there being no other absolutes, Wimsatt answers that indeed we *can* judge competence in poetry just as we can judge competence in other kinds of performance.

6. And just as Coomaraswamy cited Plato for *his* purposes, so Wimsatt cites him for *his*, quoting Socrates to the effect that poets are the ones who know the least about their own works. Wimsatt gives numerous examples of elegant and eloquent statements by poets about poetry—none of which presumably would take us far in an endeavor to comprehend poetry logically. Even were a poet-critic like Eliot, for example, consulted about his own poem, his answers would be beside the point, or beside the poem, anyway, in which alone lies the evidence.

7. The actual aesthetic achievement is neither an indication of nor a result of the intensity of the poet's feeling. (This will be an important point for the next section.)

8. Literary biography is an attractive study which is, however, not to be confused with literary studies.

9. Since the words are the poem, a word's history developing subsequent to the writing of the poem may also be considered relevant to the poem's meaning.

10. Finally, there is the difficult, often borderline, consideration of the apparatus of a work of literature. Frequently we may regard it as internal, and therefore relevant. But not always. This apparatus is of three main types:

a. Epigraphs which writers occasionally put at the beginning of a work are probably part of the work and therefore relevant. The epigraph might, in fact, be invented by the author. Wimsatt cites F. O. Matthiesen's view that an epigraph "is *designed* to form an integral part of the effect of the poem."

b. Notes—especially authors' notes—are problematical. Eliot's notes to *The Wasteland* are a case in point.

c. Allusions in a work are very problematical too. Wimsatt cites cases where the knowledge of the allusion (or reference) would help one comprehend the meaning, and other cases where it is superfluous. Frequently, if we are sensitive to the movement of a poem, the allusion will do its work even if we don't know the referent. Part of the art in the old ballad of

/ 335

Sir Patrick Spens, Wimsatt considers to lie precisely in the way the poet plunges us into the middle of the story.

To summarize: the argument about intention revolves mainly around whether what we know about an author and about the historical circumstances of the creation of a work is a part of the work and is therefore to be considered when the work is taught, or whether, on the other hand, the work, *solely*, *is* the work; and the study of matters not on the page before us, though perhaps interesting, is not literary study. There is a gray area, the main ingredient of which (for our pedagogical concern) is the matter of allusion—whether people, things, ideas, or other works referred to in a literary work are a part of the literary work, and therefore are to be studied or at least explicated.

II

PEDAGOGICAL IMPLICATIONS

The kinds of questions one asks of or about a work of literature depend on one's assumptions about the matter of intention or, stated more dramatically, they depend on one's notions of the mode of existence of a work of literature. So does the sort of classroom one conducts. So does the textbook one uses.

There are very diverse ways of considering literature in the classroom, and not everyone would agree that "teaching literature" necessarily means only teaching *about* literature (as Northrop Frye maintains), or teaching only criticism of literature. One extreme—the tacit knowing type of learning (or responding) of which I will speak in a moment, has nothing to do with criticism. There are, in fact, three theoretically distinct, though in practice often overlapping, views that could underlie the way one would conduct classes in literature.

1. There is first the view that all sorts of information outside the work are part of the work, making it what it is.

2. There is a second view which maintains that all that is on the page is to be explored minutely if one is to learn, to gain comprehension, of the work. From an examination of these items we may possibly carefully infer about the author (though

that is really beside the point). We focus on the work as it stands alone.

3. There is the third view, perhaps pejoratively put as the "I feel it but I can't express it" view of literature. More delicately put, this is a view emphasizing what may be called literary experience, as much as a literary work. I shall treat these views in inverse order since that way their pedagogical implications are most simply stated.

The renowned chemist and philosopher, Michael Polanyi, has put the case for "tacit knowing" as clearly as it can be put: *"We can know more than we can tell."*[9] Polanyi goes on to make the point that "all descriptive sciences study physiognomies that cannot be fully described in words, nor even by pictures." And Polanyi clarifies that he does not want to be thought to be limiting himself to perception of Gestalt—a passive affair—but that he is speaking of "an active shaping of experience performed in the pursuit of knowledge." Polanyi proceeds to explain rationally and objectively how this tacit knowing takes shape, though for our purposes it suffices to say that tacit knowing proceeds from internal processes which we do not originally sense, to a comprehension that cannot be itemized.

Polanyi then establishes the idea of "indwelling," of associating oneself so much with the mind of an artistic creator, or perhaps with that of a chess-player, that one attains, one knows not how, the knowledge of the artistic creator, or that, for example, one could, with sufficient study of him, anticipate the next move of the chess-player. Such a view brings us, paradoxically, rather close to Mr. Coomaraswamy's intentional fallacy, if fallacy it is. Therefore, I do not want to draw further on Polanyi's thesis, beyond availing myself of the apt term "tacit knowing," and the idea that there is possible a comprehension of an object (person, poem) which is unaccountable and different from the sum of the parts of the object.

What follows in a literature classroom from such a view?

[9] Michael Polanyi, *The Tacit Dimension* (New York: Doubleday Anchor Books, 1967), pp. 4ff.

The extreme pedagogical program that could be designed by an educator convinced that literary "knowledge" was essentially tacit and unaccountable would be to expose the student to a literary work, and then to make himself, and all planned presentation of auxiliary apparatus, scarce. Probably he would simply turn the student loose in a library. This idea is not far-fetched. It may, in fact, account for more lives dedicated to literature, for more literary careers, than we imagine. More or less, it comprised the literary education of John Stuart Mill. And once I thought to write an article on how my own university classmates who became professors of English became so absorbed by literature that they made the study of it their livelihood. I wrote perhaps a dozen of them, and received in return some fascinating letters, most of which I would say make minimal mention of teachers, or of formal classroom experiences. (If we think of the manner in which most people develop their liking and understanding of music, the idea may strike us as less strange.)

Among student teachers at Harvard, I have seen teaching on the assumption of a modified notion of tacit understanding attempted in what is called a peer teaching session.[10] The assignment was for each student teacher to teach a small group of his fellows one item of literature—preferably a poem, simply because its shortness would make the task more manageable. In this particular instance, the student teacher gave each member of the group a copy of the poem, set up a tape recorder, and had one student read the poem, which did not have an author's name attached but was in fact by LeRoi Jones and was an intense statement of the sense of racial isolation and outrage. The girl read the poem. (The tape recorder was going.) There was a pause. The girl said, "I didn't read it very well; it moved me so much." Silence again. One or two tentative probes by students in the general direction of the girl's statement of having been moved. Silence. More silence. Then

10 As I use the term "tacit understanding" I do not intend or include that part of Polanyi's use of the term which sees as the final outcome of such understanding the identification with the artist, his purpose, his intent, or his person.

a young man in the group raised a technical question about the prosody. With some relief, other members of the group took up the cue and for the next fifteen minutes discussed this and other specific prosodic points. The class then stopped, and the student teacher played back for them the tape of their responses to the poem. After about two minutes of listening to their early responses, the class asked for the tape to be turned off, and until the end of the session they talked about their responses. Now, what sort of teaching of literature is this?

The students' first individual encounter with the poem would have had to take place in any teaching of it. But as for what happened after that—the students' discussion of their own responses—we would be hard-pressed, I think, to call that "teaching literature," valuable as the experience may have been as an exercise in group dynamics, in self-realization, or whatever. And what about intention? Where could a teacher be said to be taking his conscious or unconscious stand on the question of intention, on the relevance of the background of the poem, if he employs such a method? (From the students' point of view, we must say simply we don't know what part intention played; it may or may not have been important, depending on what the student happens to have known of the work's origins.) But for the teacher, the implication is that intention or background is irrelevant, since he does nothing to present it, rather leaving understanding of the poem to whatever chance associations his students may make. In fact, the teacher may even disclaim having as his goal the effecting of anything beyond self-understanding in the first place.

David Holbrook has been perhaps the most verbal advocate of the English class as the occasion for students to delve into or "realize" themselves at the prodding of some stimulus, literary or otherwise. And some poets write, I suspect, with the intention only of touching a sensitive nerve, arousing associations of which they may have an inkling, but the precise nature of which they could not possibly predict. (This, too, may be imputing intent—but if intent it is, then it is that in a very different, much more vague and more generalized sense of the word than in the rest of this essay. And here I speak of what happens less from inside knowledge of the poet than from observation of what happens when a semantically minimal poem is read by a class.) I am thinking specifically of poems such as the following. I quote the first two of twelve stanzas:

Paul McCartney, Gustave Mahler
Alfred Jarry John Coltrane
Charlie Mingus Claude Debussy
Wordsworth Monet Bach and Blake

Charlie Parker Pierre Bonnard
Leonardo Bessie Smith
Fidel Castro Jackson Pollock
Gaudi Milton Munch and Berg.[11]

The fact that in italics before the first stanza stands the question "If you weren't you, who would you like to be?" and that the poem concludes

and
last of all
me.

after ten more stanzas of names, and that therefore the poem does make an intelligible, predicated statement, does not, I think, lessen my contention that poetry exists that lends itself to and may even be written to elicit unpredictable and entirely individual (i.e., never the same twice) responses, and that there is little a teacher could say to "educate" the student. That this poem is intended to be strongly rhythmical is probably not very helpful for the determination of its significance. And one might find it amusing to conceive of a misguided textbook publisher explicating each of the poem's ninety-two names with socio-historico-cultural footnotes. But even the most intention-minded critic would grant the questionable relevance of such an exercise—though given John Livingston Lowes's exhaustive reconstruction of Coleridge's experience and reading as it un-

---

[11] Adrian Henri, "Me," in Edward Lucie-Smith, *The Liverpool Scene* (New York: Doubleday, Copyright © 1967 by Edward Lucie-Smith), p. 68. Reprinted by permission of Doubleday & Company, Inc.

derlies the poem "Kubla Khan," even that is not certain.[12]

The pedagogical implications of the second view, that one's entire focus is to be on the work as it stands on the page, and that this work is not to be modified by information brought to it from the outside are—or would be—simple, if one could be sure what "bringing from the outside" meant. Thus, for example, Randall Jarrell's poem "The Death of the Ball Turret Gunner" stands well alone, and the line "From my mother's sleep I fell into the State" would not be made more meaningful if the reader knew the Rh factor of Jarrell's mother, nor even into which State the poet fell.[13] And yet without at least a minimal knowledge of the nature of the ball turret in airplanes of World War II, a reader's comprehension of the poem would be impoverished. It would not suffice to think a ball turret is something like a parapet. Thus even if one would argue that "outside" information is beside the point, and that the literary work carries itself, and that in the classroom one will focus on linguistic units small and large, on diction, on meter, on ironies (on those, that is, requiring no special, "outside," biographical or historical knowledge), and on rhetorical strategies, one must at the same time grant the necessity for a certain minimal sharing of experience with the author, and one must assume, too, a knowledge of the author's language on the part of the students (though that of course immediately raises the question, "What do you mean by 'knowledge'?").

Before proceeding to examine the third view—that all sorts of information outside the work are part of the work, making it what it is—let us pause a moment to see where we have come. And then let me chart very briefly in advance where we will be going in the examination of the third view, since that view has several complicating ramifications that will be easier to follow if the reader has a map in advance.

First, then, beginning inductively with some examples, we

---

[12] John Livingston Lowes, *The Road to Xanadu* (New York: Vintage Books, 1955).
[13] Randall Jarrell, *Selected Poems* (New York: Atheneum, 1964), p. 137.

suggested the general nature of the problem of "intention." Specifically, we attempted to clarify by focusing on the opposing views of Mr. Coomaraswamy and Mr. Wimsatt. The problem: "How much is 'outside knowledge' part of a work of art, and what place does such knowledge have in the appropriate response to art?"

Section II has concerned itself with the pedagogical implications of the diverse positions one may take on the matter of intention. First we looked at some length at a classroom in which the essential thing seems to have been the student's uncontaminated *response* to the work. Such a class must be considered as the extreme example of the anti-intentionalist view in practice. There is nothing the teacher can add, and in fact it would seem that the work itself is irrelevant—or at least that another would serve as well.

The more moderate anti-intentionalist view, that the work on the page is the only thing that matters, is the second possibility. In the classroom dedicated to this proposition, one finds students and teachers examining works minutely for diction, ironies, paradoxes, and the like. The difficulty lies in defining what one means by "the work alone" and whether any consideration of a work doesn't presuppose certain (varying) amounts of knowledge or common experience, even if only of the language.

That brings us to where we are now—the third position: that all sorts of information outside the work are part of the work, making it what it is; and the more one knows this outside material, the more one "knows" the work. This "outside material" is essentially of three types, each of which we will consider as it would relate to a classroom. First, there is the study of the broad socio-cultural context out of which the work comes. Second, there is the study of the author's life, considering both his general psychological state, and his specific psychological condition during the writing, as that condition may be induced both from authors' documents and from drafts of the literary work. A subcategory of the consideration of the author's state of mind is the attempt to gauge the "sincerity" of the work as a mirror of the "sincerity" of the author. And third, there is the study of the referents and the allusions in a piece of writing, on the assumption that to "know" the work one must be familiar with everything it is talking about.

So let us now proceed to look at the third view—in practice by far the most widespread one (though by no means necessarily a consciously held one)—that the more one knows of the circumstances of the composition of a work, the more one "knows" the work—or is learning what one ought to learn about it. This is the common assumption among most teachers. It is the assumption of textbook publishers. It is the assumption in teacher-employment examinations. And its ramifications and manifestations are multifold.

To begin with the broader cultural context (and to work toward the more individual and private), it is considered appropriate in some places for teachers of English to know politico-religious circumstances of the time and area in which works are written. Thus, on the "Boston Public Schools Examination for Certificates of Qualification" (December 27, 1967), applicants were asked: " 'Bunyan represents a different side of Puritanism from Milton.' Discuss this comment, noting the specific emphases of the two authors, with appropriate reference to two works of Bunyan and to three works . . . of Milton." The only answer that would (logically, if not in fact) excuse the potential teacher from having to know the cultural circumstances out of which the works came would be if he "Discuss[ed] this comment" by arguing, à la Wimsatt, that it was irrelevant to the works of Bunyan and Milton.

Likewise, even a superficial glance at catalogues of college courses will show that colleges and universities consider literature a subject to be taught in the light of its social, historical, and even coterie context. One will find courses on "The Age of Milton," "The Age of Swift and Pope," "The Pre-Raphaelites," and the like, and if memory of my own student days still serves me accurately, these courses almost invariably begin with a list of monarchs and their dates, proceed to a cursory survey of sociological conditions of the time and country, and then focus first on the life of the author and then, finally, on his works.

Often the consideration of works in terms of origins is trivial. Sometimes it is thoughtlessly sentimental, as in the frequent maudlin encomiums of "the good old nursery rhymes" or "the good old tunes." On the other hand, not to know that much of William Morris's poetry must be seen against the larger background of his taste for the Nordic and the medieval must impoverish a reader's appreciation. To read Hawthorne's *House of the Seven Gables* with no recognition of the Puritan shadow looming over it would be to lose something valuable. Not to know that Kafka had read Kierkegaard, and not to appreciate the point that in *The Castle* the story of Amelia's resistance to the demands of the Castle (which in this case is to be equated with a kind of Divine Authority) may find its parallel in Kierkegaard's obsession with the story of God's demand that Abraham sacrifice his son, is to read the story poorly and out of its own context.[14]

Similarly the matter of form. Frequently we may let the form of a piece of writing work its will on us, but there are other times when not to place a work in the context of the tradition of its form would be to miss much in the reading. To illustrate the former option first: the poet Thom Gunn has written what seems to me a spare and beautiful poem titled "Flying Above California" in which he tells of surveying that richly diverse state, and concludes

> that accuracy of the beaches,
> is part of the ultimate richness.[15]

The entire poem—not only the last two lines—is written in such lines of nine syllables, exemplifying the "accuracy" of the beaches and Gunn's vision of the whole state. That the poem

[14] Admittedly there is debate about the parallel. Heinz Politzer argues for it; Erich Heller against. Both essays may be found in the collection of essays I have edited on Kafka's *Castle* in the "Twentieth Century Interpretations" series (Englewood Cliffs, N.J.: Prentice-Hall, 1968).

[15] Thom Gunn, *My Sad Captains and Other Poems* (Chicago: University of Chicago Press, 1961), p. 34.

is not metrically loose, free, floppy, but remains firmly regular in its syllabic organization, is significant and essential to the meaning. But why nine syllables, rather than five, or the more classical decasyllabic line, I cannot imagine. Historically the nine syllables mean nothing to me, and I should guess that I am not missing any essential irony, paradox, or allusion. Internally—as far as only this poem goes—it is simply the disciplined recurrence of the nine-syllable line that does carry meaning.

But by way of contrast, one may consider a poem where the historical association of a given form is indeed very significant. Consider John Crowe Ransom's "Piazza Piece."

> —I am a gentleman in a dustcoat trying
> To make you hear. Your ears are soft and small
> And listen to an old man not at all.
> They want the young man's whispering and sighing.
> But see the roses on your trellis dying
> And hear the spectral singing of the moon;
> For I must have my lovely lady soon,
> I am a gentleman in a dustcoat trying.
>
> —I am a lady young in beauty waiting
> Until my truelove comes, and then we kiss.
> But what grey man among the vines is this
> Whose words are dry and faint as in a dream?
> Back from my trellis, Sir, before I scream!
> I am a lady young in beauty waiting.[16]

We have in this poem two actors: an old man and a beautiful young girl. And the old man wants the young girl. He is wooing her. In the penultimate line of the poem there is the suggestion that the wooer is indeed about to succeed, and to have his "lady young in beauty." And all this in a sonnet divided into an octave and a sestet, metrically most reminiscent of the Petrarchan sonnet form, precursor of a tradition of countless romantic sonnets of the Renaissance. Arbitrary? Not at all! And if we miss the formal allusion (the allusion produced by form), we miss, I should argue, an essential part of Ransom's

[16] John Crowe Ransom, *Poems and Essays* (New York: Alfred A. Knopf, 1955), p. 38.

meaning. For though this is a sonnet of wooing, there can be little doubt that the "gentleman in a dustcoat," wheedling, insinuating, importuning, and "grey," must be Death—Death come to fetch thoughtless and beautiful youth. It is the old and traditional tale of Death and the Maiden, often written about, often depicted. But the fact that Ransom thought to put this old story in something resembling the rich and historically most romantic Petrarchan sonnet form is a stroke of the poet's genius that adds to the mere semantic content in a way so as to increase infinitely the irony and the poignancy—but in such a way that someone not aware of the historical associations of the form would have missed entirely.

This consideration of form I have chosen to discuss under the general heading still of literature viewed in its social and cultural context. Actually the Ransom example verges on the topic of the relevance of allusion, since the adaptation of the Petrarchan form in this instance is, after all, an allusion. However, before we look more closely and specifically at the problem of the relevance of comprehension of allusion to the study of literature, let us consider briefly the second area deemed important by those who would argue that we should know the origins of a work, namely, the matter of the relevance of the author's biography to the work of literature.

That the facts of the author's life and person are irrelevant to the study of the work before us has been argued eloquently, as was indicated in the first section of the present essay. That many textbooks, teachers, publishers, and editors disagree is easily demonstrable.

Consider merely the matter of dust jackets, perhaps of children's books especially—how many of them tell us that the authoress is a trinominal lady, formerly a Fulbright scholar in France, and now living with her husband, her three children, and her two poodles, in a converted, remodeled barn in Connecticut. Consider the number of instances of books quoting writing of youngsters, where that writing is followed by a statement of the child's age—saying, in effect, "do not consider this work *in vacuo,* but recognize the youth of the author." It is as though a Calder mobile were labeled "by Calder, age 62."

Textbooks, too, make much of historical and biographical backgrounds for literary works. Picking simply the first one that comes to hand and opening it randomly, I find the "Song of Hiawatha" followed by a short biographical sketch and photograph of Longfellow; on another page I find an amusing poem about the stodginess but inevitability of old age, followed by a short account of the World War I experiences of e. e. cummings—which tells, in addition, how cummings attempted new ways of communicating by unconventional spelling, punctuation, etc. The squib following a poem by Countee Cullen names him as "one of America's greatest Negro poets."[17]

Also, there are statements, essays, even whole books, by authors telling how and why they write, and others (including text books) concerning themselves with successive and discarded early drafts, particularly of poems, as a way of giving insight into the nature of the writer, and—eventually, I should think —into the nature of the work.[18] Of these, of course, only the textbooks would argue by the very fact of their existence that one must know the background, the evolution of a work, to understand it fully. In the other books and essays, the presumption is that their authors think the history of a work is part of the work, though possibly the essays and statements may have

---

[17] All these examples are from Robert C. Pooley, Edythe Daniel, Edmund J. Farrell, Alfred H. Grommon, and Olive Stafford Niles, eds., *Projection in Literature* (Glenview, Ill.: Scott, Foresman, 1967).

[18] E.g. Thomas Mann, *The Story of a Novel: The Genesis of Doctor Faustus,* trans. Richard and Clara Winston (New York: Alfred A. Knopf, 1961); Rudolf Arnheim, W. H. Auden, Karl Shapiro, and Donald Stauffer, *Poets at Work: Essays Based on the Modern Poetry Collection at the Lockwood Memorial Library, University of Buffalo* (New York: Harcourt, Brace, 1948), in which Karl Shapiro's essay "The Meaning of the Discarded Poem" signifies by its title precisely the issue of which we are talking. For imaginative textbook use of photographic reproductions of poets' successive drafts, see Chad Walsh, *Doors into Poetry* (Englewood Cliffs, N. J.: Prentice-Hall, 1962). There are other books, too, having the same purpose.

been intended merely as literary chitchat, or psychological evidence of the nature of interesting people. But over all such works there hovers the assumption that insights into the author add to one's potential reading of his works and are therefore relevant. When reading such autobiographical works, we should at least keep in mind Wimsatt's or Plato's view that artists may be quite ignorant of the meaning of their own work. Wimsatt's point is, in fact, disarmingly seconded by an example of the lack of special insights a writer may have into his own creation in Herbert Kohl's account of his young elementary school student, Franklin, who wrote a fable and was subsequently questioned about it:

Franklin   Feb. 26
Once upon a time there was two men who were always fighting so one day a wise man came along and said fighting will never get you anywhere they didn't pay him no attention and they got in quarrels over and over again. So one day they went to church and the preacher said you should not fight and they got mad and knock the preacher out Can't find no ending.

The children read their fables to each other, made copies of their work, which they exchanged or pasted on the classroom walls. There were favorite fables, Barbara's two and the one of Thomas C. that had "smash or be smashed" as a moral. But the piece that fascinated the children the most was Franklin's. They wanted to know if his non-ending was an ending. Michael held that "can't find no ending" was itself the moral of Franklin's fable, and he was supported by Maurice and Ralph. Some of the other children disagreed and insisted that Franklin had not succeeded in writing a fable. Franklin wasn't sure himself what he had done and timidly agreed with both sides.[19]

Very closely related to our feelings of the relevance of an author's biography, indeed not really completely separable from it, are our feelings about the author's "sincerity." Certainly, in the classroom a work—a poem, for example—will

[19] Herbert Kohl, 36 *Children* (New York: New American Library, 1967), p. 111.

receive entirely different responses depending on our or the students' feeling for the circumstances, especially the suffering out of which it may have come. Henley's "Invictus" beginning

> Out of the night that covers me,
> Black as the Pit from pole to pole,
> I thank whatever gods may be
> For my unconquerable soul.

and ending with the famous lines,

> I am the master of my fate:
> I am the captain of my soul.

is frequently cited as one of the most glaring instances of Victorian sentimentality, really not much superior to Kilmer's "Trees" until it is pointed out from what suffering, from what personal bravery, and from what an indomitable strength of will this poem arose. Whether, after knowing the circumstances of its origin, we can thereafter perceive the poem as we did before must depend, I suppose, on the humane fallibility of our aesthetical purity.

Similar instances in the arts are legion: the paintings of crippled Toulouse-Lautrec, Christopher Smart's glorious and glorifying poem "Jubilato Agno," written in a mental institution ("For I am not without authority in my jeopardy, which I derive inevitably from the glory of the name of the Lord"; "FOR I pray the Lord JESUS that cured the LUNATICK to be merciful to all my brethren and sisters in these houses"),[20] even Alan Ginsberg's "Howl"—all could be perceived differently for knowledge of their origins, even by some stringently pure critics.

Then, too, there may be cases in which we know nothing of the author's circumstances, but where we say that we "feel" the sincerity of his grief or sorrow. And "feeling" that, we bribe the critical censor to close his eyes. In my own classes there is an example. I give my students the following poem by Jon Silkin, a contemporary English poet:

[20] Christopher Smart, *Jubilate Agno* (Cambridge: Harvard University Press, 1954), pp. 41–61.

Death of a Son

[who died in a mental hospital aged one]

Something has ceased to come along with me.
Something like a person; something very like one.
    And there was no nobility in it
        Or anything like that.

Something was there like a one year
Old house, dumb as stone. While the near buildings
    Sang like birds and laught
        Understanding the pact

They were to have with silence. But he
Neither sang nor laughed. He did not bless silence
    Like bread, with words.
        He did not forsake silence.

But rather, like a house in mourning
Kept the eye turned in to watch the silence while
    The other houses like birds
        Sang around him.

And the breathing silence neither
Moved nor was still.

I have seen stones: I have seen brick
But this house was made up of neither bricks nor stone
    But a house of flesh and blood
        With flesh of stone

And bricks for blood. A house
Of stones and blood in breathing silence with the other
    Birds singing crazy on its chimneys.
        But this was silence,

This was something else, this was
Hearing and speaking though he was a house drawn
    Into silence, this was
        Something religious in his silence,

Something shining in his quiet,
This was different this was altogether something else:
    Though he never spoke, this
        Was something to do with death.

350 /

And then slowly the eye stopped looking
Inward. The silence rose and became still.
The look turned to the outer place and stopped.
  With the birds still shrilling around him.
  And as if he could speak

He turned over on his side with his one year
Red as a wound
He turned over as if he could be sorry for this
And out of his eyes two great tears rolled, like stones,
  and he died.[21]

Then I give them Ben Jonson's well known poem, "On My First Son."

Farewell, thou child of my right hand, and joy;
My sin was too much hope of thee, loved boy.
Seven years thou wert lent to me, and I thee pay,
Exacted by thy fate, on the just day.
O, I could lose all father now. For why
Will man lament the state he should envy?
To have so soon 'scaped world's, and flesh's, rage,
And if no other misery, yet age?
Rest in soft peace, and, asked, say here doth lie
Ben Jonson, his best piece of poetry.
For whose sake, henceforth, all his vows be such,
As what he loves may never like too much.

I tell my students Wimsatt's dictum, that actual aesthetic achievement is neither an indication of nor a result of the intensity of the poet's feeling. I point out to them in the Silkin poem the sloppiness of the dangling modifier in the subtitle, "who died in a mental hospital aged one." I ask why the "near buildings," presumably either the houses with children, or the children themselves (though "building" is a curious image to represent "child"), should understand "the pact/They were to have with silence," presumably the knowledge of the in-

---

[21] Jon Silkin, "Death of a Son," in Donald Hall, Robert Pack, and Louis Simpson, eds., *The New Poets of England and America* (New York: Meridian Books, 1957), pp. 272–74. "Death of a Son" Copyright © 1954 by Jon Silkin. Reprinted from *The Peaceable Kingdom*, by Jon Silkin, by permission of Chatto and Windus Ltd., publisher, and from *Poems New and Selected*, by Jon Silkin, by permission of Wesleyan University Press, publisher.

evitability of death. I ask the class to tell me what in the world it could mean (if the other children are either singing buildings, or singing birds) to say that the "other/Birds [were] singing crazy on its chimneys." And what are the specific referents for the various *this's?* And what does it mean that the silence, which sat so heavy on the poet's child, "rose and became still," as though it had not previously been still too? The poem is vague. The metaphors are confused and don't work out.

I turn to the Jonson poem, and I point out to the class the form, the discipline of this expression of grief—knotted tight, constricted, pressured, hard as a fist, and I suggest that in the very tautness of the restraint and suppression there is the correlative of a torrential sorrow dammed, held back, as it were, by the force of the poet. But the students don't believe me. Silkin's is the greater poem, they will argue—for true grief knows no bounds. The poet's agony does not permit him to shape, trim, and model his phrases. One does not expect a cry of agony to be syntactically correct. Silkin's is the greater grief; Silkin's is the superior poem.

I tell them that by that measure a teardrop on a page would be the most perfect poem. But they are not impressed.

In the concluding section, which is about the voice of the narrator, we touch again on something very close to the matter of "sincerity." But first let us regard briefly a third manifestation of the view that the more outside information we can bring to our reading of a work, the better we will understand and appreciate it. In this case the "outside information" refers to the *allusions* in the work. In discussing this subject we must realize that there are degrees of obviousness of allusion, and we must come to a practical and reasonable understanding of what we mean when we use the term. After all, all words, since they presumably have referents or stand for *something,* are therefore allusions. And there are many instances, too, of borderline cases, where we may ask whether even a special word or reference really *ought* not to be in *any* intelligent

352 /

reader's repertoire—terms such as "God," "the Last Judgment," or even "the Bard of Avon." But in what follows I mean to raise the issue of information that may well be outside the ordinary reader's ken. And then the question is: Are both the reference and the referent part of the work? Is clarification of an author's allusions a permissible enlargement of the reader's perception of the work, and does the work itself improve for having such clarification?

Wimsatt maintains that there are some allusions which work "to a great extent even when we do not know them, through their suggestive power," but the real test and borderline case, as Wimsatt suggests, is when the poet supplies his own notes to a poem, as in the instance of Eliot's *The Wasteland*. As I read him, Wimsatt has not fully resolved the issue. Referring to other commentators on the same problem, he raises the real issue of whether the impact of the poem is more diluted by our not understanding the references, or by what "may look like unassimilated material lying loose beside the poem." What seems to me Wimsatt's own irresolution on the point is to be found in his sentence "We mean to suggest by the above analysis that whereas notes tend to seem to justify themselves as external indexes to the author's *intention*, yet they ought to be judged like any other part of a composition (verbal arrangement special to a particular context), and when so judged their reality as parts of the poem, or their imaginative integration with the rest of the poem, may come into question."[22]

Clearer instances of the problem of the organic connection of allusion to what stands alone on the printed page are numerous. Thomas Mann's novella *Death in Venice* is said by Germanists to be a veritable encyclopedia of parodies of German literary styles and authors. James Joyce's *Ulysses* (not to mention *Finnegans Wake*) is seldom studied without a library of explanatory handbooks pointing the parallels between the individual chapters and (1) organs of the body, (2) arts and sciences (divisions of learning), (3) colors, and (4)

[22] Wimsatt, "The Intentional Fallacy," in *The Verbal Icon*, p. 16.

rhetorical devices. The main analogue, reference, and allusion is of course in the very title, *Ulysses*, each of Joyce's chapters finding its appropriate character or incident in a specific section of Homer's *Odyssey*.

The example of Joyce is perhaps extreme. It is hard to imagine what may be gained from an uncontaminated and virginal reading of *Ulysses*, and it may be that this is the time to quote a statement (itself part of a broader context) by Harold C. Martin:

> There is no worse enemy to the general education of the mind, it seems to me, than the isolation of product from origin. No one doubts that some kinds of expertness can be developed by the isolation, and in a technological age it may be argued that that is exactly what ought to be developed. But in the measure that teachers are concerned with cultivation of the mind, they consent to such a goal at grave peril. If they aim at anything, it is at largeness of understanding. For that end many kinds of expertness may be needed, and teachers would be wrong to ignore their part of the responsibility to provide them . . . teachers are therefore obligated to do whatever they can to find, and exploit, the lines that lead to wholeness, the lines of connection. . . .[23]

Veering, as we have done, from the purely ontological and aesthetical problem to the practical, pedagogical ("what does it mean to 'teach' a work?"), it is appropriate to say that the teachers who find expression in the creation of English textbooks seem to see no problem. To them, by and large, anything and everything that may be hooked, pasted, wired, or footnoted onto a work is relevant, appropriate, and to be taken in by the student if the work is to be "learned." Thus, back to our previous example, the Scott, Foresman volume, *Projection in Literature*. Fearless Hiawatha, heeding not the warning of old Nokomis, strides forth into the forest, journeying ever westward, crossing the mighty Mississippi, passing the mountains of the prairie, until he

[23] Harold C. Martin, "What English Institutes Could Be," in *Speaking About Teaching: Papers from the 1965 Summer Session of the Commission on English* (Princeton, N.J.: College Entrance Examination Board, 1967), p. 8.

> Passed the land of Crows and Foxes,
> Passed the dwellings of the Blackfeet,
> Came unto the Rocky Mountains,
> To the kingdom of the West Wind,
> etc.

There is a footnote after "Blackfeet." It reads: "Crows . . . *Blackfeet*. The Crow tribe extended from North Dakota into Canada, the Fox tribe lived in northeastern Wisconsin, and the Blackfoot tribe in Montana and Canada."

The main presumption of such a note is probably that the student reading the poem ought to know where Hiawatha passed when on his journey—perhaps be able to plot his course and label it appropriately on a map of the United States. Another possible rationale for the note might be that it would be too bad if the youngster thought merely that Hiawatha traversed country in which lived blackbirds, vixen, and people with dirty feet. Such a possible misunderstanding, however, being unlikely—or even having a charm of its own—here we may have an instance in which to apply what Wimsatt said of some of Eliot's allusions—that they "work when we know them—and to a great extent even when we do not know them, through their suggestive power." That is to say, the average seventh-grader probably knows that Crows and Blackfeet are Indian tribes, even if he does not know precisely where they dwelled. What is important is the association, the general sense that Hiawatha crossed great stretches of territory, and if the youngster thinks foxes—animals—were on these mountains and prairies, so much the richer the poem.

The case is not dissimilar to the same text's footnote for Kipling's *Rikki-tikki-tavi*. Rikki-tikki, the mongoose, asks Nag, the cobra, "Who is Nag?" The cobra answers, "Who is Nag? . . . I am Nag. The great God Brahm put his mark upon all our people. . . ." The editors' footnote reads: "The great God Brahm (bräm), the supreme god of the Hindu religion, usually known as Brahma (brä'ma)."

"Well, you just can never learn too much," is about the only thing one can say to that!

/ 355

III

Now actually we could logically stop here. The nature of the discussion about intention has been stated, as have the extremes of the pedagogical consequences—on the one hand leaving the work totally unexplicated so that the student makes of it what he will, and on the other hand freighting the work copiously with notes as to its socio-historical origins, its author's state of mind, and the full explanation of all references within the work. In stating the extremes I hope I have not suggested that philosophical, curricular, or pedagogical arguments could not be made on either side of the intentional fence. Indeed we only need look at the work of the most ingenious of the puristic critics (e.g. William Empson), or the most learned of the historico-cultural ones (e.g. Marjorie Hope Nicholson or E. M. W. Tillyard) to understand immediately that we have a great deal to learn from all of them. Yet the question remains: as teachers, what is it we absolutely *must* teach our students about literature, no matter where we take our stand on the intentional argument? And why is that question placed here in this essay, which could be argued to have been concluded? Because the answer to this question, too, glances off the subject, intention.

To revert to this essay's opening tactic, what if the poem by Jon Silkin, "Death of a Son," were an invented situation? I don't know Jon Silkin, and though the intensity of the sorrow expressed in the poem would seem to argue otherwise, it is not inconceivable in the medium, literature, that the grieving voice of the speaking father should (or could) be invented. That, after all, is one of the great talents with which we so often credit Shakespeare, the ability to empathize, to—as it were—experience all conditions, stages, sexes, and individual attitudes of life. That he could seem to speak convincingly with the tongue of an Iago, a Hamlet, an Ophelia, a Malvolio, a Lear, a Jessica—that is Shakespeare's miraculous ability as the greatest dramatist. And so Shakespeare might have in-

356 /

vented a Jon Silkin speaking sorrowfully of the death of a son. And so might Jon Silkin have done, given his medium.

Consideration of this possibility is important, and it has to do with intention in literature. Though not categorically impossible, it would be very unusual if we found in another art, in another medium, an artist attempting to talk with a point of view, or from a personal vision, other than his own. And yet just such an attempt is the staple of a great deal of literature. The literary artist assumes a persona. It is often his *intention* to speak with a voice other than his daily, identifiable one. Now obviously you may reply, "but a man can speak *only* of what is a possibility for him. He cannot say things that are inconceivable for him. The potential, even for all Shakespeare's characters, must have been in the soul or the brain of Shakespeare—or he would not have been able to give birth to them." And that is of course perfectly true. Any persona, character, invention, or point of view created by a writer must indeed be within the writer's possibilities. (Whether that would make of Shakespeare a possible Iago or Shylock is not precisely relevant; the *imagining* of Iago and of Shylock *was* within Shakespeare's possibilities, as the imagining of a fourth dimension is, for most of us, not possible). And this, the frequent assumption of a voice or point of view other than one's own, distinguishes literature, at least, from normal specimens in the other arts.

This fact must be understood by the consumer of literature, and for that reason it seems most expedient to *teach* it, rather than to hope the reader will eventually discover it for himself. The man on the street has, in fact, usually not discovered it. Recently, when the motion picture of Joyce's *Ulysses* was playing in the small movie house of the town in which I lived, the management posted a hand-lettered sign in the lobby of the theater telling patrons that it sincerely regretted having the contractual obligation to the distributor to show this immoral film, this debased pornography, and that it (the management) looked forward to the day when it could resume its schedule of clean and pure family fare.

/ 357

The confusion exemplified in this instance represents almost an antecedent stage, a super-primitivity, of literary response. Attributing the musings of one character, of Molly Bloom, to an entire cast of characters, to an entire work, must certainly be as naive a response as is possible, and when the question is not even asked what it might be that the "obscene" character is saying, then the condemnation may be paralleled to the condemnation of a political study for containing the word "communism."

The above, as I say, is an even earlier state of aesthetic primitiveness than when a reader does not recognize the fact that the author in most works wears a mask, speaks through a persona the assumption of which may occasionally be unconscious, but which, in the case of literary artists, is usually purposely selected and artfully created. *To create such a narrator, or such a perspective of the events recorded, is an intention of the literary artist. Teaching the fact of the existence of this intention seems to me to be a primary and inescapable task if one wishes to educate readers in how to read.*

Teaching students to observe and appreciate the *author creating a character or observer* seems to me then one of the most important tasks of the teacher. And the lessons come in varying degrees of difficulty and in various genre. It should not be exceedingly difficult to make students aware of the fact that Jonathan Swift is not Gulliver, that Gulliver is a character like any other, and that we may take his measure (and not be put off by the fact that he seems to be narrating the book). What do we learn of him? He was trained as a surgeon. He observes empirically. He notes sizes, heights, weights, and mechanical workings. When things are technically ingenious, he admires. He has an eye for things; into human beings he has less insight. And into philosophical nuances, none at all. All this we learn (1) from what he says of himself, (2) from the things he chooses, the events he selects to report on out of the myriad possibilities he has, and (3) conversely, what he neglects to comment on. And so Gulliver's increasing misanthropy is certainly a subject of Swift's satire, though in this particular author the intricate interweavings, the cobweb filaments between creator and his creature, may be impossible to disentangle.

With poems the task may be interesting too. Take the poem "Blue Girls," by John Crowe Ransom:

Blue Girls

Twirling your blue skirts, traveling the sward
Under the towers of your seminary,
Go listen to your teachers old and contrary
Without believing a word.

Tie the white fillets then about your lustrous hair
And think no more of what will come to pass
Than bluebirds that go walking on the grass
And chattering on the air.

Practice your beauty, blue girls, before it fail;
And I will cry with my loud lips and publish
Beauty which all our power shall never establish,
It is so frail.

For I could tell you a story which is true:
I know a lady with a terrible tongue,
Blear eyes fallen from blue,
All her perfections tarnished—and yet it is not long
Since she was lovelier than any of you.[24]

A reader who tells you that the poem says "make the most of your beauty, girls, because some day your beauty will have faded, just like that of a lady I know" will have missed much that is happening. Such a reader will have missed the important point that Ransom has created a strikingly dramatic character (narrator, persona) who presents himself through his words. In other words, the poem is at least as much about the "speaker" as it is about the girls addressed by the "speaker."

To suggest only briefly what we may discover of this interesting dramatic speaker:

1. Where is the speaker? At a seminary—a fancy and somewhat old-fashioned name for a girls' (finishing) school. Possibly, but not necessarily, the speaker is relatively high up, looking down on the girls, as is *suggested* by the sort of over-all

24 Ransom, *Poems and Essays*, p. 29.

view of the girls traveling the "sward" who are compared to bluebirds walking on the grass. The speaker *may* be looking through a link fence, but the sum of what he sees suggests another perspective.

2. Who is the speaker? Well, he's someone who can see the girls at the seminary. And who might that be? It could be the janitor. Is there any way we can find out? "Style is the man" goes an old saw, and style in an instance such as this may be syntax. Even more helpfully, it may be diction. What is diction? There are word pools, reservoirs, from which, consciously or unconsciously, we select the words in which we express ourselves; and the nature of these pools, the characteristics typifying our vocabulary or our images, are excellent indications of our deeper and even of our shallower selves.[25] Images of corruption pervade the play *Hamlet*; words having to do with itching, rubbing, scraping, scabs, boils, and the like characterize the vocabulary of the abrasive character, Coriolanus. And so what do we find of the character saying the words to the girls in the poem "Blue Girls"?

What is a "sward"? What are "fillets"? Grass, ribbons—both words uncommon, stilted, somewhat archaic. And what of the peculiar word choice, turn of phrase, analogy in the third stanza? "Practice your beauty. . . ." "I will cry with my loud lips and publish/Beauty which all our power shall never establish. . . ."

"Practice your beauty," when normally we think of beauty as an attribute, a quality. One has it or one doesn't—but one doesn't go out and exercise it like a backhand, or the way one practices law or medicine. So the speaker's view or understanding of beauty is a peculiar one—one that sees it as something that these young girls here addressed actually work on. They engage, in the speaker's view, in the activity of being beautiful. That is their pastime. Curious.

And parallel to the imperative that the girls are to "practice their beauty . . . before it fail" (subjunctive mood!), what will

[25] In this vein, see Caroline Spurgeon, *Shakespeare's Imagery and What It Tells Us* (Cambridge, 1935).

the speaker do as regards Beauty (capitalized now, partly because it begins the line, but for other reasons perhaps too)?
The speaker will "publish" (*publico, publicāre*) Beauty. He
will make it known perhaps; perhaps he will publish in the
sense that one publishes a poem. But all is vanity, isn't it? For
all our power (the girls are not power figures; an authority, an
establishment housed in a tower, is a power, exercises power)
will not *establish* beauty, "it is so frail." The girls, then, are to
"practice" their beauty before they lose it or it fails them; the
speaker will announce it, but even with the publication of it
he will fail to establish it, make it firm and permanent.

Now, back again to consider the dramatic speaker. Who is
he? Located in a girls' school, looking at the girls, musing,
comparing them to the equally heedless bluebirds, he speaks
in language somewhat weighted with archaisms, and in the
subjunctive mood. (The janitor now seems unlikely.) And
stiffly, awkwardly, the speaker suggests the analogy of the girls'
practice of evanescent exercises of beauty, and his own practice
pertaining to Beauty, equally elusive no matter with what
"power" it is exercised. Original as is the perception of beauty
in the third stanza, the expression of the perception is touch-
ingly stiff, stilted, un-fluid, marmoreal, both in diction and
in tense.

There can be little question, can there, that this is a profes-
sorial type speaking, one in the humanities most certainly if
he conceives of himself as a publisher, an establisher of Beauty.
And so in that light, then, we regard the statement about the
transitoriness of young physical beauty, the un-establishability
of intellectual beauty—and the anecdotal and ironic exemplification, beautifully, incisively sharpened with the words "terrible tongue" and "blear eyes" of the girl once so beautiful,
most likely beloved by the speaker, who grew shrewish, old,
and ugly.

There is more, much more. But this should suffice to suggest
how far we are from saying merely "oh yes, that's a *carpe diem*
poem." "Make hay while the sun shines, for tomorrow you may
be dead." We have, rather, a portrait of a pedant, a scholar,

a teacher, who has seen beauty, who is overcome by its fleeting ungraspability, and who expresses this, and his own anecdotal exemplification, in words movingly stiff and awkward. And the portrait of the speaker, and the drama of his feelings, is the poem. (I once had a student suggest that the speaker was herself the "lady with a terrible tongue," reminiscing. The theory is interesting and not disprovable.)

Although one such example considered relatively closely should suffice, let us just note very briefly another poem, the well-known "Loveliest of Trees" by A. E. Housman.

Loveliest of Trees

> Loveliest of trees, the cherry now
> Is hung with bloom along the bough
> And stands about the woodland ride
> Wearing white for Eastertide.
>
> Now, of my threescore years and ten,
> Twenty will not come again,
> And take from seventy springs a score,
> It only leaves me fifty more.
>
> And since to look at things in bloom
> Fifty springs are little room,
> About the woodlands I will go
> To see the cherry hung with snow.[26]

Again the unskilled reader may say, "*carpe diem*; make the most of your youth." But again he would miss the fact that there is a speaker in the poem, and though he is less clearly characterized than is Ransom's speaker, he must be there nonetheless. The young man, after all, thinking he has only another fifty years or so to live, is going out to make the most of the moment. He's going out to see the cherry hung with snow. And who is it that is apt to have thoughts of this nature—thoughts telling him to go out and live, for life is short? Usually, at least, it's apt to be a poetical man addressing a real or an invented

[26] A. E. Housman, *The Collected Poems of A. E. Housman* (London: Jonathan Cape, 1939), p. 11. Reprinted by permission of The Society of Authors and Jonathan Cape.

audience of the young. So we have a poetical speaker, speaking his piece about taking advantage of the present, putting it in the dramatic voice of a young man. But that is only part of the story, for if I can say that this is a middle-aged voice speaking dramatically as a young man, then surely Housman himself was aware of that fact, too. And so we can carry the analysis one step further and say that this is in fact a poet (A. E. Housman) parodying, or dramatically portraying, a middle-aged man who is portraying a young man. (Jorge Luis Borges, I imagine, would press the point further—on to infinity, perhaps—saying it is a poet portraying a poet portraying a poet, etc. . . . who is . . . etc.)

The point has been made, I expect. Teaching readers to observe and to appreciate the author's *intended* and created speaker is one of the most important tasks of the teacher. Teaching this is a first step in teaching reading. And many people have never been taught to read. When the student has been taught to read such relatively simple works as the ones I have dealt with above, then he is ready to approach the really problematical. I give one last example.

The last example is essentially no different from the examples cited, except that it is much more complex, and therefore demands skills in reading that have not heretofore been required. In the cases of Swift, Ransom, and Housman, we must recognize their speakers to be characters. Similarly in the work of Franz Kafka, with the one added complication that not merely are we obliged to understand the character/narrator with all his peculiarities or limitations (e.g. Gulliver the gullible), but as both Walter H. Sokel and Wayne Booth have pointed out, in Kafka's major works the protagonist himself is ignorant, is not sure of what he sees, and sees much less than the total situation. "The protagonist's perspective," says Sokel of Kafka's character K (in *The Castle*), "operates for the purpose of blocking access to and comprehension of the truth, for the truth of the story emerges through the defeat of the protagonist's consciousness. . . . In Kafka's narratives . . . consciousness hides truth." Ironically, therefore, "The annihilation or

/ 363

refutation suffered by Kafka's protagonist, bearer of the lie, becomes the negative revelation of truth."[27] Wayne Booth has made the same point: ". . . when K stumbles, we stumble with him. The ironies work against us fully as much as they do against him."[28]

In other words, in our learning to read, we have moved first, and almost parenthetically, from learning that the views of one character (e.g. Molly Bloom) are not the book, and if the views of one character are communistic, erotic, or what have you, that says nothing at all of the book, or of the author, either of which (whom) might in fact be hostile to the views of the one character. The second major step is to the realization that *the literary artist has in fact created a literary artifact, and if one does not perceive it as such, then one does not really understand.* A primary characteristic of this literary artifact is that, whether it is through a first-person narrator obviously not the author (e.g. Gulliver, again, or Jim Hawkins in *Treasure Island*), or much more subtly in a lyric, the author has created, almost always knowingly I should think, a dramatic speaker who has his own peculiarities and distinctions, which are to be seen and understood if we wish to account for (read, understand, learn, or even "merely respond to" the work). Third, we have fascinating refinements and complications of the second point, as when (if Sokel and Booth are correct) we have a protagonist through whom we see, but who is himself so fallible that only in the negation of his perceptions and understandings (and consequently of our own) is a truth to be discovered.

If these consequences of seeing the work of art as a work of art (and not as "life itself") seem elementary, let me say merely that even if they are that, the fact seems not to be common knowledge, as anyone who has taught college freshmen, or encountered censorship in the schools, can attest. Holden

[27] Walter H. Sokel, *Franz Kafka* (New York: Columbia University Press, 1966), p. 12.
[28] Wayne C. Booth, *The Rhetoric of Fiction* (Chicago: University of Chicago Press, 1961), p. 287.

Caulfield may, because of his raw-nerved moral obsessiveness, be reciting his compulsive quest for honesty from the psychiatrist's couch—but that's not the way it's read by the censors who would take the immoral *Catcher in the Rye* with that obscene Caulfield boy out of the schools.

Whether a poem on a page encompasses all the circumstances leading to its birth or flowing from its allusions is a problem I have stated, but certainly not settled. How deeply we explore an author's circumstances and purposes when we "teach" a work of literature, I have not settled either—though I have attempted to bring out what are some pedagogical consequences of our decision. But that it *is* an author's intention to construct a literary artifact, and what being a literary artifact entails, I have said unambiguously it *is* our job to teach. When the chips are down, one may decide that one would really rather not teach literature—that it would be spoiling a beautiful thing. One would rather play therapist and wash the student in warm words. That's another problem. But *if* teaching literature means anything, it must mean at least that one teaches the student that if an author created a literary artifact, it was his intention to create a literary artifact, and that we must regard it, study it, ask questions of it in that light, and with that understanding.

Barbara Leondar

> To attempt a fundamental examination of metaphor would
> be nothing less than an investigation of the genesis of thought
> —a dangerous enterprise.
>
> J. Middleton Murry

There's one in every English class—one student whose turn of
mind is so inexorably literal as to miss the point of poetry
entirely. Reveal to such a student that Juliet is the sun, and
he will repay you with a look of pained incomprehension.
Dazzle him with a brilliant *explication de texte* and he will
respond with mute impermeable disbelief. His wrongheaded-
ness is so steadfast or—what comes to the same thing—his up-
rightness so unmitigated that he resists seduction and coercion
alike. "Why," he will grumble (but never inaudibly enough),
"why can't a poet just say what he means?"

Why indeed? The question deserves a better answer than it
usually gets. This essay proposes such an answer, or rather, pair
of answers, which, by diverse routes, move toward a single
destination. Each exploration, however, traverses a different

terrain and consequently opens its own vistas. The first investigates the metaphors of poetry, examining how their customary presentation in the classroom may distort or falsify, and suggests a less simplistic view. As it passes from consideration of individual figures to a view of the whole work of literature as metaphor, this section urges a modest strategy for outwitting the determined literalist. The second exploration contemplates a larger ecology: it disengages metaphor from its exclusively literary attachments and sets it in the context of the entire language system, the better to perceive its role therein. That it performs a role—a function unique to itself and consistent across contexts—is an assumption underlying the entire essay. How to assess that role and how to employ our knowledge of it in the classroom form the subjects of the concluding pages.

Before embarking, however, perhaps we should recall what every student of aesthetics already knows: that the concepts of his subject, however useful and familiar, suffer from a persistent inexactness. Many can compose a metaphor, or recognize one, but a comprehensive and general account of how metaphor works, or even what metaphor is, remains to be fashioned. Still, this state of affairs generates less discomfort than might be anticipated. The knowledgeable critic, whose instincts have been honed on flinty experience, learns when it is safe to trust those intuitions; he thereby achieves a surprising degree of skill and effectiveness. Confronting a statement about metaphor, even in the absence of explicit principles, such an initiate can with confidence estimate the worth of that description. He will, for instance, find the following series intelligible enough; he could, if he wished, mark each one true or false:

When we use a metaphor we have two thoughts of different things active together and supported by a single word, or phrase, whose meaning is a resultant of their interaction.[1]

[1] I. A. Richards, *Philosophy of Rhetoric* (London: Oxford University Press, 1936), p. 93.

[Metaphor] is the synthesis of several units of observation into one commanding image; it is the expression of a complex idea, not by analysis, nor by abstract statement, but by a sudden perception of an objective relation.[2]

Metaphor combines the element of necessity or universality (the prime poetic quality which Aristotle noticed) with that other element of concreteness or specificity which was implicit in Aristotle's requirement of the mimetic object. Metaphor is the union of history and philosophy which was the main premise of Sidney's *Defence*.[3]

Vital metaphor should be defined as a pluri-significative sign focus whose referents can be univocally conjoined or fused only at the expense of absurdity, but which implicitly involves a process of assimilative construing whose cognitive import cannot be entirely resolved into literal or non-tensional assertions.[4]

To the novice, however, lacking the insights of experience, such a series must seem not merely opaque but downright nonsensical. And if that novice is also a naive literalist, descriptions of this kind may only bolster his wary conviction that the study of literature is a vast hoax, a cloaking of the emperor. Those to whom his aesthetic education is entrusted, then, might find some instruction in adopting a borrowed innocence and, for a while, listening with his ears.

I

EXPLICATION

There are neither do-it-yourself manuals nor conceptual tool kits for our recalcitrant literalist. If he is ever to understand the figures of poetry, he must forge his own instruments. Let us, then, assign him a task, one which will not only provide initial momentum, but which will serve as well to test the precision of his calibrations. Let us give him some lines from T. S. Eliot:

[2] Herbert Read, *English Prose Style*, 2nd ed. (New York: Pantheon, 1952), p. 23.

[3] W. K. Wimsatt and Cleanth Brooks, *Literary Criticism: A Short History* (New York: Alfred A. Knopf, 1964), p. 749.

[4] Douglas Berggren, "The Use and Abuse of Metaphor," *Review of Metaphysics* XVI (1962): 244.

Out of the slimy mud of words, out of the sleet and hail of
  verbal imprecisions,
Approximate thoughts and feelings, words that have taken the
  place of thoughts and feelings,
There spring the perfect order of speech, and the beauty of
  incantation.[5]

And now let us require him to analyze those lines in such a
manner that (1) he provides an explication or paraphrase of
the sense of the passage; (2) he explains how the formal structure of the passage sustains and reveals those meanings; and
(3) he characterizes that formal structure in terms sufficiently
general or abstract to apply to other metaphors, although not
necessarily to *all* others. (The reasons for this exemption will
become clear subsequently.) In short, let us ask him to find,
or construct, or invent an interpretive instrument which
renders explicit those operations performed subliminally by
the experienced reader. Let us require that he produce a lucid
and rational process for analyzing metaphors—or, if not wholly
rational, at least less mysterious than the one his teachers
employ.

Probably he will turn first to his anthology. There he will find
something like this: "The most common [figures of speech]
. . . are simile and metaphor. The first is usually defined as a
stated comparison . . . the second as an implied comparison."[6]
Or "When we omit the word of comparison but imply a likeness—as in the sentence, 'That hog has guzzled all the champagne'—we are making use of metaphor."[7] Or "A metaphor is
a figure of speech that compares objects. . . ."[8] Among school
texts, at least, the consensus is virtually complete: metaphor
is a truncated simile from which the comparative term has
been deleted. Despite repeated and devastating attacks on this

[5] T. S. Eliot, "Choruses from 'The Rock,' IX," in *Collected Poems: 1909–
1935* (New York: Harcourt, Brace, 1936), p. 206.
[6] Cleanth Brooks and Robert Penn Warren, *Understanding Poetry*, 3rd ed.
(New York: Holt, Rinehart and Winston, 1960), p. 555.
[7] Morris H. Abrams *et al.*, eds., *The Norton Anthology of English Literature*
(New York: Norton, 1962), p. 1757.
[8] Marlies K. Danziger and W. Stacy Johnson, *An Introduction to Literary
Criticism* (Boston: D.C. Heath, 1961), p. 40.

oversimplified equation, it persists at the very point where it can effect the greatest mischief, among the authorities on whom the beginner relies. For that reason, it may be useful to review once more the deficiencies of a comparison theory.

To conceive of metaphor as compressed simile is to adopt what Max Black has labeled "a substitution view," one which treats metaphor "as a substitute for some other literal expression . . . which would have expressed the same meaning had it been used instead."[9] Whether such a literal equivalent can, in fact, be composed is highly problematical. Certainly the simpler instances of metaphor, those commonly adduced as illustrations, lend themselves to literal restatement. *That hog has guzzled all the champagne* translates readily enough as *that greedy creature.* But try to apply the same formula to a more subtle figure and the uncertainties multiply. At issue are not merely the intricacies of synonymy, although those difficulties surely amplify the problem. Rather, the formula fails conceptually; it proves untrue to the nature of figurative language. What, for instance, is compared in *Her beauty hangs upon the cheek of night? Cheek* with *night? Cheek* with some unnamed X? The metaphor does not tell us, and the formula cannot. Nor can it disclose the resemblances upon which a comparison might rest. This failure to uncover—or to specify a procedure for uncovering—the *tertium comparationis* renders the formula virtually useless as an instrument of explication. And not merely useless, but misleading as well, for if no explicit similarities can be cited, there would appear to be small warrant for assuming an intention to compare.

Our imaginary literalist, however, need never address himself to issues of logic; operational pragmatism will carry him to the same conclusions. Simply to measure his anthology's comparison theory against the complexities of his assigned task is to discover how little is revealed. He will find that he cannot even identify in Eliot's lines the two terms of the putative comparison. *Out of words like the slimy mud?* But surely that

[9] Max Black, "Metaphor," in Black, *Models and Metaphors* (Ithaca: Cornell University Press, 1962), p. 31.

violates, even parodies, what the verse says. Yet the comparison formula can take him no further. The explanatory power of that theory extends only to a fragment of the metaphoric population, and the least interesting fragment at that. Its domain consists of a small group of figures sharing two marked characteristics: figures which accept restoration of the term *like* without loss or corruption of sense and which, in addition, rely upon an aura of association firmly fixed by convention. From the primer onward, for example, convention teaches that wolves are rapacious and fierce, that lions are stalwart and strong. Hence, *man is a wolf* or *Richard is a lion* take on the appearance of simple comparisons. To treat them as such is probably harmless enough, provided they are not then delegated to represent the entire metaphoric populace.

For such metaphors, as we have observed, invite paraphrase; they speak figuratively but mean literally. Another kind of metaphor, however, suggests such a multiplicity of likenesses or implies such ambiguous ones as to resist paraphrase. Such figures mean what the language cannot otherwise say; they extend the resources of the lexicon. Eliot's image illustrates that capacity. To say of this figure that poetry evolving in the mind resembles the evolution of life itself is merely to graze the surface of meaning. The metaphor owes its effectiveness to its power of evoking multiple correlations between the two processes, of fabricating a web of coincident features. Such figures occupy one extreme of a metaphorical scale whose opposite pole is the compressed simile. Contingent upon their positions along that scale, particular figures will be more or less amenable to analysis as simple comparisons. But at some point on this continuum the principle of comparison ceases to explicate efficiently. Beyond that point a different descriptive scheme is required.

Such a notion, however, violates what has been an unexamined assumption about metaphor: its conception as a unitary phenomenon all of whose instances can be subsumed under a single description. The manifest inability to achieve such a description has failed even to modify this assumption.

On the contrary, the prevailing notion has supported explanatory constructions which, like the one just reviewed, systematically misrepresent important segments of their constituency.
Worse, it has served tacitly to discourage reformulation, or at
least that kind of reformulation which purchases increased
precision at the price of increased complexity. Certainly simplification is a laudable aim, but one dearly bought if its cost
is distortion. Moreover, such a commitment forecloses the
possibility that a less elegant but more accurate reconstrual
might ultimately engender a new and more comprehensive
simplification. Still, even if that eventuality were never realized,
the study of metaphor would be better served by a program
which acknowledges the subtleties of the phenomenon it observes. Accordingly, we may in that spirit urge our literalist to
examine competing notions of metaphor, in order to determine to what portion of the population each may apply.

The comparison theory, derived historically from Aristotle's
conception of metaphor as analogy,[10] still finds in that conception its most durable alternative. Because it describes
metaphor as embracing not merely two but four terms, the
analogical formula appears to encourage more precise explication. And in selected instances it serves gracefully. *The ship
plows the waves* may properly be rewritten *ship : waves : : plow
: soil*. Again, *Tis the year's midnight* implies a relation of the
winter solstice to the annual cycle like that of midnight to the
daily one. Yet should our literal-minded student attempt to
apply this formula to Eliot's image, he will arrive at an impasse. If he begins with the whole sentence, he finds it impossible to contrive a complete analogy (*evolution of life : ? : :
evolution of poetry : ?*). Whereas if he begins with the metaphoric phrase (*verbal imprecisions : evolution of a poem : : Ice
Age : evolution of life*), his analogy isolates only a single correspondence in what he rightly suspects to be a network.
Moreover, even that correlation proves unrevealing, for once
again the grounds of resemblance, the points of likeness represented by the evasive colon, remain obscure. Indeed, if the

10 Aristotle, *Poetics* 21.1457b.

colon is taken to signify a literal phrase—such a phrase, for example, as *dark, mysterious, and climactic* in the analogy *midnight : day : : winter solstice : year (Tis the year's midnight)*—then the Aristotelean scheme says no more than the comparison principle. Each illuminates a small set of figures, but each finally suffers the same insufficiencies.

And if the student reads further in his Aristotle, he will find the master himself brought up short. Homer, Aristotle notes, refers to the rock of Sisyphus as *the shameless stone*, and that metaphor, he continues, may be explicated as follows: "As the stone is to Sisyphus, so is the shameless one to him *who is shamed*."[11] Even a schoolboy can see how little such an explication explains. When an intellect of Aristotle's rank bumbles about in this fashion, the student need not blush to resume his search elsewhere.

Let him persevere and he will discover these insufficiencies addressed and to some degree ameliorated by recent explicative formulae.[12] Of those, he will find most useful one which describes metaphor metaphorically. That is, it conceives the metaphoric vehicle as a screen through which the tenor is observed, a screen whose coordinates locate the tenor's essential characteristics.[13] As a figure projects onto its tenor the cluster of connotations ordinarily attaching to the vehicle, it shapes and selects the reader's perceptions and thereby generates novel meanings. When, for instance, *The fog comes on little cat feet*, the feline vehicle endows its tenor with attributes of silence, stealth, surprise—with just such feline qualities as fog can comfortably accept. Avoiding thus the issue of literal paraphrase, this formulation also includes among its felicities an attractive account of what Richards has

[11] Aristotle, *Rhetoric* iii.11.3, 4.

[12] See, for instance, Monroe C. Beardsley, *Aesthetics: Problems in the Philosophy of Criticism* (New York: Harcourt, Brace, 1958), pp. 138–48; William K. Frankena, "Some Aspects of Language," and Paul Henle, "Metaphor," both in Paul Henle, ed., *Language, Thought, and Culture* (Ann Arbor: University of Michigan Press, 1958); Winifred Nowottny, *The Language Poets Use* (London: Oxford University Press, 1962), pp. 59ff.

[13] Black, "Metaphor," pp. 38–47.

termed the "interaction" of vehicle and tenor.[14] Such a formula provokes none of the objections incurred by the principles of comparison and analogy. In fact, it demonstrates its superior power in the very passages which disarm the earlier theories: in those metaphors, specifically, in which the grounds of comparison elude precise statement (*The red rose crowns the year*), or in which the fourth term of the analogy evades discovery (*Hitch your wagon to a star*).

But the interaction formula encounters difficulties of its own. In particular, it appears helpless before figures whose connotative auras are ambiguous, impoverished, or distorted by context. A fragment from Donne may illustrate this impotence in one of its forms:

> . . . for I
> Except you enthrall me, never shall be free,
> Nor ever chaste, except you ravish me.

Here context strips the figurative verbs of their customarily pejorative associations. *Enthrall* and *ravish* supply metaphoric vehicles for spiritual bondage and mystic union, both ardently desired by the poetic speaker. To impose upon these tenors the coloration of revulsion ordinarily connoted by rape and enslavement is to sanction folly—but a folly required by the interaction formula. Again, that instrument falters when confronted with Eliot's figure. There, however, the connotative value of the vehicle is less ambiguous than barren. Evolutionary progress evokes few associated conventions, and it is their absence which confounds the formula. If the metaphoric screen is blank, if the vehicle projects no attributes upon the tenor, no interaction can result. Such a metaphor paralyzes the explicative system.

Yet whatever the defects of the preceding conceptions—the interactive, the analogical, and the comparative—they need not be discarded out of hand. If none fully explains metaphor, each nevertheless identifies and illumines a set of its occurrences. Taken together, they comprehend nearly the entire range of figures. Only the sort of metaphor exemplified in

[14] See above, p. 367.

374 /

Eliot's elusive image continues to resist explication. In his attempt to account for that figure, the literal-minded student, if he is lucky, will find his way into an alien realm, the domain of physical science.

More often than the nonspecialist realizes, the theoretical scientist employs what he terms a "heuristic fiction," a cognitive model whose defining properties closely resemble those of metaphor. Such a model is neither a construction nor a diagram; it represents symbolically, rather than physically, some well-understood system of relations, fictional or real. That the model is verbal constitutes its essential value, for it thereby permits explanation of unfamiliar phenomena in the language of the known and manipulable. But it is not merely verbal, not merely a linguistic transaction between categories. Instead, the model postulates a crucial structural identity between itself and its original, an identity which sanctions and supports the exchange of language. Black's description illuminates this principle: "The model is an *icon* . . . designed to reproduce faithfully . . . in some new medium the *structure* or web of relationships in an original. . . . The dominating principle of the analogue model is what mathematicians call 'isomorphism.' "[15] That principle may also contribute to an understanding of metaphor.

The resemblance of models to metaphors has of course been remarked. The converse, however—the resemblance of metaphors to models—has been largely ignored. Yet that similarity may entail interesting consequences. For if the scientific analogue is a fruitful heuristic in its own sphere, the poetic analogue which it so closely resembles may perform the same role. Poetic metaphors, that is, may be conceived as models representing domains of human experience. Like a model, such a metaphor cannot be understood as merely verbal, merely a transference of language, but must be confronted as a verbal diagram of a structure, a network of relations. Exploration of the skeletal principle of such an iconic vehicle offers a strategy for discovering the isomorphic structure and reciprocal net-

[15] Max Black, "Models and Archetypes," in *Models and Metaphors*, p. 222.

work subsisting in the tenor. Consider, for instance, Belinda at her toilet:

> And now, unveiled, the toilet stands displayed,
> Each silver vase in mystic order laid.
> First, robed in white, the nymph intent adores,
> With head uncovered, the cosmetic powers.
> A heavenly image in the glass appears;
> To that she bends, to that her eyes she rears.
> The inferior priestess, at her altar's side.
> Trembling begins the sacred rites of Pride.

Here Pope invokes pagan ritual as a model by whose means vanity may be explored. In just this way, Donne's sonnet details the structure of paradoxical emotions inhering in religious surrender. And in the same way Eliot's lines discover the interrelated processes governing the genesis of poetry. *Slimy mud* and *sleet and hail* propose an evolutionary model whose essential principle is the progressive refinement of adaptation, organization, and awareness. Poetic language, the metaphor says, arises in the primordial unconscious; enters consciousness, like humanity itself, in its own Pleistocene; acquires precision, order, and ritual expression. Thus, "out of the slimy mud of words" the fittest survive as "the perfect order of speech." Thus, too, individual consciousness rehearses the ascent of the race, and ontogeny recapitulates phylogeny in the poetic image. But the model (and for "model" read "metaphoric vehicle") is itself subtly modified by its original. Speech and incantation are voluntary and purposeful. Because the ontogenetic process (the refining of poetic language) is willful, the phylogenetic one (biological evolution) is made to seem so, and the upward struggle of life becomes a striving toward perfection and apocalypse. Bodied forth on the skeletal structure of the model, the meanings of Eliot's figure take on form, flesh, and color. At this point the literalist may consider his task completed and the conditions of his assignment fulfilled.

Isomorphism and Mimesis

His teacher, however, may perceive in this solution implications which extend beyond the limits of the original problem.

Until its appropriateness is demonstrated, for instance, the scientific model remains a hypothesis. If model and metaphor are genuine equivalents, a metaphor, too, may be in some sense a hypothesis. And in that supposition resides still another: the possibility of extrapolation to the literary work as a whole. The isomorphic principle, that is, may apply not only to the individual figure, but also to the larger structure in which it is embedded.

Such a notion is less odd than it may appear; it represents, in fact, the restatement in novel language of a rather conventional view of literature as mimesis. But the new language invites some new construals and even, perhaps, new conclusions. For to read the whole work as a concrete representation of some underlying generality is to apprehend it as a metaphoric vehicle whose tenor (or tenors) is some segment of human experience. It is to conceive the work as a model, an icon, an analogue—that is, as a net of relations among person, action, and image. The work may then be said to impute to some portion of experience a relational structure isomorphic with the one it embodies. *King Lear*, for instance, may be read as a vehicle whose tenor is the structure of morality (more precisely, of order, love, and justice) in the Elizabethan universe, and whose interrelationships of action, character, and image represent (are isomorphic with, or iconic of) the network of relations obtaining in that universe. This is not to read *Lear* as an allegory, but rather as a concrete universal, an illustration which incarnates and expresses a principle not otherwise expressible. What seems true of the whole work seems true, as well, of its individual images and clusters of images. The metaphors of clothing, for instance, propose an analogue for the nature of illusion, so that Lear's experience of nakedness on the heath presumes an isomorphism with the experience of stripping away self-deceit.

The clank of heavy machinery behind such an interpretive system seems a risk worth enduring. As its jargon becomes more familiar, its worst offenses may vanish. And as a teaching strategy, it possesses manifest virtues. Not the least of these is the economy effected by encompassing within a single ex-plicative method the whole work and its component parts. Again, such a system avoids those twin hazards of literary in-struction: literalism (mistaking the paraphrase for the poem) and solipsism (mistaking the work's self-reference for its only reference). To locate literature at the intersection of life and language is to preserve for the young initiate the crucial quali-ties of immediacy and relevance, while demonstrating how that relevance must be sustained by a formal structure. Seen thus, the poem will appear less an assertion than a supposition, a hypothesis, a speculation, and so can be retrieved from the classroom moralizing which so often reduces it to homily or dogma. It can also be retrieved from the impulsive, subjective evaluation characteristic of the beginner: the hasty rejection or its obverse, the sentimental and uncritical affirmation. To treat the work as a supposition is both to entertain and to doubt it—that is, to distance it—and thus to experience it empathically and skeptically at once.

But the scientific model can be verified. As Black indicates, "We can determine the validity of a given model by checking the extent of its isomorphism with its intended application . . . we can, in principle at least, determine the 'goodness' of their 'fit.' "[16] The theoretical model entails consequences which can be tested by mathematics, experiment, or observation, and which, if verified, will tend to confirm the hypothesis. A model so validated may be said to exhibit verisimilitude. Although the poetic icon cannot attain to the universal validity of scien-tific theory, although it resists mathematical and experimental proofs, there is a sense in which every metaphor is tested in the experience of its readers. An apt figure provokes a simultaneous sense of surprise and familiarity. The proverbial shock of recog-nition attests to the frequency of this phenomenon. Such an involuntary assent to the image suggests that some sort of trial has, in fact, occurred, and the fit of the metaphor as measured against experience has been affirmed. A metaphor of this kind, then, also exhibits verisimilitude. If such an interpretation of

[16] *Ibid.*

verisimilitude violates convention, it nonetheless seems more appropriate than the common understanding of "truth to fact." Any application of the term in its customary sense to such a work as *Lear*, for instance, seems to substitute whimsy for criticism, whereas a reconstrual along the lines suggested would extend its domain, not only to *Lear* but to Kafka, Ionesco, and like fantasists. To retain verisimilitude among the defining criteria of great literature requires its interpretation, not in the narrow sense of accurate representation, but in the broader one of structural isomorphism with experience.

Perhaps, too, the conception of metaphor as hypothesis can enlighten notions of timelessness and universality in literature. Perhaps, that is, some works endure because they continue to provide valid hypotheses about important segments of human experience, hypotheses which are tested and affirmed by each generation. If universal appeal, like verisimilitude, characterizes great literature, its meaning must entail more than simple popularity. Rather, universality may indicate that the literary hypothesis—the metaphor or icon—has withstood the testing of large numbers of qualified readers, and will probably continue to be verified in this manner. The power and scope of such a metaphoric hypothesis, the variety and depth of experience which it must account for, are evidenced in the changing texture of life and the consequently changing critical emphases of history. A poem massive enough to command assent across the ages, despite reversals of taste, shifts of values, radical alterations in the style and tempo of life, must embody more than merely local and transient insights. Universality in those terms seems not so very remote from the universality of abstract theory.

II

METAPHOR AND INVENTION

The foregoing construes metaphor as a purely literary phenomenon. The contemporary revival of interest in metaphor, however, tends to overlook its aesthetic functions in favor of its extraliterary uses. Even its broader role as a pervasive component of all language goes largely ignored. Rather, recent study links metaphor with cognition, with perception, and especially with those translogical activities loosely understood as intuition, insight, and invention.

I. A. Richards, one of the first to interest himself in the relation of metaphor to thinking, provides a point of entry into the ongoing debate. He argues that all language is metaphoric, and that this is so because all thought is metaphoric.[17] Those are startling and radical claims—indefensible claims, ultimately—but provocative and fruitful to explore. All thinking, says Richards, is sorting, distributing items of ideation into conceptual bins containing other items which they resemble. These conceptual bins are, of course, provided by the lexicons of natural languages. To think, then, is to classify, and to classify, moreover, in accordance with traditional species/genus distinctions. A particular or a subordinate will be assigned to a class or superordinate on the basis of a set of relevant characteristics. And that, Richards argues, is a metaphoric process, since it is founded on the perception of similarities.

What is missing, however, from such a description of classification is an awareness of the role of presuppositions. As Strawson has taught us, the use of a term entails (or at least implies) certain prior assumptions not properly a part of the definition of that term.[18] A carnivore, for instance, is defined as a meat-eater, so that *eating meat* will be the relevant characteristic shared by all members of that class. But *eating meat* is an activity performed by animate creatures; thus, to be carnivorous presupposes vitality. Every superordinate conceals some prior requirement of this sort—covert or assumed, and rarely made explicit in a definition.

These concealed presuppositions help to account for both the remarkable versatility of language and some of its most dangerous tricks. They permit us, for instance, to tell a lie credibly,

[17] I. A. Richards, *Interpretation in Teaching* (New York: Harcourt, Brace, 1938), p. 48.
[18] P. F. Strawson, *Introduction to Logical Thinking* (New York: Wiley, 1952), pp. 48ff.

380 /

for their concealment partially obscures the faint boundary between actual and possible truth, between what is and what might be. An assertion will be true only if it assigns to a category some individual which conforms to the *definition* of that category; but an assertion will remain intelligible as long as it assigns to a category some individual which might potentially conform—that is, any individual which satisfies the *presuppositions* of that category. We may call a man a thief whether or not he steals, and although that statement might be untrue, it would not be categorically nonsensical. The statement would make sense, would be understood. Because *thief* presupposes an animate and purposeful agent, any such agent—a bird, a monkey, or a man—may meaningfully be classed under that superordinate. But to call an inanimate object (say a pebble or a cloud) a thief is to make no sense at all. The classification would be semantically impermissible. Thus, the crucial consideration in this account is the fact that the implicit presuppositions of a category, and not its explicit definition, determine what may without absurdity be classified within it.

Now it will be easier to see where Richards went astray. We need not quarrel with his assertion that all thought—or at least all predication—is sorting. But we will want to insist on an urgent distinction between literal and figurative classification. Making a literal statement, however novel or surprising, means declaring what is semantically acceptable—meaningful, if not necessarily true—and in that sense, conventional. The assertion *Tom is a thief*, even if untrue, is nonetheless semantically conventional. But to violate the presuppositions of *thief*—to claim, for instance, that *Time is a thief*—is to assert an absurdity, to commit what Ryle calls a "category mistake,"[19] and at the same time to invent a metaphor. Here, then, is the critical distinction between literal and metaphorical sorting that Richards overlooked. Metaphor is always a violation of presuppositions, a coupling of incompatibles, a semantic aber-

[19] Gilbert Ryle, *The Concept of Mind* (New York: Barnes and Noble, 1949), p. 8.

ration, a piece of arrant nonsense. That much Beardsley has made perfectly clear.[20]

Far less clear, however, are the concomitants of such odd linguistic behavior. How, for instance, does the reader comprehend a metaphor, despite its illogic? Or what amounts to the same thing, how is metaphor distinguishable from *mere* nonsense? And still more puzzling, why should such linguistic improprieties persist, even flourish, in an age whose giants have struggled to render language precise, direct, and transparent? What, in short, can metaphor accomplish that no other form of language can repeat? We have returned to the naive question of our hypothetical student, though now we find it less innocent than we had imagined. But this time we can come at it by a different approach. Rather than examining the form of metaphor, we can instead inquire into its semantic activity.

Let us begin, then, with the figures we know best, those of literature, on the assumption that they can teach us something useful about all metaphors. Thus, when Romeo proclaims that Juliet is the sun, the experienced reader comes to comprehend him perfectly. Nor does he merely understand the mood in which Romeo speaks or the emotion to which he gives vent. Indeed, he could not understand how Romeo feels without first making sense of what Romeo says. The dogma which assigns poetry to the viscera and prose to the cerebrum, holding the two forever opposed by the length of the spinal column, will not survive the test of practice. Yet even the experienced reader may not comprehend Romeo immediately; he may require a moment's contemplation. Characteristically, the initial response to metaphor is bafflement. That this should be so is hardly surprising in view of the semantic outrage perpetrated by the figure. But this very bafflement directs the reader how to proceed; he scans his lexicon for possible meanings. Is Juliet round and yellow? Is she a great gaseous mass? Is she capricious and unpredictable? From among these possibilities, the reader selects those which the context of the figure seems to ratify. It is context which permits him to assign meaning to an

[20] Beardsley, *Aesthetics*, pp. 138ff.

anomalous phrase, and context, then, which distinguishes between metaphor and nonsense. Semantically, as we have seen, metaphor *is* nonsense, but nonsense made meaningful by an environment. Disembedded from that environment and freed of local constraints, the figure invites virtually unlimited interpretation. For the metaphor does not locate Juliet in the class of suns; it is not a definition. If it were, then the need for a context would be largely abolished. Or, if metaphor were a partial definition—that is, if Romeo were assigning Juliet to the class of suns, and thus ascribing to her the definitive attributes of suns—then Romeo's would be a literal statement. (This is the trap into which the neophyte so readily tumbles. He perceives Romeo as mad or mistaken, rather than metaphoric.) In fact, the contrary is true. Those attributes of the sun which are defining or criterial are precisely the ones that are banished from the figure. Whatever Juliet may be, she is not a gaseous celestial mass.

Rather, the metaphor locates Juliet in some superordinate class to which the sun belongs, which is to say, in *any* class to which the sun might possibly be assigned. The metaphor does not deal in definitions but in presuppositions; it says that Juliet and the sun are members of the same class, although it does not tell us what that class is. Thus, whatever may be said of the sun—that it is a wheel of fire, or round and yellow, or searing and destructive—may also be said of Juliet. This is merely another way of observing what every experienced reader already knows: that figures of speech ignore, even deny, the principal meanings of their vehicles and rely instead on those subordinate values that the literature teacher calls connotations or associations. It is this shift of focus from the central to the peripheral that empowers the metaphor, for it enables the writer to transcend the gross distinctions of conventional vocabulary and to utilize the infinitely finer, more subtle meanings which lurk along the borders of speech. It is this shift, also, which endows metaphoric language with its allusive quality, its appearance of preferring the sidelong encounter to the head-on confrontation with its subject. But while it enhances the scope and subtlety of language, this same shift also increases the danger of ambiguity. *Anything* that may be said of the sun may also be said of Juliet. Of that enormous range of possibilities, some will eliminate themselves as inapplicable because contradictory (e.g., Juliet cannot have been represented in Greek mythology by Apollo). But much of the potential range of meaning waits to be eliminated by the context of the figure. Until context has done its work of narrowing, selecting, specifying, the figure remains unintelligible; that is, not metaphor at all, but nonsense. Context removes ambiguities and thereby actualizes metaphor.

Thus far, however, we have attended only to the figure's immediate environment, the text in which the metaphor occurs. But that text, too, takes *its* meaning from a larger universe of discourse, from the entire hierarchy of categories which are literal or semantically conventional in the language and the society from which the text arises. Categories, of course, vary across time, across geography, across language, and especially across cultures. Thus, what is semantically aberrant in one culture may be self-evident truth in another. A metaphor for us (e.g., *How living are the dead!*) might have been, for an ancient Egyptian, a statement of literal fact. And today, when the Borero tribesman of Brazil speaks of himself as a red parrot, he is not making metaphors; his language includes a category which equates man and parrot under a single superordinate. Metaphor is incurably relative; it exists at all only by virtue of its interlocking contexts and the cultural conventions preserved therein.

Metaphor, we have observed, is nonsense, though nonsense of a special kind. Not every incongruous coupling, then, is a figure, but every such structure may be thought of as a potential figure awaiting an actualizing environment. This, of course, is merely to say that everything in the world shares some common trait with each other thing, and thus any two diversities may be grouped together and subsumed under a single superordinate. A may be linked with B only insofar as both are not X, but even that is sufficient for classification and could

384 /

thus make a metaphor were an appropriate context to be devised. The poet's work, much of the time, consists in fabricating just such a universe of discourse.

But so, it would seem, does the work of the scientist, or at least of that highly original band which has emphasized the conceptual aspects of science. The list of seminal works built on metaphoric foundations is a familiar and substantial one. To number only a representative few: there is Torricelli's famous pronouncement, "We live submerged at the bottom of an ocean of the element air," quoted and explicated at length by Pascal in his *Physical Treatises*. There is Gilbert's pioneering work on magnetism, where astronomical bodies are described in terms of terrestrial magnets. There is Darwin, whose "natural selection" treats evolutionary processes in language borrowed from artificial stock-breeding. There is Yukawa, who, regarding atomic nuclei as a kind of corpuscular light, predicted the existence of the meson. And there is the present revival of interest in hydraulics and fluid mechanics which witnesses the reversal of an earlier figure, that of electricity as a fluid medium. Such a review need not be extended; it stands merely as a reminder of the large body of achievement supporting current inquiry into the heuristic function of metaphor.

Still, whatever the connection between *Juliet is the sun* and the fruitful figures of scientific invention, that link still seems obscure. Even granting the complexities of definition and classification underlying so simple a figure as Romeo's, those complexities do not appear to clarify the heuristic role claimed for metaphor. To do that, we will need to reexamine an observation made earlier. Recall that Romeo's figure locates Juliet in the same class as the sun (that is, under the same superordinate), but fails to name the class. It does not name the class because it cannot, because the lexicon provides no name for it. The indispensable function which only metaphor can perform is to give expression to meanings not otherwise accessible because language provides no established categories for their expression. The lexicon of a language, used literally, can only repeat what has already been said. Literal speech is conventional speech, and convention is the outgrowth of precedent. Thus, literal speech does not allow—cannot allow—for expression of the newly emergent, the peripherally conscious, the wholly novel. There are no words to say what has never been said before.

Indeed, conventional language rigidly adhered to may serve to stifle discovery precisely because it offers no ready conceptual bin in which to trap a fleeting perception or novel intuition. Much, of course, remains to be learned about the influence of language on thought and perception. But it seems difficult to deny that both are guided, and perhaps constrained, by the cultural expectations embedded in, and transmitted through, the lexicon. Most of the time we see what we expect to see, the landscape that language has pointed out to us. Most of the time, too, we operate conceptually upon the objects, activities, and relations which language has taught us to know. We have, despite the absence of precise formulations, descriptions of the awesome difficulties confronting the man who labors to think a thought which transcends the limits of his language. Metaphor is the linguistic mechanism which brings such conceptions to expression.

We have returned to an earlier point: metaphors, with certain exceptions, are not substitutes for literal speech. Rather, the figure creates a wholly novel category, an unnamed superordinate—or rather, a superordinate class namable only by its known constituents. To describe the characteristics of that class is to explicate the metaphor. If we recall the mode of explication set forth earlier, we can then begin to recognize how metaphors provide fruitful scientific hypotheses. But perhaps it should first be noted that, in the heuristic sequence, the point at which a metaphor suggests itself marks the completion, not the inception, of the inventive cycle. The metaphor expresses an already-formed hypothesis, novel because it sets its subject in an unexpected frame of reference, but not otherwise different from more conventional hypotheses. To determine the implications of such a hypothesis, then, requires a procedure like that applied earlier to Eliot's figure. The scientist will look for point-by-point correspondences of structure or behavior between tenor and putative vehicle. To explore a conception of man as immersed in an ocean of air, or a conception of astronomical bodies as terrestrial magnets, will require of the scientist precisely those skills exercised by the literary critic. Both must estimate the characteristics of the new superordinate by reference to the attributes of its conjoined subordinates as they mutually modify each other. Both are engaged in assimilating the unique to the known and familiar. Neither scientist nor critic can determine in advance how far the metaphor will carry him or how fruitful it will prove. But the scientist assumes the further obligation to test his projections in accordance with accepted procedures of verification, to assess the agreement between his fabrication and the world it professes to explain. And so, I have urged, ought the reader of literature.

METAPHOR IN THE CLASSROOM

How the scientist initially finds his metaphor remains at present beyond the boundaries of conjecture. But we might reasonably guess that such figures will not be vouchsafed to our recalcitrant literalist. His illiteracy will impoverish not only his poetic understanding, but his appreciation of a much wider range of human endeavor. Nor would it be surprising to find, accompanying his linguistic inflexibility, a correlative rigidity of thought and attitude. Whether the style of thought precedes the habit of speech, or the reverse, matters little. What results from such rigidity is a constriction of imagination in both domains, a wasteful reduction of creative capacity with all that it implies. Northrop Frye has vividly described that lamentable condition:

. . . listening to a speech by a high authority in the field, I know him to be a good scholar, a dedicated servant of society, and an admirable person. Yet his speech is a muddy river of cliches, flowing stickily into a delta of banalities at the peroration. The content of the speech does not do justice to his mind: what it does reflect is the state of his literary education. . . . He has never been trained to think rhetorically, to visualize his abstractions, to subordinate logic and sequence to the insights of metaphor and simile, to realize that figures of speech are not the ornaments of language, but the elements of both language and thought. . . . Once again, nothing can now be done for him: there are no courses in remedial metaphor.[21]

Schools rightly regard fluency not only as a desirable end in itself, but also as a means to clarity and precision of intellect. To that list of the aims of language study might be appended conceptual elasticity and inventiveness, and to the language curriculum itself might be added some lively instruction in the uses of metaphor. If schools can teach their students to harness the inventive energy of the figure, to utilize it as an instrument of thought not only in literature but in all disciplines—better yet, across disciplinary boundaries—they may enlarge not only creative impulses but cognitive powers as well. And if the notion of promoting ingenuity by teaching metaphor seems to stand logic on its head, that may be merely the measure of our present ignorance. Until educators find a more direct route to originality, metaphor may have to serve. That such instruction demands a light hand and a delicate ear for absurdity should go without saying. Even the present vacuum offends less than would a crude attempt to mechanize imagination.

How such instruction might inform the study of literature has already been suggested. But in speech-training and in composition, even more than in literature, the need for reform is urgent. In these subjects a revival of the ancient art of invention might successfully exploit the potential of metaphor. Students might be led deliberately to cultivate contradictory modes of conceiving the familiar and conventional. They might be taught to yoke incongruous pairs and then to fabricate a context which will make sense of their nonsense. Or they might be urged to explore the consequences of their own and others' metaphorical suppositions. Such practiced distortion

[21] Northrop Frye, "Elementary Teaching and Elemental Scholarship," *PMLA* LXXIX (1964): 12–13.

could serve to exorcise the ritualistic proprieties and unquestioned assumptions built into the very language system, and thus to liberate students from the clichés which imprison them. One may even hope that, eradicating the constraints of accustomed usage and systematically turning plain facts topsy-turvy, some students may attain to the innocence of vision from which fresh insight springs.

To advocate such a reform is to rediscover Kenneth Burke, and through him his master Bergson. Some years ago Burke outlined precisely such a program:

> Let us contrive not merely the flat merger of contradictions recommended by Bergson, but also the multitude of imperfect matchings, giving scientific terms for words usually treated sentimentally, or poetic terms for the concepts of science, or discussing disease as an accomplishment, or great structures of thought as an oversight, or mighty planetary movements as a mere following of the line of least resistance, a kind of glorified laziness; or using noble epithets for ignoble categories, and borrowing terms for the ephemeral to describe events for which we habitually reserve terms for the enduring. Let us not only discuss a nation as though it were an individual, but also an individual as though he were a nation, depicting massive events trivially, and altering the scale of weeds in a photograph until they become a sublime and towering forest—shifting from the animal, the vegetable, the physical, the mental, "irresponsibly" applying to one category the terms habitual to another. . . .[22]

One might even hope for more. Probably much of the school curriculum in all subjects—or perhaps regardless of subject—ought to be concerned with promoting inventiveness and fluency in the manipulation of the relevant symbol systems. Attention to the uses of metaphor might then produce an institutional bonus, an increased unity and coherence in the curriculum itself. As a common component of creativity in many disciplines, metaphors can establish an integrating principle linking often disparate realms. The student who learns

[22] Kenneth Burke, *Permanence and Change*, 2nd ed. (Los Altos, Calif.: Hermes Publications, 1954), pp. 119–22.

to perceive literature as figure, to respect the images embedded in his daily speech, to master his own experience by structuring and restructuring it in metaphoric variants, will acquire some sense of the unity of language processes. If, moreover, he practices the uses of metaphor in disciplines other than the literary, he may attain some glimpse of the singleness of all modes of symbolic knowledge, and may, indeed, begin to achieve that most valuable agility of mind, the capacity to leap categories and thus to free cognition of its bondage to habit.

Allan Shields

> *Let all you write be one and of a piece.*
> Horace

This essay is concerned with the problem of unity *in* the arts and not with the unity *of* the arts. Although my principal aim is to survey the various meanings of the concept, inferences regarding the uses of "unity" in educational contexts are also set forth. For purposes of this discussion, the expression "aesthetic unity" is used broadly to refer to whatever critics and theorists have meant when discussing the unity in works of art. Accordingly, eight meanings of aesthetic unity are identified: logical unity, material unity, ideational unity, functional unity, structural unity, formal unity, organic unity, and multiple unity.

Logical Unity

Unity in this sense means that an object, concept, or organism is or can be seen as one thing. In art, this meaning is intended whenever we simply identify a piece of music, an opera, a poem, a mural, or a pageant. The observation that "a work is a unity" is, of course, trivial in the sense that it applies with equal force to all art objects and indeed to any kind of discriminable object whatsoever. It is also inconsequential since nothing follows from the simple recognition (say) of a poem regarding any of the poem's qualities. As D. W. Prall noted, unity in this respect "is merely the fact of its being a single entity, not its structural, coherent character. It is the unity that is the distinction of one concept from another in logic, the mere distinction of this from that, which is necessary to articulate thinking."[1]

This is not to say that it is always easy to see objects even as simple units. There are unframed paintings that spill over their sides, constructions that require effort to separate them from their settings, and dances and dramas that involve audiences as participants (e.g., spontaneous happenings and aleatory music), all of which challenge the view of art as a simple discriminable unit. Still "unity as a unit" is not an aesthetically interesting idea and we may set it aside.

Material Unity

As DeWitt Parker observed, this meaning of unity involves the role or function of artistic materials.[2] That is, apart from other aspects in a work of art the material itself may constitute a unifying factor. Regarding the role of the material, Parker writes that "since the medium is valuable in itself, the mind, which craves unity everywhere, craves it there also, and lingers longer and more happily on finding it; and, since the medium can be expressive, the unity of the fundamental mood of the thought expressed will overflow into and pervade it. Hence there occurs *an autonomous development of unity in the material*, raising the total unity of the expression to a higher power."[3]

There are those who would dispute this meaning, saying it

[1] D. W. Prall, *Aesthetic Judgment* (New York: Crowell Apollo Editions, 1967), p. 359.
[2] DeWitt H. Parker, *The Principles of Aesthetics*, 2nd ed. (New York: Appleton-Century-Crofts, 1946), p. 24.
[3] *Ibid.*

marks no distinction that cannot better be expressed as a relationship between content and its formed expression. Parker, at least, sees in this kind of unity a contribution that involves more than content, for content can be given expression in different media, and when so given, we discover how much was "meant" by the medium. It does not appear to trouble some critics, for example, when a violin concerto is transcribed for trumpet, or when a painting is displayed by a photograph, but to Parker the differences are of considerable importance. Again, he says, that "to a large extent, even in the creative work of the artist, this unity is given, not made; *the very materials of the artist* consisting of elementary expressions—words, tones, colors, space-forms—*in which the unity of form and content has already been achieved*, either by an innate psycho-physical process, as is the case with tones and simple rhythms, or by association and habit, as is the case with the words of any natural language or the object-meanings which we attach to colors and shapes."[4]

Ideational Unity

It has been thought by a number of students of the arts that the primary meaning of unity lies in the capacity of the mind to entertain the work as a whole, to intuit wholeness, and to attribute unity to an otherwise segmented and disjunctive physical presentation. In the performing arts especially, it is said that interpretation alone produces unity from a complexity of varied features. It is impossible, for example, to "hear" a new musical composition the first time it is played, inasmuch as the meaning of the first part depends upon the last. Only during the second playing is a "real" hearing possible. After we have become familiar with the composition, we then construe the work to have an objective status as a whole unit. We attribute, ideationally, what in fact is not an objective characteristic of the work. Though this seems very clear in the case of opera, ballet, or symphonic works, it is less clear

---

[4] *Ibid.*, pp. 79–80; emphasis added. Cf. Rudolf Arnheim, *Art and Visual Perception* (Berkeley: University of California Press, 1954), p. 52.

with poetry, and still more debatable with the space arts. Paintings seem to be less ideational and more objective in their unity.

One theoretician has argued this point in connection with the dramatic arts. Writing about the "ideality of art" as a complete theory, Ronald Peacock says that " 'Unity' is not a sensuous experience, but an idea about it; it is an interpretation. And similarly with a work of art; the unity is the result of the artist's imaginative thought; he has constructed it."[5] Prall speaks in a similar vein: "Unity, coherence, a theme in variations, balance, symmetry, hierarchy, climax, simplicity, purity —all these are names for unification, for apprehension, and also general characteristics of the apprehended object in its completeness."[6] Without accepting Peacock's extreme theory that all art is ideational, we may conclude that at least one meaning of unity lies in the efforts of artists and performers to create unity for our apprehension.

Finally, in support of the meaning of ideational unity, we must admit that a temptation to *idealize* art objects works in favor of all concerned: artist, critic, and audience. If beauty be not in the eye of the beholder, yet such an eye will enhance the beauty it finds. To this extent, ideational unity is an important meaning of the concept of unity.

Functional Unity

Since works of fine art are generally regarded as nonutilitarian objects, it is easier to grasp this meaning of unity by speaking first of useful objects. Once learned, the purpose of utilitarian objects seems self-evident. A chair is to be sat on, a spoon to be used in eating, a hammer to drive nails. Quite apart from questions of color, texture, and design, there are other questions to be raised about a chair. A four-legged chair with one leg missing is functionally disunified. A grotesquely large chair with legs six feet high, a seat five feet across, and a five-foot back, though it may satisfy other aesthetic demands, will not be functionally unified. Or to take an even more familiar example: it may be

[5] Ronald Peacock, *The Art of Drama* (New York: Macmillan, 1957), pp. 74-75.
[6] Prall, *Aesthetic Judgment*, p. 180.

said that early automobiles were functionally unified, though they were far from aesthetically unified. The complexity of such cars with their great spatial voids, divisions, and independent units, can best be appreciated by comparing one with recent designs. With regard to functional unity there is less contrast between them.

Returning to art, architecture represents the one fine art that cannot escape being functional. But a work by an architect may fail to be functionally unified while being formally unified. A cathedral is functionally unified, though under dire circumstances it could serve as hospital, morgue, or political arena. By a close analogical transfer, we may now say that functional unity in a painting, sculpture, or other refined object of art means that all images used in the work must serve a central expression appropriately and congruously. Functional utility means a working together. Varied media provide a fair test of the discriminability of this meaning of unity. Where in poetry the *sound* of the speech enhances the ideas of the speech, there is functional unity. Where oral imagery is apt to imitate natural sounds as a result of language, we have a clear example. "The click click click of dry leaf on leaf" and other onomatopoeia are only obvious examples of such a happy marriage.

In the arts, the collaborative forms of drama, opera, and ballet most frequently exemplify functional unity. In this connection, Peacock remarks that "A similar organic coordination of the seen and the heard arises when the wind blows over a field of corn or sways the tree-tops. By contrast, the physical appearance of a person singing, and the sound of the song, are disjunctive. There is a causal physical relation between the two, but there the link breaks off; the appearance of the singer is not relevant to the song."[7]

Speaking of architecture, Parker observes how functional unity is related to other kinds: "This purpose of unity cannot well be sensed without spatial contiguity; here, as in sculpture, a unified life demands a unified material. Yet sometimes detached structures belong together functionally, and may be

---

[7] Peacock, *The Art of Drama*, p. 97.

felt as one aesthetically, provided they are similar in design and some one of them is dominant; otherwise, each claims to be a distinct individual, and aesthetic rivalry is the result. Functional unity, although necessary, is not sufficient for aesthetic unity; in addition, there must be formal unity—design, composition."[8] Just how this meaning of unity can be kept from melding with the meanings of organic unity is a problem that will be faced after we have examined the facets of organic unity.

Functional unity appears to be largely derivative from "natural" sources, in which the art image "imitates" and reminds us of those sources, purposes, and needs which we have apart from aesthetic experiences. Or perhaps we may put the matter the other way, saying that our aesthetic experiences with nature flow over into our aesthetic experiences with made objects, where, because refined, we prefer looking for their expressions.

Structural (Architectonic) Unity

Once more Parker has made one of the strongest cases for this type of unity. Structural appeal is a function of the architectonic arrangements, the forms in which works can be cast. "But even all the reasons so far invoked—the necessity for significance, the interest in unity, the demand for perspicuity—do not, I think, suffice to explain the structure of works of art. *For structure has, oftentimes, a direct emotional appeal*, which has not yet been taken into account, and *which is a leading motive for its presence. . . . Structure is not a purely intellectual or perceptive affair; it is also motor and organic, and that means emotional. It is felt with the body as well as understood by the mind."*[9]

Parker goes on to analyze and to describe different "types" of unity under the heading of "structural unity" and identifies these as unity in variety, in balance, symmetry, and related exceptions, and in "that unity characteristic of all teleologically related facts" such as we find in the developments, evolutions, sequential unfoldings of plot, and so on. His own lucid expli-

[8] Parker, *The Principles of Aesthetics*, p. 262.
[9] *Ibid.*, pp. 69–70; emphasis added.

cation makes it unnecessary to duplicate it. But it needs to be said that the position taken here is that even though these "types" of unity are basically architectonic in their creation and appeal, there are also important differences among them; for example, they are sufficiently different in execution, appeal, technique, and impact to require more refined discrimination as concepts. For this reason we reserve the "structural appeal of unity in variety" for separate treatment under "organic unity," "balance and symmetry and related exceptions" we relegate to a discussion of "formal unity," and "unity of teleological function" we have discussed under "functional unity." There is, again, no need to believe that these types are "separate." Our only philosophic task is "discrimination." Parker remarks that "The different types are by no means exclusive of each other and are usually found together in any complex work of art. Symmetry usually involves a combination of harmony and balance."[10]

Peacock, an idealist in his aesthetic theory, not surprisingly makes a great deal out of structural unity, interpreted as formal "intertextural imagery," borrowing the term from Coleridge. In poetry, for example, his argument from intertextural imagery shows "the ubiquitous presence of images—in verbal sound, rhythmic pattern, in sensuous suggestion and evocation both in the subject and in figures of speech—or, to put it another way, of a mode of expressiveness not identical with language but intralinguistic, working through language, and linking verbal art with other kinds."[11] After some technical examples he goes on to say:

The interfusion of the characteristic elements is inextricable, so that the "poetry" is not the sum of the parts but the product of mutual assimilation. . . . *Nor can a better example be found of the commanding principle of such an intertexture, that it has a unity conveniently called organic by analogy with the organic structures in nature, in which a whole is made up of perfectly functioning, mutually adapted parts, the whole being something that, exceeding the mere sum of the parts,*

[10] *Ibid.*, p. 74.
[11] Peacock, *The Art of Drama*, p. 97.

has an identity of its own. Such unity means that a single alteration in any word changes not only that word but all the relations of sense and imagery in the context.[12]

These passages show clearly the meaning of unity conceived of as structural appeal and why we delight in structure for its intrinsic values, as in the case of a fugue, round, or repeated melody in music.

Formal Unity

An object may have unity, be unified, or be a unity by virtue of its formal properties. In this sense, unity is the result of form. In the abstract, we accept such a formulation with few qualms. In a concrete case, however, formal unity cannot be disengaged from the content that makes it. Aristotle's lead was sound. No particular, no form. No form, no particular. And Aristotle's lead was sound again when he showed that what cannot be separated may nonetheless be cognitively discriminated and distinguished. Form may be discriminated from its content and its expression, but it cannot be "separated," whatever that could mean.

So thoroughly has form been discriminated in the history of aesthetics and art that there are some for whom "form" and "unity" appear to be synonymous terms. Though obviously our analysis leaves no room for such an identity, there do in fact seem to be some meanings of both terms that are synonymous. When the total arrangement of parts is said to be the unity of the work—the whole work—then we may speak also of its form, shape, and arrangement. And when we speak of the whole being more than the sum of its parts, we may substitute the term "form" for "whole" without loss of meaning, or we may substitute "unity."

On the other hand, there are cases when we cannot speak univocally. Where the form of a musical composition is said to be the fugue, it does not follow that it will have unity as an organic, functional, or material unity. A work may have more or less form while being highly unified, for example some free

12 *Ibid.*, p. 98; emphasis added.

verse. A whole may have form—an anthology of one kind of poetry—without having any significant unity as a work. Though we cannot argue independence—not yet—of form and unity, we may argue discriminability.

This discrimination stands in need of further refinement. Roman Ingarden has labored to this end, finding nine different meanings of the form-content relationship.[13] Ingarden's distinctions, objectively descriptive and reportorial, need not detain us. Only in the discussion of his ninth meaning does he find that form is consonant with "regularity" and "unity." But this last is not a contrast between form and content. It is a contrast between formed and unformed, form and shapelessness. It is a special regularity, not just a regular feature. The harmonious regularity is the main meaning of "form."

Gotshalk discusses what he calls "artistic form," approaching the question from the perspective of the creative act. He asks, "By what principles does the artist transcend 'nature' and enhance existential structure in the direction of greater intrinsic perceptual interest?"[14] and answers, "The four principles of harmony, balance, centrality, and development, with their associates and derivatives—recurrence, similarity, gradation, variation, modulation, symmetry, contrast, opposition, equilibrium, rhythm, measure, dominance, climax, hierarchy, and progression—are probably the chief formal principles used by the imagination of artists for the purification and enhancement of existential structure in works of art."[15] Though Gotshalk has more to say that has bearing on the question of form, much of it can better be discussed under the meaning of "organic unity."

Organic Unity

The metaphor of "organic" unity has a long history and the idea still appeals. To be integrated, with parts intimately inter-

---

[13] Roman Ingarden, "The General Question of the Essence of Form and Content," *Journal of Philosophy* LVII (1960): 222–33.

[14] D. W. Gotshalk, "Form," in Eliseo Vivas and Murray Krieger, eds., *The Problems of Aesthetics* (New York: Rinehart, 1953), pp. 194–208.

[15] *Ibid.*, p. 199.

related, to be a unitary whole being, to be a nondependent, freely living being in its own right, to be articulated (in both major senses of that useful term), and to be taken in all of these senses, demands a powerful, metaphorical symbol. Is there anything in the universe of living beings more inherently exciting or more radically meaningful than another living being? The chief drawback with the figure lies in our tendency to forget its analogical character. Though argument has primarily focused on the "organic" aspect of the term, it would have been more productive had advocates tried to deal more directly with the literal aspects of the problems involved. This is not the moment to pursue this logical difficulty. And it may be added that the problem is not as neat as we have just made it. After all, it is not so far-fetched to invert the issue and show that a life is often taken to be itself an artful creation, so that a living being may be said to be a metaphor of an art object.

We now face our most formidable set of distinctions. One of the difficulties is that disputants and advocates do not discuss the problems in either the same terms or the same contexts. Aristotle was discussing drama and tragedy most specifically. Harold Osborne operates in a larger aesthetic frame. Lord and Hutchings debate aesthetical theory. McTaggart and Broad write in a context of ontology, metaphysics, linguistics, and logical analysis, whereas Ernest Nagel's approach is within the context of the philosophy of science. When we remember that most aesthetic analysts have assimilated the other meanings of unity to "organic unity," we may be inclined to refuse the challenge to seek whatever clarity there may lie in the concept in favor of starting anew. Indeed, there is evidence that some analysts believe that they *have* started afresh. Were we able to find a beginning, much of our puzzlement might very well be avoided, but no such choice is open to us.

Parker's statement of the traditional concept will be a useful point of departure.

By [organic unity] is meant the fact that each element in a work of art is necessary to its value, that it contains no elements that are not thus necessary, and that all that are needful are there. The beautiful object is organized all through, "baked all through like a cake." Since everything that is necessary is there, we are not led to go beyond it to seek something to complete it; and since there are no unnecessary elements, there is nothing present to disturb its value. Moreover, the value of the work as a whole depends upon the reciprocal relations of its elements: each needs, responds to, demands, every other element. . . . In short, the meaning of the whole is not something additional to the elements of the work of art, but their cooperative deed.[16]

The conclusion to be drawn from this statement is not "so that is what organic unity means," but "what does 'organic unity' mean, when more fully explicated?" To this question we now turn.

To control the discussion, it will be convenient to divide the materials into three parts: (1) the writings of McTaggart, Broad, and Osborne; (2) Nagel's analysis; and (3) the discussion between Lord and Hutchings.

The Writings of McTaggart, Broad, and Osborne[17]

Osborne alone is concerned with the concept of organic unity as an aesthetic principle. McTaggart and Broad are interested in metaphysical-logical meanings.

McTaggart's use of the term "manifestation" is important to an understanding of his analysis. "By Manifestation I mean nothing more than the relation between a whole and its parts, when the emphasis is placed on the unity of the whole rather than the plurality of the parts, so that the parts are regarded as due to the differentiation of the whole rather than the whole as due to the union of the parts."[18] McTaggart believes that *any* "substance" may be properly conceived from either perspective, part to whole or whole to part, and *that both are valid.*

---

[16] DeWitt H. Parker, "The Problem of Aesthetic Form," in Morris Weitz, ed., *Problems in Aesthetics* (New York: Macmillan, 1959), pp. 175–76.

[17] J. McTaggart, *The Nature of Existence* (Cambridge: Cambridge University Press, 1921), I, chaps. 13, 20, 21; C. D. Broad, *Examination of McTaggart's Philosophy* (Cambridge: Cambridge University Press, 1933), I, chap. 17; Harold Osborne, "Organic Unity as an Aesthetic Principle," in Osborne, *Aesthetics and Criticism* (London: Routledge, 1955), pp. 238–48.

[18] McTaggart, *The Nature of Existence*, I, 121.

He further writes that "It is no more true that the nature of the substance is a unity of manifestation than that it is a unity of composition. Our advance consists, not in passing from one to the other, but in passing from a position in which only one is recognized as valid to a position where both are recognized."[19] Quite literally, he means that with any object composed of parts, "The unity is as essential as the plurality."[20] All of which is needed preparation for his analysis of how parts and wholes are related.

When the whole may be taken as expressing and informing each and all parts, then the object's unity is dependent upon its pervasive, qualitative character. Under these conditions of viewing the relation we may speak of the parts as being manifestations of the whole, rather than the whole being compounded of parts, as we naturally and more easily believe. "The parts are now seen to manifest the whole, taken as a unity. No part could do this, if the others did not do so also."[21] This new emphasis on interrelational structure may be expressed by saying that "To the idea of mutual indispensability is now added the more positive idea of mutual cooperation."[22] In summary, Broad says that "McTaggart's notion of organic unity is merely that nothing which is part of a whole W *would have been a part of it* if anything else which is a part of W *had failed to be a part of it.*"[23] The game, in other words, is to articulate a phrase, sentence, definition, or statement which will do linguistic justice to the concept. The question then is whether this expresses the way a unity may be read from a congeries, a variety of parts?

Broad's formulation makes McTaggart's statement emphasize the hypothetical, abstract, even conjectural *possibilities* of union. On this basis, no *other* part could possibly be a part of the whole of any union or collection, without making that union a *different* one. Being different, the first union would be

19 *Ibid.*
20 *Ibid.*, p. 122.
21 *Ibid.*, p. 158.
22 *Ibid.*
23 Broad, *Examination of McTaggart's Philosophy*, I, 316.

disunified. Hence, as Broad hints, this formulation is a tautology: "Whatever is a union by virtue of its parts in relation, is a relation of those parts such that they form a union." And every item in the universe conforms. Hence, though it is true (necessarily), it is trivial and inconsequential. Broad says so. "In this chapter I propose to take together two conceptions, which McTaggart treats separately. One is called 'Manifestation,' .... The other is called 'Organic Unity.' ... To be quite frank, I must say that both appear to me to be completely trivial, and the discussion of them is, in my opinion, 'much ado about nothing.' "[24] Nevertheless, Broad exercises considerable analytical skills trying to bring order into the conceptual chaos.

Broad's approach consists of formulating what other people have meant by organic unity. He admits, as we have seen, that McTaggart's formulation "is certainly a fact and is perfectly trivial, whilst what other people have meant by it is something which would be important but which is probably not a fact. And this is what I find about all the more exciting conceptions which occur in philosophy. I believe that other people who have called a whole W an 'organic unity' have meant that W is such that no part of it could *have existed* unless all the other parts had *existed* and had stood to each other in the relations in which they in fact did stand."[25]

Osborne tries to clarify this distinction by agreeing with Broad's remarks and by stating that since McTaggart's formulation fails to distinguish a heap of stones (as a W) from an aesthetic object, he fails utterly to do justice to what aestheticians have meant by unity. And that quality of the second formulation that distinguishes it from McTaggart's—the quality of *existence*—serves to emphasize a quality which Osborne, McTaggart, and Broad all neglect—*uniqueness*. Let me explain.

The second statement, by emphasizing the *facts* of part-whole relationships, serves to emphasize that this whole and these parts *alone* of all possible relationships stand together, *and that*

[24] *Ibid.*, p. 310.
[25] *Ibid.*, p. 316 (emphasis in original).

this is a unique arrangement. The first formulation fails to emphasize the uniqueness as an *additional* quality, and hence the second is supposed to be superior. "What is to be discussed here is the application of the notion of organic unity to aesthetic objects and specifically the contention that a beautiful work of art is a configuration such that its constituent parts could not have *existed* except as parts of precisely that whole of which they were in fact parts. Unless this can be demonstrated and is intended, the notion of organic unity is, I believe, not only valueless but conducive to mystification and obscurantism in discussions of beauty."[26] Aside from the real difficulty that there is considerable doubt whether Broad's formulation one is different from formulation two at all, we seem now to be faced by a *new* problem: clarifying the concept of "the unique as a principle of art creation and aesthetics."

Osborne's further enlightening discussion does in fact make several sound improvements in the argument of Broad and McTaggart. One improvement has to do with the question of the analogue: organic being. Broad and McTaggart lean heavily on the supposed quality of the delicacy of balance of unified forces in an organism, such that a slight change in one part, or an alteration of position of parts, would be disastrous to the whole. Regarding art objects, Osborne rightly argues that such objects, though appearing to be ephemeral and tender (a melody), are actually tough, stable, and not susceptible to major or minor changes in their setting or parts.[27]

This is not the place to extend our discussion, though it must be added that an unmistakable source of confusion about "organic unity" lies in the failure of those who use the analogue to understand the first principles about *organisms* themselves. Osborne's point about the changeability and adaptability—the recalcitrance to alteration—of works of art is well taken. But the *facts* of biology and art history render *both* of Broad's formulations nugatory. Organic unity requires a different defense and a different formulation to be a successful aesthetic

26 Osborne, "Organic Unity," p. 240.
27 *Ibid.*, pp. 240–43.

principle, from those formulations given by McTaggart, Broad, and Osborne.[28]

Nagel's Analysis[29]

Though Nagel's analysis of the meanings of these key concepts occurs in the context of logic and the philosophy of science, certain of his refinements, *mutatis mutandis*, are relevant to aesthetic problems. There is no need to dispute or challenge Nagel's results for our purposes. In summary, he finds no less than seven distinct meanings of the part-whole relationships, and four major applications of meaning through the use of the term "sum" in expressions such as "The whole is more than the sum of its parts." Regarding "organic wholes," Nagel finds it convenient to leave living bodies and organisms out of the discussion and to limit himself to physical systems to try to find in what sense or senses we may distinguish between "additive" wholes from "nonadditive" wholes. He concludes that "There are many systems whose constituent parts and processes are 'internally' related, in the sense that these constituents stand to each other in relations of mutual causal interdependence."[30] He also reports that "Although the occurrence of systems possessing distinctive structures of interdependent parts is undeniable, no general criterion has yet been proposed which makes it possible to identify in an absolute way systems which are 'genuinely functional' as distinct from systems which are 'merely summative.' "[31] A still more shaking conclusion is that "It does not seem possible to distinguish sharply between systems that are said to be 'organic unities' and those which are not."[32]

Nagel's final observation on his own findings is of particular moment.

[28] Osborne's position is not pursued here in further detail, but since he makes Broad's formulation the basic principle on which he proceeds, we are probably accurate in including him.

[29] Ernest Nagel, "Wholes, Sums, and Organic Unities," *Philosophical Studies* III (1952): 17–32.

[30] *Ibid.*, p. 27.

[31] *Ibid.*, p. 28. Cf. the discussion of "functional unity" above.

[32] *Ibid.*, p. 29.

The upshot of this discussion of organic unities is that the question whether they can be analyzed from the additive point of view does not possess a general answer. Some functional wholes certainly can be analyzed in that manner, while in the case of others (for example, living organisms) no fully satisfactory analysis of that type has yet been achieved. Accordingly, the mere fact that a system is a structure of dynamically interrelated parts does not suffice, by itself, to prove that the laws of such a system cannot be reduced to some theory developed initially for certain assumed constituents of the system. This conclusion may be meagre, but it does show that the issue under discussion cannot be settled, as so much of extant literature on it assumes, in a wholesale and a priori fashion.[33]

Discussions Between Lord and Hutchings[34]

With the specific problem of the meaning of unity, we have begun to see how other closely related questions crowd in. When we stop to ask how unity gets created in an object, how it gets injected, how an object informs unity, and how we can experience unity, we coincidentally raise other matters. In what sense are those particular parts conducive to unity in ways that others are not? Is there a way of telling in general how some elements project while others appropriately and conveniently recede? Briefly, such questions prompt pursuit of the standards of dominance, relevance, uniqueness, congruity, connexity, dependency, and the negatives of all of these and more.

In an exchange of articles, Lord and Hutchings have discussed several questions regarding organic unity as a standard of critical judgment. In her article "Aesthetic Unity," Lord pursues the difficult problem of the meaning and conditions

<hr />

[33] *Ibid.*, pp. 30–31.

[34] Catherine Lord, "Aesthetic Unity," *Journal of Philosophy* XLVII (1961): 321–27; Catherine Lord, "Organic Unity Reconsidered," *Journal of Aesthetics and Art Criticism* XXIII (1964): 263–68; P. Hutchings, "Organic Unity Revindicated?" *Journal of Aesthetics and Art Criticism* XXIII (1965): 323–27; Catherine Lord, "Unity with Impunity," *Journal of Aesthetics and Art Criticism* XXVI (1967): 103–6; Paul Grimley Kuntz, "The Art of Blotting," *Journal of Aesthetics and Art Criticism* XXV (1966): 93–103.

of aesthetic experience and its dependency upon the aesthetic object and concludes that "The aesthetic experience should be viewed as a process of growing awareness culminating in the unity of the imagination and the understanding. This unity is occasioned by the apprehension and the enjoyment of the aesthetical idea which is the source of the unity of the work of art. Thus the unity of the cognitive faculties reflects and issues from the unity of the work of art."[35]

It is against this conclusive setting that the articles following must be set. Her detailed argument rests on a tripartite division of the roving aesthetic effort. The first "stage" is ectypal, that is, the parts are examined discretely and extensively in the search for a whole. The second "stage" is the recognition of the fact of interrelationship of the parts in the whole, where their affinity for each other is grasped. The third stage allows the "imagination to function archetypally" when the imagination and undertaking (in Kantian terms) freely play, allowing us to "enjoy the parts of the work of art in terms of their connectedness."

In her later article, "Organic Unity Reconsidered," Lord argues that organic unity in its traditional sense is overly rigid, and that instead of a relatively static and inflexible part-whole relationship we must speak in terms of "grades of relevance" of parts, that some parts are more important, "important" meaning having greater or lesser dominance of impact. In literature, for example, "there are different degrees of literary unity appropriate to particular genres. An epic would not be expected to have the unity of a tragedy nor a tragedy the unity of a lyric poem."[36] One result of this position (an important one) is to give strength to the principle that "the stature of a work of art does not stem from organic unity."[37] Finally, looking beyond her results in this work, she says, "Organic unity properly understood is indeed *one* kind of unity that a work of art may exhibit, but it is not the only kind. Specifically, there

[35] Lord, "Aesthetic Unity," p. 327.
[36] Lord, "Organic Unity Reconsidered," p. 266.
[37] *Ibid.*, p. 267.

is the unity of Aristotle's cosmos (not to mention other kinds) which, though less stringent than organic unity, affords another type of model. Once we free ourselves from the spell of a single model, we may embark upon a series of detailed investigations as to the different kinds of unity which works of art are privileged to exhibit."[38]

Hutchings's criticism of Lord's position rests on a "heuristic" and "pragmatic" vindication of the principle of organic unity, and he suggests that "as a matter of critical method it is always pointful to look for organic unity, even when at first blush it does not look as though we are going to find it."[39] He goes on to argue that Lord's requirement is based upon a categorical distinction between "the indispensable or the essential, and the dispensable or padding." Lord answers Hutchings's argument, in "Unity with Impunity," by showing that they do not disagree. They agree that "the grades of relevance of a poem vary from the essential to the level of mere accident. And the merely accidental has a function."[40]

Probably the two most enlightening results from this exchange are these. First, organic unity as a critical standard rests upon the clarity of other dependent standards, such as relevance, impact, importance, and the accidental or essential. Second, we need to seek and explicate other models of unity. We may claim to have advanced the second. It yet remains to look more carefully at the first.

Multiple Unity as a Critical Criterion

Kuntz observes, almost as an aside, that critical standards themselves are dependent upon a prior manifestation of standards in works of art. "I would suggest that critical standards be clarified, like Aristotle's for Greek drama, after the great works have been produced. Before that time, a critic who sees the possibility of a new art-form cannot begin with reflecting on why the works are great but with encouraging the creative

[38] *Ibid.*, p. 268. The analysis in this essay agrees with Lord's proposal.
[39] Hutchings, "Organic Unity Revindicated," p. 324.
[40] Lord, "Unity with Impunity," p. 106.

artist."[41] The question of *sources* of critical standards is independent of their application. Nevertheless, we may strengthen Kuntz's observation by claiming that genetically there is no other way to conceive of how critical standards come to be developed at all. It is almost a truism to observe the priority of work over critical evaluation, in any sense, even following the *development* of standards. New works in a well-established genre have ways of altering those criteria. In particular, a display on the violin of what technically *can be done* musically is a dramatic proof of what might be done, might be well to do, and thus to present to the critic a neat issue on what new principles may be involved.

When Aristotle identified the keys to a proper plot of a drama as unities of time, place, and action, he seemed to be proposing criteria that would (1) help the next creative artist control his creation, (2) serve a critic in judging a new work and its aesthetic worth, (3) identify an aesthetic frame within which an audience might properly reflect on a dramatic performance, and (4) establish a position of superiority of aesthetic grasp by the philosopher. Though it is tempting to pursue each of these implications, there is a more relevant implication that must occupy our attention.

When a critic, say a teacher of painting, tells an artist, say a student, that his painting lacks unity, what is the student to understand? The answer now appears to be impossible to produce, considering the complexities we have witnessed, but there may be a way. Though it cannot now be argued in detail, the answer proposed is this: The student (read "artist," "performer," "audient") must now understand that (1) the criterion of unity is multiple, (2) the criteria can only be meaningfully applied in the context of a particular art medium, and (3) the criteria set fiduciary limits, not absolute, rational, or sensory limits. Each of these points requires further elaboration. To refer to Parker once again:

41 Kuntz, "The Art of Blotting," p. 99. The entire essay is peculiarly rewarding in its indirect reflections on unity *via* "order."

/ 409

The unity in some forms of art is tighter than in others; in a play closer than in a novel, in a sonnet more compact than in an epic. In extreme examples, like *The Thousand and One Nights*, the *Decameron*, the *Canterbury Tales*, the unity is almost wholly nominal, and the work is really a collection, not a whole. With all admissions, it remains true, however, that offenses against the principle of unity in variety diminish the aesthetic value of a work. These offenses are of two kinds— the inclusion of the genuinely irrelevant, and multiple unity, like a double composition in a picture, or ambiguity of style in a building . . . otherwise there occurs the phenomenon aptly called by Lipps "aesthetic rivalry". . . .[42]

Though we are indebted to Parker for the term "multiple unity," it is possible to show that, far from being an offense against unity, multiple unity *is a necessary condition of any art object, created or found.* The questionable sin of "the irrelevant" will not be pursued, though the obvious difficulty with Parker's criticism lies in the term "genuine."

If our prior analysis is correct, it follows that any art object will exhibit a spectrum of unifying criteria. It will be unified by virtue of its function, material, unicity, ideas expressed, structure, forms, and organismic interrelatedness of parts. We would need to retrace our steps entirely to be clearer on these meanings and to trace out particular examples in works to see how to apply each criterion. But it must at least be admitted that there is no incompatibility in having unity result from an organic relationship *and* a functional aim *and* a material expression. Only an a priori view of a restrictive kind can deny this multiple unity in art works.

Again, not all criteria of unity apply with equal force to all objects. The variability of weight of these criteria creates the great confusion in their application. It may even be the case that it will seem to be too tedious, ponderous, and inconsequential even to try to apply more than one or two criteria at a time. Is this the reason why so few critics undertake seriously to justify their judgment?

Let us indicate how various the criteria of unity can be. What

[42] Parker, *The Principles of Aesthetics*, p. 71.

makes for unity? We may list the following: balance, imbalance, dominance, recessiveness, harmony, disharmony, concinnity, congruity, incongruity, aptness, inappropriateness, hierarchy, disorder, climax, measure, theme and variations, centrality, penumbra, gradation, sameness, evolution, modulation, symmetry, asymmetry, contrast, opposition, equilibrium, etc., etc., etc. Were we to go on it would become necessary to incorporate special art terms into our discourse, terms that have been invented and adopted to discuss particular art forms. The list obviously (now) is without clear limits.

In *applying* these terms to a particular art object, say the Parthenon, we would see that some terms would be more appropriate in our evaluations than others—theme and variations, symmetry, dominance—and that some types of unity would be more apparent than others—organic unity, functional unity, formal unity.

Particular Applications

In our criteriological conclusion above we said that the criteria can only be meaningfully applied in the context of a particular art medium. This is a statement that runs counter to a great deal of theoretical expression. It is tempting to think, as many theorists do, that since there are themes and variations in music, one can speak of themes and variations in painting, drama, and architecture. In an analogical sense this must be granted. But the theme of *music* is not an architectural device or shape, is not material, cannot be seen, etc. The differences reveal the extent to which the parallel breaks down on application. It may even be conceded that the teaching (and learning) of theme and variations in music is enhanced by seeing these in painting, and vice versa. Still the literal *differences* between the space arts and time arts, between aural images and visual images, between unities of time and unities of space, mark important distinctions. The teacher of music may compare music with paintings, but he had better teach the *musical* lesson. In judging, a music critic should follow suit. Though little has been said regarding the use of compara-

/ 411

tive judgments, it needs remarking that these are among the most confusing—and confused—in the literature. "The Parthenon has more formal unity than the Pentagon" is a kind of judgment that is more defensible, assuming an initial understanding of both objects and of "formal unity," than "The Parthenon has more formal unity than a Bach fugue." The latter kind of statement is common and barely defensible, for as we have seen, there is almost *no* evidence that the key term "formal unity" is used in any clear sense. And if the basic use is cloudy, surely derivative senses will be vaguer.

An analysis of unity suggests an even more radical result. Critical evaluation and description of art works should be highly particular and specific, as specific as an individual art work itself. Thus, a music critic would not be a critic *in general*, nor would he be well described as a critic of opera, but would better be known, even as some conductors are in fact known, as specialists in Beethoven, Brahms, or whoever, and would be best known as "critic of Brahms's *Third Symphony*," or "critic of *Manon Lescaut*." This is the way of gaining maximum assurance that the meanings of the object are understood and can be communicated and assessed. Putting the matter another way, the more judgments involve theoretical elements, the less likely they will be musically precise.

Criteria as Fiduciary Limits

There is a view of "organic unity" that takes it as an ideal limit. This view recognizes the impossibility of ever achieving (or finding) an object of which it can be said to be perfect, complete, needing nothing more, having nothing in excess. The standard is accepted as a goal to which artists aspire.

A different way of reading the theoretical condition of the varied meanings of unity and their criteria is to hold them as having their origin an art *works*, being interpreted and extracted from the works, constructed as principles, and held as fiduciary limits of value. A limit of a fiduciary kind is one in which you put your trust, your confidence, without meaning to believe that the outcome is certain or foregone. It is a kind of wager, a posit, a postulation, rather than an exact limit, a "definition," a stipulation, or a restriction. In a sense, it *is* an ideal, for it is more than what has been reached or achieved, whereas what has been achieved is always less than one might expect to reach. Such fiduciary limits are flexible, bending without breaking as they get applied to novel conditions of test. Thus the form of a sonnet may vary considerably without its ceasing to be a sonnet, but it cannot vary without limit. And the materials of painting may vary considerably before painting becomes collage becomes bas relief becomes sculpture. There are limits. But these limits are never so restrictive in practice as has often been believed. The criteria of unity may thus be conceived as fiduciary criteria.

Inferences for Education

Teachers of the arts have perennially scoffed at the philosopher's efforts to theorize about art. They may be right but perhaps for the wrong reason.

Typically the art instructor teaches students to observe a particular art object in careful detail, or to create with intelligence a unique object, and to prefer the discrete, sense object to anything that might be said about it. The teacher, when he speaks, speaks about the *object*, its elements, its relations to each other, its content, materials, techniques. He may also make allusions to past influences, novelties, and perhaps, as an afterthought, some judgments and evaluations. Rarely does he attempt to justify his opinions, a philosophic effort.

More to the point, when the teacher addresses himself to the question of the unity of the work, he quite naturally will speak of the *means or techniques of unifying*, or the negative elements that tend to *disunify* the work. He may propose changes, additions, deletions, shifting of emphases, and so on, but he may never stop to question whether the unity is the unity of form or of material. All of this is a correct approach for the teacher of art. He may go further. He may also teach the student to ignore the implorings of the theorist to give consideration to philosophical issues of art; he may teach the stu-

/ 413

dent to respect the creative, intuitive urging of his own being and to ignore tradition, critic, or audience. The devoted teacher may encourage the student to disengage himself from his instruction, believing with Confucius that this is the primary responsibility of the teacher: to make himself useless to the student.

The traditional formulation of the critical principle of organic unity is useless for the creative artist facing a blank canvas or music sheet. The prescription "Put in nothing in excess, remove nothing necessary, and the remainder will be a unity" is of no help to the person who must decide, "Is this excess? What more is needed?" Though an analysis of unity may make it possible for an artist to understand the theoretical basis of his conceptions, he still may never need the theory in order to create.

If the foregoing is correct, then there are further inferences:

1. The problems of the creation of art are removed from the problems of teaching art history, theory, aesthetics, appreciation, and criticism. Though there is some overlap, they are more clearly distinct than is commonly thought.

2. Learning about different types of unity involves direct confrontations with objects of art, and since such aesthetic ends are more important than creative or performance ends for the general student, creative or performance exposure may be kept to a minimum in the schools.

3. Different types of unity dictate the use of flexible standards, care in applying standards to particular art works, cautions against imposing music standards on painting, painting vocabulary on drama, etc.; in other words caution against the misuses of the criteria of unity.

4. The traditional variability of standards of acceptable types of unity suggest that some principles be amended to conform to valuable practice: e.g., the need to recognize the importance of chance factors in creation, to recognize "proper" violations of "laws of unity," and to see the place of the accidental and nonintentional in the creative and critical processes.

Even the artist and musician will have to be taught aesthetic theory, for they cannot be expected to learn it in art and music courses; "even," because it is assumed generally that only the nonart and nonmusic student will have to be taught these matters. Artists absorb them by osmosis, it is thought.

C. M. Smith

I. Style Defined

Any discussion of style must consider the wide range of denotations and connotations the term has acquired. In linguistics, a definition can apparently be quite precise: "The style of a text is a function of the aggregate of the ratios between the frequency of its phonological, grammatical and lexical items, and the frequencies of the corresponding items in a contextually related norm."[1] But what is the meaning of "style" in expressions such as "style is the man"[2] or "style is the ultimate morality of mind"?[3] There seems to be no option but to stipulate working definitions to suit special contexts, a procedure which will be followed here. Given the nature of the present undertaking, i.e., setting forth some of the relationships that might conceivably obtain between style and education, a defi-

[1] Nils Erik Enkvist, John Spencer, and Michael J. Gregory, *Linguistics and Style* (London: Oxford University Press, 1964), p. 27.

[2] Attributed to Buffon. In A. N. W. Saunders, *Imagination All Compact* (London: Methuen, 1967), p. 104.

[3] Alfred North Whitehead, *The Aims of Education* (New York: New American Library, Mentor Books, 1949), p. 24.

nition should ideally satisfy four requirements: (1) be as noncontroversial as possible in light of accepted aesthetic theories; (2) have demonstrable application to most recognized art forms; (3) lead teachers of the arts and aesthetic education to valuable insights concerning their work; (4) provide a basis for fruitful discussion of some educational issues in general. Clearly, more than one of these requirements will have to be compromised.

It might be well to begin with the question: What sorts of things are normally said to have or exhibit style? According to F. E. Sparshott, nothing occurring in nature: "Style is a way of doing things; but what we have in nature is just the way things happen."[4] Style, then, characterizes voluntary processes, human activities; but it is also exhibited by the products of such activities, that is, artifacts. However, if only human actions and artifacts can be said to possess style, would it be correct to assume that *all* such processes and products have some kind of style?

This question requires a decision as to whether "style" is to be used normatively, a use which would make style ascription equivalent to a favorable judgment, while a negative evaluation would consist in saying that a thing has no style. If, on the other hand, "style" is a neutral term descriptive of certain sets of identifiable features found in any artifact or performance, then evaluation would have to be a separate venture from style ascription and would be in terms of "good style" and "bad style." This latter usage seems to have much to recommend it because it will be seen that seemingly value-neutral descriptions and classifications of styles are among the chief concerns of art historians, while assessment of stylistic merit or demerit is one of the occupational specialties of art critics. However, it should be recognized that both historian and critic deal with artifacts and performances specifically designed to exhibit style, among other aesthetically relevant features. Hence what appears to be neutral style description rests upon an ante-

---

[4] F. E. Sparshott, *The Structure of Aesthetics* (Toronto: University of Toronto Press, 1963), p. 99.

cedent judgment that the thing is worthy of the attention of historian and critic, that it is an aesthetic object, i.e., an artifact or performance having style. Consequently, there is some argument in favor of the normative use which would justify dividing the universe into two classes of entities: (1) works of art and artistic performances, that is, clear-cut exemplifications of style, and other artifacts and performances resembling them by virtue of having style; (2) natural events and objects, and those performances and artifacts which resemble them in one respect only: their lack of style.

If style cannot be predicated of everything, what are the proper conditions for style ascription? This question may perhaps be approached through some remarks of Whitehead's on the relationship of style to the aims of education, for this relationship will eventually become one of the topics of this discussion. Education should aim to produce a sense of style, Whitehead says, because "style hates waste . . . with style the end is attained without side issues, without raising undesirable inflammations. With style you attain your end and nothing but your end."[5] He almost seems to identify style with efficiency. But this would make the thoroughly calculated and unvarying performance of the robot the most stylish of all. And what about activities, such as the dance, which are not designed to attain any extrinsic ends; would they be devoid of style? Though efficient performance is important in education and is probably a necessary condition of style, one would hesitate to agree that it is a sufficient one. Perhaps the following moves somewhat closer to the essence of style: "Properly, the word [style] means something more than manner of being or doing, and this 'something' is not easily defined. I believe that a good style implies a kind of *organization of originality*, a harmony that excludes excesses of the imagination. Extravagance and eccentricity burst the bounds of good style."[6] Whitehead's "irrelevance" is here paralleled by "excess," "extrava-

[5] Whitehead, *The Aims of Education*, p. 24.
[6] Paul Valéry in J. V. Cunningham, ed., *The Problem of Style* (Greenwich, Conn.: Fawcett Publications, 1966), p. 19.

gance," and "eccentricity" as style-denying features. And two new notions are added; one is organization. Style presupposes some kind of unity, an order that excludes irrelevancies and excesses. Second, there is this "something more," and one could suggest that this is a feature crucial to any attempt to make of style a strictly aesthetic concept. For it might be held that style is not just any sort of order, any kind of unity. The organization and unification wrought by style is perceptual, and this means that relevance or irrelevance, excess and harmony are judged by criteria of aesthetic fittingness. What is extraneous or "just right" is seen, heard, intuited to be so, not measured, deduced, or conceptualized. To repeat, one precondition for the proper use of "style" as recommended here would be the presence of an aesthetic or perceptual order in an artifact or performance.

But what kind of organization is it, and what is being ordered and arranged? Very simply, the unity imposed by style is one of recurrence of identical, similar, or analogous elements. Consequently, perceiving style in anything means having acquired an expectation that qualities identified in one part of a work might be echoed or repeated in another, that a performance will be tied together by certain recurrences. One might even suggest that much of the emotional satisfaction associated with an experience of style can be attributed to the fulfillment of anticipations. As to the nature of the recurring elements, there is considerable difference of opinion. Some aestheticians include expressive and symbolic aspects, but for present purposes the choice is being limited mainly to the sensuous and formal properties of artifacts and performances or, in Monroe C. Beardsley's terms, to elements of texture and elements of structure.

Beardsley explicates these distinctions in the styles of different art forms and summarizes his views on style in the visual arts as follows: "First, when this term is applied to individual objects, it is best used to refer to recurrent features of texture. . . . Second, when the term is applied to groups of objects, to the *oeuvre* of a given age or painter, it usually refers to recurrent features of texture and structure."[7] For instance, of a single work one frequently says that its style consists in a characteristic manner of paint application or other ways of creating surface texture in a medium. Period styles, on the other hand, are more aptly ascribed to works displaying similarities of formal features such as the treatment of spaces and volumes. In music Beardsley holds that the style of a single composition as well as that shared by several works is definable as a recurrence of both structural and textural features within a system of probabilities. To hear the style of a piece of music is "to become aware of the relative probabilities of certain developments—for example, that certain chords will follow others, that certain melodic figures are likely to be endings or beginnings, that certain intervals belong to certain scales. . . ."[8]

It is in the literary arts that the recommended restriction of style-defining features to perceptual elements seems to become too arbitrary. Words have meanings, and meanings are not perceived. But perhaps this judgment is too harsh. In a discussion of style in literature, Beardsley differentiates between the general purport of the piece and the details of meaning. This separation, he points out, is effected for purposes of analysis only and is not felt to exist in the aesthetic experience of the work. Nonetheless, it is possible to speak of the primary purport and a web of secondary connotations and nuances of meanings which are perhaps felt or intuited rather than clearly cognized. This and the fact that these secondary meanings are referred to as texture appear to indicate that there are non-cognitive, aesthetic aspects in literature which are somehow analogous to the sensuous, perceptual, or expressive qualities in other art forms. Such an interpretation is perhaps justified in view of the definition of the style of a literary work as "the recurrent features of its texture of meaning."[9]

By way of summary, then, the following may serve as a tenta-

[7] Monroe C. Beardsley, *Aesthetics: Problems in the Philosophy of Criticism* (New York: Harcourt, Brace, 1958), p. 173.

[8] *Ibid.*, p. 189.

[9] *Ibid.*, p. 223.

tive definition of style. Amplification and refinement will be undertaken at necessary points in the discussion.

Style is a normative concept properly applied to those human performances and artifacts which exhibit a predominantly perceptual (aesthetic) order or organization of the kind characterized by the recurrence of textural and/or structural features.

II. Style and Aesthetic Education

While the above working definition does not restrict style to the fine arts, the most obvious domain for an exploration of the possible relevance of the concept of style to education would be those areas of the curriculum assigned to instruction in or about the arts. Now such instruction is carried on in elementary, secondary, and higher education with varying degrees of enthusiasm and under a variety of course headings, "Art Education," "Music Education," "Art Appreciation," "Allied Arts Program," and "Humanities" being just a few of them. For the sake of simplification, the phrase "aesthetic education" will be used hereafter. And since this, too, can mean different things to different people, a loose interpretation will be attempted to provide a consistent focus for discussion.

"Aesthetic education" will properly designate any kind of instructional program designed to educate the students' aesthetic preferences in the direction of critical connoisseurship or, as it has also been called, enlightened cherishing.[10] Very briefly, the objectives of aesthetic education are, first, to induce in the pupil a genuine appreciation of and preference for significant, serious art; second, to provide the student with the knowledge and abilities needed to justify his preferences reasonably and intelligently. However, these are not really separate aims, for one of the assumptions central to an educational program of this nature is that the appreciation of art can be cultivated best through becoming knowledgeable about

[10] The phrase "enlightened cherishing" has been used and explained repeatedly in the writings of Harry S. Broudy. See, for example, "The Role of the Humanities in the Curriculum," *The Journal of Aesthetic Education* I (1966): 17–27.

objects of preference and skilled in probing and analyzing these objects for their aesthetic values. It is suggested that aesthetic education so conceived can be promoted by (1) facilitating increasingly more sensitive discriminations of aesthetic qualities through guided encounters with works of art; (2) instruction in critical and evaluative procedures and exposition of some of the underlying theoretical problems; (3) providing for a sufficient understanding of the historical and cultural context of art.

Possible applications of the concept of style to aesthetic education will be explored in the aforementioned three areas, though in reverse order. However, some disclaimers seem in order. What follows is not meant to be a workable program for aesthetic education. No effort will be made to identify phases of instruction, indicate sequential arrangement of content, or even distinguish clearly between pedagogical and repertory content.[11] Where hoped for attainments on the part of students are mentioned, they may perhaps be construed as ideal limits. Nor are the subsequent remarks intended to furnish a theoretical framework for aesthetic education. All that is being attempted is to see how far the notion of style and its ramifications might take the inquirer into areas of educational concern; there may be much terrain in aesthetic education which is simply not accessible via style.

USES OF "STYLE" IN TEACHING HISTORICAL AND THEORETICAL FOUNDATIONS OF ART

To begin with knowledge about art. For the most part this would be the history of styles and certain fundamentals of

---

[11] "Repertory content" would be the subject matter as presented to the student. "Pedagogical content" is the knowledge the teacher must have of the subject which makes it possible for him to package the content for teaching; i.e., pedagogical content is what makes the discipline or subject functional for the teacher in teaching but is not necessarily taught to the pupil. This distinction is made by Harry S. Broudy in "Criteria for the Professional Preparation of Teachers," *Journal of Teacher Education* XVI (1965): 408–15, reprinted in Frank H. Blackington III and Robert S. Patterson, eds., *School, Society, and the Professional Educator* (New York: Holt, Rinehart and Winston, 1968), pp. 187–88.

media and techniques. It seems to have become difficult to make the history of art palatable to students, possibly because so often "art appreciation" courses rest content to trot out period styles in dull procession. But art history may very well be a most interesting and challenging subject if, along with the evolution of styles, the evolution of controversy and debate about styles also receives attention.

The different theories about the genesis and development of styles are among the best means for placing works of art within a larger cultural and historical context. For instance, one variation of a standard argument is that "In each period . . . there are certain common denominators of visual choice and aesthetic emphasis; they appear and reappear in the works of artists in certain groups and epochs, and they characterize what may be called the general style of a time, a country, or even a class. This general style is historically as real as wars, economic developments, or religious movements."[12] It is being asserted, in other words, that style is a thoroughly objective feature in the cultural landscape and a reliable clue to the "spirit of the age." In addition, styles are often thought to behave in predictable ways, moving from "early" through "high" to "late" manifestations. If these views are correct, the student should expect to be able to "read" in an individual work not only the general cultural tenor of its period but, if it be an "early" example, indications of some fulfillment or climax toward which the style is tending; if "late," some evidence of a falling away from an earlier perfection. The student may wish to test this for himself, but he should be made aware of the historical and theoretical presuppositions underlying such interpretations.

Persons convinced that artistic styles are symptomatic of something more fundamental, real, or significant are not limited to history. For instance, it has been said that different styles are expressions of different types of temperament, so that a Baroque period would merely be one in which Baroque people set the tone. Another theory relates artistic production

[12] Paul Zucker, *Styles in Painting* (New York: Dover, 1963), p. 3.

to the three basic ways in which man handles the forms and fragments of experience: generalizing, dramatizing, and recording. The corresponding styles in art, the classical, romantic, and realistic,[13] would then constitute mankind's entire stylistic repertoire. E. H. Gombrich reduces the options even further, believing that the array of period styles represents only a series of masks for two categories, the classical and the nonclassical.[14]

But Gombrich's interpretation is interesting, among other things, for the fact that he does not look beyond the sphere of art for the causes of stylistic change. There is no need to assume that the alternation of classical/nonclassical is symptomatic of other changes or events, for the explanation may lie in the way style words function. These words, says Gombrich, are used as terms of exclusion to distinguish "us" from "them."[15] Whenever an age formulates specific rules for its artists, they are usually in the form of admonitions to avoid certain things. Perhaps it was this peculiarly negative, excluding feature in style rules which led Gombrich to suggest—with due acknowledgments to K. R. Popper—that "Maybe we would make more progress in the study of styles if we looked out for such principles of exclusion, the sins any particular style wants to avoid, than if we continue to look for the common structure or essence of all the works produced in a certain period."[16] If Gombrich is right, style defines itself by negation. But there appears to be no stopping the process. "Indeed it might be argued that what ultimately killed the classical ideal was that the sins to be avoided multiplied till the artist's freedom was confined to an ever narrowing space; all he dared to do in the end was insipid repetition of solutions."[17]

To sum up this brief outline: Instruction in the history of styles might profitably be supplemented by some of the more speculative explanations of period styles, and a sampling may

[13] This is derived from Sparshott's discussion of Eric Newton's theory. Sparshott, *The Structure of Aesthetics*, p. 185.

[14] E. H. Gombrich, *Norm and Form* (London: Phaidon, 1966), p. 83.

[15] *Ibid.*, p. 88.

[16] *Ibid.*, p. 89.

[17] *Ibid.*, p. 89.

be offered of at least three different sorts of theories: (1) those which, mindful that the history of formal solutions can apply Occam's razor and do away with the "spirit of the age,"[18] explain stylistic change as developing according to an inner dynamic; (2) those which see style as a clear and direct expression of historical, social, or cultural forces; (3) those which identify styles as manifestations of basic forms of mental activity or constancies of human nature.

Thus prepared, a student may come to employ style terms with confidence and sophistication, but his confidence is unfounded as long as he remains unaware of some of the complexities inherent in these very concepts. Of what sort, for instance, are the judgments that lead him to classify one work as Byzantine, another as Romanesque? In other words, are there definite criteria governing the application of style concepts?

One recent examination of the logic of style concepts is Morris Weitz's comparison of what art historians say about a period style with how they use a particular style concept—"Mannerism" in this case—in their writings.[19] As part of his study Weitz selected essays by six art historians and found that, although they were writing about roughly the same group of paintings and supported their style-giving reasons adequately, each rested his conclusions on a different set of criteria. Further analysis disclosed that, individually and collectively, these sets of criteria were vague in a special sense.

This finding enabled Weitz to maintain that Mannerism, and probably every other style concept, is not a logically closed concept. It has no definition, no set of necessary and sufficient criteria, or even any necessary criterion. Nor does it need such criteria in order to support its style-giving reasons.[20] But while not a closed concept, "style" is not open either in the way genre

---

[18] *Ibid.*, p. 95.
[19] Morris Weitz, "Genre and Style," read at International Year of Philosophy, State University College at Brockport, New York, Feb. 18, 1968. Quotations are from a multilith copy of this paper. Quoted with permission.
[20] *Ibid.*, p. 32.

concepts, for example, are. "Drama" and "novel" are open or flexible in the sense that they will need to accommodate future instances with new properties, and disputes are generally over whether some work qualifies for membership. But in the case of style, "disagreements . . . converge more on the exchange of sets of criteria than on their enlargement to cover new cases or on the rejection of putatively necessary criteria."[21] Weitz does not foresee any settlement of these disagreements, for "the fundamental vagueness of 'Mannerism' consists in the perennial possibility of intelligibly enlarging or exchanging the criteria for its correct use."[22] Thus *irreducible* vagueness is one of the logical features of style concepts; but Weitz also calls it a "beneficial vagueness," because the very incompletability of criteria allows for new histories of Mannerism to be written.[23]

Analyses of style concepts such as the above are recommended topics not merely because they lend interest and intellectual depth to teaching about period styles. They also help explain why art history is an ongoing concern. It may be perplexing to many to see generation after generation of critics and historians turn out scholarly volumes on a largely complete body of art works. But as Weitz suggests, it may be due to the logical structure of style concepts that the last word has not been said on any style, nor is it likely to be forthcoming. Hence the rewards of keeping at an incompletable task probably lie elsewhere, and what continues to attract people to the study of the arts can perhaps be indicated by enlarging on some of the other complexities of the notion of style.

USES OF "STYLE" IN TEACHING ABOUT THEORETICAL PROBLEMS OF ANALYSIS, CRITICISM, AND EVALUATION

What went before were suggestions for dealing in educationally fruitful ways with the concept of a *period style* as used in art history and in theorizing about such usage. What remains to be done is a further exploration of the *concept of style* as such, for it can be shown that this is one way of help-

[21] *Ibid.*, p. 37.
[22] *Ibid.*, p. 32.
[23] *Ibid.*, p. 32.

426 /

ing the student understand and appreciate some of the issues in aesthetic criticism and analysis.[24] As an approach to this new subject, reference is made once more to the definition of style at the close of the first section. This definition is admittedly problematic in several respects, one of them being its stand on one side of a continuing controversy, namely, whether style can be discussed separately at all.

It seems to make good sense to state that "process and work, form and content, expression and style, must be kept apart provisionally and in precarious suspense, till the final unity: only thus are possible the whole translation and rationalization which constitute the process of criticism."[25] Paul Valéry had this to say on the matter: "Thus style signifies the manner in which a man expresses himself, *regardless of what he expresses*, and it is held to reveal his nature, quite apart from his actual thought—for thought has no style."[26] To offer a third and most succinct formulation: "Anyone who wishes to consider style must premise that something may be said in different ways and the ways may be compared."[27] Clearly, common sense and several considered opinions agree that if works of art can be analyzed, then style is a feature which can be dealt with independently of medium, form, content, expression, or whatever other critical categories may be employed. Stated differently, if style is to be understood as ordered recurrences of textural and structural features, then it should be possible to point to, describe, and secure agreement concerning these features.

However, many have expressed misgivings about this issue. Beardsley, for one, does not think there could be anything like the completely styleless thought Valéry spoke of. "There are not, then, two things, knowing what to say and knowing how

[24] For a more complete treatment of the theory and strategy of teaching critical skills, see Ralph A. Smith, "Aesthetic Education: A Role for the Humanities," *The Record* LXIX (1968): 343–54.

[25] René Wellek and Austin Warren in Cunningham, ed., *The Problem of Style*, p. 65.

[26] Paul Valéry in Cunningham, ed., *The Problem of Style*, p. 18.

[27] Cunningham, ed., *The Problem of Style*, p. 9.

to say it; but there is knowing in general or in outline, what to say, without knowing what other things to say along with it, through suggestion, connotation, and general purport."[28] In fact, the more carefully style is analyzed as a separate feature, the more one is led back to meaning, and this is the "paradox of style analysis."[29] Now if style cannot be kept distinct from meaning or expressiveness, it becomes a part of meaning[30] and will thus lose its usefulness as a separate critical category and as a classifying device in art history. This is not universally deplored. On the contrary, proponents of the theory of organic form like Benedetto Croce tend to believe that stylistic categories only do violence to the "insularity" of each individual and incommensurable work of art.[31] But since this sort of attitude would jeopardize much of what has been proposed as being the proper business of aesthetic education, a closer look is needed at the source of these difficulties with the concept of style.

The focus has now shifted from analyzing the styles of works of art for the purpose of determining their classification to the description of the style of a single work and its relation to the work's other aesthetic qualities. The question is: What characteristics recur, are distributed throughout, or in some way unify and organize the work so as to be describable as its style? There should be little trouble with certain gross features. A painting may show linear perspective, realistic drawing, or a pointillist technique; a literary work may be distinguished by repetitive idiosyncrasies of structure or idioms native to specific geographic regions; a musical composition may repeatedly employ peculiarities of orchestration. But matters tend to become more problematic once style description attempts to articulate finer shadings and differences. What if the style of a piece of music is distinguished by its "languid melodic line," that of a painting by "elegantly attenuated forms," that of a

---

[28] Beardsley, *Aesthetics*, p. 224.
[29] *Ibid.*, p. 223.
[30] Enkvist, Spencer, and Gregory, *Linguistics and Style*, p. 20.
[31] Gombrich, *Norm and Form*, p. 81.

literary work by its "air of bemused detachment"? Such judgments are quite common and purportedly refer to objective features of the works in question. However, there is no way of producing empirical proof to convince the dissenter who hears the "languid melodic line" as merely slow and perhaps sad; who sees the "elegantly attenuated forms" as merely unnaturally thin and drawn out; who finds the literary style to be not one of "bemused detachment" but of "biting sarcasm." It is at this point that the paradox of style should have become evident: descriptive statements grade into interpretation, into statements about expressiveness and meaning, and at this level agreement on the "real" nature of style elements is much less likely. Once the discussion of style has led the student to an awareness of this peculiarity of aesthetic discourse, he should be ready to be introduced to some of the difficulties with aesthetic terms, aspects, qualities, and the like. As before, some suggestions for topics appropriate to this context will follow.

One distinctive characteristic possessed by many of these descriptive-interpretive utterances in aesthetic analysis is that they ascribe qualities to a work which it cannot have in any literal sense. At times these phrases bring together words from modes of experience other than that appropriate to the work in question. Yet everyone understands what is meant by a "loud color," a "silken voice," an "acid sound," and "lively, animated architectural volumes." In other cases expressions that normally refer to states of mind, moods, feelings—such as melancholy, angry, aggressive—are used to describe a work's details or total impact. Much theorizing has been engendered by the phenomena of synaesthesia, i.e., the pairing of incongruous ways of experiencing, and metaphor, i.e., perceiving works of art as analogous to or expressive of feelings and emotions. Philosophical, psychological, and even neurological explanations abound, and any student of style stands to gain insight from familiarizing himself with several of these.

But he should also be made aware that many contemporary writers in aesthetics think it inappropriate and unnecessary to resort to metaphysical speculation in order to explain this supposed lack of objectivity and verifiability in aesthetic judgments. The answer is to be sought in the way man uses language. Frank Sibley's solution is perhaps something of a compromise. He has been interpreted as holding that aesthetic predicates are different from others only in that they require taste and sensitivity for their proper application. This means that only specially endowed individuals—those with refined taste or an "aesthetic sense"—could use these terms correctly, and Sibley's critics were quick to point out that this would make the qualities designated by aesthetic predicates somehow nonnatural.[32] Another approach has been to assert that there is something peculiar not about aesthetic predicates, but about the objective features in a work of art which they describe. These features have the property of being able to sustain different aspects, that is, they can be "perceived as" different things.[33] The difficulty here is that many aesthetic terms such as unity, harmony, balance do not refer to anything in particular which may be seen as this or that. Hope is being held out that aspect-perceiving language may be enriched so as to accommodate all aesthetic predicates.[34] However this issue may be settled, some linguistic analysts seem to yield even less to the demands of the aesthetic situation. To them, the proper business of aesthetic theory is "to strip the notion of the aesthetic of its psychological baggage—baggage which suggests that there is something like a unique state of mind that is designated by the term *aesthetic* . . . what is required is, first of all, to see whether and in what ways aesthetic predicates are like other predicates and what these other predicates are."[35] The strategy is to examine the logical properties of aesthetic

[32] Frank Sibley's essay, "Aesthetic Concepts," *Philosophical Review* LXXVII (1949) is discussed by Peter Kivy, "Aesthetic Aspects and Aesthetic Qualities," *Journal of Philosophy* LXIV (1968): 85–93.

[33] A perennial favorite is the "duck-rabbit figure" which lends itself to being seen as a duck as easily as to being seen as a rabbit. Most examples in these contexts are very simple drawings, not works of art.

[34] David Michael Levin, "More Aspects to the Concept of 'Aesthetic Aspect,'" *Journal of Philosophy* LXV (1968): 483–90.

[35] Marcia P. Freedman, "The Myth of the Aesthetic Predicate," *Journal of Aesthetics and Art Criticism* XXVII (1968): 50.

predicates and to designate their proper universe of discourse, which turns out to be simply the utterances made by persons standing in front of works of art. It is thus thought possible to define aesthetic terms without having to say anything about the nature of art, aesthetic experience, aesthetic attitude, or style, for "It is not the context which makes certain terms aesthetic and others not; it is rather the presence or absence of certain terms . . . which makes certain contexts aesthetic or not."[36] Whether a student attracted to this line of reasoning can truly be said to have developed aesthetic sensitivity may be for the teacher to judge.

The foregoing discussion was occasioned, it may be recalled, by the realization that style cannot for long be kept distinct from meaning, expressiveness, and import. There is, however, yet another shift which can easily occur in style analysis, and that is the grading of the descriptive into the normative or evaluative. E. H. Gombrich argues that every attempt to dissociate norm from form in the description of period styles is bound to fail because some hidden standard is always operative. In fact, he thinks that the norm against which all styles are measured is the "classical solution," that is, the reconciliation of ordered composition with faithful representation. How he establishes his case need not be gone into here, but his argument is suggestive for any style analysis undertaken by layman and critic alike. Are not all style descriptions colored by some unexpressed criterion, some conception of what art ought to be? For instance, a style described by one observer as well balanced and finely articulated may appear stiff and too much concerned with irrelevant detail to a person with a more flamboyant conception of artistic merit. Trying to articulate these latent standards, whether they be idiosyncratic or shared by a generation, may be a valuable exercise in helping students understand the reasons for so much divergence in aesthetic judgments and perhaps for their own attitudes as well.

However, the unconscious preferences and latent norms which may prejudice style description need not enter into the

[36] *Ibid.*, p. 55.

more deliberate evaluations of the styles of individual works. For what is involved here is not the characterization of style as an isolated feature but an assessment of its relationship to other aspects of a work. The goodness and badness of a style cannot be judged independently of the work of art.[37] Beardsley's example from literature may serve as an illustration:

Bad style . . . might then be tentatively described in these terms: the diction and syntax of a discourse are such as to produce an incoherence between primary and secondary levels of meaning, or such as to produce ambiguity or obscurity. Perhaps there is more to be said; I am mainly concerned to point out the kind of objective analysis that the evaluation of style ought to be. So far as the faults of a literary work may be called faults of *style*, they will turn out to be faults that proceed from a poor management of the details of meaning, connotation, general purport, and syntactical suggestion, in relation to the larger or more prominent parts of the meaning. On the other side, a style may be said to be appropriate to, or coherent with the rest of the work's meanings if, so to speak, the eddies of meaning it sets up work together with the main streams.[38]

Analogous examples can easily be found in the other arts. For example, does the distinctive rendering of forms in a painting support the attitude of spirituality the content seems to convey? Are the lines of a drawing appropriate to the tensions implied by the subject matter? Does a dense, confused sound texture disrupt the delicate general mood of a musical composition?

These are judgments of aesthetic fittingness and appropriateness which presuppose an interpretation of the overall meaning, import, or expressiveness of the work,[39] for as has been made clear, style is good or bad only in relationship to these main streams of meaning. Hence style evaluation requires a whole range of critical and analytical skills: ability to describe, explain, interpret, and, where meaning cannot be assessed

[37] Beardsley, *Aesthetics*, p. 226.

[38] *Ibid.*, p. 227.

[39] "Where appropriate" should perhaps be added. Some works of art are obviously decorative in character, others are purely formal arrangements; in many of these cases, interpretations should perhaps not be attempted.

properly except in the work's historical context, even a good deal of knowledge about art. For pedagogical purposes it should be noted, then, that evaluation of stylistic merit is a rather high-level critical performance and may well be used as a test of the student's progress toward connoisseurship.

USE OF STYLE IN ARRANGING ART ENCOUNTERS

Finally, another valid objective for aesthetic education is to increase a student's sensitivity to art. The problem is what teaching procedures might secure this outcome. To do criticism and analysis already presupposes a good deal of perceptiveness, as has been emphasized. Lectures using slides can, of course, point out many aspects a student might not notice on his own. He should also be encouraged to avail himself of other opportunities to experience art. But to ensure that the student's looking and listening occur in aesthetically and educationally relevant ways, the teacher may also wish to structure the student's encounters with art, and here the concept of style can be a valuable criterion for selecting works. In short, style can give focus and direction to aesthetic education even when it is not being discussed explicitly.

III. Style in Education

It remains yet to be seen whether style can be an educationally significant notion outside its obvious applications in aesthetic education. Can educators regardless of professional specialty gain valuable insights from the concept of style? It does not take much reading in educational literature to become convinced that indeed they can, for there has been a great deal of talk about learning styles, teaching styles, cognitive styles, and even styles of educational administration and personnel management. To note that in most instances "method," "habit," "standard procedure," or "manner" could be substituted without loss of meaning is not sufficient to condemn these uses of "style." And if one purpose of the rather restrictive definition of style stipulated for the present discussion was to avoid having to deal with such loose applications of the term in education, it may now be doubted that the definition is equal to that particular task without further refinement.

It will be recalled that, in order to qualify as components of style conceived in strictly aesthetic terms, recurring elements were to be perceptual. But this still leaves the concept of style too hospitable to be manageable, for a style of administration, as an example, could be said to be "perceptual" if what is meant are the things the administrator is observed doing repeatedly. Consequently, being perceived is not a sufficient condition for making anything aesthetic, and an additional consideration is now being proposed: the way perceived elements are attended to. An explanation of this will be attempted as part of the next topic.

That topic is the first of three within which the general relationship of style to education will be examined, although with varying emphasis and, as will become evident, with increasingly meager results. They are: teaching method or strategy, curriculum areas other than aesthetic education, and educational objectives.

STYLE AND THE "ART" OF TEACHING

An introductory question might be: How can style help the teacher do his work more effectively? That classroom discourse and texts are more persuasive when presented in an attractive style—provided this does not compromise intellectual content —is, of course, a valid methodological consideration. But it is also too trivial to merit much discussion. More significant is a theory, embodied in a number of recent articles in the field of education, which argues that style, or more appropriately the styling activity of the creative artist, has far-reaching implications for the conduct of classroom teaching. Only the barest outline of this theory can be presented, and discussion may at times seem to digress from the subject of style. But in the end some gain will hopefully be registered in understanding the total relationship between art and education. More specifically, one of the anticipated outcomes is a seed or two of doubt concerning the validity of the proposition that teaching is really an art and the teacher should see himself as an artist.

The writings in question are the product of a methodological inquiry into the creative process. What made such an approach seem fruitful was the recognition that art does not issue from the mysterious workings of divine inspiration but from an activity in which means are ordered toward objectives.[40] Explicated more fully, "the artistic process as methodologically conceived is essentially qualitative problem solving—the controlled procedure of instituting qualitative relationships as means to the achievement of a qualitative total or end."[41] But if artistic doing exemplifies method—that is, if it is more than just setting down one thing after another until a work of art has emerged—then there must be some way of knowing in advance where the process is going. Hence one should be able to identify something called a "qualitative end" which is evident to both the artist and the observer of the artistic process. However, "known beforehand" cannot refer to a complete mental image of the finished work in somebody's head, for this would vitiate the commitment to experimentalism insisted upon in the theory under discussion.[42] Accordingly, the qualitative end is no more than the general style, the "pervasive quality," of the end result, and it is observable in each stage of the work in progress. Pervasive quality, which characterizes process and product alike, is usually identified by style words (Cubism, Gothicness, and the like) and is at times explicitly synonymous with style. It is this close identification of pervasive quality with style, the central importance of pervasive quality to the methodological treatment of art, and its pur-

[40] Francis T. Villemain, "Democracy, Education, and Art," *The Journal of Aesthetic Education* I (1966): 29.

[41] David W. Ecker, "Some Problems of Art Education: A Methodological Definition," in *A Seminar in Art Education and Curriculum Development*, Cooperative Research Project V-0021 (University Park: Pennsylvania State University, 1966), p. 32.

[42] The theory in question is said to be a legitimate extension of John Dewey's experimentalism. The derivation is set forth in detail in Francis T. Villemain and Nathaniel L. Champlin, "Frontiers for an Experimentalist Philosophy of Education," *Antioch Review* XIX (1959), reprinted in David W. Ecker and Elliot W. Eisner, eds., *Readings in Art Education* (Waltham, Mass.: Blaisdell, 1966), pp. 444–58.

ported implications for teaching which are taken to justify the present discussion.[43]

Since the general pervasive quality (or style) of the finished work is "set in advance" in the sense indicated, this same pervasive quality also functions as the control or criterion for selecting and rejecting further qualitative components; therefore, pervasive quality is called a *method*. The artist's criterion and his method are one and the same.[44] Until the artist has arrived at a style which will control his work, he does not know how to proceed.[45] But once a pervasive quality is supplied—as in the case of the architect who is instructed to design a Gothic building—creative potential is released. Gothicness, for instance, "sets the format or pattern, prescribes the elements employed in the designing, and acts as a point of reference for determining what is to be rejected as inappropriate . . . the fact that these elements are possible *means* is determined by that to which we refer with the term 'Gothicness.' This regulative device which controls or directs the designing procedure is the architect's *method*."[46]

To repeat, art yields to methodological inquiry because it is an activity controlled by pervasive quality or style. This activity also serves as a paradigm for qualitative orderings wherever they occur. "While the so called fine arts do provide us with some of the finest examples of qualitative ordering and achievement, qualitative problems may also be found and chosen in personal relations and in the larger social units of the family and community, as well as in *all teaching and learn-*

[43] It is said, for instance, that it is pervasive quality which permits a clever artist to finish a work begun by another; which makes forgeries successful; and which enables the restorer to design a fitting head for an ancient statue. In all these examples, pervasive quality is obviously identical with style. Nathaniel L. Champlin, "Methodological Inquiry and Educational Research," in A Seminar in Art Education, p. 314.

[44] David W. Ecker, "Some Inadequate Doctrines in Art Education and a Proposed Resolution," Studies in Art Education V (1963): 79.

[45] In the absence of any control (or style), and before an empty canvas, an artist is without control." Champlin, "Methodological Inquiry," p. 318.

[46] Villemain and Champlin, "Frontiers for an Experimental Philosophy of Education," p. 449.

ing situations. . . ."[47] Specific recommendations for teacher-training include the study of the performing arts as examples of qualitative means-ends relatings which employ human components as means.[48] One could conclude, then, that to create and sustain teaching situations pervaded by a quality of drama and interest the teacher would manipulate the qualitative aspects of persons and of the learning environment much in the manner of the artist who composes with the qualities of his medium, under the guidance of a style or desired pervasive quality.

Whether or not this kind of methodological inquiry constitutes an adequate description of the creative process is not at issue here.[49] What needs to be examined is the justifiability of extending a methodology discovered in the artist's studio to other sorts of activities, including teaching. The reasoning that led to this extension may be reconstructed as having been something along the following lines. For purposes of classifying the kinds of activities and experiences available to man, the categories of cognitive and noncognitive/qualitative are established.[50] The arts are then singled out as exemplars of the purely qualitative, and it is noticed that the activity of the artist is

[47] Ecker, "Some Problems of Art Education," p. 33; emphasis added.

[48] "The qualitative dimension of good teaching may indeed be characterized as a series of events or situations created by the teacher and students, which have dramatic unity and interest for teacher and students." *Ibid.*, p. 33.

[49] Monroe C. Beardsley, for example, has objected to using the means-ends terminology in art: "On the Creation of Art," *Journal of Aesthetics and Art Criticism* XXIII (1965): 291–304, reprinted in Ralph A. Smith, ed., *Aesthetics and Criticism in Art Education* (Chicago: Rand McNally, 1966), p. 158. The theory may also be held suspect because it is not falsifiable by any conceivable experience. Anything an artist does in the process of completing his work is describable as ordering qualitative means toward qualitative ends, the artist's verbal protests to the contrary notwithstanding.

[50] To be precise, there can be mixed types along a spectrum, and the differentiation is according to cognitive or qualitative predominance. "Qualitative mediations are instrumental to focally cognitive operations at one end of the spectrum, while on the other they become focal with cognitive elements assuming the instrumental role. When qualities are of equal if not primary interest, when they become ends to be obtained, we have the experience of [art]." Villemain, "Democracy, Education, and Art," p. 30.

describable in terms of qualitative means-ends ordering toward a qualitative outcome which also functions as method or control. It is then argued that because this kind of ordering is exemplified in the arts, it can also be applied wherever qualities are present or predominant.

But without doing violence to the popular conception of the fine arts, a counterargument could easily be constructed which would suggest that the equation of qualities in the arts with qualities in other contexts rests on a category mistake. For it is not unreasonable to hold that the fine arts are distinctive areas of human endeavor, experience, and satisfaction precisely because they alone feature artifacts and performances which are purely qualitative or noncognitive in the sense of (1) having resulted from a process of qualitative ordering directed by predominantly aesthetic (qualitative, noncognitive) judgments and (2) being designed specifically for aesthetic (qualitative, noncognitive) experience. If it is this special way of functioning in works of art and aesthetic experience that makes some qualities aesthetic qualities, then nothing follows necessarily for the ordering of qualities in general, if indeed it does occur. One legitimate conclusion might be that whenever it is discovered that qualities have in fact been arranged and are being experienced according to aesthetic criteria, the artifact or performance in question can make some claim to being considered a work of art of aesthetic object. Is teaching an art in this sense?

To be sure, much of what goes on in the classroom is "qualitative" in the very loose meaning which identifies quality with anything noncognitive. A teacher may perceive a classroom atmosphere of inattention and restlessness and wish to restructure the situation to one pervaded by attentiveness and interest. But assuming attentiveness and interest to be qualitative ends, setting the "style" for what is to be done, what, precisely, would the teacher be structuring, and how would he go about it? No doubt the teacher receives perceptual clues from his students—bored or bewildered looks on their faces, for example. But he does not note these looks aesthetically, as perceptually gratifying, unfitting, or whatever. In other words, perceptions are not registered in terms of their intrinsic aesthetic value but are interpreted as *symptoms* of an underlying state of affairs: the pupils are not learning well. Judging appearances to signal mental or psychological states is not the "seeing as" of aesthetic perception; it is a cognitive affair, depending, among other things, on prior experience and knowledge of causal relationships.[51] This difference between aesthetic and nonaesthetic ways of experiencing qualities is further illustrated by how the teacher attends to the situation. What he decides to do is controlled not by aesthetic judgments, but by the intellectual demands of the subject matter, the types of logical moves appropriate to the lesson content, the student's mental capacity, and so forth. Should the classroom quality transform itself into one of attentiveness, this will again be taken merely as a sign that the teaching episode is now progressing well and not as something to be enjoyed for its own

[51] The difference between noticing qualities aesthetically and nonaesthetically may perhaps be illuminated by a distinction Charles S. Peirce makes in his theory of signs. This is a distinction not according to what kind of thing the sign is, but according to the properties which allow it to be interpreted as standing for its object or referent. In Peirce's terms, what one would be willing to call an aesthetic sign would be a qualisign or icon. "An Icon is a sign which refers to the Object that it denotes merely by virtue of characters of its own . . ." (2.247). "The Icon has no dynamical connection with the object it represents; it simply happens that its qualities resemble those of that object, and excite analogous sensations in the mind for which it is a likeness" (2.299). The kind of noticing which was described as seeing a quality as a symptom of something else may be called an index, according to Peirce. "An index is a sign which refers to the object that it denotes by virtue of being really affected by, or existentially related to, that object" (2.248). "The index is physically connected with its object; they make an organic pair, but the interpreting mind has nothing to do with this connection except remarking it, after it is established" (2.299). References are by volume and paragraph number to Charles Hartshorne and Paul Weiss, eds., *Collected Papers of Charles Sanders Peirce* (Cambridge: Harvard University, Belknap Press, 1932). Now an index may be qualitative—a gesture, the appearance of a weather vane, or a cloud—but what is noticed is the existential connection with the object or referent: the cloud indicating the imminence of rain, the weather vane the direction of the wind, the gesture a person's impatience or displeasure. An index, Peirce says, refers to a *fact*, no matter what sort of thing it is as a sign; and whatever refers to a fact is not a sign of qualitative "suchness."

sake. In sum, there appears to be little support for the contention that teaching is in any important way analogous to the
creative process and that the teacher should refurbish his professional image by thinking of himself as arranging aesthetic
qualities with style and dramatic flair.

STYLE IN OTHER SUBJECT AREAS

The next point is whether the concept of style can find any
meaningful application in subjects other than those dealing
explicitly with the arts and literature. Perhaps one should look
to the general curriculum area of history and the social studies
and no further. Richard Hofstadter, for instance, has suggested that the study of style can lend an added dimension to
history and political culture. Although style is not an appropriate category for explaining the formation of institutions and
the distribution of powers, it should receive attention for two
reasons: ". . . first, that our political and historical writing,
until recently, has tended to emphasize structure at the cost
of substantially neglecting milieu; and second, that an understanding of political styles and of the symbolic aspects of politics is a valuable way of locating ourselves and others in relation
to public issues."[52] To rephrase this as a modest proposal to
educators: when style refers to the recurrent types of imagery
distinctive of an era or to an aesthetic order deliberately imposed on certain public events, it can serve as a useful concept
in conveying to students the ambiance of an age and in explaining the attractiveness of otherwise meaningless political rituals
and exercises.

Another conceivable topic for the social studies is the cultural
and social phenomenon of misplaced emphasis on style. A preoccupation with style is, of course, most apparent in much of
contemporary art where content and firm character delineation have receded into irrelevance. But aestheticizing tendencies, if this is what they are, are also in evidence elsewhere.
There has been talk of the style of violence, the politics of

[52] Richard Hofstadter, *The Paranoid Style in American Politics* (New York:
Vintage Books, 1967), p. viii.

style, and style as the essence of democracy, implying, it seems, that style makes violence acceptable or attractive; that it should be an objective for politicians; and that without it democracy is not worth having. Now it may be that these expressions are just hyperbole, but more likely they are symptomatic of a general tendency to import aesthetic categories into areas of life where they are of dubious worth. Several responsible critics have commented, for example, that it is the aesthetic appeal of flamboyant styles of dress, speech, gesture, and the like rather than commitment to any consistent ideology or well-defined program of action which attracts followers to some of the more extreme movements. Thus the "style of rebellion" can easily become an end in itself.[53]

Since these and related phenomena have given rise to some uneasiness, it has now become necessary to elaborate and refine the originally proposed normative use of the concept of style. Although style is generally a good-making feature, much depends on the context. Possession of style will enhance the total value potential of a thing by making it a fit candidate for aesthetic experience; but style does not improve objects and performances for other purposes. In fact, in some instances style, by eliciting a favorable aesthetic response and thus one kind of positive assessment, may help conceal deficiency in or the absence of other values—the functionality of an object or the motives of an agent, for example. Perhaps this is another "paradox of style": that style, though commonly a most desirable feature, tends to become evaluated negatively the more consciously and single-mindedly it is pursued. In the arts, this

[53] A parallel may perhaps be seen in the behavior of the "aristocratic rebel," as exemplified by Lord Byron. According to Bertrand Russell, "The aristocratic rebel, since he has enough to eat, must have other sources of discontent" (p. 747). This discontent has its source in the strong emotional urges of the romantic temper, which Russell describes and roundly condemns. "It is not the psychology of the romantics that is at fault: it is their standard of values" (p. 681). "The romantic movement is characterized, as a whole, by the substitution of aesthetic for utilitarian standards . . . The morals of the romantics have primarily aesthetic motives" (p. 678). References are to Bertrand Russell, *A History of Western Philosophy* (New York: Simon and Schuster, 1960).

/ 441

can lead to judgments such as "merely decorative," "mannered," "empty," or "effete." In other contexts, condemnation might well be justified on moral grounds. Consequently, the problem of whether and under what circumstances "style for style's sake" could become reprehensible might make for animated classroom debate and should certainly be an object of concern to the educator wanting to understand the kinds of values that seem to be gaining acceptance, particularly among the young.

STYLE AS AN AIM IN EDUCATION

Finally, what about style as an educational objective? Previously expressed doubts concerning the advisability of elevating style to the status of an end or aim in some areas make this an unpromising subject to begin with. However, three points deserve attention; two are rather negligible, but the third goes to the very heart of the educational enterprise.

First of all, would it be reasonable to insist that students should acquire not only skills, but also a knack for deploying these skills with style? Probably not. The stylish performance is one which, in addition to being faultless and efficient, is also graceful, effortless, rhythmical—in short, pleasant to behold. But style in this sense appears only as a concomitant of a high degree of mastery, when skill has become second nature, so to speak. Schools cannot spare the time to polish performances to this extent; they have to rest content with competence.

Then there is the notion that students should be expected to attain an appealing personal style; or rather, a disposition so to arrange their appearance, voice qualities, gait, etc., as to be aesthetically acceptable to their fellow men, hence more pleasant to have around. In this interpretation, style would be a part of good manners in general and could be condemned by the kind of currently fashionable arguments voiced in opposition to making good personal style and polite deportment legitimate educational objectives. It is said, for instance, that emphasis on style and manners would tend to foster superficiality, insincerity, and conformity; that it would stifle cre-

442 /

ativity, self-expression, and authenticity; and so forth. It should therefore be difficult to make a convincing case.

By far the most important educational objective expressed in terms of style is the "life style." Of course, this expression refers to the quality of the adult life and is thus of the nature of a high-level or remote educational aim. The philosophical problems involved in justifying this kind of objective need not be gone into here except to indicate briefly two tendencies which can be frustrating in combination. The first is that when educators are pressed to state reasons for what they are trying to accomplish in their profession, they will sooner or later refer to a set of principles, some social or ethical ideal, and to the kind of person or character type exemplifying these.[54] In other words, something describable as a life style is ultimately cited as justifying whatever is being done in school. On the other hand, it is impossible to deduce and very difficult to derive consistently from such a stated objective any one set of practical procedures as the only or best one for producing this outcome.

However, these difficulties with the life style objective are not the ones of immediate interest here. Rather, the problem is one posed by the restrictive definition of style maintained throughout most of this discussion. Since style was to be conceived as a strictly aesthetic term, it could be ruled that life style as an educational objective evidently involves a looser or metaphorical use of the term "style" and would therefore not be an appropriate subject in the present context. For surely life style implies evaluations according to ethical standards rather than primarily aesthetic ones; one would assess a man's moral worth and social usefulness rather than whether he lives "in style." Yet there is resistance to stipulating the matter away by definition, a feeling that style should retain aesthetic con-

[54] "Every aspect of the educational enterprise implies some theory of education, as every theory of education implies some conception of the nature of man, of the meaning of good and the public welfare. . . ." W. O. Stanley, "The Social Foundations Subjects in the Professional Education of Teachers," *Educational Theory* XVIII (1968): 232.

notations when designating a way of life. And perhaps this has something to do with the ancient identification of the good with the beautiful, i.e., the notion that contemplation of a good life should also give rise to aesthetic satisfaction. Unfortunately, this does not square with the facts of life. The pillar of the community may be the drabbest character around; conversely, the rogue may display a most beguiling style. Thus real life does not accommodate the educator who would like to have aesthetic persuasiveness as an ally in his endeavor to convince the student of the worthiness of a particular way of living. But art does, and this is why discussion must finally return to aesthetic education.

It is now suggested that aesthetic education can contribute greatly to general value education by fostering in students an appreciation of the life styles exhibited in aesthetically persuasive form in works of art. Naturally, this demands a decision on what sorts of works should constitute the content of aesthetic education. Critical skills and aesthetic perceptiveness can probably be exercised about minor works or even ordinary things taken as aesthetic objects. But since the arts do not display any logical order which would require moving from the simple to the complex, from the familiar to the unfamiliar, there is also little to discourage the use of established masterpieces at most levels of schooling. Through thoughtful selection of exemplars it should be possible to lend to desirable life styles dramatic impact in the theater arts, vividness in literature, expressiveness and sensuous appeal in painting, and noble form in sculpture, to name only the most obvious cases. It is in this sense that aesthetic education could support the larger ends of formal schooling while at the same time promoting its own objective of enlightened preference.

Bibliographical Note

Access to the philosophical literature pertinent to aesthetic education has been greatly facilitated by the publications at the University of Illinois Philosophy of Education Project. See Harry S. Broudy, Michael J. Parsons, Ivan A. Snook, and Ronald D. Szoke, *Philosophy of Education: An Organization of Topics and Selected Sources* (Urbana: University of Illinois Press, 1967), and Christiana M. Smith and Harry S. Broudy, *Philosophy of Education: Supplement,* 1969 (Urbana: University of Illinois Press, 1969). Sources and topics pertinent to aesthetic education are listed under the following headings: Aesthetics: Philosophy; Aesthetics: Nature and Aims of Education; Aesthetics: Curriculum Design and Validation; Aesthetics: Organization and Policy; and Aesthetics: Teaching-Learning. There will be further publications of the project as the literature develops. Listings include both books and articles.

The periodical literature in aesthetics and aesthetic education can also be followed in the *Journal of Aesthetic Education,* published by the University of Illinois Press at Urbana-Champaign; the *Journal of Aesthetics and Art Criticism,* published by the American Society for Aesthetics at Wayne State University; the *British Journal of Aesthetics,* published by the British Society for Aesthetics, London, and *The Philosopher's Index,* published by the Philosophy Documentation Center, Bowling Green State University, Ohio.

/ 445

Name Index

Abrams, M. H., 306, 369
Aquinas, T., 189
Aldrich, V. C., 267, 271, 319
Alschuler, R. H., 132
Archambault, R. D., 4
Aristotle, 116, 122, 372–73, 398, 409
Armstrong, L., 38
Arnheim, R., xi, 132, 280, 347, 393
Arnstine, D., 15–17, 38, 41, 43, 44, 449
Auden, W. H., 347
Austin, J. L., 155
Axline, V. M., 130–31

Baier, K., 166–69
Baker, C., 307
Balzac, H., 318
Barnett, G., 5
Baudelaire, C., 308
Beach, F. A., 34
Beardsley, M. C., x, xi, xiii, 11, 140, 141, 149, 158–59, 174, 188–91, 265, 266, 290–91, 298, 330, 332, 373, 382, 419–20, 427–28, 432, 437, 449
Beberman, M., 42
Belth, M., 5, 8
Benn, S. I., 262
Bentham, J., 308
Berenson, B., 135
Berggren, D., 368
Berlinger, R., 142
Berlyne, D. E., 34
Biederman, C., 124
Birkhoff, G. D., 179
Black, M., 282, 370, 375, 378
Blackington, F. H., 422
Booth, W., 363–64
Borges, J. L., 363
Bosanquet, B., 73
Braly, K., 94
Broad, C. D., 400–405
Brooks, C., 368, 369
Broudy, H. S., 99, 321, 324, 421–22, 449
Bruner, J. S., 5

Burke, K., 389
Burnett, J. R., 321

Caillois, R., 110, 118–19
Campbell, D. T., 94
Cassirer, E., 102
Caulfield, H., 365
Cézanne, P., 315–17, 324–25
Champlin, N., 14–15, 435–39
Chase, R., 325
Child, I. L., 43
Clark, W. H., Jr., 449
Coleman, F. J., 311
Coleridge, E. H., 307
Coleridge, S. T., 235, 306–9, 323, 340, 397
Collingwood, R. G., 73, 159, 229, 268
Coomaraswamy, A. K., 332–35, 337, 342
Copleston, F., 189
Crane, H., 312
Crawford, D. W., 44
Crittenden, B., xv, 449
Croce, B., 73, 98, 159, 161, 310, 428
Cunningham, J. V., 418, 427
Curran, C. E., 42

Daniel, E., 347
Danziger, M. K., 369
Darwin, C., 385
Dearden, R. F., 114–15, 117
DeGeorge, R. T., 131
Descartes, R., 137–38, 142, 144
Devine, T. G., 330
Dewey, J., xii, 4, 11–14, 30, 33, 43, 61, 140–41, 158, 277, 304, 311, 314, 319, 326, 435
Dickens, C., 130
Dickie, G., 11–12, 146
Dickinson, E., 315
Donne, J., 374
Dryden, J., 305
Ducasse, C., 93, 123
Dürer, A., 317
Dworkin, M. S., 43

/ 447

Ecker, D. W., 140–41, 158–61, 435–39

Edie, J., 152

Edman, I., 277

Eisner, E. W., 140, 435

Eliot, T. S., 317, 335, 353, 355, 368–72, 374–76

Elton, W., 146

Empson, W., 356

Enkvist, N. E., 416

Ernst, M., 312

Farrar, A., 52

Farrell, E. J., 347

Festinger, L., 38

Findlay, J. J., 61

Fleming, N., 197

Flew, A., 237

Frankena, W. K., 373

Freedman, M. P., 430

Freud, S., 79

Fry, R., 123, 242

Frye, N., 336, 387–88

Gallie, W. B., 67, 311–12

Garrer, J. N., 262

Ghiselin, B., 158

Gilbert, W., 385

Gombrich, E. H., 123, 424, 431

Gordon, W. J. J., 198

Gotshalk, D. W., xii, 103, 290, 296, 297, 299, 399, 449

Green, T. F., 321–22

Greene, M., 449

Gregory, M. J., 416

Grene, M., 84

Grommon, A. H., 347

Groos, K., 126

Gunn, M. A., 330

Gunn, T., 344

Hambridge, J., 179

Hanson, N. R., 184, 198, 231

Hare, R. M., 171

Harlow, H. F., 34

Hartshorne, C., 286, 439

Hattwick, L. W., 132

Hawthorne, N., 344

Hebb, D. O., 37

Hegel, G. W. F., 73

Heidegger, M., 96–97, 152, 163

Heller, E., 344

Hendrix, G., 99

Henle, P., 373

Henley, W. E., 349

Hofstadter, A., 306, 310

Hofstadter, R., 440

Holbrook, D., 339

Holton, G., 274

Homer, 354, 373

Hook, S., 277

Horace, 391

Hospers, J., 159

Houseman, A. E., 362–63

Huizinga, J., 118, 122

Hume, D., 138, 144, 306

Hunt, J. M., 34

Husserl, E., 141–47, 154, 156–57, 163

Hutchings, P., 400–401, 406–8

Ingarden, R., 142, 153, 399

James, H., 309

Jarrell, R., 341

Jenkins, I., 450

Johnson, W. S., 369

Jones, D., 292

Jonson, B., 351–52

Joyce, J., 311, 314, 353–54, 357

Kaelin, E. F., 97, 140, 450

Kafka, F., 344, 363

Kant, I., 72, 118, 144, 165, 306

Kaprow, A., 123

Katz, D., 94

Kaufmann, W., 117

Keats, J., 308

Kelley, G. A., 37–38

Kennedy, J. F., 102

Kepes, G., 274

Kierkegaard, S., 97–98, 344

Kimball, S., 321

Kivy, P., 430

Kohl, H., 348

Komisar, B. P., 322

Kozol, J., 18

Krieger, M., 35, 318, 399

Kronovet, E., 288

448 /

Contributors

1. *Donald Arnstine* is Associate Professor of Philosophy of Education at Boston University. His publications include *Philosophy of Education: Learning and Schooling* and articles in *Educational Theory, Studies in Philosophy and Education, The Journal of Educational Philosophy,* and *The Journal of Aesthetic Education.* His major interest is the relation of value theory to philosophy of education. In the fall of 1970 he will be at the University of California, Davis.

2. *Monroe C. Beardsley* is Professor of Philosophy at Temple University, having previously served for several years as Chairman of the Department of Philosophy and Religion at Swarthmore College. His publications include *Practical Logic, Aesthetics: Problems in the Philosophy of Criticism, Aesthetics from Classical Greece to the Present,* and *Philosophical Thinking* (with Elizabeth L. Beardsley). He is one of the leading aestheticians writing today.

3. *Harry S. Broudy* is Professor of Philosophy of Education at the University of Illinois (Urbana-Champaign). His publications include *Building a Philosophy of Education, Paradox and Promise, Democracy and Excellence in American Secondary Education* (with B. Othanel Smith and Joe R. Burnett), *Exemplars of Teaching Method* (with John R. Palmer), and *Philosophy of Education: An Organization of Topics and Selected Sources* (with associates). In recent years he has been in demand as a speaker and writer on both aesthetic education and the professional preparation of teachers, and has done much to stimulate contemporary interest in both topics.

4. *Walter H. Clark, Jr.* received his Ph.D. from Harvard University and is now an Assistant Professor in the Department of English at the University of Michigan. He has published a book of verse, *Nineteen Poems,* and his article "The Role of Choice in Aesthetic Education" has been reprinted in Jane Roland Martin (ed.), *Readings in Philosophy of Curriculum.* His major interest is theory of criticism.

5. *Brian S. Crittenden* is Associate Professor at the Ontario Institute for Studies in Education. His publications include an edited anthology, *Philosophy and Education,* and articles in *Studies in Philosophy and Education, Educational Theory, Journal of Value Inquiry,* and *The Journal of Aesthetic Education.* His major interest is the relation of value theory to philosophy of education.

6. *D. W. Gotshalk* is Professor Emeritus of Philosophy at the University of Illinois (Urbana-Champaign). His publications include *Structure and Reality, Metaphysics in Modern Times, Art and the Social Order, The Promise of Modern Life, Patterns of Good and Evil, Human Aims in Modern Perspective,* and *The Structure of Awareness.* He continues to write in the areas of value theory and general philosophy.

7. *Maxine Greene* is Professor of English and a member of both the Department of Philosophy and Social Sciences and the Department of Languages and Literature at Teachers College, Columbia University. Her publications include

The Public School and the Private Vision and a collection of readings, *Existential Encounters for Teachers*. She has also served as Editor of *The Record* (formerly *Teachers College Record*). Her major interests are literature and the politics of education.

8. *Iredell Jenkins* is Professor of Philosophy and a member of the Law Faculty at the University of Alabama, having previously taught philosophy for several years at Harvard University. His publications include *Art and the Human Enterprise* and numerous articles in philosophical and legal journals.

9. *Eugene F. Kaelin* is Chairman of the Department of Philosophy at Florida State University. His pubilcations include *An Existentialistic Aesthetic* and numerous articles in philosophical and educational journals. His major interest is phenomenological analysis, and he has written several articles on the uses of phenomenology in aesthetic education.

10. *Barbara Leondar* received her Ph.D. from Harvard University and is now Assistant Professor of English and Coordinator of the Teacher Certification Program at the University of Massachusetts in Boston. Her major interests are literary theory and urban education.

11. *Joseph Margolis* is currently Professor of Philosophy at Temple University, having been a visiting professor at several universities. His publications include *The Language of Art and Art Criticism* and *Psychotherapy and Morality*, and he has edited *Philosophy Looks at the Arts, Contemporary Ethical Theory, An Introduction to Philosophical Inquiry,* and *Fact and Existence*.

12. *Peter F. Neumeyer* is currently Associate Professor of English at State University of New York, Stony Brook, after having previously taught in the Harvard Graduate School of Education. His publications include an edited anthology of essays on Kafka's *The Castle* and numerous articles in literary and educational journals. In addition to children's literature and the teaching of English in the schools, his major interests are seventeenth-century English and modern comparative literature.

13. *Michael J. Parsons* is an Assistant Professor in the College of Education at the University of Utah. His publications include the co-authoring of *Philosophy of Education: An Organization of Topics and Selected Sources* and several articles in educational journals. His major interests are aesthetics and philosophy of education.

14. *Louis Arnaud Reid* is Professor Emeritus of the Philosophy of Education at the University of London, where he was the first holder of the Chair of the Philosophy of Education. His major publications include *A Study in Aesthetics, Ways of Knowledge and Experience, Philosophy and Education,* and most recently, *Meaning in the Arts*. He has long been interested in the philosophical foundations of aesthetic education.

15. *Allan Shields* is Dean of the College of Humanities and Fine Arts at the University of Northern Iowa, after having previously taught philosophy at San Diego State College for several years. His publications include *A Complete*

Bibliography of F. C. S. Schiller (with H. L. Searles) and numerous articles in music, philosophical, and educational journals. He is also an active musical performer. In the fall of 1970 he will return to San Diego State College.

16. *C. M. Smith* served as a Research Assistant on the Philosophy of Education Project at the University of Illinois (Urbana-Champaign). She co-authored (with H. S. Broudy) the 1969 *Supplement* to *Philosophy of Education: An Organization of Topics and Selected Sources,* and is currently Book Review Editor for *The Educational Forum.* Her major interest is the relation of aesthetic theory to philosophy of education.

17. *F. E. Sparshott* is Professor and Chairman of the Department of Ethics at Victoria College, University of Toronto. His publications include *An Enquiry into Goodness and Related Concepts, The Structure of Aesthetics, A Divided Voice* (poems), and *The Concept of Criticism.* He is one of the most systematic writers doing work in aesthetics today.